LADIES AND GENTLEMEN OF THE JURY

Greatest
Closing Arguments
in Modern Law

Michael S Lief, H. Mitchell Caldwell
and Benjamin Bycel

A LISA DREW BOOK
SCRIBNER

SCRIBNER
1230 Avenue of the Americas
New York, NY 10020

SCRIBNER and design are trademarks of
Simon & Schuster Inc.

A LISA DREW BOOK is a trademark of Simon & Schuster Inc.

Designed by Colin Joh
Set in Bembo

Manufactured in the United States of America

5 7 9 10 8 6

Library of Congress Cataloging-in-Publication Data is available.

Lief, Michael, S
Ladies and gentlemen of the jury: greatest closing arguments in
modern law/Michael S Lief, H. Mitchell Caldwell, and Benjamin
Bycel.
p.   cm.
"A Lisa Drew Book"
1. Summation (Law)—United States. 2. Jury—United States.
3. Trial practices—United States. 4. Forensic orations.
I. Caldwell, Harry M. II. Bycel, Ben. III. Title.
KF8924.L54 1998   97–50267
347.73'75—dc21   CIP

ISBN 0-684-83661-0

This book is dedicated to our families:

For Joyce, Denise, Lee, Nicole, and Eric—H.M.C.
For Laura, Josh, and Sarah—B.B.
For my parents, Shirley and Gerald—M.S L.

Acknowledgments

We are deeply indebted to the Honorable Bruce Einhorn, Senior U.S. Immigration Judge, Professor of Law Barbara Babcock of Stanford University, and Dean Geoffrey Cowan of the Annenberg School of Communications, for their invaluable assistance in the preparation of this book. Judge Einhorn's vast expertise and experience in the prosecution of war criminals lent depth and perspective to the Nuremberg chapter. Likewise, Professor Babcock was most gracious and helpful in resurrecting the remarkable life and career of Clara Shortridge Foltz; but for her efforts, Foltz's story would have been lost. Finally, Dean Cowan's exhaustive knowledge of all things darrow was graciously offered to—and accepted by—the authors; the chapters on this famed litigator are the better for Cowan's help. We would also like to thank Lee Jackson Caldwell for his time spent digging through dusty boxes and musty records at the National Archives in search of elusive trial transcrips.

The authors must also acknowledge the work of a number of Pepperdine law students who have assisted with the research over the years, first and foremost Robin Sax. Thank you all.

Contents

CONTENTS

Introduction

An advocate can be confronted with few more formidable tasks
than to select his closing arguments. . . .
—*Robert H. Jackson,*
chief counsel for the United States at the Nuremberg Trial, 1946

How does a trial advocate manage in just a few hours to summarize
months of testimony and documentary evidence, transforming it into a
compelling story that will persuade the jurors—and win the case?

The closing argument is the lawyer's final opportunity to give perspective, meaning, and context to the evidence introduced throughout
a lengthy trial. It is the last chance for the lawyer to forcefully communicate his position to the jury, to convince them why his version of the
"truth" is correct.

Every argument here is a finely crafted verbal work of art. Remember, closing arguments are heard—not read—by the jurors. Because of
this, they represent the modern-day, highest form of an ancient profession and art: that of the storyteller. Like the wandering bards of yore, the
attorney must command the attention of the courtroom. He must use
every psychological and emotional tool at his command to tell his
client's story. The advocate must use his summation to touch not just
the intellect of the jurors, but also their emotions. But there is one vital
difference between yesterday's storytellers and today's advocates. Where
the bard sat at the foot of the king and entertained, the lawyer's storytelling has the power to put evil men to death, to free the innocent, and
to make whole the injured. Such is the power of the words, the tale, the
closing argument.

The purpose of this book is to present to the reader a selection of the
finest closing arguments in American history. The authors are acutely
aware that for every closing argument presented in the book, there are

countless others, many by unknown attorneys in little-known cases, that rival the ones we selected. Each of the summations we've chosen for inclusion share common themes and presentations.

Each case was selected for the quality of its summation, as well as for its historical significance. A deliberate effort has been made to exclude those that achieve fleeting fame—or notoriety. We have concentrated instead on trials that have withstood the test of time, that will continue to fascinate and educate decades after the verdicts were read. These are trials that hold men responsible for war crimes, take the nuclear power industry to task, demand equal rights for women, and prove that the mere passage of time will not excuse the deeds of a killer.

It may well be—and in fact probably is—terribly presumptuous of us to "choose" the ten greatest arguments. Of necessity, we limited our prospective list to noteworthy trials. Then the trial record had to be available; unfortunately, this has not always been the case. Astonishingly, the transcripts of some of the most noteworthy trials have simply disappeared. And finally, the closing argument must have been terrific.

Certain trials that the reader might expect to find are not represented, and are conspicuous by their absence. The Scopes Monkey Trial, pitting Clarence Darrow against William Jennings Bryan, cannot appear, because these two courtroom legends agreed not to make closing arguments in that case.

Sorely missed in this work is Louis Nizer, who for more than thirty years was without peer before a jury. Transcripts of his closing arguments simply can't be found.

The book is organized in the following manner. Each chapter contains a brief historical introduction which places the case in a social, historical context. Along with the introduction is a biographical sidebar about the lawyer who delivered the closing. This is followed by an analysis of the argument, focusing on notable aspects of the close, and then the argument itself.

Most of the arguments have been edited, some more, some less. It is our thought that occasionally an argument will go into very specific factual detail, more than is necessary for us to appreciate its brilliance. With that exception, we have taken nothing out. And, of course, nothing has been added.

So relax, read how these experts weave their tales of betrayal, violence, oppression, and hope, and see what can be done by a quick-thinking lawyer, armed with his wits—and the power of his words.

CHAPTER ONE

Architects of Genocide

The Victorious Allies Put Hitler's Henchmen in the Defendant's Box at Nüremberg

The Guns Fall Silent

Dawn came early to Reims, France, on the morning of May 7, 1945. This was not nature's dawn, but then the darkness which it ended was not the brief and pretty peace of nature's night. The darkness was a maelstrom made of men, bent on Holocaust and war. As the dawn finally came, the light of Europe's liberation from National Socialism illuminated the deeds of those evil men, who now faced judgment for having turned much of the world on a perverted Axis of persecution, the darkest point of which was Nazi Germany.

At Reims, France, at 2:41 A.M., May 7, 1945, General Alfred Jodl, chief of the Operations Staff of the German High Command, signed the instrument of unconditional surrender of all German land, sea, and air forces.

The newborn peace found more than 30 million dead, many of them civilians and Allied prisoners of war who endured a crimson march of displacement, internment, enslavement, deprivation, involuntary labor, quasimedical experimentation, and a myriad of other tortures, before their demise.

Genocide, the wholesale slaughter of the Jews wherever they could be found, was to be the legacy of Hitler's Third Reich. The entire industrial might of a modern Western nation had been subverted, harnessed, to create an industry of death. German companies submitted bids, hoping to win lucrative contracts to build ovens in which to burn Jews, to build chambers in which to gas Jews, and the right to slave labor, supplied by the Jews and captured Slavs. It was clear to the victors that something new was necessary, to assign blame for the terrible war and its very modern atrocities. They decided that there were to be war crimes trials, something that had never been done before. Rather than dispense summary judgment and execute the Nazi leadership, the rule of law would be reestablished in Germany, after twelve lawless years of Nazi rule.

The bringing to justice of those still alive and responsible at the highest level of Nazi authority for these perfidious acts was part of the unfinished business of World War II, which the unconditional surrender of Germany made possible but did not itself accomplish. Bringing that grave and arduous task to a conclusion became the job of the International Military Tribunal at Nüremberg, Germany, which heard and decided the Trial of the Major War Criminals of the European Axis between November 20, 1945, and September 30, 1946. It is no wonder, then, that the chief counsel for the United States at the Nüremberg trial, Justice Robert H. Jackson, declared that "Never before in legal history has an effort been made to bring within the scope of a single litigation the developments of a decade, covering a whole continent, and involving a score of nations, countless individuals, and innumerable events. . . . This trial has a scope that is utterly beyond anything that has ever been attempted that I know of in judicial history."

The Road to Nüremberg

Just as V-E Day made good the Allied promise of unconditional surrender, so the Nüremberg trial was the culmination of Allied declarations of intention to bring to justice the major figures in the European Axis for their acts of aggression and the atrocities committed by their minions during the Second World War. On October 25, 1941—even before the entry of the United States into the war—President Roosevelt and Prime Minister Churchill made simultaneous statements warning Axis leaders that their "crimes" would not go unpunished.

In order to gather evidence against such suspected war criminals, fifteen nations, including the United States and Britain (but not the Soviet Union), formed the United Nations War Crimes Commission, which first convened in London on October 26, 1943. Shortly thereafter, on November 1, 1943, the leaders of the United States, Britain, *and* the Soviet Union issued the Moscow Declaration, which called for the following:

> [A]t the time of the granting of any armistice to any government which may be set up in Germany, those German officers and men and members of the Nazi party who have been responsible for, or

have taken a consenting part in the atrocities, massacres, and executions, will be sent back to the countries where their abominable deeds were done in order that they may be judged and punished according to the laws of these liberated countries and of the free government which will be erected therein . . . [but this policy] *is without prejudice to the case of German criminals whose offenses have no particular geographical localization, and who will be punished by joint decision of the Governments of the Allies.* (Emphasis added.)

It was this latter category of alleged war criminals which formed the caseload of the International Military Tribunal at Nüremberg, and which gave to Robert Jackson the greatest litigative challenge of his career.

In a memorandum to President Roosevelt, dated January 22, 1945, the secretaries of state and war and the attorney general recommended "ways and means for carrying out the policy regarding the trial and punishment of Nazi criminals," as follows:

> After Germany's unconditional surrender the United Nations could, if they elected, put to death the most notorious Nazi criminals, such as Hitler or Himmler, without trial or hearing. We do not favor this method. While it has the advantage of a sure and swift disposition, it would be violative of the most fundamental principles of justice, common to all the United Nations. This would encourage the Germans to turn over these criminals, and, in any event, only a few individuals could be reached in this way.
>
> We think that the just and effective solution lies in the use of the judicial method. Condemnation of these criminals after a trial, moreover, would command maximum public support in our own times and receive the respect of history. The use of the judicial method will, in addition, make available for all mankind to study in future years an authentic record of Nazi crimes and criminality.

The three cabinet officers further recommended that "the trial of the prime leaders [be] by an international military commission or military court, established by Executive Agreement of the heads of State of the interested United Nations." Such a court, the officers added, could consist of persons appointed by the "Big Four" powers of Britain, France, the United States, and the Soviet Union, and by other Allied countries.

The cabinet officers also suggested that the prosecution of the major Nazi leaders be directed by "a full-time executive group" composed of lead counsel from the same Big Four powers.

At first, the cabinet officers' call for a war crimes tribunal met with less enthusiasm abroad than at home. In an aide-mémoire to the U.S. administration dated April 23, 1945, the British government held "that it is beyond question that Hitler and a number of arch-criminals associated with him (including Mussolini) must, so far as they fall into Allied hands, suffer the penalty of death for their conduct leading up to the war and for the wickedness which they have either themselves perpetrated or have authorized in the conduct of the war." Consequently, London argued "that execution without trial is the preferable course."

The Honorable Robert Jackson, associate justice of the United States Supreme Court, disagreed. In a speech prepared for delivery to the American Society of International Law on April 13, 1945 (the day after President Roosevelt's death), Jackson stated that "I am not so troubled as some seem to be over the problems of jurisdiction of war criminals or of finding existing and recognized law by which standards of guilt may be determined." However, Jackson also cautioned that "if you are determined to execute a man in any case, there is no occasion for a trial. The world yields no respect to courts that are merely organized to convict."

Thusly armed, Jackson set about forming a staff of attorneys for the coming war crimes litigation. Among the deputy prosecutors selected by Jackson were U.S. Army Gen. Telford Taylor, who later served as chief of counsel for War Crimes at the second round of trials held at Nüremberg before American judges between 1946 and 1949, and Thomas Dodd, who later served as a United States senator from Connecticut. He also opened an office in London, where he would meet with British, French, and Soviet representatives on the constitution and composition of the upcoming war crimes tribunal and its proceedings.

Jackson was not only America's chief prosecutor at Nüremberg, but also the president's representative at the Big Four talks in London during June–August 1945, where the rules of engagement for the International Military Tribunal would be written. Thus, Jackson possessed a power few prosecutors before or since him would have: to create the court before which he would appear, and to shape the substantive and procedural law which that court would apply to the cases he would present to it.

In giving shape to the Nüremberg trial, however, Jackson did not exercise absolute authority. Rather, he was obliged to work compromises in London with representatives of Britain, France, and the Soviet Union, each with its own separate legal tradition. In particular, Jackson attempted in London to reconcile the Anglo-American and Continental systems of jurisprudence. For example, Jackson and his London interlocutors had to fashion an indictment of those to be tried before the tribunal. In doing so, Jackson admitted that he "would not know how to proceed with a trial [as in Continental countries] in which all of the evidence had been included in the indictment. I would not see anything left for a trial, and, for myself, I would not know what to do in open court." In the end, Article 16 of the Charter of the International Military Tribunal, drafted as a compromise by Jackson and company at London, provided that "the Indictment shall include full particulars specifying in detail the charges against the Defendants."

Furthermore, Article 15(a) of the charter required the chief Allied prosecutors to undertake the "investigation, collection, and production *before or at the Trial* of all necessary evidence" (emphasis added). Arguing in favor of a more Continental approach, including an expedited form of trial practice and of a less rigid separation of the judicial and prosecutorial functions, was the Soviet representative, General Nikititchenko: "[T]he Soviet Delegation considers that there is no necessity in trials of this sort to accept the principle that the judge is a completely disinterested party with no previous knowledge of the case."

For his part, Jackson responded that the tribunal's "judges will have to inquire into the evidence and reach an independent decision. . . . That is the reason why, at the very beginning, the position of the United States was that there must be trials, rather than political executions . . . (I) have no sympathy with these men [i.e., the likely defendants], but, if we are going to have a trial, then it must be an actual trial."

On August 8, 1945, Jackson was able to negotiate and obtain the Big Four's signatures on a Charter of the International Military Tribunal (IMT), an international executive agreement which provided for an independent panel of four judges (one each to be appointed by the American, British, French, and Soviet governments) responsible for drawing up its own rules of procedure, and empowered to impose convictions and sentences on war crimes defendants only upon the approval of at least three of its members. Furthermore, the charter which Jackson negotiated guaranteed to defendants the rights to detailed notice of the charges against them, to the assistance of counsel, to cross-examination of prosecution witnesses, to presentation of a defense, and to a full translation of court proceedings.

In return, Jackson agreed with his negotiating partners that the proceedings of the tribunal "need not be encumbered with the legalisms of Anglo-Saxon law." Article 19 of the charter stated: "The Tribunal shall not be bound by technical rules of evidence. It shall adopt and apply to the greatest possible extent expeditious and nontechnical procedure, and shall admit any evidence which it deems to have probative value." Also, Article 18 required the tribunal to "confine the trial strictly to an expeditious hearing of the issues raised by the charges. . . ."

On the subject of charges, Jackson helped in defining the following acts as crimes within the jurisdiction of the tribunal for which individual responsibility could be found:

(a) Crimes Against Peace: namely, planning, preparation, initiation, or waging of a war of aggression, or a war in violation of international treaties, agreements or assurances, or participation in a common plan or conspiracy for the accomplishment of any of the foregoing:

(b) War Crimes: namely, violations of the laws or customs of war. Such violations shall include, but not be limited to, murder, ill-treatment or deportation to slave labor members of the civilian population in occupied territory, murder or ill-treatment of prisoners of war or persons on the seas, killing of hostages, plunder of public or private property, wanton destruction of cities, towns or villages, or devastation not justified by military necessity:

(c) Crimes Against Humanity: namely, murder, extermination, enslavement, deportation, and other inhumane acts committed against any civilian population, before or during the war, or persecutions on political, racial, or religious grounds in execution of or in connection with any crime within the jurisdiction of the Tribunal, whether or not in violation of the domestic law of the country where perpetrated.

Leaders, organizers, instigators and accomplices participating in the formulation or execution of a common plan or conspiracy to commit any of the foregoing crimes are responsible for all acts performed by any persons in execution of such plan.

The charter's definition of war crimes was largely compatible with longstanding prohibitions in United States and international law, including Francis Lieber's *Instructions for the Government of Armies of the United States in the Field,* promulgated as General Orders No. 100 by President Abraham Lincoln on April 24, 1863, and the Hague Conventions of 1899 and 1907 Respecting the Laws and Customs of War on Land. However, the inclusion of crimes against peace among the charter's litany of actionable offenses was a bolder, more novel stroke by Jackson and the U.S. administration to, in the words of Telford Taylor, "establish the initiation of aggressive war as a crime under universally applicable international law." Also, the separate category accorded to crimes against humanity gave heightened legal attention and importance to the concept of "genocide"—a concept newly named by a member of Jackson's Nüremberg staff—the extermination of Jews and other minority groups under Nazi rule. The deputy prosecutor in question was Raphael Lemkin, who in later years lobbied intensively for U.S. ratification of the United Nations Genocide Convention.

Also on the subject of charges, Article 9 of the charter authorized the tribunal that a group or organization of which an individual defendant had been a member (e.g., the SS) "was a criminal organization." Article 10 in turn permitted any signatory state to the charter to bring individuals to trial in separate proceedings on charges that they had been members of such a criminal organization. "In any such case[s] the criminal nature of the group or organization is considered proved and shall not be questioned." Jackson pressed hard for the enactment of these provisions, because they "constitute[d] the means through which . . . a large number of people can be reached with a small number of long trials—perhaps one main trial. The difficulty in our case [i.e., that of the United States] is that we have in the neighborhood of perhaps 200,000 prisoners. We don't want to have 200,000 trials."

On the subject of defenses, Jackson and the other Allied representatives prevented those at the top and those at the bottom of the Nazi chain of command from escaping legal responsibility for the criminal orders they gave or the ones they followed:

> Article 7. The official position of defendants, whether as Heads of State or responsible officials in Government Departments, shall not be considered as freeing them from responsibility or mitigation punishment.

Article 8. The fact that the Defendant acted pursuant to order of his Government or of a superior shall not free him from responsibility, but may be considered in mitigation of punishment if the Tribunal determines that justice so requires.

In his report to President Truman dated October 7, 1946, Jackson correctly concluded that the Charter of the IMT "made explicit and unambiguous what was theretofore . . . implicating International Law"—that the planning and waging of aggressive war and the mass dislocating and killing of racial, religious, and ethnic minorities are crimes whose perpetrators, high and low, individual and organizational, will be held accountable for before the bar of justice. To Jackson, the charter was more than the rules of a particular court: "It is a basic charter in the international law of the future."

The Nüremberg Trial

On August 29, 1945, Jackson and the other Allied prosecutors announced the indictment of twenty-four persons for trial before the IMT. The defendants included:

Hermann Goering, Reichmarschal of the German Air Force, chief of War Economy, minister-president of Prussia, and, from 1939 until April 23, 1945, Adolf Hitler's designated successor.

Rudolf Hess, the person to whom Hitler dictated his venomous political testament, *Mein Kampf* ("My Struggle"), and Nazi party chairman, who in May 1941 had parachuted into Scotland (where he was interned as a British prisoner of state for the duration of World War II) in a madcap effort to negotiate peace with King George VI.

Joachim von Ribbentrop, the Nazi German foreign minister who negotiated Japan's adherence to the European Axis and who collaborated in the identification, deportation, and extermination of European Jewry.

Wilhelm Keitel, Hitler's closest military adviser, head of the High Command of the German Armed Forces, who issued orders for the wartime execution of Soviet commissars and of non-German civilians who acted in opposition to Nazi rule.

Ernst Kaltenbrunner, head of the Reich Security Main Office of the SS, and in that regard, overseer of the German Gestapo (secret state police).

Alfred Rosenberg, Reich minister of Eastern Occupied Territories and principal Nazi party ideologist.

Hans Frank, Hitler's main legal adviser and his governor over much of Poland.

Wilhelm Frick, author of the Nüremberg Laws of 1935 which dispossessed German Jews, Nazi minister of the Interior, and Reichsprotector of Bohemia and Moravia (now the Czech Republic).

Julius Streicher, self-proclaimed "Jew-Baiter Number One," publisher of the anti-Semitic Nazi newspaper *Der Stuermer* ("The Storm"), and principal organizer of the 1935 Nüremberg Rally at which Hitler announced his new laws against the Jews.

Walter Funk, Nazi minister of Economic Affairs and president of the Reichsbank which helped finance German wartime aggression and the Final Solution of the Jewish Question.

Hjalmar Horace Greeley Schacht, high-ranking prewar Reich economic adviser who later joined the German resistance to Hitler.

Karl Doenitz, grand admiral of the German Navy, Hitler loyalist, and acting German head of state from April 30, 1945 (the date of Hitler's suicide) to May 22, 1945 (the date of Doenitz's arrest by Allied authorities).

Erich Raeder, German Admiral Doenitz's predecessor as naval commander in chief.

Baldur von Schirach, head of the Hitler Youth and Wartime *Gauleiter* (Nazi leader) of Vienna, Austria, whose paternal grandfather had served as a major in the U.S. Army during the American Civil War and as an honorary pallbearer at Abraham Lincoln's funeral.

Fritz Sauckel, Nazi party leader and governor of Thuringia, Germany, and Reich plenipotentiary for the mobilization of labor, including slave labor.

Alfred Jodl, chief of the Operations Staff of the German High Command.

Martin Bormann, Hitler's private secretary and head of the chancellery of the Nazi party, who was missing at the time of the Nüremberg trial and so was prosecuted there in absentia.

Franz von Papen, who preceded Hitler as German chancellor and who helped engineer Hitler's appointment as chancellor in January 1933.

Artur Seyss-Inquart, SS general, Reich governor of Austria, and Reich commissioner of the German-occupied Netherlands.

Albert Speer, a Hitler confidant and wartime German minister for Armaments and Munitions.

Konstantin von Neurath, von Ribbentrop's predecessor as Nazi foreign minister.

Hans Fritzsche, Nazi newscaster and second-ranking official under Josef Goebbels in the Nazi Propaganda Ministry.

Two other persons were also indicted: Robert Ley, founder and head of the Nazi German Labor Front and anti-Semitic agitator; and Gustav Krupp, dean of the German arms industry which supplied Hitler with the means for his war of aggression. However, Ley committed suicide in his Nuremberg cell on October 25, 1945, and Krupp was found unable to stand trial for health reasons by the IMT. By a three-to-one vote, the tribunal rejected Jackson's November 1945 request to substitute Gustav's son, Alfried Krupp, as a defendant. (Alfried Krupp was an SS member who had managed his family's armaments industry since his father's first stroke in 1941, and who had participated in the use of slave labor to achieve war production aims.) Only the Soviet judge voted to grant Jackson's motion.

The resulting proceedings before the Tribunal at Nüremberg were an enormous exercise, as reported by Jackson himself:

> The trial began on November 20, 1945, and occupied 216 days of trial time. Thirty-three witnesses were called and examined for the prosecution. Sixty-one witnesses and 19 defendants testified for the defense; 143 additional witnesses gave testimony by interrogatories for the defense. The proceedings were conducted and recorded in four languages—English, German, French, and Russian—and daily transcripts in the language of his choice was provided for each prosecuting staff and all counsel for defendants. The English transcript of the proceedings covers over 17,000 pages.
>
> In preparation for the trial, over 100,000 captured German documents were screened or examined and about 10,000 were selected for intensive examination as having probable evidentiary value. Of these, about 4,000 were translated into four languages and used, in whole or in part, in the trial as exhibits.

By far the most damaging evidence introduced against the defendants at Nüremberg were the "documents of their own making, the authenticity of which has not been challenged except in one of two cases." Jackson, his fellow prosecutors, and their staffs, therefore deserve great credit for their meticulous preparation of the paper trail which led the majority of the defendants from the dock to the gallows or prison.

It is therefore unfair and unfortunate that Jackson's performance at

Nüremberg has been criticized, disproportionately so, for his March 1946 cross-examination of Hermann Goering. The expectations placed on Jackson for that examination were unrealistically high. For example, the alternate British judge at Nüremberg, Sir Norman Birkett, asserted that "It will be a duel to the death between the representative of all that is worthwhile in civilization and the last important surviving protagonist of all that was evil." Judged by such hyperbole, Jackson's plodding and somewhat long-winded manner of interrogation was deemed a failure in the face of Goering's confident and quick-witted style of response. At one point during his examination of Goering, Jackson's frustration with the witness, exacerbated by his fatigue from months of litigation and by his sense of public disappointment in his confrontational skills, caused him to dissolve into confusion as he asked, "Now, was the leadership principle supported by and adopted by you [Goering] in Germany because you believed that no people are capable of self-government, or that you believed that some may be, but not the German people: or for that matter whether some of us are capable of using our own system but it should not be used in Germany." In reply, Goering arrogantly but effectively stated that although he did not understand the question, he would try to answer it anyway. Goering was not to get away with murder, but he at least succeeded in getting Jackson's goat.

Nevertheless, Jackson and his fellow Nüremberg prosecutors were largely successful in their courtroom efforts. In its judgment of September 30, 1946, the International Military Tribunal found nineteen of the twenty-two defendants guilty on one or more of the counts of the indictment. Five defendants—Goering, von Ribbentrop, Keitel, Rosenberg, and Jodl—were convicted on all four counts of "a common plan or conspiracy," crimes against peace, war crimes, and crimes against humanity. Those five defendants, and the also criminally convicted Kaltenbrunner, Frank, Frick, Streicher, Sauckel, Bormann, and Seyss-Inquart, were sentenced to death. The remaining criminally convicted defendants received sentences ranging from fifteen years to life imprisonment. Only three Nüremberg defendants—Schacht, von Papen, and Fritasche—were wholly acquitted. The tribunal's Soviet judge, Nikitchenko, dissented from these acquittals and also argued for a death sentence for Hess. Furthermore, the tribunal found four Nazi organizations to be criminal in character: the leadership corps of the Nazi party; the SS; the SD, or Security Service of the SS; and the Gestapo. In the end, Jackson achieved the goal he and the U.S. government had set for the Nüremberg proceedings: a fair trial, with culpability apportioned to individuals and groups based only on the evidence provided to an independent tribunal.

Jackson's Closing Argument

Jackson's closing argument to the tribunal of July 26, 1946, was the first of four final speeches for the prosecution. Jackson in his argument focused on count one of the indictment and the evidence of a common plan or conspiracy. The British lead prosecutor, Lord Shawcross, then argued for convictions for crimes against peace under count two of the indictment. The French and Soviet prosecutors then spoke as to counts three and four—war crimes against humanity.

In his closing argument, Jackson was clearly in his element. As one of his Nuremberg colleagues, Telford Taylor, noted: "Jackson had shaken off the malaise contracted in his encounter with Goering. He was most comfortable and skilled beyond his fellows, in the preparation and presentation of courtroom arguments. At the lectern he was the picture of confidence."

Jackson rose to the occasion of his argument and spoke as the advocate for civilization against those who had sought and almost achieved the conquest of the world.

Biography

An associate justice of the United States Supreme Court doesn't get to try cases; those days are long gone by the time an attorney makes his way to the most prestigious position in the American legal system—unless that attorney happens to be Robert Houghtwout Jackson. Appointed to the Supreme Court in 1941 by President Franklin D. Roosevelt, Jackson was granted a leave of absence in 1945 to participate in the prosecution of Nazi war criminals. Jackson was to head the U.S. delegation and serve as the lead prosecutor.

The path that led Jackson to Nüremberg began in 1892, in Spring Creek, Pennsylvania. He received his legal training at Albany Law School, in Albany, New York. After graduating and passing the bar, he practiced law in Jamestown, New York, until 1934, when he was appointed general counsel for the U.S. Bureau of Internal Revenue in 1934.

Jackson prospered in Washington, D.C., and was tapped by FDR in 1936 to serve as assistant attorney general of the United States, where he distinguished himself by his skillful prosecutions of major U.S. corporations charged with violating antitrust laws. Promoted in 1938, he served as solicitor general of the United States for two years. In 1940 Jackson headed the Justice Department after he was chosen to become U.S. attorney general. In 1941, FDR appointed him to the Supreme Court. He was also FDR's frequent fishing and poker-playing companion.

Four years after his appointment to the bench, Jackson's service was interrupted when President Harry S. Truman sent word to Jackson that his trial expertise was needed in Germany, asking him to serve as American chief counsel for the prosecution in the trials at Nüremberg. On May 2, 1945, Truman issued Executive Order 9547, appointing the fifty-three-year-old Jackson "as the Representative of the United States and as its Chief of Counsel in preparing and prosecuting charges of atrocities and war crimes against such of the leaders of the European Axis powers and their principal agents and accessories as the United States may agree with any of the United Nations to bring to trial before an international military tribunal." He accepted; and on May 3, 1945, Jackson took the reins of what would prove to be one of the most significant trials in the history of humanity.

Following the Nüremberg trials, Jackson returned to the United States and his place on the Supreme Court. His writings include *The Case Against the Nazi War Criminals* (1946) and *The Nürnberg Case* (1947).

He remained a sitting (if sometimes absent) Justice until his death on October 9, 1954.

Commentary

Jackson's summation at Nüremberg ranks among the finest arguments ever delivered; if ever there was a blueprint for a prosecution close, this is it. There are so many outstanding aspects of this argument it is difficult to know where to begin. First and foremost, Jackson recognized his role in this extraordinary trial. He had to take the vast scope of the Nazis' atrocities and give it a contextual framework in order to allow his jury, made up of the members of the IMT, to deal with the sheer enormity of the deeds. Next, he had to strike a clear and compelling central theme, one which would faithfully serve him through the argument and more importantly, strike a resounding chord with his jury. Third, he had to separate the wheat from the chaff, clear the trial of the peripheral material brought by the defense, and keep the jurors focused on the significant facts and relevant issues. Finally, Jackson had to organize the evidence to assist the jurors in dealing with the huge amount of evidence that was introduced.

It is difficult for the mind to come to grips with the Holocaust. The sheer enormity of the crimes is so beyond ordinary human experience that there is no context in which to begin evaluating the defendants' misdeeds, assess blame, and then move on to assign punishment. One of Jackson's main tasks was to put the crimes of the Nazi leadership into historical perspective. Very early in his masterful close he sets about the job: "No half-century ever witnessed slaughter on such a scale, such cruelties and inhumanities, such wholesale deportations of peoples into slavery, such annihilations of minorities. The terror of Torquemada pales before the Nazi inquisition. These deeds are the overshadowing historical facts by which generations to come will remember this decade."

In this passage and several others early in the close, Jackson captures the vast scope of events and thus begins the process of allowing the tribunal—sitting as jury—to place these crimes into a context where they might more readily be able to make their evaluations.

Jackson clearly establishes his central theme, "It is their overt acts which we charge to be crimes," very early and ties the balance of his close to the theme. Throughout this fairly lengthy argument, Jackson returns to a simple conspiracy theory, one supported by the Nazis' overt acts. Again and again, Jackson pounds home that the defendants are being tried not for the reprehensible beliefs they held, but for the reprehensible deeds they had done.

Jackson recognized that there is a dynamic in all trials whereby one side will attempt to keep the trial focused on clearly defined issues. This side—here the prosecution—will struggle to keep peripheral issues from coming center stage and somehow obfuscating what they perceive to be relevant concerns of the trial. In stark contrast, the opposing side will find it to their advantage to bring in matter not always central to the case. This time-honored tactic of attempting to shift the focus of the trial to a more agreeable footing was undertaken by the defense. However, early in his summation, Jackson squarely and forcefully discounts the defense attempt and zeroes in on the main issue: "But justice in this case has nothing to do with some of the arguments put forth by the defendants or their counsel. We have not previously and we need not now discuss the merits of all their obscure and tortuous philosophy. We are not trying them for possession of obnoxious ideas. . . . It is not their thoughts, it is their overt acts which we charge to be crimes . . ." Jackson brushed aside the peripheral issues the defense attempted to interject into the trial and focused the jury on the only relevant issue, that of a conspiracy. Once focused on the conspiracy and the overt acts establishing it, all else is surplusage. Jackson told the jury: "I perhaps can do no better service than to try to lift this case out of the morass of detail with which the record is full and put before you only the bold outlines of a case that is impressive in its simplicity . . . I must leave it to experts to comb the evidence and write volumes on their specialties, while I picture in broad strokes the defenses whose acceptance as lawful would threaten the continuity of civilization. I must, as Kipling put it, 'splash at a ten-league canvas with brushes of comet's hair.' "

The prosecutor reaps a bitter harvest if the jury does not understand its function. It is the prosecution that drives the criminal trial; the prosecution must make its case clear before the jury. Confusion results in hung juries, or even acquittals. The prosecution must therefore be at pains to keep the law and the facts as clear as possible. Jackson, recognizing his obligation, told his multinational jury: "The strength of the case against these defendants under the conspiracy count, which it is the duty of the United States to argue, is in its simplicity. It involves but three ultimate inquiries: first, have the acts defined by the charter as crimes been committed; second, were they committed pursuant to a common plan or conspiracy; third, are these defendants among those who are morally responsible?" Having clearly established the law that the jury will use, Jackson then spent the balance of his argument laying out the overt acts that proved the conspiracy.

Jackson recognized that it is difficult for any jury to retain mountains of information. There are times when the jurors are so overburdened with facts and details they lose the ability to retain the most meaningful material. The Nüremberg trial presented such a problem. There was so much testimony that the jurors' ability to retain the important evidence was severely strained. A lawyer who can help organize the evidence into manageable chunks has done a tremendous service to the jury and, more importantly, to his client. The most efficient and effective tool in this regard is a simple list, which allows for meaningful compilation of material. Jackson employed a list, one that consisted of the five groups of overt acts which made up the conspiracy. Under each of the five headings he was able to bunch a number of events without having to fear that he was overburdening his audience to the point where he would lose them. And in one deft moment near the end of his close, Jackson summed up the defendants and the key role each had played in the just-ended war:

These men in this dock, on the face of the record, were not strangers to this program of crime, nor was their connection with it remote or obscure. We find them in the very heart of it. The positions they held show that we have chosen defendants of self-evident responsibility. They are the very top surviving authorities in their respective fields and in the Nazi state.

No one lives who, at least until the very last moments of the war, outranked Göring in position, power, and influence.

No soldier stood above Keitel and Jodl, and no sailor above Raeder and Dönitz.

Who can be responsible for the duplicitous diplomacy if not the Foreign Ministers, von Neurath and [von] Ribbentrop, and the diplomatic handy man, von Papen?

Who should be answerable for the oppressive administration of occupied countries if *Gauleiters,* protectors, governors, and commissars such as Frank, Seyss-Inquart, Frick, von Schirach, von Neurath, and Rosenberg are not?

Where shall we look for those who mobilized the economy for total war if we overlook Schacht, and Speer, and Funk? Who was the master of the great slaving enterprise if it was not Sauckel? Where shall we find the hand that ran the concentration camps if it is not the hand of Kaltenbrunner?

And who whipped up the hates and fears of the public, and manipulated the party organizations to incite these crimes, if not Hess, von Schirach, Fritzsche, Bormann, and the unspeakable Julius Streicher?

The list of defendants is made up of men who played indispensable and reciprocal parts in this tragedy.

Jackson had left the jury with a clear picture of who each defendant was, and what each had done to merit a guilty verdict. Finally, justice would be done, reborn out of the ashes of war, in the courtroom at Nüremberg.

Closing Argument

The War Crimes Trial
Delivered by Robert H. Jackson
Nüremberg, Germany, July 26, 1946

Mr. President and Members of the Tribunal:

An advocate can be confronted with few more formidable tasks than to select his closing arguments where there is great disparity between his appropriate time and his available material. In eight months—a short time as state trials go—we have introduced evidence which embraces as vast and varied a panorama of events as ever has been compressed within the framework of a litigation. It is impossible in summation to do more than outline with bold strokes the vitals of this trial's mad and melancholy record, which will live as the historical text of the twentieth century's shame and depravity.

It is common to think of our own time as standing at the apex of civilization, from which the deficiencies of preceding ages may patronizingly be viewed in the light of what is assumed to be "progress." The reality is that in the long perspective of history the present century will not hold an admirable position, unless its second half is to redeem its first.

These two-score years in this twentieth century will be recorded in the book of years as one of the most bloody in all annals. Two world wars have left a legacy of dead which number more than all the armies engaged in any war that made ancient or medieval history. No half-century ever witnessed slaughter on such a scale, such cruelties and inhumanities, such wholesale deportations of peoples into slavery, such annihilations of minorities. The terror of Torquemada pales before the Nazi inquisition. These deeds are the overshadowing historical facts by which generations to come will remember this decade. If we cannot eliminate the causes and prevent the repetition of these barbaric events, it is not an irresponsible prophecy to say that this twentieth century may yet succeed in bringing the doom of civilization.

I shall not labor the law of this case. The position of the United States was explained in my opening statement. My distinguished colleague, the attorney general of Great Britain, will reply on behalf of all the chief prosecutors to the defendants' legal attack. At this stage of the proceedings, I shall rest upon the law of these crimes as laid down in the charter. The defendants, who except for the charter would have no right to be heard at all, now ask that the legal basis of this trial be nullified. This tribunal, of course, is given no power to set aside or to modify the Agreement Between the Four Powers, to which eighteen other nations have adhered. The terms of the charter are conclusive upon every party to these proceedings.

Of one thing we may be sure. The future will never have to ask, with misgiving: "What could the Nazis have said in their favor?" History will know that whatever could be said, they were allowed to say. They have been given the kind of a trial which they, in the days of their pomp and power, never gave to any man.

But fairness is not weakness. The extraordinary fairness of these hearings is an attribute of our strength. The prosecution's case, at its close, seemed inherently unassailable because it rested so heavily on German documents of unquestioned authenticity. But it was the weeks upon weeks of pecking at this case by one after another of the defendants that has demonstrated its true strength. The fact is that the testimony of the defendants has removed any doubts of guilt which, because of the extraordinary nature and magnitude of these crimes, may have existed before they spoke. They have helped write their own judgment of condemnation.

But justice in this case has nothing to do with some of the arguments put forth by the defendants or their counsel. We have not previously and we need not now discuss the merits of all their obscure and tortuous philosophy. We are not trying them for possession of obnoxious ideas. It is their right, if they choose, to renounce the Hebraic heritage in the civilization of which Germany was once a part. Nor is it our affair that they repudiated the Hellenic influence as well. The intellectual bankruptcy and moral perversion of the Nazi regime might have been no concern of international law had it not been utilized to goose-step the *Herrenvolk* across international frontiers. It is not their thoughts, it is their overt acts which we charge to be crimes. Their creed and teachings are important only as evidence of motive, purpose, knowledge, and intent.

We charge unlawful aggression but we are not trying the motives, hopes, or frustrations which may have led Germany to resort to aggressive war as an instrument of policy. The law, unlike politics, does not concern itself with the good or evil in the status quo, nor with the merits of grievances against it. It merely requires that the status quo be not attacked by violent means and that policies be not advanced by war. We may admit that overlapping ethnological and cultural groups, economic barriers, and conflicting national ambitions created in the 1930s, as they will continue to create, grave problems for Germany as well as for the other peoples of Europe. We may admit too that the world had failed to provide political or legal remedies which would be honorable and acceptable alternatives to war. We do not underwrite either the ethics or the wisdom of any country, including my own, in the face of these problems. But we do say that it is now, as it was for sometime prior to 1939, illegal and criminal for Germany or any other nation to redress grievances or seek expansion by resort to aggressive war.

Let me emphasize one cardinal point. The United States has no interest which would be advanced by the conviction of any defendant if we have not proved him guilty on at least one of the counts charged against him in the indictment. Any result that the calm and critical judgment of posterity would pronounce unjust would not be a victory for any of the countries associated in this prosecution. But in summation, we now have before us the tested evidences of criminality and have heard the flimsy excuses and paltry evasions of the defendants. The suspended judgment with which we opened this case is no longer appropriate. The time has come for final judgment and if the case I present seems hard and uncompromising, it is because the evidence makes it so.

I perhaps can do no better service than to try to lift this case out of the morass of detail with which the record is full and put before you only the bold outlines of a case that is impressive in its simplicity. True, its thousands of documents and more thousands of pages of testimony deal with an epoch, and cover a continent, and touch almost every branch of human endeavor. They illuminate specialties, such as diplomacy, naval development and warfare, land warfare, the genesis of air warfare, the politics of the Nazi rise to power, the finance and economics of totalitarian war, sociology, penology, mass psychology, and mass pathology. I must leave it to experts to comb the evidence and write volumes on their specialties, while I picture in broad strokes the offenses whose acceptance as lawful would threaten the continuity of civilization. I must, as Kipling put it, "splash at a ten-league canvas with brushes of comet's hair."

The strength of the case against these defendants under the conspiracy count, which it is the duty of the United States to argue, is in its simplicity. It involves but three ultimate inquiries: first, have the acts defined by the charter as crimes been committed; second, were they committed pursuant to a common plan or conspiracy; third, are these defendants among those who are criminally responsible?

The charge requires examination of a criminal policy, not of a multitude of isolated, unplanned, or disputed crimes. The substantive crimes upon which we rely, either as goals of a common plan or as means for its accomplishment, are admitted. The pillars which uphold the conspiracy charge may be found in five groups of overt acts, whose character and magnitude are important considerations in appraising the proof of conspiracy.

I. The Seizure of Power and Subjugation of Germany to a Police State

The Nazi party seized control of the German state in 1933. "Seizure of power" is a characterization used by defendants and defense witnesses, and so apt that it has passed into both history and everyday speech.

The Nazi *junta* in the early days lived in constant fear of overthrow. Göring, in 1934, pointed out that its enemies were legion and said: "Therefore the concentration camps have been created, where we have first confined thousands of Communists and Social Democrat functionaries."

In 1933, Göring forecast the whole program of purposeful cruelty and oppression when he publicly announced: "Whoever in the future raises a hand against a representative of the National Socialist movement or of the state, must know that he will lose his life in a very short while."

New political crimes were created to this end. It was made a treason, punishable with death, to organize or support a political party other than the Nazi party. Circulating a false or exaggerated statement, or one which would harm the state or even the party, was made a crime. Laws were enacted of such ambiguity that they could be used to punish almost any innocent act. It was, for example, made a crime to provoke "any act contrary to the public welfare."

The doctrine of punishment by analogy was introduced to enable conviction for acts which no statute forbade. Minister of Justice Gürtner explained that National Socialism considered every violation of the goals of life which the community set up for itself to be a wrong per se, and that the act could be punished even though it was not contrary to existing "formal" law.

The Gestapo and the SD were instrumentalities of an espionage system which penetrated public and private life. . . .

With all administrative offices in Nazi control and with the Reichstag reduced to impotence, the judiciary remained the last obstacle to this reign of terror. But its independence was soon overcome and it was reorganized to dispense a venal justice. Judges were ousted for political or racial reasons and were spied upon and put under pressure to join the Nazi party.

The result was the removal of all peaceable means either to resist or to change the government. Having sneaked through the portals of power, the Nazis slammed the gate in the face of all others who might also aspire to enter. Since the law was what the Nazis said it was, every form of opposition was rooted out, and every dissenting voice throttled. Germany was in the clutch of a police state, which used the fear of the concentration camp as a means to enforce nonresistance. The party was the state, the state was the party, and terror by day and death by night were the policy of both.

II. The Preparation and Waging of Wars of Aggression

From the moment the Nazis seized power, they set about by feverish but stealthy efforts, in defiance of the Versailles treaty, to arm for war. In 1933 they found an air force.

By 1939, they had twenty-one squadrons, consisting of 240 echelons or about 2,400 first-line planes, together with trainers and transports. In 1933 they found an army of three infantry and three cavalry divisions. By 1939 they had raised and equipped an army of fifty-one divisions, four of which were fully motorized and four of which were Panzer divisions. In 1933, they found a navy of one cruiser and six light cruisers. By 1939, they had built a navy of four battleships, one aircraft carrier, six cruisers, twenty-two destroyers, and fifty-four submarines. They had also built up in that period an armament industry as efficient as that of any country in the world.

These new weapons were put to use, commencing in September 1939, in a series of undeclared wars against nations with which Germany had arbitration and nonaggression treaties, and in violation of repeated assurances. On September 1, 1939, this rearmed Germany attacked Poland. The following April witnessed the invasion and occupation of Denmark and Norway, and May saw the overrunning of Belgium, the Netherlands, and Luxembourg. Another spring found Yugoslavia and Greece under attack, and in June 1941 came the invasion of Soviet Russia. Then Japan, which Germany had embraced as a partner, struck without warning at Pearl Harbor in December 1941 and four days later Germany declared war on the United States.

We need not trouble ourselves about the many abstract difficulties that can be conjured up about what constitutes aggression in doubtful cases. I shall show you, in discussing the conspiracy, that by any test ever put forward by any responsible authority, by all the canons of plain sense, these were unlawful wars of aggression in breach of treaties and in violation of assurances.

III. Warfare in Disregard of International Law

It is unnecessary to labor this point on the facts. Göring asserts that the Rules of Land Warfare were obsolete, that no nation could fight a total war within their limits. He testified that the Nazis would have denounced the conventions to which Germany was a party, but that General Jodl wanted captured German soldiers to continue to benefit from their observance by the Allies.

It was, however, against the Soviet people and Soviet prisoners that Teutonic fury knew no bounds, in spite of a warning by Admiral Canaris that the treatment was in violation of international law.

We need not, therefore, for purposes of the conspiracy count, recite the revolting details of starving, beating, murdering, freezing, and mass extermination admittedly used against the eastern soldiery. Also, we may take as established or admitted that the lawless conduct such as shooting British and American airmen, mistreatment of western prisoners of war, forcing French prisoners of war into German war work, and other deliberate violations of the Hague and Geneva Conventions, did occur, and in obedience to highest levels of authority.

IV. Enslavement and Plunder of Populations
in Occupied Countries

The defendant Sauckel, plenipotentiary general for the Utilization of Labor, is authority for the statement that "out of five million foreign workers who arrived in Germany, not even 200,000 came voluntarily." It was officially reported to defendant Rosenberg that in his territory "recruiting methods were used which probably have their origin in the blackest period of the slave trade." Sauckel himself reported that male and female agents went hunting for men, got them drunk, and "shanghaied" them to Germany. These captives were shipped in trains without heat, food, or sanitary facilities. The dead were thrown out at stations, and the newborn were thrown out the windows of moving trains.

Sauckel ordered that "all the men must be fed, sheltered, and treated in such a way as to exploit them to the highest possible extent at the lowest conceivable degree of expenditure." About two million of these were employed directly in the manufacture of armaments and munitions. The director of the Krupp locomotive factory in Essen complained to the company that Russian forced laborers were so underfed that they were too weakened to do their work, and the Krupp doctor confirmed their pitiable condition. Soviet workers were put in camps under Gestapo guards, who were allowed to punish disobedience by confinement in a concentration camp or by hanging on the spot.

Populations of occupied countries were otherwise exploited and oppressed unmercifully. Terrorism was the order of the day. Civilians were arrested without charges, committed without counsel, executed without hearing. Villages were destroyed, the male inhabitants shot or sent to concentration camps, the women sent to forced labor, and the children scattered abroad. The extent of the slaughter in Poland alone was indicated by Frank, who reported: "If I wanted to have a poster put up for every seven Poles who were shot, the forests of Poland would not suffice for producing the paper for such posters."

International law at all times before and during this war spoke with precision and authority respecting the protection due civilians of an occupied country, and the slave trade and plunder of occupied countries were at all times flagrantly unlawful.

V. Persecution and Extermination of Jews and Christians

The Nazi movement will be of evil memory in history because of its persecution of the Jews, the most far-flung and terrible racial persecution of all time. Although the Nazi party neither invented nor monopolized anti-Semitism, its leaders from the very beginning embraced it, incited it, and exploited it. They used it as "the psychological spark that ignites the mob." After the seizure of power, it became an official state policy. The persecution began in a series of discriminatory laws eliminating the Jews from the civil service, the professions, and economic life. As it became more intense it included segregation of Jews in ghettos and exile. Riots were organized by party leaders to loot Jewish business places and to burn synagogues. Jewish property was confiscated and a collective fine of a billion marks was imposed upon German Jewry. The program progressed in fury and irresponsibility to the "final solution." This consisted of sending all Jews who were fit to work to concentration camps as slave laborers, and all who were not fit, which included children under twelve and people over fifty, as well as any others judged unfit by an SS doctor, to concentration camps for extermination.

Adolf Eichmann, the sinister figure who had charge of the extermination program, has estimated that the anti-Jewish activities resulted in the killing of six million Jews. Of these, four million were killed in extermination institutions, and two million were killed by *Einsatzgruppen,* mobile units of the Security Police and SD, which pursued Jews in the ghettos and in their homes and slaughtered them by gas wagons, by mass shooting in antitank ditches, and by every device which Nazi ingenuity could conceive. So thorough and uncompromising was this program that the Jews of Europe as a race no longer exist, thus fulfilling the diabolic "prophecy" of Adolf Hitler at the beginning of the war.

Of course, any such program must reckon with the opposition of the Christian church. This was recognized from the very beginning. Defendant Bormann wrote all *Gauleiters* in 1941 that "National Socialism and Christian concepts are irreconcilable," and that the people must be separated from the churches and the influence of the churches totally removed. Defendant Rosenberg even wrote dreary treatises advocating a new and weird Nazi religion.

The Gestapo appointed "church specialists" who were instructed that the ultimate aim was "destruction of the confessional churches." The record is full of specific instances of the persecution of clergymen, the confiscation of church property, interference with religious publications, disruption of religious education, and suppression of religious organizations.

The chief instrumentality for persecution and extermination was the concentration camp, sired by defendant Göring and nurtured under the overall authority of defendants Frick and Kaltenbrunner.

The horrors of these iniquitous places have been vividly disclosed by documents and testified to by witnesses. The tribunal must be satiated with ghastly verbal and pictorial portrayals. From your records it is clear that the concentration camps were the first and worst weapon of oppression used by the National Socialist state, and that they were the primary means utilized for the persecution of the Christian church and the extermination of the Jewish race. This has been admitted to you by some of the defendants from the witness stand. In the words of defendant Frank: "A thousand years will pass and this guilt of Germany will still not be erased."

These, then, were the five great substantive crimes of the Nazi regime. Their commission, which cannot be denied, stands admitted. . . .

I pass now to the inquiry [as to] whether these groups of criminal acts were integrated in a common plan or conspiracy.

The Common Plan or Conspiracy

The prosecution submits that these five categories of premeditated crimes were not separate and independent phenomena but that all were committed pursuant to a common plan or conspiracy. The defense admits that these classes of crimes were committed but denies that they are connected one with another as parts of a single program.

The central crime in this pattern of crime, the kingpin which holds them all together, is the plot for aggressive war. The chief reason for international cognizance of these crimes lies in this fact. Have we established the plan or conspiracy to make aggressive war?

Certain admitted or clearly proven facts help answer that question. First is the fact that such war of aggression did take place. Second, it is admitted that from the moment the Nazis came to power, every one of them and every one of the defendants worked like beavers to prepare for *some* war. . . .

The plans of Adolf Hitler for aggression were just as secret as *Mein Kampf,* of which over six million copies were published in Germany. He not only openly advocated overthrowing the Treaty of Versailles, but made demands which went far beyond a mere rectification of its alleged injustices. He avowed an intention to attack neighboring states and seize their lands, which he said would have to be won with "the power of a triumphant sword." Here, for every German to hearken to, were the "ancestral voices prophesying war."

Göring has testified in this courtroom that at his first meeting with Hitler, long before the seizure of power: "I noted that Hitler had a definite view of the impotency of protest and, as a second point, that he was of the opinion that Germany should be freed of the peace of Versailles. . . . We did not say we shall have to have a war and defeat our enemies; this was the aim and the methods had to be adapted to the political situation."

When asked if this goal were to be accomplished by war if necessary,

Göring did not deny that eventuality but evaded a direct answer by say-ing: "We did not even debate about those things at that time." He went on to say that the aim to overthrow the Treaty of Versailles was open and notorious and that "every German in my opinion was for its modifica-tion, and there was no doubt that this was a strong inducement for join-ing the party." Thus, there can be no possible excuse for any person who aided Hitler to get absolute power over the German people, or took a part in his regime, to fail to know the nature of the demands he would make on Germany's neighbors.

Immediately after the seizure of power, the Nazis went to work to implement these aggressive intentions by preparing for war. They first enlisted German industrialists in a secret rearmament program. Twenty days after the seizure of power, Schacht was host to Hitler, Göring, and some twenty leading industrialists. Among them were Krupp von Bohlen of the great Krupp armament works and representatives of I. G. Farben and other Ruhr heavy industries. Hitler and Göring explained their program to the industrialists, who became so enthusiastic that they set about to raise three million Reichsmarks to strengthen and confirm the Nazi party in power. Two months later Krupp was working to bring a reorganized association of German industry into agreement with the political aims of the Nazi government. Krupp later boasted of the suc-cess in keeping the German war industries secretly alive and in readi-ness despite the disarmament clauses of the Versailles treaty, and recalled the industrialists' enthusiastic acceptance of "the great intentions of the führer in the rearmament period of 1933 to '39."

The spirit of the whole Nazi administration was summed up by Göring at a meeting of the Council of Ministers, which included Schacht, on May 27, 1936, when he said, "All measures are to be con-sidered from the standpoint of an assured waging of war."

As early as November 5, 1937, the plan to attack had begun to take definiteness as to time and victim. In a meeting which included defen-dants Raeder, Göring, and von Neurath, Hitler stated the cynical objec-tive: "The question for Germany is where the greatest possible conquest could be made at the lowest possible cost."

Six months later, emboldened by the bloodless Austrian conquest, Hitler, in a secret directive to Keitel . . . stated his "unalterable decision to smash Czechoslovakia by military action in the near future." On the same day, Jodl noted in his diary that the führer had stated his final deci-sion to destroy Czechoslovakia soon and had initiated military preparations all along the line. By April the plan had been perfected to attack Czecho-slovakia "with lightning-swift action as the result of an 'incident.' "

All along the line, preparations became more definite for a war of expansion, on the assumption that it would result in worldwide conflict.

By May 1939, the Nazi preparations had ripened to the point that Hitler confided to defendants Göring, Raeder, Keitel, and others his readiness "to attack Poland at the first suitable opportunity," even though he recognized that "further successes cannot be attained with-out the shedding of blood."

While a credulous world slumbered, snugly blanketed with perfidi-ous assurances of peaceful intentions, the Nazis prepared not merely as before for *a* war, but now for *the* war. The defendants Göring, Keitel, Raeder, Frick, and Funk, with others, met as the Reich Defense Coun-cil in June 1939. The minutes, authenticated by Göring, are revealing evidence of the way in which each step of Nazi planning dovetailed with every other. These five key defendants, three months before the first Panzer unit had knifed into Poland, were laying plans for "employment of the *population* in wartime," and had gone so far as to classify industry for priority in labor supply "after five million servicemen had been called up." They decided upon measures to avoid "confusion when mobilization takes place," and declared a purpose "to gain and maintain the lead in the decisive initial weeks of a war." They then planned to use in production prisoners of war, criminal prisoners, and concentration camp inmates. They then decided on "compulsory work for women in wartime."

Here also comes to the surface the link between war labor and con-centration camps, a manpower source that was increasingly used and with increasing cruelty. An agreement between Himmler and Minister of Justice Thierack in 1942 provided for "the delivery of antisocial ele-ments from the execution of their sentence to the Reichsführer SS to be worked to death." An SS directive provided that bedridden prisoners be drafted for work to be performed in bed. The Gestapo ordered 45,000 Jews arrested to increase the "recruitment of manpower into the con-centration camps." One hundred thousand Jews were brought from Hungary to augment the camps' manpower. On the initiative of the defendant Dönitz, concentration camp labor was used in the construc-tion of submarines. Concentration camps were thus geared into war production on the one hand, and into the administration of justice and the political aims of the Nazis on the other.

The use of prisoner-of-war labor as here planned also grew with German needs. At a time when every German soldier was needed at the front and forces were not available at home, Russian prisoners of war were forced to man anti-aircraft guns against Allied planes. Field Marshal Milch reflected the Nazi merriment at this flagrant violation of international law, saying, "This is an amusing thing, that the Russians must work the guns." The orders for the treatment of Soviet prisoners of war were so ruthless that Admiral Canaris, pointing out that they would "result in arbitrary mistreatments and killings," protested against them as breaches of international law. The reply of Keitel was unambiguous: "The objections arise from the military conception of chivalrous warfare! This is the destruction of an ideology! Therefore I approve and back the measures."

Other crimes in the conduct of warfare were planned with equal thoroughness as a means of insuring the victory of German arms. In October 1938, almost a year before the start of the war, the large-scale violation of the established rules of warfare was contemplated as a policy, and the Supreme Command circulated a most secret list of devious explanations to be given by the propaganda minister in such cases. Even before this time, commanders of the armed forces were instructed to employ any means of warfare so long as it facilitated victory. After the war was in progress the orders increased in savagery. A typical Keitel order, demanding use of the "most brutal means," provided that: "It is the duty of the troops to use all means without restriction, even against women and children, so long as it insures success."

The German naval forces were no more immune from the infection than the land forces. Raeder ordered violations of the accepted rules of warfare whenever necessary to gain strategic successes. Dönitz urged his submarine crews not to rescue survivors of torpedoed enemy ships in order to cripple merchant shipping of the Allied nations by decimating their crews.

Thus, the war crimes against Allied forces and the crimes against humanity committed in occupied territories are incontestably part of the program of making the war because, in the German calculations, they were indispensable to its hope of success.

Similarly, the whole group of prewar crimes, including the persecutions within Germany, fall into place around the plan for aggressive war like stones in a finely wrought mosaic. Nowhere is the whole catalogue of crimes of Nazi oppression and terrorism within Germany so well integrated with the crime of war as in that strange mixture of wind and wisdom which makes up the testimony of Hermann Göring. In describing the aims of the Nazi program before the seizure of power, Goring said: "The first question was to achieve and establish a different political structure for Germany which would enable Germany to obtain against the Dictate [of Versailles], and not only a protest, but an objection of such a nature that it would actually be considered."

From Göring's cross-examination we learn how necessarily the whole program of crime followed. Because they considered a strong state necessary to get rid of the Versailles treaty, they adopted the *Führerprinzip*. Having seized power, the Nazis thought it necessary to protect it by abolishing parliamentary government and suppressing all organized opposition from political parties. This was reflected in the philosophy of Göring that the opera was more important than the Reichstag. . . . In order to eliminate incorrigible opponents, it was necessary to establish concentration camps and to resort to the device of protective custody. Protective custody, Göring testified, meant that: "People were arrested and taken into protective custody who had committed no crime but who one might expect, if they remained in freedom, would do all sorts of things to damage the German state."

The same purpose was dominant in the persecution of the Jews. In the beginning, fanaticism and political opportunism played a principal part, for anti-Semitism and its allied scapegoat mythology were a vehicle on which the Nazis rode to power. It was for this reason that the filthy Streicher and the blasphemous Rosenberg were welcomed to a place at party rallies and made leaders and officials of the state or party. But the Nazis soon regarded the Jews as foremost amongst the opposition to the police state with which they planned to put forward their plans of military aggression. Fear of their pacifism and their opposition to strident nationalism was given as the reason that the Jews had to be driven from the political and economic life of Germany. Accordingly, they were transported like cattle to the concentration camps, where they were utilized as a source of forced labor for war purposes.

A glance over the dock will show that, despite quarrels among themselves, each defendant played a part which fitted in with every other, and that all advanced the common plan. It contradicts experience that men of such diverse backgrounds and talents should so forward each other's aims by coincidence.

The large and varied role of Göring was half militarist and half gangster. He stuck a pudgy finger in every pie. He used his SA musclemen to help bring the gang into power. In order to entrench that power, he contrived to have the Reichstag burned, established the Gestapo, and created the concentration camps. He was equally adept at massacring opponents and at framing scandals to get rid of stubborn generals. He built up the Luftwaffe and hurled it at his defenseless neighbors. . . . He was, next to Hitler, the man who tied the activities of all the defendants together in a common effort.

The parts played by the other defendants, although less comprehensive and less spectacular than that of the Reichsmarshal, were nevertheless integral and necessary contributions to the joint undertaking, without any one of which the success of the common enterprise would have been in jeopardy. There are many specific deeds of which these men have been proven guilty. No purpose would be served—nor indeed is time available—to review all the crimes which the evidence has charged up to their names. Nevertheless, in viewing the conspiracy as a whole and as an operating mechanism, it may be well to recall briefly the outstanding services which each of the men in the dock rendered to the common cause.

The zealot Hess, before succumbing to wanderlust, was the engineer tending the party machinery, passing orders and propaganda down to the Leadership Corps, supervising every aspect of party activities, and maintaining the organization as a loyal and ready instrument of power. When apprehensions abroad threatened the success of the Nazi scheme for conquest, it was the duplicitous von Ribbentrop, the salesman of deception, who was detailed to pour wine on the troubled waters of suspicion by preaching the gospel of limited and peaceful intentions. Keitel, weak and willing tool, delivered the armed forces, the instrument of aggression, over to the party and directed them in executing its felonious designs.

Kaltenbrunner, the grand inquisitor, took up the bloody mantle of Heydrich to stifle opposition and terrorize compliance, and buttressed the power of National Socialism on a foundation of guiltless corpses. It was Rosenberg, the intellectual high priest of the "master race," who provided the doctrine of hatred which gave the impetus for the annihilation of Jewry, and who put his infidel theories into practice against the eastern occupied territories. His woolly philosophy also added boredom to the long list of Nazi atrocities. The fanatical Frank, who solidified Nazi control by establishing the new order of authority without law, so that the will of the party was the only test of legality, proceeded to export his lawlessness to Poland, which he governed with the lash of Caesar and whose population he reduced to sorrowing remnants. Frick, the ruthless organizer, helped the party to seize power, supervised the police agencies to insure that it stayed in power, and chained the economy of Bohemia and Moravia to the German war machine.

Streicher, the venomous vulgarian, manufactured and distributed obscene racial libels which incited the populace to accept and assist the progressively savage operations of "race purification." As minister of Economics, Funk accelerated the pace of rearmament, and as Reichsbank president banked for the SS the gold teeth fillings of concentration camp victims—probably the most ghoulish collateral in banking history. It was Schacht, the facade of starched respectability, who in the early days provided the window dressing, the bait for the hesitant, and whose wizardry later made it possible for Hitler to finance the colossal rearmament program, and to do it secretly.

Dönitz, Hitler's legatee of defeat, promoted the success of the Nazi aggressions by instructing his pack of submarine killers to conduct warfare at sea with the illegal ferocity of the jungle. Raeder, the political admiral, stealthily built up the German Navy in defiance of the Versailles treaty, and then put it to use in a series of aggressions which he had taken a large part in planning. Von Schirach, poisoner of a generation, initiated the German youth in Nazi doctrine, trained them in legions for service in the SS and Wehrmacht, and delivered them up to the party as fanatic, unquestioning executors of its will.

Sauchel, the greatest and cruelest slaver since the pharaohs of Egypt, produced desperately needed manpower by driving foreign peoples into the land of bondage on a scale unknown even in the ancient days of tyranny in the kingdom of the Nile. Jodl, betrayer of the traditions of his profession, led the Wehrmacht in violating its own code of military honor in order to carry out the barbarous aims of Nazi policy. Von Papen, pious agent of an infidel regime, held the stirrup while Hitler vaulted into the saddle, lubricated the Austrian annexation, and devoted his diplomatic cunning to the service of Nazi objectives abroad.

Seyss-Inquart, spearhead of the Austrian fifth column, took over the government of his own country only to make a present of it to Hitler, and then, moving north, brought terror and oppression to the Netherlands and pillaged its economy for the benefit of the German juggernaut. Von Neurath, the old-school diplomat, who cast the pearls of his experience before Nazis, guided Nazi diplomacy in the early years, soothed the fears of prospective victims, and as Reich protector of Bohemia and Moravia, strengthened the German position for the coming attack on Poland. Speer, as minister of Armaments and War Production, joined in planning and executing the program to dragoon prisoners of war and foreign workers into German war industries, which waxed in output while the laborers waned in starvation. Fritzsche, radio propaganda chief, by manipulation of the truth goaded German public opinion into frenzied support of the regime and anesthetized the independent judgment of the population so that they did without question their masters' bidding. And Bormann, who has not accepted our invitation to this reunion, sat at the throttle of the vast and powerful engine of the party, guiding it in the ruthless execution of Nazi policies, from the scourging of the Christian church to the lynching of captive Allied airmen.

The activities of all these defendants, despite their varied backgrounds and talents, were joined with the efforts of other conspirators not now in the dock, who played still other essential roles. They blend together into one consistent and militant pattern animated by a common objective to reshape the map of Europe by force of arms. Some of these defendants were ardent members of the Nazi movement from its birth. Others, less fanatical, joined the common enterprise later, after successes had made participation attractive by the promise of rewards. This group of latter-day converts remedied a crucial defect in the ranks of the original true believers, for as Dr. Seimers has pointed out in his summation: "There were no specialists among the National Socialists for the particular tasks. Most of the National Socialist collaborators did not previously follow a trade requiring technical education." It was the fatal weakness of the early Nazi band that it lacked technical competence. It could not from among its own ranks make up a government capable of carrying out all the projects necessary to realize its aims. Therein lies the special crime and betrayal of men like Schacht and von Neurath, Speer and von Papen, Raeder and Dönitz, Keitel and Jodl. It is doubtful whether the Nazi master plan could have succeeded without their specialized intelligence which they so willingly put at its command. They did so with knowledge of its announced aims and methods, and continued their services after practice had confirmed the direction in which they were tending. Their superiority to the average run of Nazi mediocrity is not their excuse. It is their condemnation.

The dominant fact which stands out from all the thousands of pages of the record of this trial is that the central crime of the whole group of Nazi crimes—the attack on the peace of the world—was clearly and deliberately planned. The beginning of these wars of aggression was not an unprepared and spontaneous springing to arms by a population excited by some current indignation. A week before the invasion of Poland, Hitler told his military commanders: "I shall give a propagandist cause for starting war—never mind whether it be plausible or not. The victor shall not be asked later on whether we told the truth or not. In starting and making a war, not the right is what matters, but victory." The propagandist incident was duly provided by dressing concentration camp inmates in Polish uniforms, in order to create the appearance of a Polish attack on a German frontier radio station. The plan to occupy Belgium, Holland, and Luxembourg first appeared as early as August 1938 in connection with the plan for attack on Czechoslovakia. The intention to attack became a program in May 1939, when Hitler told his commanders that: "The Dutch and Belgian air bases must be occupied by armed forces. Declarations of neutrality must be ignored." Thus, the follow-up wars were planned before the first was launched. These were the most carefully plotted wars in all history. Scarcely a step in their terrifying succession and progress failed to move according to the master blueprint or the subsidiary schedules and timetables until long after the crimes of aggression were consummated.

Nor were the war crimes and the crimes against humanity unplanned, isolated, or spontaneous offenses. Aside from our undeniable evidence of their plotting, it is sufficient to ask whether six million people could be separated from the population of several nations on the basis of their blood and birth, could be destroyed and their bodies disposed of, except that the operation fitted into the general scheme of government. Could the enslavement of five millions of laborers, their impressment into service, their transportation to Germany, their allocation to work where they would be most useful, their maintenance—if slow starvation can be called maintenance—and their guarding have been accomplished if it did not fit into the common plan? Could hundreds of concentration camps located throughout Germany, built to accommodate hundreds of thousands of victims, and each requiring labor and materials for construction, manpower to operate and supervise, and close gearing into the economy—could such efforts have been expended under German autocracy if they had not suited the plan?

Has the Teutonic passion for organization become famous for its toleration of nonconforming activity? Each part of the plan fitted into every other. The slave labor program meshed with the needs of industry and agriculture, and these in turn synchronized with the military machine. The elaborate propaganda apparatus geared with the program to dominate the people and incite them to a war their sons would have to fight. The armament industries were fed by the concentration camps. The concentration camps were fed by the Gestapo.

The Gestapo was fed by the spy system of the Nazi party. Nothing was permitted under the Nazi iron rule that was not in accordance with the program. Everything of consequence that took place in this regimented society was but a manifestation of a premeditated and unfolding purpose to secure the Nazi state a place in the sun by casting all others into darkness.

Common Defenses Against the Charge of Common Responsibility

The defendants meet this overwhelming case, some by admitting a limited responsibility, some by putting the blame on others, and some by taking the position, in effect, that while there have been enormous crimes there are no criminals. Time will not permit me to examine each individual and peculiar defense, but there are certain lines of defense common to so many cases that they deserve some consideration.

Counsel for many of the defendants seek to dismiss the conspiracy or common-planning charge on the ground that the pattern of the Nazi plan does not fit the concept of conspiracy applicable in German law to the plotting of a highway robbery or a burglary. Their concept of conspiracy is in the terms of a stealthy meeting in the dead of night, in a secluded hideout, in which a group of felons plot every detail of a specific crime. The charter forestalls resort to such parochial and narrow concepts of conspiracy taken from local law by using the additional and nontechnical term, "common plan." Omitting entirely the alternative term of "conspiracy," the charter reads that "leaders, organizers, instigators, and accomplices participating in the formulation or execution of a common plan to commit" any of the described crimes "are responsible for all acts performed by any persons in execution of such plan."

The charter concept of a common plan really represents the conspiracy principle in an international context. A common plan or conspiracy to seize the machinery of a state, to commit crimes against the peace of the world, to blot a race out of existence, to enslave millions, and to subjugate and loot whole nations cannot be thought of in the same terms as the plotting of petty crimes, although the same underlying principles are applicable. Little gangsters may plan which will carry a pistol and which a stiletto, who will approach a victim from the front and who from behind, and where they will waylay him. But in planning a war, the pistol becomes a Wehrmacht, the stiletto a Luftwaffe. Where to strike is not a choice of dark alleys, but a matter of world geography. The operation involves the manipulation of public opinion, the law of the state, the police power, industry, and finance. The baits and bluffs must be translated into a nation's foreign policy. Likewise, the degree of stealth which points to a guilty purpose in a conspiracy will depend upon its object. The clandestine preparations of a state against international society, although camouflaged to those abroad, might be quite open and notorious among its own people. But stealth is not an essential ingredient of such planning.

The defendants contend, however, that there could be no conspiracy involving aggressive war because: 1) none of the Nazis wanted war; 2) rearmament was only intended to provide the strength to make Germany's voice heard in the family of nations; and 3) the wars were not in fact aggressive wars but were defensive against a "Bolshevik menace."

When we analyze the argument that the Nazis did not want war it comes down, in substance, to this: "The record looks bad indeed—objectively—but when you consider the state of my mind—I subjectively hated war. I knew the horrors of war. I wanted peace." I am not so sure of this. I am even less willing to accept Göring's description of the general staff as pacifist. However, it will not injure our case to admit that as an abstract proposition none of these defendants liked war. But they wanted things which they knew they could not get without war. They wanted their neighbors' lands and goods. Their philosophy seems to be that if the neighbors would not acquiesce, then they are the aggressors and are to blame for the war. The fact is, however, that war never became terrible to the Nazis until it came home to them, until it exposed their deceptive assurances to the German people that German cities, like the ruined one in which we meet, would be invulnerable. From then on war was terrible.

But again the defendants claim: "To be sure, we were building guns. But not to shoot. They were only to give us weight in negotiating." At its best, this argument amounts to a contention that the military forces were intended for blackmail, not for battle. The threat of military invasion which forced the Austrian *Anschluss,* the threats which preceded Munich, and Göring's threat to bomb the beautiful city of Prague if the president of Czechoslovakia did not consent to the protectorate, are examples of what the defendants have in mind when they talk of arming to back negotiation.

Did these defendants then intend to withdraw German demands, or was Germany to enforce them and manipulate propaganda so as to place the blame for the war on the nation so unreasonable as to resist? Events have answered that question, and documents such as Admiral Carls's memorandum, quoted earlier, leave no doubt that the events occurred as anticipated.

But some of the defendants argue that the wars were not aggressive and were only intended to protect Germany against some eventual danger from the "menace of communism," which was something of an obsession with many Nazis.

At the outset this argument of self-defense fails because it completely ignores this damning combination of facts clearly established in the record; first, the enormous and rapid German preparations for war; second, the repeatedly avowed intentions of the German leaders to attack, which I have previously cited; and third, the fact that a series of wars occurred in which German forces struck the first blows, without warning, across the borders of other nations.

Even if it could be shown—which it cannot be—that the Russian war was really defensive, such is demonstrably not the case with those wars which preceded it.

It may also be pointed out that even those who would have you believe that Germany was menaced by communism also compete with each other in describing their opposition to the disastrous Russian venture. Is it reasonable that they would have opposed that war if it were undertaken in good faith self-defense?

The frivolous character of the self-defense theory on the facts is that it sought to compensate, as advocates often do, by resort to a theory of law. Dr. Jahrreiss, in his scholarly argument for the defense, rightly points out that no treaty provision and no principle of law denied Germany, as a sovereign nation, the right of self-defense. He follows with the assertion, for which there is authority in classic international law, that: ". . . Every state is alone judge of whether in a given case it is waging a war of self-defense." It is not necessary to examine the validity of an abstract principle which does not apply to the facts of our case. I do not doubt that if a nation arrived at a judgment that it must resort to war in self-defense, because of conditions affording reasonable grounds for such an honest judgment, any tribunal would accord it great and perhaps conclusive weight, even if later events proved that judgment mistaken.

But the facts in this case call for no such deference to honest judgment because no such judgment was even pretended, much less honestly made.

In all the documents which disclose the planning and rationalization of these attacks, not one sentence has been or can be cited to show a good faith fear of attack. It may be that statesmen of other nations lacked the courage forthrightly and fully to disarm. Perhaps they suspected the secret rearmament of Germany. But if they hesitated to abandon arms, they did not hesitate to neglect them. Germany well knew that her former enemies had allowed their armaments to fall into decay, so little did they contemplate another war. Germany faced a Europe that not only was unwilling to attack, but was too weak and pacifist even adequately to defend, and went to the very verge of dishonor, if not beyond, to buy its peace. The minutes we have shown you of the Nazis' secret conclaves identify no potential attacker. They bristle with the spirit of aggression and not of defense. They contemplate always territorial expansion, not the maintenance of territorial integrity.

If these defendants may now cynically plead self-defense, although no good faith need of self-defense was asserted or contemplated by any responsible leader at the time, it reduces nonaggression treaties to a legal absurdity. They become only additional instruments of deception in the hands of the aggressor, and traps for well-meaning nations. If there be in nonaggression pacts an implied condition that each nation may make a bona fide judgment as to the necessity for self-defense against imminent, threatened attack, they certainly cannot be invoked to shelter those who never made any such judgment at all.

In opening this case, I ventured to predict that there would be no serious denial that the crimes charged were committed, and that the issue would concern the responsibility of particular defendants. The defendants have fulfilled that prophecy. Generally, they do not deny that these things happened, but it is contended that they "just happened," and that they were not the result of a common plan or conspiracy.

One of the chief reasons the defendants say there was no conspiracy is the argument that conspiracy was impossible with a dictator. The argument runs that they all had to obey Hitler's orders, which had the force of law in the German state, and hence obedience cannot be made the basis of a criminal charge. In this way it is explained that while there have been wholesale killings, there have been no murderers.

This argument is an effort to evade Article 8 of the charter, which provides that the order of the government or of a superior shall not free a defendant from responsibility but can only be considered in mitigation.

Like much of the defense counsel's abstract arguments, the contention that the absolute power of Hitler precluded a conspiracy crumbles in face of the facts of record. The *Führerprinzip* of absolutism was itself a part of the common plan, as Göring has pointed out. The defendants may have become slaves of a dictator, but he was *their* dictator. To make him such was, as Göring has testified, the object of the Nazi movement from the beginning. Every Nazi took this oath: "I pledge eternal allegiance to Adolf Hitler. I pledge unconditional obedience to him and the führers appointed by him." Moreover, they forced everybody else in their power to take it. This oath was illegal under German law, which made it criminal to become a member of an organization in which obedience to "unknown superiors or unconditional obedience to known superiors is pledged." These men destroyed free government in Germany and now plead to be excused from responsibility because they became slaves. They are in the position of the fictional boy who murdered his father and mother and then pleaded for leniency because he was an orphan.

What these men have overlooked is that Adolf Hitler's acts are their acts. It was these men among millions of others, and it was these men leading millions of others, who built up Adolf Hitler and vested in his psychopathic personality not only innumerable lesser decisions but the supreme issue of war or peace. They intoxicated him with power and adulation. They fed his hates and aroused his fears. They put a loaded gun in his eager hands. It was left to Hitler to pull the trigger, and when he did they all at that time approved. His guilt stands admitted, by some defendants reluctantly, by some vindictively. But his guilt is the guilt of the whole dock, and of every man in it.

But it is urged that these defendants could not be in agreement on a common plan or in a conspiracy because they were fighting among themselves or belonged to different factions or cliques. Of course, it is not necessary that men should agree on everything in order to agree on enough things to make them liable for a criminal conspiracy. Unquestionably there were conspiracies within the conspiracy, and intrigues and rivalries and battles for power. Schacht and Göring disagree, but over which of them should control the economy, not over whether the economy should be regimented for war. Göring claims to have departed from the plan because through Dahlerus he conducted some negotiations with men of influence in England just before the Polish war. But it is perfectly clear that this was not an effort to prevent aggression against Poland but to make that aggression successful and safe by obtaining English neutrality. Rosenberg and Göring may have had some differences as to how stolen art should be distributed but they had none about how it should be stolen. Jodl and Goebbels may have disagreed about whether to denounce the Geneva Convention, but they never disagreed about violating it. And so it goes through the whole long and sordid story. Nowhere do we find an instance where any one of the defendants stood up against the rest and said: "This thing is wrong and I will not go along with it." Wherever they differed, their differences were as to method or disputes over jurisdiction, but always within the framework of the common plan.

Some of the defendants also contend that in any event, there was no conspiracy to commit war crimes against humanity because cabinet members never met with the military to plan these acts. But these crimes were only the inevitable and incidental results of the plan to commit the aggression for *Lebensraum* purposes. . . . This was *Lebensraum* on its seamy side. Could men of their practical intelligence expect to get neighboring lands free from the claims of their tenants without committing crimes against humanity?

The last stand of each defendant is that even if there was a conspiracy, he was not in it. It is therefore important in examining their attempts at avoidance of responsibility to know, first of all, just what it is that a conspiracy charge comprehends and punishes.

In conspiracy we do not punish one man for another man's crime. We seek to punish each for his own crime of joining a common criminal plan in which others also participated. The measure of the criminality of the plan and therefore of the guilt of each participant is, of course, the sum total of crimes committed by all in executing the plan. But the gist of the offense is participation in the formulation or execution of the plan. These are rules which every society has found necessary in order to reach men, like these defendants, who never get blood on their own hands but who lay plans that result in the shedding of blood. All over Germany today, in every zone of occupation, little men who carried out these criminal policies under orders are being convicted and punished. It would present a vast and unforgivable caricature of justice if the men who planned these policies and directed these little men should escape all penalty.

These men in this dock, on the face of the record, were not strangers to this program of crime, nor was their connection with it remote or obscure. We find them in the very heart of it. The positions they held show that we have chosen defendants of self-evident responsibility. They are the very top surviving authorities in their respective fields and in the Nazi state. No one lives who, at least until the very last moments of the war, outranked Göring in position, power, and influence. No soldier stood above Keitel and Jodl, and no sailor above Raeder and Dönitz. Who can be responsible for the duplicitous diplomacy if not the foreign ministers, von Neurath and [von] Ribbentrop, and the diplomatic handy man, von Papen? Who should be answerable for the oppressive administration of occupied countries if *Gauleiters,* protectors, governors, and commissars such as Frank, Seyss-Inquart, Frick, von Schirach, von Neurath, and Rosenberg are not? Where shall we look for those who mobilized the economy for total war if we overlook Schacht, and Speer, and Funk? Who was the master of the great slaving enterprise if it was not Sauckel? Where shall we find the hand that ran the concentration camps if it is not the hand of Kaltenbrunner? And who whipped up the hates and fears of the public, and manipulated the party organizations to incite these crimes, if not Hess, von Schirach, Fritzsche, Bormann, and the unspeakable Julius Streicher? The list of defendants is made up of men who played indispensable and reciprocal parts in this tragedy. The photographs and films show them again and again together on important occasions. The documents show them agreed on policies and on methods, and all working aggressively for the expansion of Germany by force of arms.

Each of these men made a real contribution to the Nazi plan. Every man had a key part. Deprive the Nazi regime of the functions performed by a Schacht, a Sauckel, a von Papen, or a Göring, and you have a different regime. Look down the rows of fallen men and picture them as the photographic and documentary evidence shows them to have been in their days of power. Is there one whose work did not substantially advance the conspiracy along its bloody path toward its bloody goal? Can we assume that the great effort of these men's lives was directed toward ends they never suspected?

To escape the implications of their positions and the inference of guilt from their activities, the defendants are almost unanimous in one defense. The refrain is heard time and again: these men were without authority, without knowledge, without influence, indeed without importance. Funk summed up the general self-abasement of the dock in his plaintive lament that, "I always, so to speak, came up to the door. But I was not permitted to enter."

In the testimony of each defendant, at some point there was reached the familiar blank wall: nobody knew anything about what was going on. Time after time we have heard the chorus from the dock: "I only heard about these things here for the first time."

These men saw no evil, spoke none, and none was uttered in their presence. This claim might sound very plausible if made by one defendant. But when we put all their stories together, the impression which emerges of the Third Reich, which was to last a thousand years, is ludicrous. If we combine only the stories from the front bench, this is the ridiculous composite picture of Hitler's government that emerges. It was composed of:

A number-two man who knew nothing of the excesses of the Gestapo which he created, and never suspected the Jewish extermination program although he was the signer of over a score of decrees which instituted the persecutions of that race;

A number-three man who was merely an innocent middleman transmitting Hitler's orders without even reading them, like a postman or delivery boy;

A foreign minister who knew little of foreign affairs and nothing of foreign policy;

A field marshal who issued orders to the armed forces but had no idea of the results they would have in practice;

A security chief who was of the impression that the policing functions of his Gestapo and SD were somewhat on the order of directing traffic;

A party philosopher who was interested in historical research, and had no idea of the violence which his philosophy was inciting in the twentieth century;

A governor general of Poland who reigned but did not rule;

A *Gauleiter* of Franconia whose occupation was to pour forth filthy writings about the Jews, but who had no idea that anybody would read them;

A minister of the Interior who knew not even what went on in the interior of his own office, much less the interior of his own department, and nothing at all about the interior of Germany;

A Reichsbank president who was totally ignorant of what went in and out of the vaults of his bank;

And a plenipotentiary for the War Economy who secretly marshaled the entire economy for armament, but had no idea it had anything to do with war.

This may seem like a fantastic exaggeration, but this is what you would in actuality be obliged to conclude if you were to acquit these defendants.

They do protest too much. They deny knowing what was common knowledge. They deny knowing plans and programs that were as public as *Mein Kampf* and the party program. They deny even knowing the contents of documents they received and acted upon.

These defendants, unable to deny that they were the men in the very top ranks of power, and unable to deny that the crimes I have outlined actually happened, know that their own denials are incredible unless they can suggest someone who is guilty.

The defendants have been unanimous, when pressed, in shifting the blame on the other men, sometimes on one and sometimes on another. But the names they have repeatedly picked are Hitler, Himmler, Heydrich, Goebbels, and Bormann. All of these are dead or missing. No matter how hard we have pressed the defendants on the stand, they have never pointed the finger at a living man as guilty. It is a temptation to ponder the wondrous workings of a fate which has left only the guilty dead and only the innocent alive. It is almost too remarkable.

The chief villain on whom blame is placed—some of the defendants vie with each other in producing appropriate epithets—is Hitler. He is the man at whom nearly every defendant has pointed an accusing finger.

I shall not dissent from this consensus, nor do I deny that all these dead or missing men shared the guilt. In crimes so reprehensible that degrees of guilt have lost their significance, they may have played the most evil parts. But their guilt cannot exculpate the defendants. Hitler did not carry all responsibility to the grave with him. All the guilt is not wrapped in Himmler's shroud. It was these dead whom these living chose to be their partners in this great conspiratorial brotherhood, and the crimes that they did together they must pay for one by one.

It may well be said that Hitler's final crime was against the land that he had ruled, he was a mad messiah who started the war without cause and prolonged it without reason. If he could not rule he cared not what happened to Germany. As Fritzsche has told us from the stand, Hitler tried to use the defeat of Germany for the self-destruction of the German people. He continued the fight when he knew it could not be won, and continuance meant only ruin.

But let me for a moment turn devil's advocate. I admit that Hitler was the chief villain. But for the defendants to put all blame on him is neither manly nor true. We know that even the head of a state has the same limits to his senses and to the hours of his day as do lesser men. He must rely on others to be his eyes and ears as to most that goes on in a great empire. Other legs must run his errands; other hands must execute his plans. On whom did Hitler rely for such things more than upon these men in the dock? Who led him to believe he had an invincible air armada if not Göring? Who kept disagreeable facts from him? Did not Göring forbid Field Marshal Milch to warn Hitler that in his opinion Germany was not equal to the war upon Russia? Did not Göring, according to Speer, relieve General Galland of his air force command for speaking of the weaknesses and bungling of the air force? Who led Hitler, utterly untraveled himself, to believe in the indecision and timidity of democratic peoples if not von Ribbentrop, von Neurath, and von Papen? Who fed his illusion of German invincibility if not Keitel, Jodl, Raeder and Dönitz? Who kept his hatred of the Jews inflamed more than Streicher and Rosenberg? Who would Hitler say deceived him about conditions in concentration camps if not Kaltenbrunner, even as he would deceive us? These men had access to Hitler, and often could control the information that reached him and on which he must base his policy and his orders. They were the Praetorian Guard, and while they were under Caesar's orders, Caesar was always in their hands.

If these dead men could take the witness stand and answer what has been said against them, we might have a less distorted picture of the parts played by these defendants. Imagine the stir that would occur in the dock if it should behold Adolf Hitler advancing to the witness box, or Himmler with an armful of dossiers, or Goebbels, or Bormann with the reports of his party spies, or the murdered Röhm or Canaris. The ghoulish defense that the world is entitled to retribution only from the cadavers, is an argument worthy of the crimes at which it is directed.

We have presented to this tribunal an affirmative case based on incriminating documents which are sufficient, if unexplained, to require a finding of guilt on count one against each defendant. In the final analysis, the only question is whether the defendants' own testimony is to be credited as against the documents and other evidence of their guilt. What, then, is their testimony worth?

The fact is that the Nazi habit of economizing in the use of truth pulls the foundations out from under their own defenses. Lying has always been a highly approved Nazi technique. Hitler, in *Mein Kampf,* advocated mendacity as a policy. Von Ribbentrop admits the use of the "diplomatic lie." Keitel advised that the facts of rearmament be kept secret so that they could be denied at Geneva. Raeder deceived about rebuilding the German Navy in violation of Versailles. Göring urged [von] Ribbentrop to tell a "legal lie" to the British Foreign Office about the *Anschluss,* and in so doing only marshaled him the way he was going. Göring gave his word of honor to the Czechs and proceeded to break it. Even Speer proposed to deceive the French into revealing the specially trained among their prisoners.

Nor is the direct lie the only means of falsehood. They all speak with a Nazi doubletalk with which to deceive the unwary. In the Nazi dictionary of sardonic euphemisms, "final solution" of the Jewish problem was a phrase which meant extermination; "special treatment" of prisoners of war meant killing; "protective custody" meant concentration camp; "duty labor" meant slave labor; and an order to "take a firm attitude" or "take positive measures" meant to act with unrestrained savagery. Before we accept their word at what seems to be its face, we must always look for hidden meanings. Göring assured us, on his oath, that the Reich Defense Council never met "as such." When we produced the stenographic minutes of a meeting at which he presided and did most of the talking, he reminded us of the "as such" and explained this was not a meeting of the Council "as such" because other persons were present. Göring denies "threatening" Czechoslovakia—he only told President Hácha that he would "hate to bomb the beautiful city of Prague."

Besides outright false statements and doubletalk, there are also other circumventions of truth in the nature of fantastic explanations and absurd professions. Streicher has solemnly maintained that his only thought with respect to the Jews was to resettle them on the island of Madagascar. His reason for destroying synagogues, he blandly said, was only because they were architecturally offensive. Rosenberg was stated by his counsel to have always had in mind a "chivalrous solution" to the Jewish problem. When it was necessary to remove Schuschnigg after the *Anschluss,* von Ribbentrop would have had us believe that the Austrian chancellor was resting at a "villa." It was left to cross-examination to reveal that the "villa" was Buchenwald concentration camp. The record is full of other examples of dissimulations and evasions. Even Schacht showed that he, too, had adopted the Nazi attitude that truth is any story which succeeds. Confronted on cross-examination with a long record of broken vows and false words, he declared in justification: "I think you can score many more successes when you want to lead someone if you don't tell them the truth than if you tell them the truth."

This was the philosophy of the National Socialists. When for years they have deceived the world, and masked falsehood with plausibilities, can anyone be surprised that they continue the habits of a lifetime in this dock? Credibility is one of the main issues of this trial. Only those who have failed to learn the bitter lessons of the last decade can doubt that men who have always played on the unsuspecting credulity of generous opponents would not hesitate to do the same now.

It is against such a background that these defendants now ask this tribunal to say that they are not guilty of planning, executing, or conspiring to commit this long list of crimes and wrongs. They stand before the record of this trial as bloodstained Gloucester stood by the body of his slain king. He begged of the widow, as they beg of you: "Say I slew them not." And the queen replied, "Then say they were not slain. But dead they are. . . ." If you were to say of these men that they are not guilty, it would be as true to say there has been no war, there are no slain, there has been no crime.

CHAPTER TWO

Darrow in the Docket

In a Time of Labor Unrest, America's Greatest Litigator and Friend of the Workingman Fights for His Professional Life

Union Unrest

In 1910, the leaders of American industry sought to keep labor unions from gaining a toehold in the workplace, and perhaps no city appeared more dedicated to keeping the forces of organized labor out than Los Angeles.

In this era of labor organizing, violence was common: more than 100 bombings—without a single fatality—were attributed to the unions over a four-year period, from 1906 to 1910. Strikes called by the workers would be broken by scab labor imported by employers.

Los Angeles was an open-shop town, where the unions enjoyed little success in organizing the workers, unable to loosen the stranglehold employers—led by *Los Angeles Times* owner Harrison Gray Otis—had on the burgeoning city. And, in a time when newspapers rarely considered impartial reporting a virtue, the *Times* could be counted on to fire the latest broadside of hot type and tainted reportage across the bows of the labor movement. Any business owner sympathetic to union demands would find his local suppliers suddenly unable to fill orders, bankers unwilling to extend a line of credit.

San Francisco, by contrast, was exclusively made up of closed shops, where union membership was required to obtain work. The disparity between labor costs in San Francisco and Los Angeles led business leaders in the northern half of the state to give the unions an ultimatum: equalize costs throughout the state or contracts would not be renewed. The unions could either sacrifice their hard-won gains and lower wages to match those in Los Angeles, or raise them by forcing the "scabbiest town" in the nation to accept organized labor.

When the West Coast head of the Bridge and Structural Iron Workers Union heard that demands for an eight-hour workday and a four-dollar minimum wage had been rejected, he contacted John J. McNamara, thirty-four, the union's national secretary-treasurer, and requested that the union's top dynamite expert be sent to California. The man wasn't available, so McNamara instead sent his twenty-eight-year-old brother, James Barnabas "J. B." McNamara.

The *Times*'s owner, Otis, reportedly knew that the unions had targeted the newspaper because of its leading role in the antilabor fight. Made cautious by the likelihood the union would dynamite the Times Building, Otis delayed renovations and made sure that no important records were stored there.

On September 30, 1910, at 5:45 P.M., James "J. B." McNamara concealed a suitcase containing sixteen sticks of dynamite set to explode at 1:00 A.M. among barrels of ink, rubbish, and paper in a covered passage called Ink Alley, which ran through the Times Building. A little more than six hours later, a tremendous explosion rent the night air, shock waves sending bleary-eyed Angelenos running into the streets, afraid an earthquake had decimated the city. The curious crowds soon followed horse-drawn fire wagons to the shattered Times Building and watched in horror as flames raced through the structure, fed by ink and newsprint, consuming men and machines. Two firemen and a police officer struggled to position a rope fire net usually handled by a crew of twelve. An editor leapt from the fifth floor of the burning building, hitting the net with such force the three rescuers were knocked to the ground. The editor picked himself up and walked away, but four other employees were killed attempting the same escape, some missing the net entirely.

When the fires died down later that morning, the extent of the damage was awe-inspiring: the explosion had been so powerful it reduced portions of the alley's concrete floor to powder, sending debris crashing into the basement pressroom below, and blew a hole extending from the basement to the roof measuring up to twenty feet in diameter. Twenty employees lay dead.

Within hours, the *Times* had a paper on the streets blaming "Unionists" for the blast. But the bomb makers had greater ambitions than the destruction of the newspaper. Nine hours after the blast, a suitcase containing fifteen sticks of dynamite, a battery, and an alarm clock were discovered propped against the outside wall of the home of the secretary of the Merchants and Manufacturers Association. And just in case *Times* owner Otis hadn't gotten the union's message, his gardener discovered yet another dynamite-filled suitcase, this one concealed in the shrubs outside the Otis mansion. Altogether, fifty pounds of explosives had been used in the three bombs, just 10 percent of the 500 pounds purchased by the suspects.

Responding to the antiunion invective, Socialist presidential candidate and labor leader Eugene V. Debs put a new spin on the bombing, claiming industrialists had planted the explosives and framed the union. A grand jury was impaneled to investigate the blast, and quickly discounted the possibility that a gas leak had been its cause. The grand jury was able to identify the purchasers of the dynamite and trace its origin to a San Francisco–area manufacturer.

The first break in the case came on April 12, 1911, when James McNamara and Ortie McManigal were arrested by private detectives in Detroit. According to prominent L.A. attorney Oscar Lawler, who was heading the prosecution's investigation, the two were acting under the orders of McNamara's elder brother, John. James was not a member of his brother's union; he was a printer and belonged to the typographers union. McNamara and McManigal were to blow up a series of factories to divert attention away from the L.A. bombing and throw the police off the trail. The conspirators were brought under guard to Chicago the next day, where they were held incommunicado in the home of a police officer while their captors waited for extradition papers. McManigal had built and planted a number of bombs that closely resembled those discovered in L.A. after the explosion at the Times Building. After a week of captivity, McManigal confessed, saying that he had planted the bomb at the Llewellyn Iron Works at the request of John McNamara, and that James McNamara had planted the bomb at the Times Building, along with two accomplices. The next day, April 21, the detectives and the two suspects left for Indianapolis.

On Saturday, April 22, Los Angeles Chief Deputy District Attorney W. Joseph Ford presented papers seeking the extradition of James B. and John J. McNamara to Indiana Governor Thomas Marshall. A warrant for John was issued and he was arrested that same day.

The unions rallied for their jailed McNamara brothers, claiming they'd been the victims of a frame job; the American Federation of Labor (A.F. of L.) began raising funds for their defense. In June of 1911, A.F. of L. founder Samuel Gompers began courting Clarence Darrow, first with flattery, later with veiled threats. Darrow, the greatest trial lawyer in the nation, had defended union men in the past, winning acquittals by turning trials upside down, converting inquiries into the innocence or guilt of his clients into searing indictments of the treatment of workingmen at the hands of greedy capitalists. Darrow, weary of trial practice, feeling physically frail and not up to the rigors of what promised to be a lengthy fight, didn't want the McNamara case. The prosecution appeared to have the makings of an airtight case, and Darrow believed the McNamaras to be guilty. Gompers, convinced of the brothers' innocence, would not be refused. He told Darrow that he'd be denounced as a traitor to the labor cause if he refused the McNamaras in their time of need. Unwilling to sever his ties to the labor movement, Darrow agreed to take the case under certain conditions: that he be able to set the trial strategy and pick his cocounsel; that he receive a fee of $50,000, and that $200,000 be placed at his disposal. Gompers agreed. This was an enormous sum; $250,000 in 1911 is the equivalent of $3 million in 1998.

On July 5, 1911, Darrow entered "not guilty" pleas for the McNamaras. Questioning of prospective jurors began in October, with voir dire continuing through November.

Jury Tampering

On Friday, October 6, 1911, Darrow's lead investigator, Bert Franklin, approached the home of Robert Bain, an elderly Civil War veteran who was one of forty-three men in the pool of potential jurors. Bain, a carpenter, was out on a job, but his wife was drawn into conversation by Franklin, who soon discovered the couple had an $1,800 mortgage on their new home and were having difficulty with the payments. Franklin spun a tale of corruption for Mrs. Bain, explaining that the prosecution was buying jurors and witnesses in an effort to convict two innocent men. Franklin said he was prepared to pay her husband a total of $4,000 for a vote to acquit the McNamaras. That evening, Bain reluctantly agreed to accept the money. Bain was subsequently picked as a juror and Darrow had one "not guilty" in his pocket.

Meanwhile, tensions continued to rise between the forces of labor, industry, and the establishment. President Taft was coming to Los Angeles, and thirty-nine sticks of dynamite were discovered beneath a bridge over which the presidential train was to pass. Lawler, who'd developed a friendly relationship with Taft while serving as assistant U.S. attorney general, met October 17 with the president during his visit to Los Angeles. Lawler believed that documents confirming the union's role in the bombings were hidden in the union headquarters in Indianapolis. He needed access to those records, and a federal indictment would provide him entree. Lawler convinced Taft that federal laws had been broken by the Iron Workers Union; Attorney General George Wickersham contacted Lawler the next day, informing him the Justice Department would begin moving. Within two weeks, a grand jury probe resulted in the union's facing charges it was illegally transporting explosives across state lines, a federal offense. The documents Lawler needed were quickly seized in Indianapolis and sent to Los Angeles.

By early November, Darrow became aware of a prosecution witness who would testify he'd been asked by John McNamara to shelter his brother James in the days following the bombing. The prosecution began gathering so many witnesses who could connect James to the purchase of the explosives and the placing of the bomb that Darrow complained to his client "that he'd left a trail a mile wide." Meanwhile, District Attorney Fredericks was being approached by members of the business community about the possibility of a plea bargain. The Socialist candidate stood a good chance of winning the Los Angeles mayoral campaign, and it was felt that an admission of guilt by James McNamara would take the wind out of the Socialists' sails. Fredericks wanted some admission of guilt from John McNamara; James was willing to plead guilty to the bombing, but only if his brother, the union leader John, not be held accountable for the Times bombing. Fredericks countered, agreeing to waive John's involvement in the Times explosion, where twenty-three lives were lost, if John would plead guilty to the Llewellyn Iron Works explosion, where there were no fatalities.

Later in November, with plea bargain talks still pending, Franklin had the misfortune of trying to bribe a prospective juror named Lockwood, a rancher, former deputy sheriff, and friend of District Attorney Fredericks. Angered by the attempted bribe—$500 up front, $3,500 after acquittal—Lockwood contacted the DA, who asked him to play along with Franklin, and Lockwood agreed. A meeting was arranged at Lockwood's ranch, but was canceled at the last minute. Franklin set up another meeting for the following day, November 28, at 9:00 A.M., on the corner of Los Angeles Street and Third, where the prospective juror was to receive the first installment of the bribe. Lawler had his agents in place, one pretending to fix his motorcycle. Lockwood received $500 from the third party designated by Franklin to hold the bribe, when Franklin noticed a Los Angeles police detective nearby. Steering Lockwood away from the cop, Franklin spotted Darrow approaching. Before he could speak to Darrow, the watching police moved in, arresting Franklin.

Plea Bargain

On Thanksgiving Day, 1911, Darrow told cocounsel Joseph Scott that the district attorney had a witness who would testify that J. B. McNamara had placed the bomb in the Times Building. Darrow said he believed the defense theory that a gas leak had destroyed the building wouldn't hold up in the face of McManigal's confession and this new corroboratory testimony. McManigal had refused to recant his confession, despite the tearful entreaties of his wife and uncle, all at Darrow's behest.

The defense lawyers met with the McNamaras, trying to convince the brothers to accept Fredericks's terms for a deal. Darrow explained that the case looked hopeless, and the unfolding scandal involving juror tampering might further inflame public opinion against them. James was nonetheless willing to go to trial and risk martyrdom on the gallows if it meant his brother could go free. John McNamara was also ready to admit his complicity in the Llewellyn bombing if it meant James could avoid the hangman, but his brother unexpectedly refused any deal that left John imprisoned and tainted the labor movement. Darrow asked his cocounsel Scott to talk to James, convince him to accept the plea, but again he refused. Scott said James told him, "I'm ready to plead guilty because I'm only a scrub printer and labor won't suffer if a scrub printer like me is found guilty, but my brother is an outstanding labor leader . . . with an international reputation, and it would be a big body blow to labor if he pleads guilty." Scott told James he'd likely hang if he didn't accept the offer, but James remarked that it would suit him just fine to hang as a matter of principle. In desperation, Scott turned to the jail chaplain, who agreed to talk to McNamara. After more than a hour, the chaplain emerged from the cell: McNamara was prepared to accept the plea if his brother John thought it was the right thing to do.

On Friday, December 1, 1911, Darrow entered the courtroom and said, "May it please the court, our clients wish to change their pleas from not guilty to guilty." Pandemonium ensued, with reporters rushing from the courtroom and labor supporters stunned and infuriated by the betrayal of their trust. Darrow told the press, "There was no loop-hole. There was no hope. I hope I have saved a human life out of the wreckage. I have known for months our fight was hopeless. From the first there was never the slightest chance to win." The unions and their supporters were aghast at the sudden turn of events. Gompers wryly commented, "It won't do the labor movement any good." On December 5, the McNamaras were sentenced: James was to spend the rest of his life in prison, while John received a fifteen-year sentence.

Defendant Darrow

Darrow had gone from being the defender of the workingman to class traitor in one day. But Darrow's troubles had just begun. Franklin pleaded guilty to attempting to bribe jurors Lockwood and Bain in the McNamara case, and on January 29, 1912, he testified before the grand jury, implicating Darrow. That afternoon, Darrow was indicted on charges of jury tampering.

Darrow's trial for the attempted bribery of Lockwood began on May 15, with his former investigator as the prosecution's star witness. Franklin was clear in his testimony; he'd never acted on his own, only and always at the bidding of Clarence Darrow. The prosecutor Joe Ford started his closing argument with a vicious and stunning attack on Darrow. He compared him to other once-great men who had turned sour, men like Judas Iscariot and Benedict Arnold. "History," he said, "is filled with the examples of men whose minds are brilliant, whose sentiments are noble, but whose practices are ignoble." Ford reminded the jurors that Judas's integrity and honesty were so great "that Christ made him the treasurer of that little band," and he described Benedict Arnold's courage, valor, and "great reputation for truth, for honesty, for integrity." Yet all of those great men had committed crimes. "Previous good reputation," he said, "is no guaranty against the commission of an offense."

Ford argued that Darrow was actually responsible for the bombings which he labeled the crime of the century, because Darrow had shown criminals through his courtroom maneuverings that virtually any crime could be explained away, as long as the perpetrator had Clarence Darrow as his lawyer.

Late Tuesday afternoon, Earl Rogers on behalf of Darrow began his closing. It was agreed that both Rogers and Darrow would share the defense's closing argument. Rogers pared the prosecution's case down to just two witnesses, Franklin and Harrington, both of whom claimed to have had damning—but uncorroborated—conversations with Darrow. Rogers asked, why attempt to bribe jurors when a plea bargain was in the works? Rogers even used Darrow's tightness with a buck as evidence that no motive existed. "Do you think Darrow would throw $4,000 to the birds when he had the McNamara case practically settled? No!" Rogers thundered, "When [Darrow] lets go of a dollar it squeals! It's a mental, moral, physical impossibility for him to do it." Rogers finished by recounting the active role Darrow had played in the fight for social justice. "In this country of ours there are many things that must be settled and settled quick. We can't go on like this. We can't do it. So Darrow, through all these years, with all his heart and mind and conscience, has been doing what he can to help those who can't help themselves."

Rogers finished just in time for the noon recess. The emotions of all those in the courtroom were spent. A reporter observed that Rogers had "moved his audience to tears and to laughter at will." It had been a masterly performance.

And Clarence Darrow was scheduled to begin his summation at 2 P.M.

During the lunch break, there was a mad rush for seats in the courtroom, or even places in the outside corridor. The word was out. Darrow was about to begin. According to the *Record*, two thousand spectators "fought and struggled with bailiffs in the narrow corridor for two hours." Half of them had to be turned away. By two o'clock, when court was ready to start again, "hundreds of people were crowded into a space ten feet wide and a thousand pressed in on them in a wild effort to gain entrance to the courtroom. The bailiffs shut the doors in the faces of the crowd to keep the courtroom from being taken by storm. Women fainted and men gasped for breath. Mrs. Earl Rogers and her daughter (Adela) were caught in the crush and attorneys for both sides were imprisoned. Reserves were called in from the sheriff's office to quell the crowd and clubs had to be drawn before it could be handled. Finally, when the doors were opened, the mob surged into the room and filled all of the standing space."

At least one woman fainted, and others were knocked down, as people scrambled to get near the open doors, to find positions from which they could hear Darrow's self-defense. The bailiffs had to erect a wooden bar to block entrance to those without tickets. The men and women who did have tickets had to struggle through the mob, arriving in the courtroom with their hair and clothes awry. It took Earl Rogers ninety minutes just to force his way through the hallway crowd and into the courtroom.

At precisely two 2:22 P.M., with the commotion still continuing in the hallway, Clarence Darrow rose to speak. He walked forward slowly, wearing the same gray suit that he had worn in the McNamara case. His hair was unkempt; an unruly lock fell down over his forehead.

Darrow's close continued over a two-day period, during which he wept, spectators were moved to tears, and, to the prosecutor's horror, the jurors—and the judge—sobbed. When the jury returned a verdict of not guilty on August 17, the *Times* was quick to note the judge's reaction: "Now that the case is ended, I consider it entirely proper for me to congratulate Mr. Darrow upon his acquittal. I know that millions of hallelujahs will go up through the length and breadth of the land."

Darrow wasn't so successful in the second trial, this time for allegedly bribing Bain. He couldn't claim that it made no sense to bribe Bain as he had in the Lockwood trial, for Bain had been approached before any talks had begun with the brothers about settling. Clearly the motive, fear of a trial, still existed when Bain sold his vote. Darrow had changed strategies, this time appearing to condone the murders in the name of social reform. The jury wasn't swayed and in March, 1913, deadlocked, eight to four in favor of convicting. The DA agreed not to retry the case after Darrow promised never to practice law in California again.

Biography

The finest American trial lawyer, Clarence Darrow was born in 1857 near Kinsman, Ohio. The man who would go on to capture headlines as a public speaker, debater, and courtroom warrior only spent one year in law school before being admitted to the Ohio bar in 1878.

Darrow's first involvement in a high-profile case came in 1887, after he moved to Chicago. There he worked to free the anarchists who were charged with murder in the Haymarket Riot of 1886. By 1890, Darrow had parlayed his friendship with a judge and future governor of Illinois into a job: Chicago city corporation counsel. Darrow then moved on, to become the general counsel for the Chicago and North Western Railway.

By 1894, Darrow had moved away from corporate law, taking on the defense of Eugene V. Debs, the head of the American Railway Union. Debs, along with other labor leaders, had been charged with federal contempt of court during the Pullman strike. Although Darrow lost the case and Debs was convicted, Darrow had established a reputation as the defender of organized labor.

During the Pennsylvania coal strike of 1902, Darrow represented the striking miners. His cross examination masterfully illustrated the horrendous working conditions the men labored in, and told of the extensive use of child labor in the mining industry.

In 1907, Darrow won the acquittal of labor leader William "Big Bill" Haywood, who had been charged with the assassination of the former governor of Idaho. Then in 1911, Darrow became enmeshed in the case of the McNamaras, his swan song as the defender of labor. It was during his defense of the McNamara brothers that Darrow became embroiled in the jury-tampering scandal that is the subject of this case.

Darrow went on to defend antiwar protestors after World War I ended, trying to clear them of violating antisedition charges. In 1924, Darrow's name was back in the headlines, with his defense of Nathan Leopold and Richard Loeb (see chapter 5).

Dayton, Tennessee, was the site of his next big case, when in 1925 he defended schoolteacher John T. Scopes in what was to become known as the Scopes Monkey Trial. Scopes was being prosecuted for teaching the theory of evolution to his young students, in violation of a state law, and Darrow squared off in court against another famed orator, William Jennings Bryan. The trial was later immortalized in the film *Inherit the Wind,* starring Spencer Tracy as Darrow.

Darrow moved into civil rights litigation with his defense in Detroit of Henry Sweet, a black doctor who had used violence to defend his family from a white mob trying to force the Sweets out of their home in a white neighborhood. Darrow's impassioned closing in the 1926 trial helped carry the day and win freedom for his client.

Darrow was well known outside the courtroom for his public speeches and articles on behalf of his favorite causes: unlimited free speech, the closed shop, and his opposition to the death penalty and Prohibition.

He died in 1938, in Chicago.

Commentary

Clarence Darrow delivered an eight-hour closing argument in his own defense that left his jury spellbound by his virtuoso performance. The jurors who listened closely in a sweltering courtroom over a two-day period in August 1912 were quite different from the jurors of the 1990s; with attention spans undiminished by years of exposure to television and film, they were able to follow and maintain interest in Darrow's lengthy defense. Unfortunately, the jurors of the nineties would label Darrow a windbag—or worse. Today's attorneys face a more sophisticated, jaded, and media-savvy jury box. Consequently, an attorney who fails to keep tabs on the pace, production, and entertainment that jurors are exposed to in film and on television runs the risk of losing the jury's attention, interest, and possibly the case itself. Nonetheless, taking into account the special care and feeding that modern jurors require, there are several features of this closing that will serve modern lawyers well.

First, Darrow quickly developed his central theme, repeatedly returning to it throughout the summation. Realizing that jurors, like most audiences, will retain only very limited amounts of information, Darrow made the juror's task easier by essentially boiling his case down to a central idea and tying the balance of the close to that theme. Second, Darrow was able successfully to shift the focus of the trial from a fact-based argument, where he was vulnerable, to more of an emotion-based grounding, where he had a greater chance of success. While this was a relatively straightforward bribery trial, wherein the evidence painted a convincing picture of Darrow's guilt, he was able to refocus the trial into a larger examination of the American labor movement.

Third, Darrow, with the precision of a master craftsman, utilized finely honed phrases, phrases that framed key points for the jury in memorable packages.

Finally and perhaps most importantly, Darrow "talked" to his jury in a perfect horizontal dialogue, speaking neither above nor beneath them.

In reading the summation, note how quickly Darrow was able to develop his theme. In the second paragraph he tells the jurors that he is faced with the real prospect of incarceration. In the third paragraph he paints himself as a victim of a corrupt system. The resounding theme of this closing argument is *corrupt system, harsh punishment*. As he develops each of his points throughout, Darrow continually comes back to the central and abiding conclusion, that a corrupt system is about to pack him off to prison. Darrow truly was only selling one idea, hammering home: corrupt system, harsh punishment. If the jurors remembered nothing else of Darrow's comments, they would surely remember his central theme.

The second characteristic of this closing argument was Darrow's ability to shift the focus from a fact-based evaluation to a peripheral issue in which he was on stronger ground. Again, the theme was struck early and reiterated often. In the seventh paragraph, Darrow says, "I am on trial because I have been a lover of the poor, a friend of the oppressed, because I have stood by labor for all these years, and have brought down upon my head the wrath of the criminal interests in this country."

Significant portions of Darrow's close are devoted to talk of "just cause" and how he is but a small player caught up in a larger maelstrom of the growing labor movement. Even though the charges against Darrow involved the alleged bribing of a juror, he chose to shift the battleground from a specific bribery charge to a passionate defense of his involvement with the American labor movement. Indeed, if the jurors were to convict Darrow, they would, in a sense, be damning the entire labor movement. This diversionary tactic was certainly not unique to Darrow. In fact, the bulk of criminal defense attorneys employ this tactic from time to time. The diversion is as time-tested as the trial process itself. If your case cannot withstand the "hot-white" of close factual scrutiny, shift the focus. Find an issue and seize the high ground to gain a better perspective, one that enables you to more ably wage the battle. Darrow clearly recognized the necessity of this tactic and was masterful in its use.

The third characteristic of this summation is the one that renders it so persuasive: Darrow's use of carefully crafted, striking phrases that create vivid visualizations as well as powerful visceral reactions. Early in the summation, Darrow says, "I am a stranger in a strange land, two thousand miles from home and friends. . . ." These words paint a striking picture of a righteous warrior battling the forces of evil in a far-off place. Who among us would not feel a certain empathy for such a man, a Don Quixote de La Mancha, tilting at windmills. Later in the argument, Darrow scores again with a memorable turn of phrase, evoking a hint of Christ himself on the cross at the end. "Oh, you wild, insane members of the Steel Trust and Erectors' Association! Oh, you mad hounds of detectives who are willing to do your master's will! Oh, you district attorneys! You know not what to do."

Darrow also addresses the passions he arouses in his detractors, telling the jurors, "If you haven't made three or four enemies, gentlemen, you have lived a very weak and useless life." Darrow was able to create a sense of urgency, an excitement, that the jury found irresistible, and with his oratory won them over.

Finally, foremost among Darrow's considerable powers was his rapport with his audience. In the first paragraph, Darrow lays the foundation: "I felt that at least I ought to say something to you twelve men besides what I have already said upon the witness stand." Throughout this remarkable close there is no evidence of pontificating or preaching; rather, it is as if Darrow is discussing a serious matter with his friends. Notice the use of simple words. Throughout his closing, Darrow never uses a word that might be above his audience. He truly spoke with the jurors as an equal. And even though the jurors are mute during the argument, it is as if a dialogue, a conversation is taking place between Darrow and the jurors. This is persuasive public speaking at its finest.

Closing Argument

The State of California v. Clarence Darrow
Delivered by Clarence Darrow
Los Angeles, California, May 15, 1912

Gentlemen of the jury,

An experience like this never came to me before, and of course I cannot say how I will get along with it. I am quite sure there are very few men who are called upon by an experience of this kind, but I have felt, gentlemen, after the patience you have given this case for all these weeks, that you would be willing to listen to me, even though I might not argue it as well as I would some other case. I felt that at least I ought to say something to you twelve men besides what I have already said upon the witness stand.

In the first place, I am a defendant charged with a serious crime. I have been looking into the penitentiary for six or seven months, and now I am waiting for you twelve men to say whether I shall go there or not. In the next place, I am a stranger in a strange land, two thousand miles from home and friends—although I am proud to say that here, so far away, there have gathered around me as good and loyal and faithful friends as any man could have upon the earth. Still I am unknown to you.

I think I can say that no one in my native town would have made to any jury any such statement as was made of me by the district attorney in opening this case. I will venture to say he could not afterward have found a companion except among detectives and crooks and sneaks in the city where I live if he had dared to open his mouth in the infamous way that he did in this case.

But here I am in his hands. Think of it! In a position where he can call me a coward—and in all my life I never saw or heard so cowardly, sneaky, and brutal an act as Ford committed in this courtroom before this jury. Was any courage displayed by him? It was only brutal and low, and every man knows it.

I don't object to a lawyer arguing the facts in his case and the evidence in his case, and drawing such conclusions as he will, but every man with a sense of justice in his soul knows that this attack of Ford's was cowardly and malicious in the extreme. It was not worthy of a man and did not come from a man.

I am entitled to some rights until you, gentlemen, shall say differently, and I would be entitled to some even then, and so long as I have any, I shall assert them the best I can as I go through the world wherever I am.

What am I on trial for, gentlemen of the jury? You have been listening here for three months. What is it all about? If you don't know then you are not as intelligent as I believe. I am not on trial for having sought to bribe a man named Lockwood. There may be and doubtless are many people who think I did seek to bribe him, but I am not on trial for that, and I will prove it to you. No man is being tried on that charge. I am on trial because I have been a lover of the poor, a friend of the oppressed, because I have stood by labor for all these years, and have bought down upon my head the wrath of the criminal interests in this country. Whether guilty or innocent of the crime charged in the indictment, that is the reason I am here, and that is the reason that I have been pursued by as cruel a gang as ever followed a man.

Now, let's see if I can prove this. If the district attorney of this county thought a crime had been committed, well and good, let him go ahead and prosecute, but has he done this? Has he prosecuted any of the bribe takers and givers?

And who are these people back of him and back of the organization of this county who have been hot on my trail and whose bark I can remember from long ago! Will you tell me, gentlemen of the jury, why the Erectors' Association and the Steel Trust are interested in this case way out here in Los Angeles? Will you tell me why the Erectors' Association of Indianapolis should have put up as vicious and as cruel a plot to catch me as was ever used against any American citizen? Gentlemen, if you don't know you are not fit to be jurors.

Are those people interested in bribery? Why almost every dollar of their ill-gotten gains has come from bribery. When did the Steel Trust, which owns the Erectors' Association and is the Erectors' Association— when did it become interested in prosecuting bribery? Was it when they unloaded a billion of dollars of watered stock upon the American people—stock that draws its life and interest from the brawn, the brain, and the blood of the American workingman? Are they interested in coming all the way out to this state and to Los Angeles to prosecute a man merely for bribery? There are a good many states between this city and New York City. There are a good many state's attorneys in this broad land of ours. They can begin at home if they would, these men who have made bribery a profession and a fine art.

Gentlemen of the jury, it is not that any of these men care about bribery, but it is that there never was a chance before since the world began to claim that bribery had been committed for the poor. Heretofore, bribery, like everything else, had been monopolized by the rich. But now they thought there was a chance to lay this crime to the poor and "to get" me. Is there any doubt about it?

Suppose I am guilty of bribery, is that why I am prosecuted in this court? Is that why the most infamous methods known to the law and outside the law, these men, the real enemies of society, are trying to get me inside the penitentiary?

No, that isn't it, and you twelve men know it. Your faces are unfamiliar to me. There may not be a man on this jury who believes as I believe upon these great questions between capital and labor. You may all be on the other side, but I have faced the other side over and over again, and I am going to tell you the truth this afternoon. It may be the last chance that I shall ever get to speak to a jury.

These men are interested in getting me. They have concocted all sorts of schemes for the sake of getting me out of the way. Do you suppose they care what laws I might have broken? I have committed one crime, one crime which is like that against the Holy Ghost, which cannot be forgiven. I have stood for the weak and the poor. I have stood for the men who toil. And therefore I have stood against them, and now this is their chance. All right, gentlemen, I am in your hands, not in theirs, just yet.

In examining you before you were accepted as jurors, Mr. Fredericks asked you whether, if I should address you, you would be likely to be carried away by sympathy? You won't be if you wait for me to ask for sympathy. He has cautioned you against my argument. You will find I am a plain-speaking man, who will try to talk to you as one man to another. I never have asked sympathy of anybody, and I am not going to ask it of you twelve. I would rather go to the penitentiary than ask for sympathy.

I have lived my life, and I have fought my battles, not against the weak and the poor—anybody can do that—but against power, against injustice, against oppression, and I have asked no odds from them, and I never shall.

I want you to take the facts of this case as they are, consider the evidence as it is, and then if you twelve men can find on your conscience and under your oath any reason to take away my liberty, well and good, the responsibility will be on you. I would rather be in my position than in yours in the years to come.

As I have told you, I am tried here because I have given a large part of my life and my services to the cause of the poor and the weak, and because I am in the way of the interests. These interests would stop my voice—and they have hired many vipers to help them do it. They would stop my voice—my voice, which from the time I was a prattling babe, my father and mother taught me to raise for justice and freedom, and in the cause of the weak and the poor. They would stop my voice with the penitentiary.

Oh, you wild, insane members of the Steel Trust and Erectors' Association! Oh, you mad hounds of detectives who are willing to do your master's will! Oh, you district attorneys! You know not what to do. Let me say to you, that if you send me to prison, within the gray, dim walls of San Quentin there will brood a silence more ominous and eloquent than any words that my poor lips could ever frame. And do you think that you could destroy the hopes of the poor and the oppressed if you did silence me? Don't you know that upon my persecution and destruction would arise ten thousand men abler than I have been, more devoted than I have been, and ready to give more than I have given in a righteous cause?

I have been, perhaps, interested in more cases for the weak and poor than any other lawyer in America, but I am pretty nearly done, anyhow. If they had taken me twenty years ago, it might have been worth their while, but there are younger men than I, and there are men who will not be awed by prison bars, by district attorneys, by detectives, who will do this work when I am done.

If you help the Erectors' Association put me into the penitentiary, gentlemen, and Mr. Ford stands outside the doors licking his picturesque chops in glee at my destruction, then what? Will the labor cause be dead? Will Ford's masters ride roughshod over the liberties of me? No! Others will come to take my place, and they will do the work better than I have done it in the past.

Gentlemen, I say this is not a case of bribery at all. You know the men who have been after me, and the interests that have been after me, and the means that have been used. What have they done? They say a bribery was seriously intended down here on Main Street, close to my office, which I will speak about later, but have they tried to get a bribe giver or a bribe taker? No, not one. Let us see what they have done. They have taken Bert Franklin and given him his liberty, without costing him a cent. They have taken White and let him go scot-free. They have taken Mr. Bain and Mrs. Bain and have not even filed any information against them. They have taken Harrington and Behm and brought them here and given them immunity. They have taken Cooney and Fitzpatrick and Mayer and let them go unwhipped of justice. More than that, gentlemen, they have said boldly to Franklin, if he told the truth, and the circumstances would show that he did—in this instance—they have said boldly to him, "If you know anything against anybody in Los Angeles, keep your mouth closed, but help us put Darrow inside the penitentiary." Is there any question that they have done all this? If I am guilty, others associated with me are guilty, too. But the crimes of all the others are washed away in order "to get" me.

Gentlemen, suppose I did this bribery, suppose I did, then what? Is there any man in whose soul lurks a suspicion of integrity and fair dealing, is there any civilized man on earth who would convict me under circumstances like that? If there is, gentlemen, I would rather dwell among the savages with District Attorney Ford as a chief, much rather, because I might raise an insurrection against him and get some justice.

Will you tell me if anywhere there could be an American jury, or anywhere in the English-speaking world there could be found a jury that would for a moment lend itself to a conspiracy so obvious and foul as this? If there is, gentlemen, then send me to prison. Anyway, when I reach prison, they can do nothing more to me, and if I stay here, they will probably get me for murder after awhile. I do not mean the murder of Ford, he is not worth it; but they will put up a job and get me for something else. If any jury could possibly, in a case like this, find me guilty, the quicker it is done the better. Then I will be out of my trouble.

Gentlemen, if the state of California can afford to stand it, I can. If the state of California, and the fair city of Los Angeles, can lend itself to a crime like this, the victim will be ready when the time comes. But let me tell you, that, if under such testimony as you have heard here, and under the sort of conspiracy you have seen laid bare here, you should send me to prison, it would leave a stain upon the fair name of your city and your state that would last while these hills endure, and so long as the Pacific waves should wash your sandy coast.

Tell me that any American jury would do it! Gentlemen, I could tell you that I did this bribery, and you would turn me loose. If I did not think so, I would not think you were Americans of spirit or heart, or sense of justice. Gentlemen, if within this courthouse, men could be bought and bribed with immunity, could be threatened and coached and browbeaten, and if the gold of the Erectors' Association could be used to destroy human life—if that could succeed, it would be better that these walls should crumble into dust.

I do not know you twelve men. I never saw you before, but you have heard my story on the stand, you have seen me here from day to day. You have seen the class of people who have come here to condemn me and befoul my name. You know the class of people who have come here to tell you what my reputation has been. You have seen the witnesses who have come forward to testify in this case, and you are not insane, and I tell you, gentlemen, I do not want you to think I am worried about it now; but I have spent troubled days and sleepless nights over the misery that they have already caused me and those near and dear to me. But now I have no doubt about any jury under these circumstances. No more doubt than I had as a child when I laid my head on my mother's breast. Men cannot lose all their heart, except by a surgical operation, and there are not here in Los Angeles twelve men without some heart. If there were, they would have been in the employ of the district attorney long ago.

Now, gentlemen, let's see what they have made by their conspiracy. These are strong-arm men. They have the grand jury, two of them; with one they can reach across the continent and get whom they want; and when they get him, they take him before the other body, and they say to him—what, gentlemen? They don't say, "Your money or your life," but they say, "Your liberty or your manhood. Take your choice." And the kind of men they choose give up their manhood. How much credit can you give to the word of a man who finds his liberty held before him as a bait for his testimony?

Gentlemen, I have tried a good many cases in my time! I have been thirty-five or thirty-six years in this profession, and did you send me to prison, why, I have practiced law long enough anyhow. I was going to have a vacation. Of course, there are pleasanter places to take vacations than the one where Ford wants to put me—but I have practiced law a good long time, and I tell you I never saw or heard of a case where any American jury convicted anybody, even the humblest, upon such testimony as that of Franklin and Harrington, and I don't expect to live long enough to find that sort of a jury.

Let me say this, gentlemen, there are other things in the world besides bribery, there are other crimes that are worse. It is a fouler crime to bear false witness against your fellowman, whether you do it in a cowardly way in an address to a jury, or from a witness chair—infinitely fouler.

Now, let me put it to you as to men who value your own liberty—because you all value your own liberty, and I trust you value mine, and I have no doubt you do—suppose any infamous scoundrel taken in criminal conduct could know that he could turn on you or on me to save himself, would your liberty be safe? It would not be as safe as mine, for you might not go before as fair-minded a jury as I feel that I am before today. Suppose your hired man could be taken in some act of crime, and the district attorney could say to him, "All right, here is the penitentiary, but I will let you out if you will fasten the crime on your employer." Gentlemen, would you be safe?

Suppose you thought that I was guilty, suppose you thought so—would you dare as honest men, protecting society, would you dare to say by your verdict that scoundrels like this should be saved from their own sins, by charging those sins to someone else? If so, gentlemen, when you go back to your homes, you had better kiss your wives a fond good-bye, and take your little children more tenderly in your arms than ever before, because, though today it is my turn, tomorrow it may be yours. This consideration, gentlemen, is more important to orderly government, to the preservation of human liberty, than "to get" any one man, no matter how hard they want "to get" him.

Now, gentlemen, I am going to be honest with you in this matter. The McNamara case was a hard fight. I will tell you the truth about it; then, if you want to send me to prison, go ahead. It is up to you. It was a hard fight. Here was the district attorney with his sleuths. Here was Burns with his hounds. Here was the Erectors' Association with its gold. A man could not stir out of his home or out of his office without being attacked by these men ready to commit all sorts of deeds.

Besides, they had the grand jury, we didn't. They had the police force, we didn't. They had organized government, we didn't. We had to work fast and hard. We had to work the best we could, and I would like to compare notes with them. I wish, gentlemen of the jury, that some power had been given to us to call before this jury all the telegrams sent by the district attorney's office and sent by Mr. Burns. I wish some grand jury could be impanelled to inquire into their misdeeds. But no, we cannot. They sent out their subpoenas and they got two or three hundred telegrams, public and private, that had been sent from our office. What did they get? Have they shown you anything? Do you think you could run a Sunday school without any more incriminating evidence than they got from those telegrams? I have never tried to run one, but I don't believe you could.

What did they get? By the wonderful knowledge of Mr. Ford and by his marvelous genius, they found the key to our code. He forgot his bile and bitterness for one night and worked out a key—and then what? A telegram to Rappaport on the twenty-ninth, saying that we would give him a thousand dollars, and then a telegram on the first of December—"Better not spend the thousand."

They had detectives in our office. They had us surrounded by gumshoe and keyhole men at every step, and what did they secure? Nothing, nothing. I am surprised, gentlemen, that we were so peaceful in fighting the district attorney and Burns. I scarcely know why we had a code, except that it looked better, and men in business generally use codes, and I knew they had one, for here and there a stray telegraph operator would send me their dispatches to Burns. The poor would help me and the rich would help them, but the help of the rich was always of greater avail than the help of the poor, because they were the stronger.

What did they get with all their grand juries and all their powers, gentlemen? They got conclusive evidence, it seems to me, that everything was regular, that nothing illegal was done, and with all the witnesses—

we interviewed some hundreds—with all the time of twenty or thirty men day and night spent upon that cause, with all the money which we were obliged to spend—now let us look at the pitiful thing that they have brought to this jury to try to have you think badly of me. No matter if I had killed my grandmother, it would not prove that I had sought to bribe Lockwood. It might cause you to have a bad opinion of me, but you could not convict me of bribery on that opinion.

But what did they get? Why, it is shown here that before I left the city of Chicago in May, a Burns sleuth set a trap to catch me, and he was here and testified—Biddinger. Who is Biddinger? You saw him, you heard him testify. If there is any man on this jury who could see Biddinger, and would not take my word against his, then put me away, put me away. If there is any man on earth excepting Ford who would not take my word against Biddinger, then I wish somebody would shoot me if you cannot get rid of me in any other way.

What did he say? I will analyze his story for a minute—his story which anybody with any brains would know was a fabrication—except what he told on cross-examination, when he very nearly admitted the whole truth. Under the guise of proving to this jury that he was an important witness, Mr. Ford got him to tell of an alleged conversation with J. B. McNamara, which was probably never held; and then, when Ford came to argue his case, he willfully, maliciously, feloniously, criminally, cruelly distorted the evidence from the purpose for which it was introduced, to show that J. B. McNamara mentioned me before I ever saw him. Therefore, I must have been one of the people who inspired his deed!

For God's sake, Ford, if you are ever made district attorney of this county, if you are able to climb up the ladder of fame, higher and higher still, I would rather spend my days in the meanest prison pen that the wit and the malice of men can contrive than change places with you, infinitely rather. There are some things worse than prison. Ford introduced that statement, and then he told you it showed that I inspired McNamara's act. What do you twelve men think about a person, who could make a statement like that?

Biddinger testified that he had a conversation with McNamara. He said he came to my office and told me about it, and told me about some trinkets that he had, that another detective came with him, one who I had employed in other matters and that part was true. He admitted on cross-examination that he did tell me that Burns had traitors in our camp with whom he was consulting, and that he offered to tell me about them. He told me that some of the members of the executive board of the organization I was defending were in the pay of Burns, and this, perhaps, was true. They had traitors of ours in their employ. These traitors infest every labor union in this country. The money of the employer is used to hire men to betray their comrades into the commission of crime. I know this. I have fought many of these cases, gentlemen, and I have fought them as squarely as I could possibly fight with such men.

One of the cheapest, meanest, littlest, one of the most contemptible lies that he uttered to this jury was when he discussed the testimony of ex-Senator William E. Mason of Chicago, who testified to my reputation. Ford says, "You mean Mason, the seatmate of Lorimer?" Now, he did not even know better, he did not know anything about Mason, he was willing to perpetrate any lie to take away my liberty. Mason left the Senate ten years before Lorimer ever entered it—and they were always bitter enemies. And yet because Lorimer had been expelled from the Senate, Ford thought if he made that lying, malicious statement, you twelve men would be more apt to send me to the penitentiary. Why, gentlemen, if I have to do one or the other, if I must choose, I will go down on Main Street and bribe jurors rather than bear false witness like Ford. Is there any comparison? There is some boldness, some courage, or at least some recklessness to the one. There is nothing but cowardice and infamy in the other.

Well, Biddinger comes out here, and he telephones me to meet him at the Alexandria Hotel, and I go, and I write on an envelope the number of my telephone. Wonderful discovery! Sherlock Holmes! Burns! Ford! Wonderful! Here is an envelope that has various figures on it, "Home 6745–10"—whatever you are a mind to call it. Crime in August, heard of for the first time a year later! The testimony of Biddinger, prompted by Ford—not by the mind of Ford, but by the jaw of Ford. Crime! He met me at the hotel, he told me he was ready to give me information about spies, that he was going to San Francisco in a few days and could put me in touch with somebody who had betrayed us up there. I was not sure of him. Nobody is sure of a double-crosser. Sometimes he is your fellow, and sometimes the other man's. You are taking your chances. I had others besides Biddinger—some who kept their money and rendered me service, and gave me back reports of their detectives in my office.

Biddinger sent me a telegram, as I testified, and here comes Ford and says, "Did you send this mysterious telegram to Biddinger, saying that you would be in San Francisco?" I said, "Yes, I sent a telegram, I don't remember the wording." "Is it in your handwriting?" "No." "Whose is it?" "I don't know." "Is it your wife's?" How much would you take to have a mind like Ford's? I will tell you what you would take if you had a mind like Ford, you would take arsenic. What difference who wrote the dispatch, if I said I sent it?

He picks out a little piece of paper on which is written "6097," which he says was the number of the room I occupied in the Palace Hotel, and asks me who wrote those numbers—asks me!—Ford, Ford—Ford asks me! I cannot help it: I am here. I may die. "To every man on this earth death cometh soon or late." I do not mind death. It is rather galling though to be eaten alive by ants. That is all that worries me over this transaction. He asked me whether I wrote that. I did not think so. Probably Biddinger wrote it. I might have. I don't care, and I said so. Then he asked me to write those figures. Then what did he do? He! Why, he tells this jury I disguised my hand when I wrote those figures. Did I? Do you know whether I did nor not? Did you see the figures I wrote? Did anybody testify as to whether it was my natural handwriting or not? Did he introduce them? Did he show them to the jury? Why, no, nothing of the sort. But he told this jury that I tried to disguise my hand in writing a set of figures, which I testified might have been the number of my room.

And I went to San Francisco and saw Biddinger, and he told me he would take me where I could see a meeting between Burns and one member of our executive board, and I gave him $200 after giving him $500 for the same purpose, and of course Biddinger did not keep his faith.

And here comes in another little miserable bit of perjury to help strengthen their case, a miserable little bit of perjury that is as plain as sunrise. No man, gentlemen, honestly believes that I had anything to do with bribing or attempting to bribe Lockwood down at the corner of Third and Los Angeles streets. Of course, there may be men who think I would do it. Ford thinks so, I guess. He would think anything to send a man to the penitentiary. But could anybody else on earth think that?

I am not talking about my goodness, gentlemen. I have not too much goodness, but I always had all that I could carry around; sometimes more than I ought to have carried around. And I have played according to the rules of the game, and have taken a little hand in this trial, and you can compare my work, as to whether it is according to the rules of the game, with any of the other lawyers in the case; and I have played it that way for thirty-five years, and I have never done anything of this kind nor had to do anything of this kind. But that is not what I am discussing.

If you twelve men think that I, with thirty-five years of experience, general attorney of a railroad company of the city of Chicago, attorney for the Elevated Railroad Company, with all kinds of clients and important cases—if you think that I would pick out a place half a block from my office and send a man with money in his hand in broad daylight to go down on the street corner to pass $4,000 and then skip over to another street corner and pass $500—two of the most prominent streets in the city of Los Angeles; if you think I did that, gentlemen, why find me guilty. I certainly belong in some state institution. Whether you select the right one or not is another question, but certainly I belong in some one of them, and I will probably get treated in one of the same as in the other.

I say, nobody in their senses could believe that story, and Ford knew it, and to bolster it up by a contemptible liar, he has Biddinger say that I passed $500 in the elevator, and that Biddinger then told me that it was a careless way to do business. I know who told him to say that. I know who inspired that perjury. Of course, I did not pass $500 in the elevator, but if I had, I had just as much right to give him that $500 for that purpose as I would have to buy $500 worth of hogs, just exactly. I was doing exactly what they were doing, what Burns admitted he was doing, what was done in all their cases, what Sam Browne says they did, when he testified that they filled our office with detectives.

And here comes this wonderful man, so honest, so pure, so high, so mighty, Ford, who says the state has the right to do that, who says the state has a right to put spies in the camp of the "criminal," but the "criminal" hasn't the right to put spies in their camp. Isn't that wonderful, gentlemen? Here is a contest between two parties in litigation; the prosecution has a right to load us up with spies and detectives and informers, and we cannot put anyone in their office. Now, what do you think of that? Do any of you believe it?

Ford speaks of me as though I were a cheap jury briber, ready to give a bribe to anybody who happened along. It is a wonder that I didn't try to bribe Ford. You do not know me. Counsel would not let you read my books. If you turn me loose, I hope some time you will have a chance to read my books, so you will see if you have made a mistake. Now I am as fitted for jury bribing as a Methodist preacher for tending bar. By all my training, inclination, and habit, I am about the last person in all this world who could possibly have undertaken such a thing. I do not intimate for a moment that anybody else would, but in all this situation, mine was the position which needed to be guarded the most carefully, as these events have shown.

This is the most wonderful case in criminology that I have ever encountered in my profession. You will notice that Franklin had a great penchant for bribing people we couldn't possibly have used as jurors. The more honest the man, the quicker he would offer him something, try to "slip him a little money."

There was George Lockwood, a man of "the strictest integrity." Maybe he is—I don't know him. I wouldn't think so from his having been a friend of Franklin so long. Guy Yonkin was an honest man, and John Underwood was honest, and Smith was honest; every one of them honest men, every last one, and Franklin goes and visits with their wives, and asks them whether they will take a bribe in the McNamara case.

Now, gentlemen, we have got to use a little common sense in this matter. If I am going to the penitentiary, it will be a great solace to me in the long days of my confinement, to think you used a little common sense in this case, and were not carried away by Ford.

Does it look like a case of jury bribing? Or does it look like something that was framed up? Out of all these men whose names Franklin mentioned he swears that he believes that Yonkin, Smith, Underwood, and the man Lockwood, captain of the chain gang, were honest and incorruptible—and he goes forth to bribe them. But Krueger was not honest—something else was the matter with him. Krueger had been in trouble with the district attorney and Franklin says he knew the district attorney would not take him, and he testified that he told me so. So he tried to force money on to Krueger, when he knew that Krueger could not possibly have been a juror; and it took two men to get this fellow whom the district attorney would not possibly have accepted as a juror.

Gentlemen, am I dreaming? Is this a real case and have I been practicing law for thirty-five years and built up some position in the community where I live and where I don't live, and now am I brought to the doors of the penitentiary charged with a crime like this?

Gentlemen, don't ever think that your own life or liberty is safe; that your own family is secure. Don't ever think that any human being is safe, when under evidence like this and circumstances like these, I, with some influence, and some respect, and some money, am brought here and placed in the shadow of the penitentiary for six long months. Am I dreaming? And will I awaken and find it all a horrible nightmare, and that no such thing has happened?

Ford tells you that you do not have to do anything but return a verdict. Now, what do you suppose he said that for? Did he want to take from the minds of this jury, the responsibility involved in their verdict? Gentlemen, I don't ask for any mercy at your hands. I want a fair deal. I am going to get it. But no man has a right to take from any jurors the responsibility that they bear to the case they are judging, and tell them that they are to hold a man's life in their keeping without thoughts. If you think I deserve conviction, then convict me, but do it with your eyes open, and your minds clear.

Now, here is a fellow that goes down to bribe Bain, and he doesn't talk with Mr. Bain, but goes to a neighbor. And later he goes back to the house and does not find Bob at home, so he talks with Bob's wife. If Bob's wife had not been at home, he would have talked with the dog. If the dog had not been at home, he would have talked with the cat. He was out after jurors, it is a wonder he didn't send a letter. So he goes back to Mrs. Bain. Mrs. Bain asked him to subscribe for the *Examiner* so she could get a premium, and Franklin subscribed. He wrote his name, and Mrs. Bain said, "Is that all?" Franklin said, "No, you want the money, don't you?" And then he said, "Can you change a fifty or a hundred?" That is what Mrs. Bain said and it is no doubt true. Franklin said to her, "Can you change a fifty or can you change a hundred?—one or the other." He had come right straight from the bank where the teller swears he gave him five hundred dollars in one hundreds and fifties, and Mrs. Bain said that he asked her to change a fifty or a hundred. So if the bank teller needs any corroboration, here it comes from the mouth of Mrs. Bain, that he did get fifties and hundreds. If he had gotten one twenty-dollar bill in the bunch, wouldn't he have asked her to change the twenty? He finally pulled out his wallet and managed to find some small change, Mrs. Bain says. And he went back that night and saw Robert Bain give him $400, every penny in twenty-dollar bills.

Now, gentlemen, there it is. A man is presumed to be honest and not a criminal, and a jury presumed to be sensible and fair, and to understand the responsibility involved in passing on the liberty of a fellow-man. Now tell me, did he get these twenties from me or through any check of mine? The bank teller says no, and Mrs. Bain says no. Where did he get these twenties? I cannot tell. That money did not come from the bank on my check, and there is no way on earth to figure that it did, and if I didn't furnish the money, where did it come from? Whose hand working out here in the darkness, unknown to me and unknown to the other attorneys—whose hand was it that stretched out in the night and was working my ruin? Of all the cases upon which a grand jury ever acted, the Bain case is the silliest. Gentlemen, there isn't a chance in ten thousand that I could have been guilty in the Bain case. Not a chance in ten thousand.

Here comes Robert Bain on the witness stand, he has immunity, and we will assume that he tells the truth. I will tell you why I took him on the jury. He said he belonged to the first labor union ever organized in Los Angeles. His hair was white, and somehow, as we get along in years, we think more of the few years that are left, than do the young. So, especially in a murder case, when I find a man with white hair, I know he will be as tender and kind and careful of his brother's life as he is of his own. We know as we grow in age and experience—we understand more and more what great influence circumstances have upon our lives, and how near alike are all men after all is said and done. And we grow kindlier in our judgments, more charitable to our fellowman than we were when filled with hot blood and the intemperate passions of youth. So Bain was taken on the jury. Franklin said he was a good man for the jury.

Franklin was consulted in the case of every juror, as Davis and I testified, and as naturally would be the case. And what did Bain tell Franklin? You remember the story. He says that when Franklin gave him the money, he told Franklin that if he found the evidence against McNamara convincing, he would render a verdict of guilty, didn't he? He told Franklin that if the evidence convinced him he would vote guilty. He said he would not have voted guilty anyhow unless the evidence was convincing. Now, here is the man himself to whom they have given immunity, and who is here in some mysterious way to testify against me, and he says that he told Franklin then that if the evidence was convincing he would find my client guilty, and yet Franklin thrust $400 on to him, which he swears he got from me and told me about it. Gentlemen, do you believe it? Isn't it the stuff that dreams are made of? Do you believe it? Bribe this man with $400 when he was not bribed at all, when he told Franklin that if the evidence was convincing he would find my client guilty!

And that is not all; after he got into the jury room and stayed there with his fellows day after day—of course, you know the jury is instructed that they must not talk with their fellows about the case, must not form any opinion—of course, you know they do not. I know they do. I have lived in courts for thirty-five years. Well, Bain told a juror in that jury room that if he stayed on the jury the SOB would get what was coming [to] them. That is the evidence of witness Webb. Fredericks spent longer in cross-examining Webb than he did any other witness, but could not stir him. Webb's evidence remained unshaken.

Gentlemen, it is simply insanity to talk about the Bain case. First the check was given before bribery was ever spoken of. Second, Franklin got no money from that check to give to Bain. Third, Franklin went to the neighbor's wife, and to Bain's wife and they called at his office. Fourth, Bain was not bribed at all, and fifth, Bain says himself that he would have found my client guilty after he got in the jury room. And yet, after all this, I am guilty of bribing Bain!

Let me tell you something, gentlemen, which I know District Attorney Fredericks will use in his argument against me, and which I have no reason to feel will meet with favor in the minds of you twelve men, but it is what I believe. I will just take a chance.

Did you ever think of the other side of this question? Lincoln Steffens was right in saying that this was a social crime. That does not mean that it should have been committed, but it means this—that it grew out of a condition of society for which McNamara was in no wise responsible. There was a fierce conflict in this city, exciting the minds of thousands of people, some poor, some weak, some irresponsible, some doing wrong on the side of the powerful as well as upon the side of the poor. It inflamed their minds—and this thing happened.

Let me tell you gentlemen, and I will tell you the truth, you may hang these men to the highest trees, you may hang everybody suspected, you may send me to the penitentiary if you will, you may convict the fifty-four men indicted in Indianapolis, but until you go down to fundamental causes, these things will happen over and over again. They will come as the earthquake comes. They will come as the hurricane that uproots the trees. They will come as the lightning comes to destroy the poisonous miasmas that fill the air. We as a people are responsible for these conditions, and we must look results squarely in the face.

And I want to say to you another thing in justice to that young man who was my client, and for whom I risked my life, my liberty, and my reputation to save. He had nothing on earth to gain; his act was not inspired by love of money; he couldn't even get fame, for if he had succeeded he could never have told any human being as long as he lived. He had nothing to gain. He believed in a cause, and he risked his life in that cause. Whether rightly or wrongly, it makes no difference with the motives of the man. I would not have done it. You would not have done it, but judged in the light of his motives, which is the only way that men can be judged—and for that reason only the infinite God can judge a human being—judged in the light of his motives, I cannot condemn the man, and I will not.

I want to say more, when you know the man, no matter whom—I have known men charged with crime in all walks of life, burglars, bankers, murderers—when you come to touch them and meet them and know them, you feel the kinship between them and you. You feel that they are human. They love their mothers, their wives, their children. They love their fellowman. Why they did this thing or that thing remains the dark mystery of a clouded mind, which all the science of all the world has never yet been wise enough to solve. But this act of McNamara has again been brought before this jury that it may work upon your passions against me—for nothing else.

None of the perpetrators of this deed was ever morally guilty of murder. Never. No one knows it better than the people who were prosecuting them. Sixteen sticks of dynamite were placed under a corner of the Times Building to damage the building, but not to destroy life, to intimidate, to injure property, and for no other reason. It was placed there wrongfully, criminally, if you will, but with no thought of harming human life. The explosion itself scarcely stopped the printing presses. Unfortunately, there was an accumulation of gas and other inflammable substances in the building which ignited, and the fire resulting destroyed these human lives.

Gentlemen, do you think my heart is less kind than Ford's? Do you think he would care more than I for the suffering of his fellowmen? Do you think for a moment that I did not feel sorry at the destruction of those lives, and for the wives and the children and the friends that were left behind? Wouldn't I feel it as much as he? And yet, gentlemen, this Times matter is paraded before this jury, in the hope that in some way it may awaken a prejudice in your hearts against me.

Gentlemen, I wish in no way to modify anything I have ever said or thought upon this subject. There never was a man charged with crime that I was not sorry for; sorry for him and sorry for his crime; that I could not imagine the motives that moved his poor weak brain; and I tell you today as Mr. Steffens told you from the witness stand, there will come a time when crime will disappear, but that time will never come or be hastened by the building of jails and penitentiaries and scaffolds. It will only come by changing the conditions of life under which men live and suffer and die.

(Recess for the day)

The next day, Darrow continued:

Gentlemen of the jury,

You cannot have listened here for three months and not have understood this case. No intelligent person could, and I know you do understand it. For the balance of my argument, I shall confine my talk almost entirely to the main charge brought against me, and say no more about these outside issues, which mean nothing, except an effort on the part of the state, cruel, unjust, and unlawful, to prejudice you against me.

The question which you are to decide here is this: Did I give Franklin four thousand dollars on the morning of the twenty-eighth of November to seek to bribe Lockwood? That is all there is to it.

Now is Franklin's story true or is it a lie? If I am to be convicted it must be upon the story which Franklin tells and the evidence which he presents. It must be upon the story that on Monday morning, the twenty-eighth, he met me in my office, that I called up Job Harriman, who came there and handed me the four thousand dollars, which I then gave to Franklin, and told him to go down on the streets and bribe a juror. That is all there is of it.

Now, what is the evidence on that? Job Harriman comes on the witness stand and swears there is not a single word of truth in it. Are you going to say that he is a perjurer? Mr. Ford says that he believes it. But where in this record is there any evidence, or any indication that Job Harriman committed perjury and was guilty of bribery?

Next, Frank Wolfe testifies that I came down with him on the street car that morning, that he went with me to my office, that we discussed the political campaign and other matters, until I was called up on the phone and said that I was going to Job Harriman's political headquarters, and that I went out with him. Who is Frank Wolfe? A man who was managing editor of the *Herald* for years. A man who has held important newspaper positions for twenty years, and who is now one of the editors of the municipal paper in this city—a man upon whose countenance truth is stamped as plainly as upon any man who lives. Is he a liar? A perjurer? For what? He is not charged with bribery, and he is not interested in this case. Are you likely to throw away the evidence of Frank Wolfe, and replace it with the lies of Franklin?

I will guarantee, gentlemen, that your observation would lead you to trust me before you would trust Franklin, if my word stood alone. I believe you would take my word if it stood alone against every one of these informers and crooks and immunity hunters.

Gentlemen, I do not know whether you have had much to do with lawyers or not. You probably have more money if you have not. I am not saying anything about that, but if any of you get into trouble, you generally tell your lawyer the truth. And good men do get into trouble now and then, and bad men stay out of trouble now and then. You can't tell whether a man is good or bad because he gets into trouble or stays out. But if you do get into trouble, you tell your lawyer the truth, just as you tell your doctor the truth.

What did Franklin tell Johnston on the twelfth day of January? He told him that I had never given him a cent of money for bribery, never. He told him that the bribe money was given to him by someone else, and he told him that I never knew anything about it. Now are you going to convict me on Franklin's word, when that is the statement which he made to his lawyer in confidence? It is unthinkable. Johnston may be a liar—may be, but you don't believe it. And Johnston goes to Mr. Ford and he comes back to Franklin and reports: "That won't do, nothing will do but to make a statement against Darrow." And what does Franklin reply? He says to Johnston, "If I made a statement against Darrow, I would be a goddamn liar." Now, Franklin said in January that if he made a statement against me he would be a blankety-blank liar. In May he makes that statement. What is he? What is he? I will not characterize him. He has characterized himself. And I hope the wonderful district attorney's office got its money's worth, when it bribed him with liberty to make his statement against me.

Then Franklin meets Davis and me, Davis having called me to his office on the fourteenth, two days later, and according to Davis and me, Franklin told us then together that Johnston had come to him, reporting that he had been to the district attorney's office and telling him if he would turn up evidence against me, he need not say a word about anybody in Los Angeles, that I was the one they were after. And Franklin replied, "I could not do it. I have no evidence against you, I could not do it."

Maybe Davis and I are liars. Ford says I have corrupted Davis. Maybe

I have. Maybe I have corrupted everybody I have met, excepting Ford. But it takes some evidence to show that, doesn't it? Davis, a man of standing and high character in the city where he has lived and practiced law. He is a liar, and Franklin is telling the truth!

Suppose we took a change of venue and tried this case before twelve bushmen in Africa, do you suppose they would stick me? Do you suppose that you could find a man who would take a club and knock me on the head if a jury did find me guilty on the evidence of Franklin?

Gentlemen, I have practiced law a good many years, and this is the first time in my life that I have ever known of a lawyer seeking to impeach the integrity of a man by men who have had personal difficulties with him. Did any of you ever have any trouble with anybody? Can there be a man on this jury who has not had difficulty with three or four men who would be willing to speak ill of him and injure him if it came their way? If you haven't made three or four enemies, gentlemen, you have lived a very weak and useless life. A man who can go through life as far as you twelve men have gone, and not make three or four enemies, is not worthwhile. You had better begin on me, so you will have something to your credit before you get through.

I have said about all I care to about Franklin. I have said enough. I have said too much. I have no feeling against him. He is the way God made him. He can't help it any more than you can help being you, or I can help being I. It was a hard choice he had to make. It is a hard choice for a weak man, to offer him honor or comparative honor on the one hand, and security at least from the penitentiary on the other. Some men will take one, some will take the other. It depends on the man. He is not responsible for his brain or his skull. I don't want anybody to think that I would judge him with hardness or bitterness. I have never judged any human being that way in my life, I never shall. I am only asking you, gentlemen of the jury, to consider the reasonableness and the probabilities and the improbabilities and the absurdities of his story—nothing else.

Would I take a chance of that kind surrounded by detectives from the beginning to the end. Leave out the moral question. Leave out the tradition of a profession that I have followed for thirty-five years. Leave out everything except the bare chance; would I take that chance with these gumshoe men everywhere, their eyes on everyone connected with this case—detectives—nine of them testifying in this case—detectives over the town as thick as lice in Egypt, detectives everywhere?

Detectives to the right of me,
Detectives to the left of me,
Detectives behind me,
Sleuthing and spying,
Theirs not to question why—
Theirs but to sleuth and lie—
Noble detectives?

I hadn't a chance with those fellows. Yet, I did take a chance, I took the chance of being alive where they were, as every man does, unless he could rely on twelve men to judge him honestly and kindly and carefully, as I feel I can rely on you.

Gentlemen, show me, in all their watching and their spying—show me with all the money they have spent, with all the efforts of the strong and the powerful to get me—show me in all these long weary months, where one honest man has raised his voice to testify against me. Just one. Just one. And are you ready, gentlemen, in this day and generation, to take away the name and the liberty of a human being upon the testimony of rogues, informers, crooks, vagabonds, immunity hunters, and detectives—such testimony as has been massed against me? God, if my word and my character do not weigh more than all the trash that has been presented to the jury, I don't want to live. I don't want to live in a world where such men could cause the undoing of an American citizen. If they could, are you safe, am I safe? Is there any man who is so high and powerful that his life and his liberty would be safe? You know better. It cannot happen, and it won't happen.

Was there any reason in the world for me seeking to bribe a juror on the twenty-eighth day of November? There are two things in this case that are not even disputed. One is that the dictagraph contained nothing in the world to my detriment. Here was the place they would have evidence if there was any honest evidence in the world. They needed it, or they would not have taken the trouble to do such an infamous act. There is another fact in this case that stands out so clear that every human being who has heard it must know it and understand it, and that is that the McNamara case was disposed of so far as I was concerned prior to the twenty-eighth day of November. Fredericks has said before this jury that he was going to send out for some of these people who formed the committee that made the settlement. Did you see them? He brought Tom Gibbon before you for a few minutes one day, and after talking with him, he sent him off on his business, and we haven't seen Mr. Gibbon since. Neither he nor Harry Chandler, nor any member of that committee, has denied a single word of Steffens's testimony that the case was practically settled prior to the twenty-eighth.

Now, gentlemen, perhaps most of you don't believe in all the philosophy which Lincoln Steffens believes in. What of it? Suppose some evening when you are in your jury room, and you, being instructed not to talk about this case, get into an argument among yourselves about matters of philosophy, and the old question of free will and necessity crops up. I wonder if you will all agree, and if you don't, will you say that the man who disagrees with you is a liar, because he has a different philosophy? You won't, not unless your own philosophy is very poor. Suppose you start a little discussion on politics or religion, or who is the best baseball player in America, as you have before now, will you agree? Not at all, and there may not be one man on this jury who would believe as Lincoln Steffens believes as to what we call crime, and what is punishment, and what are social crimes, and what are not. But he is a big man with a broad vision, a man who sees further than most men.

Gentlemen, because you don't believe a thing today is no sign that it is not true. There are dreams, and the dreams of today become facts tomorrow. Every effort toward humanizing the world, every effort in dealing with crime and punishment has been toward charity and mercy and better conditions, and has been in the direction of showing that all men are at least partly good, and all men are partly bad, and that there isn't so much difference in men as we had been taught to believe. Every effort that will last beyond the day and the year must have a humane idea, must have for its purpose the uplifting of man, must have its basis in charity and pity and humanity, or else it cannot live. Lincoln Steffens believes that; you believe it, too. You may not believe this way or that, but it is aspiration that has raised man from the savage drinking the blood of his fellow from his skull, and has led him up through trials and toil and tribulation by which he has arrived at the place where he can have mercy and charity and justice and can look forward to an ideal time when there will be no crime and no punishment, no sin, no sorrow, and when man will visit no cruelty upon his fellowman.

Almost everything that you believe now was scouted at and hissed, scarcely a hundred years ago. Most acts of humanity that we practice today would have been despised and denied two hundred years ago.

The world is moving, and as it moves brutality is further off, and humanity is nearer at hand. I don't care for Steffens's views. It is the facts that I am interested in.

Was my practice humane in this case? Among the other heinous charges that Mr. Ford saw fit to bring against me was that I had betrayed my clients—I, who had almost given my life's blood for this service—I, who never had a client in my life that I didn't consider my friend—I, who under the traditions of the profession, and under the feelings of my heart have put myself in the place of every client that I ever served—I, who worked day and night to save those lives that fate had placed in my hands, and who had bared my breast to the hostility of the world to serve them! I betrayed them.

Gentlemen, I wish you knew, I wish I could make you understand. I didn't need to do it, I was not on trial then. I was living in peace. It was nothing to me, except that I made their case my own. And what happened? It was as if I were a boy walking upon the sand by the sea and the sky was clear above me, excepting here and there a fleeting cloud, as there always is in every clear sky. The waves were calm and peaceful, and in a moment the heavens fell and the ocean overwhelmed me. If it shall be written in the Book of Fate that I have not made sacrifice enough for them, well and good, let me drink the cup of the dregs.

Did I think the McNamara case was disposed of? Is there any question but that we began the settlement of that case on the twentieth of November.

Mr. Ford said I knew these people were guilty from the beginning. Where is the evidence? I did not. I have practiced law for many a year. I do not go to a client and say, "Are you guilty, are you innocent?" I would not say it to you. Every man on earth is both guilty and innocent. I know it. You may not know it. I know it. I find a man in trouble. In a way his troubles may have come by his own fault. In a way they did not. He did not give himself birth. He did not make his own brain. He is not responsible for his ideas. He is the product of all the generations that have gone before. And he is the product of all the people who touch him directly or indirectly through his life, and he is as he is, and the responsibility rests on the infinite God that made him. I do what I can for him kindly, carefully, as fairly as I can, and do not call him a guilty wretch.

I had no knowledge whatever about the McNamaras until it was borne in on me day by day that this man I knew who trusted everything to me could not be saved if he went to trial. Just as the doctor finds that his patient must die, so it came to me that this client was in deadly peril of his life. Do you think that if I had thought there was one chance in a thousand to save him I would not have taken that chance? You may say I should not. That if I believed that he was guilty I should not have tried to save him. You may say so. I do not. If this man had suffered death, it would have brought more hatred and violence, more wrong and crime than anything else; for after all, gentlemen, the source of everything is the human heart. You can change man by changing his heart. You can change him by changing his point of view of life. You cannot change him by scaring him, by putting him in the pen, by violence and cruelty. If you look on him as a doctor looks on his patient, and ascertain the cause of his conduct, then you may change him. These acts of violence will occur over and over again until the human race is wise enough to bring more justice and more equality to the affairs of life than has ever obtained before.

And let me tell you about these acts that grow from social conflict. The men who stand for the workers strike out in their blindness. True, they strike out in the night and often wrongly. These men who built the civilization which we enjoy; these men who have built the railroad bed and laid the tracks, and who man the locomotives when you and I ride peacefully across the country in Pullman cars; these men who go ten, twenty, or thirty stories in the air to the top of the high buildings, taking their lives in their hands, and whose mangled remains are so often found on the earth beneath—these are the men who have built our civilization, and let me say to you that every step in the progress of the race, every step the world has taken has been for the elevation of the poor. There is no civilization without it—there can be no civilization without it. The progress of the world means the raising of these through organization, through treating them better, through treating them kindlier, through treating them more justly. Every step in civilization means the elevation of the poor, means helping the weak and the oppressed, and don't ever get it into your head that though these people often do wrong, that though they are blind, rebellious, and riotous, that after all they are not doing their part and more in the progress of the world. I knew it, I felt it then.

I knew that though terrible were the consequences of this blind act, consequences which nobody foresaw, still it was one of those inevitable acts, which are a part of a great industrial war. I believe that the loss of life was an accident. Nobody meant to take human life in the Times disaster, and the position of the state in the settlement of the matter showed that nobody meant to take human life. I heard these men talk of their brothers, of their mothers, of the dead. I saw their human side. I wanted to save them, and I did what I could to save them, and I did it as honestly and devotedly and unselfishly as I ever did an act in my life, and I have nothing to regret, however hard it has been.

Gradually it came to me that a trial could not succeed. Gradually another thing came to me. It was expensive—money of the Erectors' Association, of the state of California, the power of the Burns Agency, everything was against us. It needed money on our side, and a great deal of it. It needed money that must be taken from the wages of men who toil—men whose cause I have always served, and whether they are all faithful to me or not, the cause that I will serve to the end.

I could not say to them that my clients would be convicted. I could not say to the thousands who believed in them, and who believed in me, that the case was hopeless. The secrets that I had gained were locked in my breast, and I had to act—act with the men who I had chosen to act with me. I had to take the responsibility, grave as it was, and I took it.

Was this case disposed of before Franklin was arrested? Why gentlemen, there is no more question about that than there is that you twelve men are in front of me. Lincoln Steffens testified that on the twentieth day of November after he and I came from San Diego, he made the proposition for a settlement to me. The idea grew out of a conversation we had with Mr. Scripps, and I said I wished it could be done, but I said, "If anything is done it must come from you." On that very day he went to Meyer Lissner and Thomas Gibbon. At first, I had so little confidence in the possibility of a settlement that I scarcely thought about it for a day or two, but soon Mr. Steffens brought back reports which gave me the confidence to wire my friend Mr. Older, and ask his advice.

All the leading men connected with the labor movement on this coast were then at Atlanta. I could not get to them. I had to take the responsibility, and the other lawyers had to take it with me. What else could we do? I could not consider politics. I would not consider my own interests. I had to consider those accused men, nothing else, and there isn't one of you twelve men who would ever hire a lawyer who you didn't believe would consider your interests first of all—and if he did not, he wouldn't be true to his profession, or true to his own manhood. Those things alone could I consider; I wired on Wednesday, the twenty-second. I wired to Fremont Older and I wired to Gompers to send me a man at once, and I named certain men. Mr. Older came down here on Wednesday morning. Now, is that all a lie? Did I wire to these men on that day? If so, why?

Ford says I might have got up all this scheme, so as to cover up a case of jury bribing. Well, I might—I might. Sometimes his bitter heart might be touched by feelings of kindness and charity, it might—if the days of miracles had not passed. And so I might have got up this elaborate scheme, because I foresaw that I was going to give Franklin four thousand dollars, on the next Tuesday morning and start him off with the money to bribe a juror. Why, gentlemen, I might have done it—and therefore you will argue, says Ford, that I did. And this in a civilized country, presumed to be.

Older and Davis and Steffens and I met together. Was I betraying my clients? Davis spoke up and said to me, "Mr. Darrow, you can't afford to do it." Judge McNutt was there; he was as fine a man as ever lived in the world, as loyal to me as any friend I have ever known, as true to his profession, and as true to the higher ideals of manhood as any man I have ever met.

Davis said, "You will be misunderstood by union labor." I told him I had no right to consider myself, I had no right to consider the men who furnished the money. My duty was over there in the county jail with those two men, whose lives depended upon my courage and my fidelity and my judgment. Whatever befell me I must be true to them, and no lawyer lives who is true to his profession and true to himself who ever hesitates in an emergency like that.

McNutt at once agreed with me. Davis went to the district attorney— and this in uncontradicted. The first proposition that came from Lissner and Steffens was that J. B. McNamara should plead guilty and all other prosecution should stop. Davis then went over to the district attorney, and brought back word that it would require a term of years at least for J. J. McNamara. That was discussed on Wednesday, November twenty-second, between Older and Davis and Steffens and myself. And Judge McNutt is dead, dead, says Mr. Ford. I couldn't help it. If the Angel of Death hovering around the courtroom had come and asked my advice, I would probably have told him, "Take Ford and spare McNutt," but he didn't. I cannot help it because the Angel of Death made a mistake.

The matter was considered on Wednesday. Steffens said that he would see that the original proposition went through, and he went back to Chandler, the manager of the *Times.* Chandler was meeting with Steffens, and then word came from the East—from the East—from the seat of money and power and wealth and monopoly; word came that it was not enough to take J. B., but that J. J. must plead guilty to something; and we worked on that. We worked on it the rest of the week, and Steffens swears that he went and interviewed these defendants. Each brother was willing to suffer himself, but J. J. didn't want his brother to be hanged and J. B. didn't want J. J. to plead guilty to anything. J. B. agreed to plead guilty and take a life sentence, and J. J. said to us that after his brother's case was out of the way he would plead guilty and take a ten years' sentence.

Ford said that I should have told J. B. that J. J. was to plead guilty. Why? I was defending J. B., and it was my business to get the best terms I could for him. I was also defending J. J., and it was my business to get the best terms I could for him. I had no right to play either one against the other—no right, let alone what a man would naturally do. Now, that was the condition, going back and forth before Saturday. We had agreed to accept the district attorney's terms, if no better terms could be had. On Saturday, when that jury list was drawn, it was not handed over to Franklin for him to look up the missing names. It was kept until night, until he himself called to me for it, and I gave it to him.* There was nothing else to do. In the face of the world, and in the face of our employee, we were bound to go on as we had. On Sunday, Steffens, McNutt, and I spent most of the day at the jail, where, finally, each of the brothers separately agreed with our plan. On Sunday night, McNutt called Davis to his house and told him that the McNamaras had agreed to our plan.

Now gentlemen, what is there against all that, anything but the breath of counsel? Nothing! The testimony as to the settlement of the McNamara case stands here clear as sunlight. On Monday morning, Mr. Davis went to Fredericks and Fredericks agreed that he would accept the pleas of guilty—J. B. to take life and J. J. ten years. Now, what about it, gentlemen? Is all this a lie? Is it another dream? Why, even Franklin doesn't testify against this. If they had got Franklin and Harrington to contradict it, then they might argue that I had some motive

---

*Of course, if the case were really settled and no jury bribery were intended, Darrow was clever enough to think of some excuse to delay Franklin a few more days as far as jury "investigation" was concerned.

on the twenty-eighth of November for seeking to bribe a juror. But nobody testifies against it. Fredericks doesn't deny it, Chandler doesn't deny it, nor Lissner, nor Gibbon. There is no denial.

In the meantime, I had received a telegram from Ed Nockles on Friday, and in reply I wired him to come on immediately. Was that dispatch a fake? Was it sent to cover up a case of jury bribing at the beginning of the next week? On Monday every one of the parties interested had formally agreed to the plan of settlement. We had agreed to it on Sunday. We had agreed to it on Saturday, but we were still trying to do better if we could. Davis had told us that the settlement must be made at once. And with this condition of affairs, when I had no thought whatever that the McNamara case would be tried, is it likely that on Tuesday morning I would take four thousand dollars, not of my own money, but of money that was sorely needed, and not only waste that money, but take a chance of the destruction of my life and a term of years in the penitentiary, by sending Franklin down on the corner of Third and Los Angeles streets to bribe a juror?

Gentlemen, if you can believe it, I do not know what your minds are made of. If there is anybody whose prejudice and hatred are so deep that they cannot be removed, who can believe a thing like that, I would like to search him with an X ray, look inside of his skull and see how the wheels go around.

The settlement of the McNamara case cost me many friends, friends that have been coming back slowly, very slowly, as more and more this matter is understood. I am not a fool. I can prove that by Ford. I knew I was losing friends. Was I saving myself? Can any man on this jury or any person point to a single place in this whole matter, where I ever sought to save myself? Was I trying to save myself when Steffens came to me, after Franklin's arrest and asked if the settlement could still be made, and I said it could, and then he turned to me and said, "Someone may think that some of you lawyers are connected with this Franklin matter," and I said to him promptly, "If anybody has suspicions of anything like that, you tell them for me that this matter is never to be in any way considered in disposing of the McNamara case. Let the law take its course in that." And have I ever haggled or bargained or sought to throw myself into the balance anywhere? I was thinking of my clients, not of myself.

You may pursue me with all the infamy and venom you wish, but I know in my inmost heart that in all the sacrifices and responsibilities I have taken in my life, I never made one so hard as this, gentlemen. With the eyes of the world upon me, knowing that my actions would call down the doubt, and in many cases, the condemnation of my friends, I never hesitated for the fraction of a second. Perhaps if I had hesitated, my flesh would have been too weak to have taken the responsibility. But I took it, and here I am gentlemen, and I am not now trying to get rid of the responsibility. Was it wise or unwise? Was it right or wrong? You might have done differently, I don't know.

I have been a busy man. I have never had to look for clients, they have come to me. I have been a general attorney of a big railroad, I have been the attorney several different times, and general counsel, as it were, of the great city of Chicago. I have represented the strong and the weak—but never the strong against the weak. I have been called into a great many cases for labor unions. I have been called into a great many arbitration cases. I believe if you went to my native town, that the rich would tell you that they could trust not only my honor, but my judgment, and my sense of justice and fairness. More than once have they left their disputes with the laboring men with me to settle, and I have settled them as justly as I could, without giving the workingman as much as he ought to have. It will be many and many a long year before he will get all he ought to have. That must be reached step by step. But every step means more in the progress of the world.

This McNamara case came like a thunderclap upon the world. What was it? A building had been destroyed, and twenty lives had been lost. It shocked the world. Whether it was destroyed by accident or violence no one knew, and yet everyone had an opinion. How did they form that opinion? Everybody who sympathized with the corporations believed it was dynamite. Everyone who sympathized with the workingman believed it was something else. All had opinions. Society was in open rupture. Upon the one hand all the powerful forces thought, "Now we have these men by the throat, and we will strangle them to death. Now we will reach out the strong arm of money and the strong arm of the law, and we will destroy the labor unions of America."

On the other hand were the weak, and the poor, and the workers, whom I had served; these were rallying to the defense of the unions and to the defense of their homes. They called on me. I did not want to go. I urged them to take someone else, but I had to lay aside my own preferences and take the case.

There was a direct cleavage in society. Upon the one hand, those who hated, growing fiercer and bitterer day by day. It was a class struggle, gentlemen of the jury, filled with all the venom and bitterness born of a class struggle. These two great contending armies were meeting in almost mortal combat. No one could see the end.

I have loved peace, all my life. I have taught it all my life. I believe that love does more than hatred. I believe that both sides have gone about the settlement of these difficulties in the wrong way. The acts of the one have caused the acts of the other, and I blame neither. Men are not perfect. They had an imperfect origin, and they are imperfect today, and the long struggle of the human race from darkness to comparative civilization has been filled with clash and discord and murder and war, and violence and wrong, and it will be, for years and years to come. But ever we are going onward and upward toward the sunshine, where the hatred and war and cruelty and violence of the world will disappear.

Men were arrayed here in two great forces—the rich and the poor. None could see the end. They were trying to cure hate with hate.

I know I could have tried the McNamara case, and that a large class of the working people of America would honestly have believed, if these men had been hanged, that they were not guilty. I could have done this and have saved myself. I could have made money had I done this—if I had wanted to get money in that way. I know if you had hanged these men and the other men, you would have changed the opinion of scarcely a man in America, and you would have settled in the hearts of a great mass of men a hatred so deep, so profound, that it would never die away.

And I took the responsibility, gentlemen. Maybe I did wrong, but I took it, and the matter was disposed of and the questions set at rest. Here and there I got praise for what you called an heroic act, although I did not deserve the praise, for I followed the law of my being—that was all. I acted out the instincts that were within me. I acted according to the teachings of the parents who reared me, and according to the life I had lived. I did not deserve praise, but where I got one word of praise, I got a thousand words of blame! And I have stood under that for nearly a year.

This trial has helped clear up the McNamara case. It will all finally be cleared up, if not in time for me to profit by it, in time for my descendants to know. Some time we will know the truth. But I have gone on about my way as I always have regardless of this, without explanation, without begging, without asking anything of anybody who lived, and I will go on that way to the end.

I know the mob. In one way I love it, in another way I despise it. I know the unreasoning, unthinking mass. I have lived with men and worked with them. I have been their idol and I have been cast down and trampled beneath their feet. I have stood on the pinnacle, and I have heard the cheering mob sound my praises. I have gone down to the depths of the valley, where I have heard them hiss my name—this same mob—but I have summoned such devotion and such courage as God has given me, and I have gone on—gone on my path unmoved by their hisses or their cheers.

I have tried to live my life and to live it as I see it, regarding neither praise nor blame, both of which are unjust. No man is judged rightly by his fellowmen. Some look upon him as an idol, and forget that his feet are clay, as are the feet of every man. Others look upon him as a devil and can see no good in him at all. Neither is true. I have known this, and I have tried to follow my conscience and my duty the best I could and to do it faithfully; and here I am today in the hands of you twelve men who will one day say to your children, and they will say to their children, that you passed on my fate.

Gentlemen, there is not much more to say. You may not agree with all my views of philosophy. I believe we are all in the hands of destiny, and if it is written in the book of destiny that I shall go on to the penitentiary, that you twelve men before me shall send me there, I will go. If it is written that I am now down to the depths and that you twelve men shall liberate me, then, so it will be. We go here and there, and we think we control our destinies, and our lives, but above us and beyond us and around us are unseen hands, and unseen forces that move us at their will.

I am here and I can look back to the forces that brought me here, and I can see that I had nothing whatever to do with it, and could not help it, any more than any of you twelve men had to do with or could help passing on my fate. There is not one of you that would have wished to judge me, unless you could do it in a way to help me in my sore distress, I know that. We have little to do with ourselves.

As one poet has expressed it,

> *Life is a game of whist. From unknown sources*
> *The cards are shuffled and the hands are dealt.*
> *Blind are our efforts to control the forces*
> *That though unseen are no less strongly felt*

I do not like the way the cards are shuffled,
But still I like the game and want to play
And through the long, long night, I play unruffled
The cards I get until the break of day.

I have taken the cards as they came. I have played the best I could. I have tried to play them honestly, manfully, doing for myself and for my fellow the best I could, and I will play the game to the end, whatever that end may be.

Gentlemen, I came to this city as a stranger. Misfortune has beset me, but I never saw a place in my life with greater warmth and kindness and love than Los Angeles. Here to a stranger have come hands to help me, hearts to beat with mine, words of sympathy to encourage and cheer, and though a stranger to you twelve men and a stranger to this city, I am willing to leave my case with you. I know my life, I know what I have done. My life has not been perfect. It has been human, too human. I have felt the heartbeats of every man who lived. I have tried to be the friend of every man who lived. I have tried to help in the world. I have not had malice in my heart. I have had love for my fellowman. I have done the best I could. There are some people who know it. There are some who do not believe it. There are people who regard my name as a byword and a reproach, more for the good I have done than for the evil.

There are people who would destroy me. There are people who would lift up their hands to crush me down. I have enemies powerful and strong. There are honest men who misunderstand me and doubt me, and still I have lived a long time on earth, and I have friends—I have friends in my old home who have gathered around to tell you as best they could of the life I have lived. I have friends who have come to me here to help me in my sore distress. I have friends throughout the length and breadth of the land, and these are the poor and the weak and the helpless, to whose cause I have given voice. If you should convict me, there will be people to applaud the act. But if in your judgment and your wisdom and your humanity, you believe me innocent, and return a verdict of not guilty in this case, I know that from thousands and tens of thousands and yea, perhaps of the weak and the poor and the helpless throughout the world, will come thanks to this jury for saving my liberty and my name.

CHAPTER THREE

Disorder in the Court

The Trial of the Chicago Seven Pits the Establishment Against the Woodstock Generation

The 1960s were a time of stunning contrasts for most Americans, with mind-boggling triumphs in outer space bumping up against headlines announcing the latest earthbound atrocity. The movement for civil rights leapt to the fore, as freedom marchers carried the ideals of equality into hostile territory. Segregationists responded with gunpowder and dynamite. In 1963, a church in Birmingham was blown up; black children were killed. Civil rights leader Medgar Evers was murdered attempting to plant the seeds of civil rights in the South. And in 1968, the Reverend Martin Luther King Jr. was assassinated on the balcony of a Memphis motel.

While the war for civil rights raged at home, another exploded in Southeast Asia. In the early 1960s, U.S. military advisers began arriving in the Republic of Vietnam, the Kennedy administration sanctioned a coup which resulted in the murder of the South Vietnamese leader, and the escalation began.

American soldiers started coming home in body bags. Lt. William Calley led his GIs in the slaughter of Vietnamese civilians (see chapter 10). Perhaps most shocking of all was the sight of a pitched battle on the grounds of the U.S. embassy in Saigon, as the North Vietnamese launched their Tet Offensive, in living color on the six o'clock news. Americans watched over dinner and argued.

The war polarized the country like nothing had since the Civil War. Father against son, mother against daughter, brother against brother. The dispute spilled over into the streets and protests spread like wildfire. To the generation that had answered the call to arms after Pearl Harbor, the sight of long-haired hippies burning their draft cards was treasonous. The summer of '68 was fast approaching, and the country was a powder keg.

In June 1968, Robert F. Kennedy, on his way to clinching the

Democratic nomination on a campaign of racial tolerance and getting American servicemen home from Vietnam, made a triumphant appearance at the Ambassador Hotel in Los Angeles. There was one more month until the convention in Chicago and Kennedy looked unbeatable. Moments after finishing his speech, shots rang out and the nation saw another Kennedy martyred, cradled in the arms of a busboy on the floor of a hotel kitchen.

Two months later, Chicago Mayor Richard Daley was preparing for the upcoming Democratic convention and was ready for the hippies, yippies, and antiwar "freaks" that he figured were about to descend on the "city with broad shoulders." Never one to shirk from confrontation, Daley gave his police shoot-to-kill orders to quell any rioting.

For the antiwar protesters, Chicago was D day, their last chance to influence the process and demand a candidate who would end the war. Thousands descended upon Lincoln and Grant Parks, uncowed by the nightsticks and tear gas of the Chicago Police Department. The clash was violent and bloody. Delegates on the convention floor were sickened by the images being broadcast from right outside. The country watched as their sons and daughters received a Chicago-style greeting— gas, clubs, and handcuffs.

Someone would have to pay for the violence, the disorder, and someone did.

In 1969, eight men were charged with conspiracy to cross state lines to incite riot. The defendants were a diverse group: Abbie Hoffman and Jerry Rubin, the "leaders" of the yippies; Bobby Seale of the Black Panthers; and Tom Hayden, Rennie Davis, David Dellinger, John Froines, and Lee Weiner of the Students for a Democratic Society (SDS).

At the onset of the proceedings, Seale, the only black defendant, was loud and outspoken when his lawyer fell ill and could not represent him at trial. Rejecting the authority of the court, Seale was less than deferential, referring to the judge as a "pig," "racist," and "fascist." Judge Julius Hoffman responded by ordering the bailiffs to gag and bind Seale to a metal folding chair in the courtroom, creating an unintended counterpoint to the blindfolded figure of Justice herself presiding over the proceedings. At this point William Kunstler, representing the other defendants, spoke out:

> KUNSTLER: Your Honor, are we going to stop this medieval torture that is going on in this courtroom? I think this is a disgrace.

RUBIN: This guy is putting his elbow in Bobby's mouth and it wasn't necessary at all.

KUNSTLER: This is no longer a court of order, Your Honor; this is a medieval torture chamber. It is a disgrace. They are assaulting the other defendants also.

RUBIN: Don't hit me in the balls, motherfucker.

SEALE: This motherfucker is tight and it is stopping my blood.

KUNSTLER: Your Honor, this is an unholy disgrace to the law that is going on in this courtroom and I as an American lawyer feel it's a disgrace.

[DISTRICT ATTORNEY] FORAN: Created by Mr. Kunstler.

KUNSTLER: Created by nothing other than what you have done to this man.

ABBIE HOFFMAN: You come down here and watch this, Judge.

FORAN: May the record show that the outbursts are the defendant Rubin.

SEALE: You fascist dogs, you rotten lowlife son of a bitch. I am glad that I said it about Washington used to have slaves, the first president—

THE COURT: Everything you say will be taken down.

KUNSTLER: Your Honor, we would like the names of the marshals. We are going to ask for a judicial investigation of the entire condition and the entire treatment of Bobby Seale.

THE COURT: Don't point at me, sir, in that manner.

KUNSTLER: If we are going to talk about words, I'd like to exchange some.

THE COURT: Don't point at me in that manner.

KUNSTLER: I just feel utterly ashamed to be an American lawyer at this time.

THE COURT: You should be ashamed of your conduct in this case, sir.

MR. KUNSTLER: What conduct, when a client is being treated in this manner?

THE COURT: We will take a brief recess.

MR. KUNSTLER: Can we have somebody with Mr. Seale? We don't trust—

At this point, Seale's case was severed from that of the other defendants, and thus was born the trial of the "Chicago Seven."

The trial of the seven was as contentious as the riots that had preceded it. Judge Hoffman was targeted for abuse by the defendants; "old man" and "Mr. Magoo" were the choice forms of address, rather than the usual "Your Honor." The Chicago Seven made sure that the protests that had started in the streets continued in the courtroom. The defendants wore judicial robes to court, then took them off and jumped on the robes. They tried to throw a birthday party in court. Dellinger commented upon a ruling of the judge by screaming "bullshit"; he was forcibly removed from court. When the court refused to reinstate Dellinger's bail, the following ensued:

> ABBIE HOFFMAN: Your idea of justice is the only obscenity in the room. You schtunk! Obviously it was a provocation. That's why it has gone on here today, because you threatened him with the cutting of his freedom of speech in the speech he gave in Milwaukee.
>
> THE COURT: Mr. Marshal, will you ask the defendant Hoffman to—
>
> HOFFMAN: Oh, tell him to stick it up his bowling ball. How is your war stock doing, Julie [Judge Hoffman]? You don't have any power. They didn't have any power in the Third Reich either.
>
> THE COURT: Will you ask him to sit down, Mr. Marshal?
>
> THE MARSHAL: Mr. Hoffman, I am asking you again to shut up.
>
> RUBIN: Gestapo.
>
> HOFFMAN: Show him your .45. Show him a .45. He ain't never seen a gun.

The behavior of the defendants affected all present. Spectators often erupted, joining in shouting matches. Singer Judy Collins began singing "Where Have All the Flowers Gone?" from the witness stand, falling silent only when a bailiff covered her mouth with his hand. Beat poet Allen Ginsberg responded to an outburst in the courtroom during his testimony by chanting, "Ommmmm, ommmmm." Judge Hoffman allowed his dislike for the defendants and their counsel to show, refusing to refer to defense attorney Weinglass by the correct name.

In February 1970, after four days of deliberation, the jury acquitted all seven of conspiracy, and returned guilty verdicts against Hoffman, Rubin, Hayden, Davis, and Dellinger on the incitement charge. Weiner and Froines were acquitted on all counts. Each of the defendants and their lawyers had been cited by Judge Hoffman for contempt of court. Kunstler was sentenced to four years in jail; Weinglass to twenty months. Neither served any time. Within nine months, the U.S. Court of Appeals for the Seventh Circuit took the case up. The court ruled that Judge Hoffman had erred by failing to question potential jurors about their prejudices; by refusing to allow defense witnesses, including former Attorney General Ramsey Clark, to testify; and by sending notes to the jury during its deliberations without informing the defense. The court's harshest criticism was directed at Judge Hoffman's behavior. The court held that Judge Hoffman made sarcastic comments that implied that the defense was incompetent and dishonest, and that the defense case was lacking in merit. "The demeanor of the judge would require reversal even if errors did not," the court said—it overturned every conviction.

Biography

William Kunstler was, in the tradition of Clarence Darrow, one of America's great "cause" lawyers. Where Darrow was the courtroom defender of the workingman, shielding him from the depredations of greedy capitalist captains of industry, Kunstler was the champion of defendants and causes that were decidedly unpopular with most Americans—workingman and tycoon alike. For throughout the 1960s, seventies, eighties, and nineties, whenever a "radical" was being prosecuted, Kunstler would come to his defense. Whether yippies, hippies, Black Panthers, assassins, or terrorists, Kunstler—much like Darrow—viewed his clients not as defendants in criminal cases, but instead as courageous figures, battling an unjust system. Kunstler tried his cases with a take-no-prisoners style. Everyone, including the judge, was the enemy of justice, and the only way to succeed was to be unrelenting and fearless. Kunstler brought the dedication, the fervor of the true believer to every trial.

William Moses Kunstler was born July 7, 1919, the son of a Jewish doctor. Raised in Manhattan, he attended Yale University, where he was a French major, earned his varsity letter on the swim team, and graduated Phi Beta Kappa in 1937.

Kunstler served in the army during World War II, and was awarded the Bronze Star for his efforts as an intelligence officer in the Pacific Theater. In 1946, Major Kunstler was discharged from the army and enrolled at Columbia University Law School, in Manhattan, graduating in 1948. He taught English at Columbia from 1946 to 1950, and then married, moved to the suburbs, and opened a practice with his brother. The Kunstlers specialized in family law and estate planning, and

William found himself comfortably ensconced in the legal mainstream. There was little hint of the radical attorney that he would become.

By the 1960s, Kunstler had tired of defending corporate clients. He became involved in the civil rights movement, where his exposure to the racism and injustice of the South radicalized him, and he began what he called his crusade to defend "the poor, the persecuted, the radicals and the militants, the black people, the pacifists, and the political pariahs."

Kunstler dedicated himself to taking on the power of the state. He deflected criticism of his love for the spotlight, saying, "I enjoy the spotlight, as most humans do, but it's not my whole raison d'être. My purpose is to keep the state from becoming all-domineering, all powerful."

His string of courtroom successes was legendary: he defended a Palestinian accused of assassinating militant Rabbi Meir Kahane in front of a room filled with witnesses, and won an acquittal.

He framed his defense of Larry Davis, charged with trying to kill nine New York City cops during a shoot-out, as an indictment of the way police treat "young Third-World people in the depressed communities of our city." Davis was acquitted.

Perhaps the highlight of Kunstler's career was the defense of the Chicago Seven. In later years, Kunstler made numerous appearances on TV and in movies, often portraying a characteristically ardent defender of the civil rights of the downtrodden. He died in 1995.

Commentary

In this brilliant summation, Kunstler provided a textbook example—a four-part clinic on how to excel in persuasive argument. First and foremost was Kunstler's courage in the face of a hostile judge. It is difficult to battle a trial judge; he has the weight of the judicial system backing him up, and the power to enforce his will. "Courage" is a word not frequently associated with lawyers. Yet it is courage that allows a lawyer to champion his client's cause in the most hostile of environments: a courtroom presided over by an antagonistic judge. Black-robed jurists can be an intimidating lot, and it is the rare lawyer who can withstand the wrath of the trial judge. Kunstler faced such a judge in this trial. The hostility of Judge Hoffman was evident even during closing arguments. Yet Kunstler did not blink in the face of this hostility; he even seemed to feed off the judge's anger. Note about one-third into the close, where Hoffman admonished Kunstler in the strongest terms to discontinue his line of argument. Kunstler responded, "I do so under protest, Your Honor, I will get down, because the judge has prevented me from going into the material that I wanted to. . . ." Throughout this trial, Kunstler went toe-to-toe with the judge, and was cited for contempt 181 times. Kunstler tried his case as he saw fit.

Second, Kunstler—like all great attorneys—quickly established his central theme, referring back to it often. Kunstler recognized that jurors can only focus on limited amounts of information and it was his job to identify the main issue. Third, in the time-honored tradition of the criminal defense attorney, Kunstler shifted the focus of the trial to the grounds most favorable to his clients. At first blush, this was a conspiracy case with the facts overwhelmingly favoring the prosecution. Kunstler managed to remake this case, turning it instead into an inquiry on the right of assembly and of free speech. Finally, Kunstler kept his summation short and biting.

From the beginning of his closing argument, Kunstler established his central premise: that his clients were rebels agitating against an unjust system. He quoted Clarence Darrow: "When a new truth comes upon the Earth, or a great idea necessary for mankind is born, where does it come from? . . . It comes from men who have dared to be rebels and think their thoughts, and their faith has been the faith of rebels." This theme is the core of the argument, and throughout the summation Kunstler conjured up visions of the righteous rebel, analogizing his clients to the patriots of the American Revolution. This theme has the virtue of being simple and straightforward, and Kunstler never strayed far from it. It is a certain sign of a great closing argument when the jurors are left with one major idea echoing in their minds as they begin deliberations. Kunstler crafted the notion that the defendants were great patriots, planted the seed in the jurors' minds, and his clients reaped what he had sown.

The third aspect of this close is Kunstler's clever shifting of the focus of the trial. If the trial is about people conspiring to start a riot and trespassing, the defendant can't win. But if instead the rights of freedom of assembly and the freedom of association are on trial, the focus of the jury changes. Kunstler harkened back to the American Revolution by casting his clients in the role of patriotic revolutionaries. Kunstler told the jurors that a great demonstration took place in 1770 at the Custom House in Boston, where rebels—patriots—picketed because it was where the unjust taxes were being collected. Likewise, in this case the amphitheater was the focus of the demonstrations. Kunstler reminded the jurors that the authorities specifically prohibited the marchers from going to the amphitheater. Kunstler said "that was like telling the Boston Patriots, 'Go anywhere you want, but don't go to Custom House,' because it was at the Custom House and it was at the amphitheater that the protesters wanted to show that something was terribly and totally wrong." By using language to paint compelling visual images of great events and establishing that his clients were part of a greater cause, Kunstler successfully moved the jurors to view his clients in a far more positive light than the prosecution desired.

The fourth aspect of this close that helped establish it as an outstanding example of advocacy in action is its relative brevity. It is difficult for any speaker in this era of sound bites and MTV-style editing to grab and hold the attention of an audience for hours. Clarence Darrow did it, but he did so before the advent of radio and television, in a time when storytelling was valued and audiences would listen, caught up in the ebb and flow of the teller's tale. The electronic media has decimated the attention span of most people, and any effective advocate will do well to take heed, like Kunstler, and be brief. To do otherwise means the long-winded trial advocate runs the risk of watching jurors' eyes glaze over as chances for acquittal fade away, along with their attention.

Closing Argument

The State of Illinois v. *Abbie Hoffman, et al.*
Delivered by William M. Kunstler
Chicago, Illinois, February, 1970

MR. KUNSTLER: Ladies and gentlemen of the jury:

This is the last voice that you will hear from the defense. We have no rebuttal. This government has the last word.

In an introductory fashion, I would just like to state that only you will judge this case as far as the facts go. This is your solemn responsibility and it is an awesome one.

After you have heard the prosecutor and Mr. Weinglass, there must be lots of questions running in your minds. You have seen the same scenes described by two different people. You have heard different interpretations of those scenes by two different people. But you are the ones that draw the final inference. You will be the ultimate arbiters of the fate of these seven men.

In deciding this case we are relying upon your oath of office and that you will decide it only on the facts, not on whether you like the lawyers; that is unimportant. Whether you like or don't like the judge, that is unimportant, too. Whether you like the defendants or don't like the defendants—

THE COURT: I am glad you didn't say I was unimportant.

MR. KUNSTLER: No. The likes or dislikes are unimportant.

And I can say that it is not whether you like the defendants or don't like the defendants. You may detest all of the defendants; for all I know, you may love all of them, I don't know. It is unimportant. It shouldn't interfere with your decision, it shouldn't come into it. And this is hard to do.

You have seen a long defense here. There have been harsh things said in this court, and harsh things to look at from your jury box. You have seen a man bound and gagged. You have heard lots of things which are probably all not pleasant. Some of them have been humorous. Some have been bitter. Some may have been downright boring, and I imagine many were. Those things really shouldn't influence your decision. You have an oath to decide the facts and to decide them divorced of any personal considerations of your own, and I remind you that if you don't do that, you will be living a lie the rest of your life, and only you will be living with that lie.

Now, I don't think it has been any secret to you that the defendants have some questions as to whether they are receiving a fair trial. That has been raised many times.

MR. FORAN: Your Honor, I object to this.

THE COURT: I sustain the objection.

MR. KUNSTLER: They stand here indicted under a new statute. In fact, the conspiracy, which is count one, starts the day after the president signed the law.

MR. FORAN: Your Honor, I object to that. The law is for the court to determine, not for counsel to determine.

THE COURT: I sustain the objection.

MR. KUNSTLER: Your Honor, I am not going into the law. They have a right to know when it was passed.

THE COURT: I don't want my responsibility usurped by you.

MR. KUNSTLER: I want you to know, first that these defendants had a constitutional right to travel. They have a constitutional right to dissent and to agitate for dissent. No one would deny that, not Mr. Foran, and not I, or anyone else.

Just some fifty years ago, I think almost exactly, in a criminal court building here in Chicago, Clarence Darrow said this:

> When a new truth comes upon the earth, or a great idea neces-
> sary for mankind is born, where does it come from? Not from the
> police force, or the prosecuting attorneys, or the judges, or the
> lawyers, or the doctors. Not there. It comes from the despised and
> the outcasts, and it comes perhaps from jails and prisons. It comes
> from men who have dared to be rebels and think their thoughts,
> and their faith has been the faith of rebels.
>
> What do you suppose would have happened to the workingmen
> except for these rebels all the way down through history? Think of
> the complacent cowardly people who never raise their voices
> against the powers that be. If there had been only these, you gentle-
> men of the jury would be hewers of wood and drawers of water.
> You gentlemen would have been slaves. You gentlemen owe what-
> ever you have and whatever you hope to these brave rebels who
> dared to think, and dared to speak, and dared to act.

This was Clarence Darrow fifty years ago in another case.

You don't have to look for rebels in other countries. You can just look at the history of this country.

You will recall that there was a great demonstration that took place around the Custom House in Boston in 1770. It was a demonstration of the people of Boston against the people who were enforcing the Sugar Act, the Stamp Act, the Quartering of Troops Act. And they picketed at the one place where it was important to be, at the Custom House, where the customs were collected.

You remember the testimony in this case. Superintendent Rochford said, "Go up to Lincoln Park, go to the bandshell, go anywhere you want, but don't go to the amphitheater."

That was like telling the Boston patriots, "Go anywhere you want, but don't go to the Custom House," because it was at the Custom House and it was at the amphitheater that the protesters wanted to show that something was terribly and totally wrong. They wanted to show it at the place it was important, and so the seeming compliance of the city in saying, "Go anywhere you want throughout the city. Go to Jackson Park. Go to Lincoln Park," has no meaning. That is an excuse for preventing a demonstration at the single place that had meaning, which was the amphitheater.

The Custom House in Boston was the scene of evil and so the patriots demonstrated. They ran into a Chicago. You know what happened. The British soldiers shot them down and killed five of them, including one black man, Crispus Attucks, who was the first man to die, by the way, in the American Revolution. They were shot down in the street by the British for demonstrating at the Custom House.

You will remember that after the Boston Massacre which was the name the colonies gave to it, all sorts of things happened in the colonies. There were all sorts of demonstrations—

MR. FORAN: Your Honor, I have sat here quite a while and I object to this. This is not a history lecture. The purpose of summation is to sum up the facts of the case and I object to this.

THE COURT: I do sustain the objection. Unless you get down to evidence, I will direct you to discontinue this lecture on history. We are not dealing with history.

MR. KUNSTLER: But to understand the overriding issues as well, Your Honor—

THE COURT: I will not permit any more of these historical references and I direct you to discontinue them, sir.

MR. KUNSTLER: I do so under protest, Your Honor, I will get down, because the judge has prevented me from going into material that I wanted to—

MR. FORAN: Your Honor, I object to that comment.

THE COURT: I have not prevented you. I have ruled properly as a matter of law. The law prevents you from doing it, sir.

MR. KUNSTLER: I will get down to the evidence in this case. I am going to confine my remarks to showing you how the government stoops to conquer in this case.

The prosecution recognized early that if you were to see thirty-three police officers in uniform take the stand that you would realize how much of the case depends on law enforcement officers. So they strip the uniforms from those witnesses, and you notice you began to see almost an absence of uniforms. Even the deputy police chief came without a uniform.

The prosecutor said, "Look at our witnesses. They don't argue with the judge. They are bright and alert. They sit there and they answer clearly."

They answered like automatons—one after the other, robots took the stand. "Did you see any missiles?"

"A barrage."

Everybody saw a barrage of missiles.

"What were the demonstrators doing?"

"Screaming. Indescribably loud."

"What were they screaming?"

"Profanities of all sorts."

I call your attention to James Murray. That is the reporter, and this is the one they got caught with. This is the one that slipped up. James Murray, who is a friend of the police, who thinks the police are the steadying force in Chicago. This man came to the stand, and he wanted you to rise up when you heard "Vietcong flags," this undeclared war we are fighting against an undeclared enemy. He wanted you to think that the march from Grant Park into the center of Chicago in front of the Conrad Hilton was a march run by the Vietcong, or have the Vietcong flags so infuriate you that you would feel against these demonstrators that they were less than human beings. The only problem is that he never saw any Vietcong flags. First of all there were none, and I call your attention to the movies, and if you see one Vietcong flag in those two hours of movies at Michigan and Balbo, you can call me a liar and convict my clients.

Mr. Murray, under whatever instructions were given to him, or under his own desire to help the police department, saw them. I asked him a simple question: describe them. Remember what he said? "They are black." Then he heard laughter in the courtroom because there isn't a person in the room that thinks the Vietcong flag is a black flag. He heard a twitter in the courtroom. He said, "No, they are red."

Then he heard a little more laughter.

Then I said, "Are they all red?"

He said, "No, they have some sort of symbol on them."

"What is the symbol?"

"I can't remember."

When you look at the pictures, you won't even see any black flags at Michigan and Balbo. You will see some red flags, two of them, I believe, and I might say to you that a red flag was the flag under which General

Washington fought at the Battle of Brandywine, a flag made for him by the nuns of Bethlehem.

I think after what Murray said you can disregard his testimony. He was a clear liar on the stand. He did a lot of things they wanted him to do. He wanted people to say things that you could hear, that would make you think these demonstrators were violent people. He had some really rough ones in there. He had, "The Hump Sucks," "Daley Sucks the Hump"—pretty rough expressions. He didn't have "Peace Now." He didn't hear that. He didn't give you any others. Oh, I think he had "Charge. The Street is Ours. Let's Go."

That is what he wanted you to hear. He was as accurate about that as he was about the Vietcong flag, and remember his testimony about the whiffle balls. One injured his leg. Others he picked up. Where were those whiffle balls in this courtroom?

You know what a whiffle ball is. It is something you can hardly throw. Why didn't the government let you see the whiffle ball? They didn't let you see it because it can't be thrown. They didn't let you see it because the nails are shiny. I got a glimpse of it. Why didn't you see it? They want you to see a photograph so you can see that the nails don't drop out of the photograph. We never saw any of these weapons. That is enough for Mr. Murray. I have, I think, wasted more time than he is worth on Mr. Murray.

Now, I have one witness to discuss with you who is extremely important and gets us into the alleged attack on the Grant Park underground garage.

This is the most serious plan that you have had. This is more serious than attacking the pigs, as they tried to pin onto the yippies and the National Mob. This is to bomb. This is frightening, this concept of bombing an underground garage, probably the most frightening concept that you can imagine.

By the way, Grant Park garage is impossible to bomb with Molotov cocktails. It is a pure concrete garage. You won't find a stick of wood in it, if you go there. But, put that aside for the moment. In a mythical tale, it doesn't matter that buildings won't burn.

In judging the nonexistence of this so-called plot, you must remember the following things.

Lieutenant Healy in his vigil, supposedly in the garage, never saw anything in anybody's hands, not in Shimabukuro's, whom he says he saw come into the garage, not in Lee Weiner's hands, whom he said he saw come into the garage, or any of the other four or five people whom he said he saw come into the garage. These people that he said he saw come into the garage were looking, he said, in two cars. What were they looking into cars for? You can ask that question. Does that testimony make any sense, that they come in empty-handed into a garage, these people who you are supposed to believe were going to firebomb the underground garage?

Just keep in mind when you consider this fairy tale when you are in the jury room.

Secondly, in considering it you have the testimony of Lieutenant Healy, who never saw Lee Weiner before. You remember he said, "I never saw him before. I had looked at some pictures they had shown me."

But he never had seen him and he stands in a stairwell behind a closed door looking through a one-foot-by-one-foot opening in that door with chicken wire across it and a double layer of glass for three to four seconds, he said, and he could identify what he said was Lee Weiner in three to four seconds across what he said was thirty to forty yards away.

MR. FORAN: Your Honor, I object to "three or four seconds." It was five minutes.

MR. KUNSTLER: No, sir. The testimony reads, Your Honor, that he identified him after three or four seconds and if Mr. Foran will look—

MR. FORAN: Then he looked at him for five minutes.

MR. KUNSTLER: He identified him after three or four seconds.

THE COURT: Do you have the transcript there?

MR. FORAN: Your Honor, I would accept that. He identified him immediately but he was looking at him for five minutes.

MR. KUNSTLER: I just think you ought to consider that in judging Lieutenant Healy's question. This officer was not called before the grand jury investigating that very thing. And I think you can judge the importance of that man's testimony on whether he ever did tell the United States attorney anything about this in September of 1968.

I submit he didn't because it didn't happen. It never happened. This is a simple fabrication. The simple truth of the matter is that there never was any such plot and you can prove it yourselves. Nothing was ever found, there is no visible proof of this at all. No bottles. No rags. No sand. No gasoline. It was supposed to be a diversionary tactic, Mr. Schultz told you in his summation. This was a diversionary tactic. Diversionary to what? This was Thursday night.

If you will recall, the two marches to the amphitheater that got as far as Sixteenth and Eighteenth Streets on Michigan had occurred earlier. The only thing that was left was the Downers Grove picnic. It was a diversionary operation to divert attention from the picnic at Downers Grove. It was diversionary to nothing. The incident lives only in conversations, the two conversations supposedly overheard by Frapolly and Bock, who are the undercover agents who were characterized, I thought, so aptly by Mr. Weinglass.

Now just a few more remarks. One, I want to tell you that as jurors, as I have already told you, you have a difficult task. But you also have the obligation if you believe that these seven men are not guilty to stand on that and it doesn't matter that other jurors feel the other way. If you honestly and truly believe it, you must stand and you must not compromise on that stand.

MR. FORAN: Your Honor, I object to that. Your Honor will instruct the jury what their obligations are.

THE COURT: I sustain the objection. You are getting into my part of the job.

MR. KUNSTLER: What you do in that jury room, no one can question you on. It is up to you. You don't have to answer as to it to anybody and you must stand firm if you believe either way or not—

MR. FORAN: Your Honor, I object to that.

THE COURT: I sustain the objection, I told you not to talk about that, Mr. Kunstler.

MR. KUNSTLER: I think I have a right to do it.

THE COURT: You haven't a right when the court tells you not to and it is a matter of law that is peculiarly my function. You may not tell the jury what the law is.

MR. KUNSTLER: Before I come to my final conclusion, I want to thank you both for myself, for Mr. Weinglass, and for our clients for your attention. It has been an ordeal for you, I know. We are sorry that it had to be so. But we are grateful that you have listened. We know you will weigh, free of any prejudice on any level, because if you didn't, then the jury system would be destroyed and would have no meaning whatsoever. We are living in extremely troubled times, as Mr. Weinglass pointed out. An intolerable war abroad had divided and dismayed us all. Racism at home and poverty at home are both causes of despair and discouragement. In a so-called affluent society, we have people starving and people who can't even begin to approximate the decent life.

These are rough problems, terrible problems, and as has been said by everybody in this country, they are so enormous that they stagger the imagination. But they don't go away by destroying their critics. They don't vanish by sending men to jail. They never did and they never will.

To use these problems by attempting to destroy those who protest against them is probably the most indecent thing that we can do. You can crucify Jesus, you can poison a Socrates, you can hang John Brown or Nathan Hale, you can kill a Che Guevara, you can jail a Eugene Debs or a Bobby Seale. You can assassinate John F. Kennedy or a Martin Luther King, but the problem remains. The solutions are essentially made by continuing and perpetuating with every breath you have the right of men to think, the right of men to speak boldly and unafraid, the right to be masters of their souls, the right to live free and die free. The hangman's rope never solved a single problem except that of one man.

I think if this case does nothing else, perhaps it will bring into focus that again we are in that moment of history when a courtroom becomes the proving ground of whether we do live free and whether we do die free. You are in that position now. Suddenly all importance has shifted to you—shifted to you as I guess in the last analysis it should go, and it is really your responsibility, I think, to see that men remain able to think, to speak boldly and unafraid, to be masters of their souls, and to live and die free. And perhaps if you do what is right, perhaps Allen Ginsberg will never have to write again as he did in "Howl," "I saw the best minds of my generation destroyed by madness," perhaps Judy Collins will never have to stand in any courtroom again and say as she did, "When will they every learn? When will they ever learn?"

CHAPTER FOUR

Death by Plutonium

Fallout from Karen Silkwood's Death Brings the Nuclear Industry to Its Knees

One of the most controversial issues of the 1970s was America's development of and growing reliance on nuclear power as a major energy source. The uncertainty of a reliable source of petroleum, in the wake of the oil embargoes, created near panic for an American public with a seemingly insatiable need for oil. America was receptive to the siren song of the atom, confident that nuclear power was the panacea for its energy woes. But there had been no close scrutiny of the potential hazards of nuclear power. Environmentalists raised the issues of nuclear waste disposal and the potential health hazards associated with operating these plants. But the public did not focus on these issues until a deadly dose of plutonium, a dead woman, a grieving father, and a zealous advocate resulted in *The Estate of Karen Silkwood* v. *Kerr-McGee.*

Karen Silkwood was a young woman who worked as a lab analyst for Kerr-McGee's Cimarron plant near Crescent, Oklahoma. The plant made plutonium fuel pins to be used in nuclear power plants. Plutonium, a radioactive chemical element used to develop nuclear power and weapons, is extremely toxic, deadly to humans in even the smallest amounts.

Silkwood discovered health and safety problems at the plant and moved to alert Kerr-McGee, as well as her coworkers. She eventually went so far as to report her concerns to outside regulatory agencies. Silkwood spearheaded a union battle to expose Kerr-McGee in an attempt to correct the safety hazards. She was a member of the negotiating team for the Oil, Chemical and Atomic Workers Union (OCAW), and she traveled to Washington, D.C., to represent employees of the Kerr-McGee plant, alleging numerous health and safety violations to the Atomic Energy Commission (AEC). The AEC asked Silkwood to document, tape record, and collect evidence to support her allegations.

From September 1974 until her death that November, Karen Silkwood pursued her investigation covertly while continuing to work at Kerr-McGee.

Silkwood's work at the plant included use of a glove box to grind and polish plutonium pins. A glove box is an enclosure designed to make it impossible for any plutonium to escape. It has sealed gloved openings which permit the worker to reach inside and perform work, presumably without exposing the worker to the contaminated substances inside. Even so, the employees were required to monitor themselves for contamination both before and after working in the boxes. The employees morbidly referred to being contaminated as being "cooked," and would question how "hot" they were with the contamination.

On November 5, 1974, Karen got cooked. She was contaminated on her left hand, right wrist, upper arm, neck, hair, and nostrils. She was immediately taken to a decontamination room where she was stripped, her skin scrubbed with an abrasive, and her nose flushed with high-power water sprayers in an attempt to eliminate the contamination.

The next day she again tested positive for plutonium contamination when leaving the plant at the end of her shift. Once again she underwent the humiliation and torture of the decontamination process. That evening, she was given containers for urine and fecal samples to test whether the plutonium had entered her system.

The next day, November 7, after still testing positive for plutonium contamination, she once again endured the invasive decontamination procedure. On that same day, the company sent a team out to her apartment, fearing it might be contaminated. The team arrived at the apartment, woke up her roommate, monitored the area, and found that it tested positive for contamination. High levels of contamination were found throughout the apartment right down to the food in the kitchen.

Kerr-McGee sent Silkwood to the Los Alamos Scientific Laboratory in New Mexico, where Karen's lungs tested positive for radioactive contamination. Notwithstanding the contamination, Karen was confident upon her return from Los Alamos that the tide had begun to turn against Kerr-McGee. She had an appointment to meet a reporter from *The New York Times* the following day, November 13, 1974. Before Silkwood left for the meeting with the reporter she told her boyfriend, "We've got them now." At the meeting, Silkwood anticipated bringing all the information she had collected over the previous months. She was going to provide data not only on the hazards of working at Kerr-McGee, but also on how the quality-control records of the fuel rods had been falsified.

The meeting was to be with David Burnham of *The New York Times* and Steve Wodka of the OCAW. The reporters waited at the Holiday Inn in Oklahoma City for more than an hour before they telephoned a union official to inquire as to Silkwood's whereabouts. On her way to the meeting, she was killed in a mysterious and suspicious one-car accident. The next day, the men went to the garage where Silkwood's car was held to pick up a box containing her possessions. The documents and evidence she had been gathering over the last months were missing and were never found.

Silkwood's apartment was quarantined and the personal property inside was confiscated and buried in a nuclear waste dump. It took three months to decontaminate the apartment. In the meantime, anyone entering the apartment was required to wear a respirator.

Kerr-McGee had an opportunity to make the matter go away, quietly and cheaply. Karen Silkwood's personal belongings were worth about $5,000. After her death, that's all her father really wanted from her employer. The money would pay for those items destroyed when plutonium contamination was found in her apartment. The cash would go to her three children now facing life without their mother. But Kerr-McGee offered only $1,500 and that was, for Bill Silkwood, the final straw. Her father contacted well-known attorney Gerry Spence and brought suit on behalf of Karen's children. Both Bill Silkwood and Spence knew it would be a long and difficult battle against a large and wealthy company that could finance top-notch experts, a David and Goliath matchup. A victory for the Silkwood family would set a precedent for the entire nuclear industry—and would also bring a measure of peace of mind to the Silkwood family, knowing that Karen had not died in vain. Thus began the lawsuit which would forever change the nuclear industry and the public's perception of it.

Bill Silkwood sued Kerr-McGee for $10,505,000: $500,000 for the physical and mental pain Karen suffered as a result of the contamination, $10 million* in punitive damages for Kerr-McGee's egregious behavior, and the original $5,000 for Karen's personal property, confiscated when plutonium was found in her apartment.

---

*Spence later increased the request for punitive damages to $70 million.

The trial began in March 1979 in Oklahoma City and lasted eleven weeks. Spence called numerous union members as witnesses; they all corroborated the union position regarding the hazardous working conditions at the plant. Various expert witnesses testified during the trial. One doctor who was an expert in the effects of low-level radiation testified that if Silkwood had not died in the car crash, she would certainly have died from cancer resulting from her exposure to plutonium. A former colleague of Silkwood's testified that when she died, Karen was in the middle of an investigation. She was going to prove that Kerr-McGee created a hazardous work environment and falsified the plutonium pin reports that were in her possession at the time of the car crash. The colleague also testified that the evidence Silkwood had obtained proved that forty pounds of plutonium with a black market value of $10 million was missing from the plant.

Kerr-McGee defended the claim of misplaced plutonium by stating that it had simply disappeared from the pipe system at the plant. The company also alleged that Silkwood deliberately contaminated herself in an attempt to discredit the company.

The jury, consisting of six people, three men and three women, returned a verdict for the entire $10,505,000. Kerr-McGee appealed the $10 million punitive damages all the way to the Supreme Court. Punitive damages were eventually settled at $1.38 million.

Silkwood v. *Kerr-McGee* was the first time that an employee of a nuclear facility was awarded damages. It set a precedent for the nuclear industry by putting it on notice that the states would play a role in the federally regulated industry, and provided the means—punitive damages—to make sure the industry paid attention.

Biography

Gerry Spence was born in Laramie, Wyoming, in 1929, the son of a deeply religious mother and anti-authoritarian father who identified strongly with working people. The elder Spence was a chemist who worked in factories and practiced frontier self-reliance; he fed his family by hunting and growing his own vegetables. Spence's mother sewed clothes for her children using animal skins, and enforced a strict regimen of church attendance for them.

He eventually attended law school because, as he put it, practicing law beat the hell out of manual labor. Spence married, had three children, and graduated at the top of his class from the University of

Wyoming in Laramie. He failed the bar exam on his first attempt, passed it on his next try, and moved to a small town in central Wyoming.

Spence had a difficult time with private practice, and threw his hat in the public sector, winning election as county attorney, and then as a district attorney. He spent his eight years in the office learning the trial skills that would serve him so well in the coming years.

In 1962, Spence ran for Congress as a right-wing Republican and was soundly defeated by a descendant of President William Henry Harrison—Spence carried just one precinct. Rejected by his law school for a teaching spot, unable to gain a judgeship, Spence turned to taking cases for insurance companies.

Spence credits his turn from corporate work to a chance encounter with a former "foe." Out shopping with his wife, Spence saw an old man he had recently beaten out of an insurance settlement after a woman ran her car into him and left him crippled. According to Spence, he told the man, "I'm sorry how your case turned out." "Don't feel bad," the old man replied. "You were just doing your job," he said, and patted Spence on the back and smiled. Spence soon began taking high-profile cases, representing the underdog.

He won a $1.3 million verdict for a secretary who caught gonorrhea from the son of an ambassador. He successfully defended Ed Cantrell, a Wyoming highway patrolman who shot an undercover agent between the eyes. The agent was a key witness in a statewide corruption case, but Spence convinced a jury that Cantrell was acting in self-defense. The Karen Silkwood case in 1979 vaulted Spence to national attention when he won the $10,505,000 award for her estate.

The Utah nursing care industry was forced to clean up its act after Spence won a $4 million medical malpractice verdict. He represented the widow of deposed Philippines president Marcos, winning an acquittal after a three-and-a-half month trial. He defended white separatist Randy Weaver on murder, assault, conspiracy, and gun charges in the Ruby Ridge case, winning an acquittal for his client.

The author of six books, Spence is the founder and director of the nonprofit Trial Lawyer's College, as well as the founder of Lawyers and Advocates for Wyoming, a nonprofit public interest law firm.

Commentary

Gerry Spence's closing argument on behalf of the Silkwood family is as fine a closing argument as has ever been delivered in an American courtroom. It ranks with Darrow's argument in Leopold and Loeb and his self-defense in his jury-tampering trial. Spence has style, and during his mesmerizing argument he rings in his points with a clear and compelling resonance. Woven throughout this closing argument is a thread of justice and righteous conviction. His structure is well thought out, a light and engaging introduction that builds to a powerful, compelling crescendo.

One of the most striking aspects of this close is his use of the horizontal dialogue (previously discussed in chapter 2). He never talks at his jurors; he chats with them. His engaging "country lawyer" style builds credibility with his jurors, as he avoids the dreaded "attorney-speak" of legal jargon and convoluted sentences that are indecipherable to the nonlawyer. Early in the close, he says:

> What I need to do is have you understand what needs to be understood. And I think I'll get some help from you. My greatest fear in my whole life has been that when I would get to this important case—whatever it was—I would stand here in front of the jury and be called upon to make my final argument and suddenly you know, I'd just open my mouth and nothing would come out. I'd just stand there and maybe just wet my pants, or something. But I feel the juices—they're going, and I'm going to be all right.

Those engaging from-the-heart words allow Spence to practically slip into the jury box and take a seat with his jurors.

Another striking aspect of this close is Spence's ability to take this trial and place it in its proper historical perspective. Of course, it is only historically significant if the plaintiff wins, a factor Spence was counting on. He lets the jurors know that he has never had a more important trial, putting them on notice that they have an opportunity to join with the Silkwood family and make history. Early in the close, Spence says:

> It's the longest case in Oklahoma history, they tell me. And, before the case is over, you will know, as you probably already know, that this is probably the most important case, as well.
>
> . . . .
>
> Well, ladies and gentlemen, I want you to know that I don't know how—excepting because Bill Silkwood happened to want me—a country lawyer from Wyoming got out to Oklahoma. It sort

of seems that if anything good comes out of this trial that it was providence, and it's the most important case of my career. I'm standing here talking to you now about the most important things I have even said in my life. And, I have a sense that I have spent a lifetime, fifty years, to be exact, preparing somehow for this moment with you. And, so, I'm proud to be here with you, and I'm awed, and I'm a little frightened.

A third noteworthy aspect of this closing argument is Spence's ability to take a difficult and sophisticated legal theory and not only make it easily understood, but explain it in such a way that significantly advances his case. As any lawyer will attest, the concept of strict liability is not easily grasped. Spence, through a simple yet vivid story, reduces this complex legal notion to terms anyone could understand.

Well, we talked about "strict liability" at the outset, and you'll hear the court tell you about "strict liability," and it simply means: "If the lion got away, Kerr-McGee has to pay." It's that simple—that's the law. You remember what I told you in the opening statement about strict liability? It comes out of the Old English common law. Some guy brought an old lion on his ground, and he put it in a cage—and lions are dangerous—and through no negligence of his own—through no fault of his own, the lion got away. Nobody knew how—like in this case, "nobody knew how." And, the lion went out and he ate up some people—and they sued the man. And they said, you know: "Pay. It was your lion, and he got away." And, the man says: "But I did everything in my power—I had a good cage—had a good lock on the door—I did everything that I could—I had security—I had trained people watching the lion—and it isn't my fault that he got away." Why should you punish him? They said: "We have to punish him—we have to punish you—you have to pay. You have to pay because it was your lion—unless the person who was hurt let the lion out himself. That's the only defense in this case: unless in this case Karen Silkwood was the one who intentionally took the plutonium out, and "let the lion out," that is the only defense.

Strict liability: "If the lion gets away, Kerr-McGee has to pay," unless Karen Silkwood let the lion loose. What do we have to prove? Strict liability. Now, can you see what that is? The lion gets away. We have to do that. It's already admitted. It's admitted in the evidence. They admit it was their plutonium. They admit it's in Karen Silkwood's apartment. It got away. And, we have to prove that Karen Silkwood was damaged. That's all we have to prove. Our case has been proved long ago, and I'm not going to labor you with the facts that prove that. It's almost an admitted fact, that it got away, and that she was damaged.

In two paragraphs, Spence has breathed life into a dry legal concept.

In his strict liability explanation, Spence boils the whole concept down to one memorable phrase: "If the lion gets away, Kerr-McGee has to pay." Throughout the balance of the close, Spence comes back to that phrase, and by simply uttering it, his explanation of strict liability is immediately recalled.

As Spence goes deeper into the argument, his anger at the actions of Kerr-McGee begins to build, culminating in the following passages in which he rages at the transgressions of the defendant:

> I couldn't get over it—I couldn't sleep—I couldn't believe what I had heard. I don't know how it affected you. Maybe you get so numb after awhile—I guess people just stand and say, "Exposure, exposure, exposure, exposure, exposure—cancer, cancer, cancer, cancer, cancer, cancer, cancer, cancer, cancer, cancer, cancer, cancer, cancer, cancer, cancer, cancer, cancer, cancer," until you don't hear it anymore. Maybe that is what happens to us. I tell you, if it is throbbing in your breast—if cancer is eating at your guts, or it's eating at you lungs, or it's gnawing away at your gonads, and you're losing your life, and your manhood, and your womanhood, and your child, or your children, it then has meaning—they are not just words. You multiply it by hundreds of workers, and thousands of workers, that is why this case is the most important case, maybe, in the history of man. That is why I'm so proud to be here with you. That's why I'm so glad you're on this jury, and that we are a part of this thing together.

Later in the argument, he goes on to say:

> I've prosecuted murderers and thieves, and drunk and crazy people, and I've sued careless corporations in my life, and I want to tell

you that I have never seen a company who misrepresented to the workers [so] that the workers were cheated out of their lives. These people that were in charge knew about plutonium. They knew what alpha particles did. They hid the facts, and they confused the facts, and they tried to confuse you, and they tried to cover it, and they tried to get you in the mud springs. You know and I know what it was all about. It was about a lousy $3.50-an-hour job. And, if those people knew they were going to die from cancer twenty or forty years later, would they have gone to work. The misrepresentations stole their lives. It's sickening. It's willful, it's callous.

The sincerity, the passion of his words, all work to make the jurors identify with his outrage over the treatment Karen Silkwood received at the hands of her employer. And by carefully crafting his argument, Spence puts the jurors in the position of having to choose whether to identify themselves with Silkwood, Spence, and the working men and women, or with the "sickening," "callous," and careless corporation that let loose the lion.

Spence's fears were unfounded; the jury got it.

Closing Argument

The Estate of Karen Silkwood v. *Kerr-McGee, Inc.*
Delivered by Gerry Spence
Jackson, Wyoming, May 14, 1979

Thank you, Your Honor. Well, here we are. Every good closing argument has to start with "Ladies and Gentlemen of the Jury," so let me start that way with you. I actually thought we were going to grow old together. I thought maybe we would just kind of go down to Sun City, and get us a nice complex there and sort of live out our lives. It looked like that was the way it was going to happen. I had an image in my mind with the judge at the head of the block, and then the six jurors with nice little houses beside each other—and I hadn't made up my mind whether I was going to ask Mr. Paul [*attorney for Kerr-McGee*] to come down or not—but I didn't think this case was ever going to get over and I know you didn't think so, either. And, as a matter of fact, as Mr. Paul kept calling witnesses and calling witnesses, I sort of got the impression that he's fallen in love with us over here and just didn't want to quit calling witnesses.

Ladies and gentlemen, it was winter in Jackson, Wyoming, when I came here, and there was four feet of snow at Jackson. We've spent a season here together. I haven't been home to Jackson for two and a half months. And, although I'm a full-fledged Oklahoman now, and have been for over a month and a half, nevertheless I'm homesick. And I'm sure you're homesick, too. I'm sure this has been a tough one on you.

Well, I know lots of you have had to do extra work, and I know you've had to work at night, and I know you've had to drive long distances. Every morning—now, I'm a jury watcher—you watch me watching you every morning, and I'd look at you to see if my jury was all right, and see if they were feeling okay. Sometimes they weren't feeling too good, but mostly we made it through this matter together, and I'm pretty proud of that. It's the longest case in Oklahoma history, they tell me. And, before the case is over, you will know, as you probably already know, that this is probably the most important case, as well.

Well, ladies and gentlemen, I want you to know that I don't know how—excepting because Bill Silkwood happened to want me—a country lawyer from Wyoming got out to Oklahoma. It sort of seems that if anything good comes out of this trial that it was providence, and it's the most important case of my career. I'm standing here talking to you now about the most important things that I have ever said in my life. And, I have a sense that I have spent a lifetime, fifty years, to be exact, preparing somehow for this moment with you. And, so, I'm proud to be here with you, and I'm awed, and I'm a little frightened, and I know that's hard for you to believe because I don't look frightened. But, I've been frightened from time to time throughout this trial. I've learned how to cover that up pretty well. And, what I am setting out to do today is frightening to me. I hope I have the intelligence, the insight, and the spirit, and the ability, and just the plain old guts to get to you what I have to get to you.

What I need to do is to have you understand what needs to be understood. And, I think I'll get some help from you. My greatest fear in my whole life has been that when I would get to this important case—whatever it was—I would stand here in front of the jury and be called upon to make my final argument and suddenly you know, I'd just open my mouth and nothing would come out. I'd just sort of stand there and maybe just wet my pants, or something. But I feel the juices—they're going, and I'm going to be all right.

Well, what we're going to talk about here isn't hard. If a country lawyer from Wyoming can understand it—if I can explain it to my kids—if Mr. Paul can understand it—and his kids—then we all can understand it. "What's going on, and who proves what?"

Well, we talked about "strict liability" at the outset, and you'll hear the court tell you about "strict liability," and it simply means: "If the lion got away, Kerr-McGee has to pay." It's that simple—that's the law. You remember what I told you in the opening statement about strict liability? It came out of the Old English common law. Some guy brought an old lion on his ground, and he put it in a cage—and lions are dangerous—and through no negligence of his own—through no fault of his own, the lion got away. Nobody knew how—like in this case, "nobody knew how." And, the lion went out and he ate up some people—and they sued the man. And they said, you know: "Pay. It was your lion, and he got away." And, the man says: "But I did everything in my power—I had a good cage—had a good lock on the door—I did everything that I could—I had security—I had trained people watching the lion—and it isn't my fault that he got away." Why should you punish him? They said: "We have to punish him—we have to punish you—you have to pay." You have to pay because it was your lion—unless the person who was hurt let the lion out himself. That's the only defense in this case: unless in this case Karen Silkwood was the one who intentionally took the plutonium out, and "let the lion out," that is the only defense, and that is why we have heard so much about it.

Strict liability: "If the lion gets away, Kerr-McGee has to pay," unless Karen Silkwood let the lion loose. What do we have to prove? Strict liability. Now, can you see what that is? The lion gets away. We have to do that. It's already admitted. It's admitted in the evidence. They admit it was their plutonium. They admit it's in Karen Silkwood's apartment. It got away. And, we have to prove that Karen Silkwood was damaged. That's all we have to prove. Our case has been proved long ago, and I'm not going to labor you with the facts that prove that. It's almost an admitted fact, that it got away, and that she was damaged.

Does Silkwood prove how the lion got away? You remember this— Mr. Paul walking up to you and saying, at the beginning of the trial, "Well, listen, it's important to find out how the lion got away." Well, it is important, because they have to prove how—but we don't. And the court will instruct you on that. As a matter of fact, I think you will hear the court say exactly this, and listen to the instruction: it is unnecessary for you to decide how plutonium escaped from the plant—how it entered her apartment—or how it caused her contamination, since it is a stipulated fact—stipulated between the parties—that the plutonium in Silkwood's apartment was from the defendants' plant. So, the question is: "Who has to prove how the lion got away?" "They have to prove it." They have to prove that Karen Silkwood carried it out. If they can't prove that by a preponderance of the evidence, they've lost, Kerr-McGee has to prove that. Why? Well, it's obvious. It's their lion—not Karen Silkwood's lion. It's the law. It's that simple.

Now, I told you there was only one legal defense, didn't I? That's the defense of Karen Silkwood having supposedly taken this stuff from the plant. Well, I'll tell you a bigger defense than that—and that's getting drowned in mud springs. Now, that isn't an original statement by me. One of my favorite—I guess my favorite—jurist, and one you know very well, has an old saying he has told us many times: he says if you want to clear up the water, you've got to get the hogs out of the spring. And, if you can't get the hogs out of the spring, I guarantee you can't clear up the water. And I want you to know that getting jurors confused is not a proper part of jurisprudence—and getting people down in the mud springs is not the way to try a case. Somehow, somebody has the responsibility, as an attorney, to help you understand what the issues are—to come forward and hold their hand out and say, "These are the honest issues, this is the law, this is what you can rely on," because I am reliable, and I'm not going to confuse you with irrelevancies, and number-crunching, and number games, and word games, and gobbledygook, and stuff, and details, and on and on and on. And the thing that I say to you is "keep out of the mud springs" in your deliberations. You are not scientists—I'm not a scientist—my only power is my common sense. Keep out of the mud springs. You'll be invited there. Use your common sense. You'll be invited to do number-crunching of your own. You'll be invited to play word games. You'll be invited to get into all kinds of irrelevancies. And I only say to you that you have one hope—don't get into mud springs—keep your common sense, and take it with you into the jury room.

Now, what is this case about? What is the $70 million claim about? I want to talk about it, because my purpose here is to do some changes that has to do with stopping some things. I don't want to see workers in America cheated out of their lives. I'm going to talk to you about that a lot. It hurts me. It hurts me. I don't want to see people deprived of the truth—the cover-ups. It's ugly. I want to stop it, with your help, the exposing of the public to the hidden dangers, and operating grossly, and negligently, and willfully, and recklessly, and callously. Those are words that you have heard from world experts that you respect—that you believe. I want to stop the misrepresentation to the workers, and to the public, and to the government, and I want to stop it to the juries, and I want to stop it having been made to you.

What is the case not about? The case is not about being against the nuclear industry. You will never hear me say that I stand here against the nuclear industry—I do not. But it is about being responsible, about responsible progress. . . . And without the truth, the progress that we all need, and want, can't be had. It is that simple—that is what the case is not about.

But it is about the power of truth, that you have to use in this case somehow, because it has been revealed to you now—you know it—and if there is only one thing that can come from this case, I will go home and sleep for two solid weeks, and rest and catch up, and I will feel that I have done my life's work in one case, and I hope that you would, too—and that if this case makes it so expensive to lie, and to cover up, and to cheat, and not to tell the truth, and to play number games, that it makes it so expensive for industry—this industry—to do that, that the biggest bargain in life, the biggest bargain for those companies is the truth.

You know, I was amazed to hear that Kerr-McGee has eleven thousand employees—eleven thousand employees. That's more than most of the towns in the state that I live in—that it is in thirty-five states—well, I guarantee that corporation does not speak "South," it doesn't speak "Okie," it doesn't speak "Western," it doesn't speak "New York." And it is in five states—or in five countries. It doesn't speak any foreign language. It speaks one language universally. It speaks the language of money. That is the only language that it speaks—the only language that it understands—and that is why the case becomes what it is. That's why we have to talk back to that corporation in money.

I want to talk about the design of that plant very quickly. It was designed by Mr. Utnage. He never designed any kind of a plant. He never designed any plant, plutonium or otherwise. And I confronted him with scores of problems—you remember those 574 reports of contaminations—they were that thick [*indicating*], in two volumes—you remember them; they were paraded out in front of you a number of times. Page after page of them are based upon equipment failure, design failure, equipment failure, design failure, equipment failure, equipment went wrong, design went wrong. Look at them yourself. I asked him about a leak detection system. "We do not need a leak detection system," he said. "What do we need a leak detection system for? We can see it. We can see it." Here is the man who told you that as long as you can't see it, you're safe. And we know that the amount of plutonium, a half a gram of plutonium, will contaminate the whole state of Oklahoma, and you can't see it. They let it flop down into the rooms, and Jim Smith said one time it was in the room a foot thick on the floor. Do you remember the testimony? He said he designed a safe plant. And he believed the company lie that plutonium doesn't cause cancer. He sat there on that stand under his oath and looked at every one of you under his oath, and he said plutonium has never been known to cause cancer. Well, now, either he lied, or he bought the company lie and didn't know. But he was the man who designed the plant. You wouldn't have to design a very good plant if you didn't think plutonium caused cancer, it wouldn't bother you. You wouldn't work very hard. There wouldn't be much to worry about. Like mayonnaise.

Well, he's the man who told you this—do you remember his testimony?—it must have shocked you—you must have stayed awake all night thinking of it: that a pound of plutonium—when it was hit by a tornado, and I know that you know what I know, and that is that just during the course of this trial, we had all kinds of tornados. One of them came within six miles of the Cimarron plant. I know you know that if a tornado hit that plant and a pound—what will happen if a pound goes up? He said, "Nothing." A pound. Well, you know, I tell you, one of these Oklahoma twisters will sure distribute that, won't it? It is a pretty good distributing agency. A pound of plutonium might mean death for every man, woman, and child in the state.

And I want to tell you something else—that it is danger—that is why we are talking about exemplary and punitive damages, to stop those kind of lies, to stop that kind of action. Right today, sitting out there at that plant are the trailers with the waste in them. They are not covered by any kind of a vault. They are full of radioactivity. All you have to have is a good strong wind to hit one of those trailers that are sitting there today at this moment as my words come out of my mouth, and pollute the whole countryside.

I talked about negligent construction of the plant—that is one of our claims. Can you imagine?—do you remember young Apperson sitting there [*indicating*]? You remember his open face—I liked him a lot—an open, honest boy—blond, curly hair—you remember him, two and a half months ago? He said, "Thirty percent of the pipes weren't welded when I came, when the plant was opened. Thirty percent of the pipes were welded after the plant was in operation, and I was there and I saw those old welds." And he wasn't a certified welder himself, and he was teaching people in an hour or two to be welders themselves—not a certified welder on the job. "There was things leaking everywhere," he said. You remember how he was describing how he was there welding the pipe and they jerked the oxygen out, and he had to gasp for air—the contamination—to survive the moment? Jim Smith talked about the valves breaking up from the acid. So much for the design of the plant.

What about the attitude of the management that followed? You know, you can have a gun—most of us in my country know about guns—we use guns—we use guns to go hunting, and it's just a tradition in the West. They probably are for many of us folks. Now, a gun is safe in the hands of somebody that believes it is dangerous. If you do not believe it is dangerous, it isn't safe—if you don't understand a gun—if you don't respect it. Now, what about management? The first manager out there said, "Sure, you can breathe in a pollen-size particle of plutonium and it won't even hurt you." You heard the experts say that a pollen-size of plutonium is lethal.

Hammock, the highway patrolman, was talking about how they shoveled up the contamination in the dirt, threw it over the fence, and how the rocks and dirt contaminated—how they played with the uranium, threw it around. One person was telling us about how they took it home and gave it to one of their children. Would $70 million stop that? Is it enough? Is two weeks' pay enough to dock them for that? Plowman [*one of the Kerr-McGee managers*] said, you could give $500 million if you think that is right. Plowman said that he resigned his job because of his concern for the plant operations. Here's a quote: "The major factor was that I didn't like the way the plant was running. I felt that the plutonium plant program was going the same way the uranium plant program was going. I just didn't think I could take much more of it. It seems like things were going from one emergency to another. Nothing was right. I hardly knew where to begin. Contamination was everywhere. The equipment leaked. There was no real effort to control it." No real effort to control it. Can you hear their witness saying, "Containment is the name of the game. The men were so contaminated on their arms and hands that you couldn't get it off without peeling their hides. They went home like this nearly every night." And then he stopped them taking the truck to town, because they always washed it in the car wash, and it would contaminate the town, and the sewer system in the town.

Well, I look at Zitting [*supervising manager at Kerr-McGee*]. He was the man over everybody. He was an adverse, hostile witness—and I called him in my case. Why would anybody do something that silly? Well, I wanted you to see with your own eyes and hear with your own ears what that man knew, who was in charge of this whole lashup. The buck stopped with him. He's like the commander in chief, like our president. Now, the president doesn't need to know everything, but when he sends a bomb, he knows it. When he sends the troops, he knows it, when he's involved with the lives of thousands of people, he knows it, because the buck stops with him, and he's the one with all the ultimate responsibility, and so was Mr. Zitting, who didn't know a damn thing about that plant, or what was going on. He said repeatedly, "I don't recall." I showed him 574 worker contamination reports. Five hundred seventy-four were marched up and dumped right here on this stand, and I said, "What about those?" And do you know what he said to me— you remember? "This is the first time I have ever seen those," in this courtroom. That is the kind of management, that is the kind of caring. I asked him about the truck that was leaking, that they buried parts of. He said he never heard of it before. Is there any wonder that Mr. Keppler of the AEC [*Atomic Energy Commission*]—poor Mr. Keppler—I probably pushed him a little further than I should have—I hope you don't hold that against me, but I wanted to shake out the last bit of information I could from him so you could see it. Poor Mr. Keppler said, "I was of the opinion I couldn't find anybody knowledgeable enough in management who knew anything about it, or who cared." This is the man who said, when I asked him, "Were you ever"—here is an actual question—"Were you ever advised by anybody that employees were of the opinion that any amount of plutonium could be taken out of that plant?" He said, "No, I never heard of it."

Was production put over safety? What did they do with a contaminated room? Did they ever stop production? Is there any evidence that they even once stopped production? If they did stop production for a contaminated room, don't you think they would have brought somebody in, in five years? Not once. They painted it—one hundred gallons of paint, and—"It is chipping off today"—to this very day.

Dr. Morgan [*expert witness called by Spence*] called that reckless. You know why it is reckless? Because as it chips off, it comes down in a fine powder form and can be breathed into your lungs. "How big a piece do you breathe into your lungs?" "Nobody knows." "Do you know when you breathe it into your lungs?" "No. Nobody knows if you breathe it. It is too late after you breathe it, and once you get it from the air sample, by the time you get it in the air sample, it is twenty-four hours too late, or longer now." By the time you understand you have been poisoned, the poisoning has already happened. That is why it is negligence. That is why it is callous. That is why Dr. Morgan said, "It is worse than reckless."

Documented doctored X rays. They were always behind. Always behind. They denied that, but they were always behind. Finally Zitting admitted, when I took him through the monthly reports—you remember that—"Yes, they were behind." And Hammock said they were shipping defective pins. It just turns my guts. They were shipping defective pins to a breeder reactor knowing they were defective, to Washington where people—the state of Washington—where people are going to somehow be subjected to the first breeder reactor in this country. Here is the actual testimony of Hammock. Now, hear this. He said, "The rods were defective because they had a bad weld, or too large a weld sealing in the plutonium pellets." This is an exact quote. "Even though we rejected them, we would go ahead and ship them because we were too far behind in production. The workers, on orders from the supervisors, would simply sand down the welds, which weakened them." Now, I want to tell you something. That evidence is before you. It is uncontradicted. If that wasn't true, they would have brought somebody here to tell differently.

Now, here we are next on training. I talked a good bit about that. I was satisfied, I will admit I was satisfied with my $10 million request—which the judge now says the sky is the limit—I was satisfied with that $10 million request until I heard about the training. I almost didn't come out for the next round after that. I couldn't get over it—I couldn't sleep—I couldn't believe what I had heard. I don't know how it affected you. Maybe you get so numb after a while—I guess people just stand and say, "Exposure, exposure, exposure, exposure, exposure—cancer, cancer, cancer, cancer, cancer, cancer, cancer, cancer, cancer, cancer, cancer, cancer, cancer, cancer, cancer, cancer, cancer, cancer," until you don't hear it anymore. Maybe that is what happens to us. I tell you, if it is throbbing in your breast—if cancer is eating at your guts, or it's eating at your lungs, or it's gnawing away at your gonads, and you're losing your life, and your manhood, and your womanhood, and your child, or your children, it then has meaning—they are not just words. You multiply it by hundreds of workers, and thousands of workers, that is why this case is the most important case, maybe, in the history of man. That is why I'm so proud to be here with you. That's why I'm so glad you're on this jury, and that we are a part of this thing together.

It wasn't until I read this document—that came to me almost like it was divinely given—and, you know, I don't know how you feel about things like that, but I reached out my hand, and that man had it, that man right there, Mr. Paul, put it in my hand. This is the '59 data that you saw, that [*defense expert*] Mr. Valentine had in his possession. Now, Dr. Morgan told you there were thousands of articles written, available to people that wanted to read them, about the danger of plutonium. Thousands. This is the one, the only one that their expert, Valentine, could tell us he read, and he had it clutched in his own little hand, and it was this document, from which he had put together this infamous manual, the manual that hides, and is full of gobbledygook so that workers who took that home in their hands and sat down at the table with their children, ladies and gentlemen, as they sat down at the table with their family around, and they said we should read this, and here it is [*indicating*]. That infamous piece of junk said nothing about cancer of the lungs, it said nothing about anything excepting once a word about— the fancy word "malignancy"—and with respect to the respiratory problems and of the lungs, it said nothing. And I read it to you, and you heard it, and you will have it in your jury room, and you can read it to yourselves and see if it told you anything. And this is the document that told him about the radium workers clear back in '59 and the uranium workers clear back in the 1800s that were dying like flies from alpha particles and they knew it. That man knew it. It is the most dastardly crime in the history of man, to cheat workers of their right to live, of their right to make a free choice. How would you like it if somebody wanted your body for $3.50 a lousy hour, and to get it, told you—like those books told you—like the big man told them, "that the nuclear industry is probably the safest industry ever developed."

I wish I could just tell you how bad that makes me feel. I wish I could just express to you how dastardly a trick that is. It would be one thing, you know, if they said to workers, "Listen, we've known for years that uranium people have died like flies, we know that radium dial people have died from alpha particles just like in the plutonium business. Here is a picture, ladies and gentlemen, my dear workers, people that are going to give your lives to my company—here is a picture of a particle, an alpha particle—millions of those will be in your lungs if you breathe any, and we don't know how much it takes to cause cancer. You have the right to know that is the danger you're exposed to." If you're working with electricity, nobody goes around and says, you know, "There isn't any danger in electricity if you grab that wire—it won't hurt you." If you're working with a structure where men's lives are involved, you don't tell them it is safe if it is not safe. You tell them the truth.

It was that night, ladies and gentlemen, that I woke up the next morning, after a fitful night's sleep, and decided that I was going to ask you to make this case meaningful, and I increased my request for a prayer from ten to seventy million—two weeks' wages. I hope it is enough. I leave it to your good judgment.

How does this all tie in with Karen Silkwood? Well the court says that they're liable if the lion got away, even if they used the utmost care. If the lion got away, they have to pay—they have to pay for what happened to her. If it is willful, wanton, and gross negligence, they have to pay such sum as you feel is correct, even if it is half a billion—even if it is five hundred million. The assessment of the damages is left for you.

I want to quote an instruction that you will hear. It is the basis of punitive damages—that's the $70 million to punish. Punitive. To exemplify. Exemplary. So that the rest of the uranium plutonium, and the nuclear industries in this country, will have to tell the truth. The basis of punitive and exemplary damages rests upon the principle that they are allowed as punishment of the offender for the general benefit of society, both as a restraint upon the transgressor—restraint upon the transgressor—that is against Kerr-McGee, so they won't do it anymore, and a meaningful warning and example—to deter the commission of like offenses in the future. If the defendants are grossly or wantonly negligent—listen to this language in the court's instructions—you may allow exemplary or punitive damages, and you may consider the financial worth. I didn't bring that out to try to have you be prejudiced against a large corporation, I brought it out because what is fair punishment for one isn't for another. It is fair punishment to take a paper boy who makes five dollars a week, and it might be fair punishment to take away five dollars from him for not coming home when he was suppose to, or to lie, if he lied. If one of your children lied about something—one of your children lied about something that had to do with the life and health of a brother or sister, and he covered it up, and he lied about it, and he said that the brother and the sister were safe when he knew that he had exposed them to death—I suppose that you might not find it unreasonable to hold him responsible for two weeks, two piddling weeks, allowance in bucks, and leave fifty weeks left for him. That is what seventy million is to this corporation—two weeks—leaving fifty weeks' income. Maybe it isn't enough, but I was afraid to ask for more. You know why I'm afraid? This case is so important that I'm afraid that if I stand here and ask you what I really think the case is entitled to, you will laugh at me, and I can't have that—I can't have you thinking that I'm silly—I can't have you thinking that I'm ridiculous, because it is important to me, it is important for what I'm trying to do that you find me credible. And I've tried to retain my credibility with you through this trial. To my knowledge, I've never stood in front of you and told you a lie. That doesn't mean I haven't ever lied; because that would be a lie. But, it doesn't mean that I have never lied to a jury—because I suppose some people would say that I have—but I try not to. I try very hard to tell it the way it is. I have tried very hard to tell it the way it is in this case.

Now, Dr. Karl Morgan said the plant employees themselves were deceived into entering a lion's cage—it was his language—not even meeting permissible standards. They were sent into a lion's cage—this actually quoting him—being told there were no animals in the cage. He said they had unqualified people there. He took great exception to the fact they weren't told about cancer, and he said that is willful. "Is it wanton?" "Yes, it is wanton." "Is it reckless?" "Yes, it is reckless." "What would you call it, doctor?" He said: "I would call it callous." He said—and I want to give you a quote from that great man of science—the father of health physics, who has taught the teachers and professors, and he's a fine, old, beautiful man—and if I were a little child wanting to be protected from the great exposures of plutonium I would curl up in his lap and close my eyes and put my hands and my faith in him, and I do. And, he said: "I could not imagine that such a lackadaisical attitude could be developed in an organization toward the health and safety of people. It was callous, willful, and wanton negligence."

Who is Karen Silkwood? Who was she? Well, it's a fear that sometimes the whole truth doesn't get to you. What would have happened in your mind about Karen Silkwood if all you had ever heard was [*Kerr-McGee supervisor*] Longaker, who was full of his own vindictiveness against her? You would have believed, by his statements: "Karen Silkwood was [an] uncouth, moody, unreliable, vindictive, sloppy woman, a miserable hate monger, and tried to get even with the company by intentionally contaminating herself—that is what she was, she was an unmitigated moody bitch," to put it plainly. Is that who she really was? You know yourself, and you know your friends, and you know me by where we come from. She was a happy child, a good child, she was reared correctly in the church, and she had her life in the church, and she loved church, and she was a scholarship student, and she was a chemistry major. She was bright, she could understand. But, more than anything else, she cared. At that corporation plant there was somebody who cared, and it was Karen Silkwood. Somebody who cared a lot about others. She had the courage that many of us wouldn't have, to walk up to her boss and say: "Your damn oxygen didn't work on one of those poor people who fainted. It didn't work, and I'm going to report it. You should have it available for these people." And, it didn't work on the people who gave her—who administered first aid to her—they didn't even know how to pop the pill, the smelling salt.

You know, I got this here so that you could hear her voice once more. This is the voice when she was talking to [*union representative*] Steve Wodka. She never knew it would be played in a courtroom with her bones rotting in the grave. But her voice is still quite alive. Now, you judge for yourself who Karen Silkwood was. [*Reporter's note: The following portion of a cassette, Plaintiff's Exhibit 31, played in open court.*]

> KAREN SILKWOOD: And, I've got one here that we're still passing all welds no matter what the pictures look like, no matter what the welds look like. We either grind down too far—and I've got a weld I would love for you to see just how far they ground it down till we lost the weld trying to get rid of the voids and inclusions and the cracks. And, I kept it.

"And, I kept it." And, I had Wally get this other part so that you could hear it. [*Reporter's note: The following portion of a cassette, Plaintiff's Exhibit 31, played in open court.*]

KAREN SILKWOOD: Ah, in the laboratory we've got eighteen- and nineteen-year-old boys, you know, twenty and twenty-one, I mean, and they didn't have the schooling so they don't understand what radiation is. They don't understand, Steve, they don't understand.

"They don't understand, Steve, they don't understand." Who was she? I say she was a prophet, an ordinary woman who cared, and could understand, doesn't have to be anything other than an ordinary woman who cared and understood in order to be a prophet. I don't mean that she's anything, you know, biblical—I mean, she was an ordinary person who cared, and she prophesied it this way: "If there is something going on"—this was an actual quote—"If there is something going on, we're going to be susceptible to cancer, and we are not going to know about it for years." She says this to you, ladies and gentlemen: "Something has to be done."

What did [*Kerr-McGee supervisor*] Morgan Moore do? How does he fit in the picture? He accused her from the beginning—pointed his finger, didn't have any evidence then—and five years later in this courtroom was still willing to point his finger, his long, white, bony finger at her. It is easy to blame. It is the blame syndrome that we see everywhere. When there was anything wrong, they blamed. They blamed her. They blamed the faulty equipment—that shut the plant down finally—on sabotage; it was always to blame.

Mr. Paul, you remember him walking up to you in the opening statement and telling you how he blamed Karen Silkwood? He didn't have any more evidence then than he has now. He said first access—first access—you remember he said about her "she had access to it, to her apartment." "Who could get into her apartment?" "Well, she could get into her apartment." The next point is an important one—I'm sure no one of you has wondered about it—"the opportunity to remove small quantities of plutonium from the plant." Then he did this business with his pocket, trying to get your mind ready to blame her and to join the "company line." But the point is he says, is that "there are many ways for a laboratory worker, including Karen Silkwood, to have removed a very small quantity from the laboratory." "Could she have intentionally removed it without detection at the plant if she wanted to get it out of there?" "Could she have?" He asked the same questions he asked during the trial: "Yes," he says. It is like a mystery—somebody spiked her urine samples—which we all know. Now, he says, and even you remember this business about how he really tried to explain to you that "she did it intentionally to herself."

Morgan Moore says: "All I have is suspicions. I can't prove a thing." Their own witnesses, witness after witness, who was willing to point the finger without any evidence—how do you like that? How would you like that if it was your child who is dead, and whose lips are sealed by death, who can't come forward and tell her side?

Now, I think it is shameful to point the finger in accusation, and know, as Mr. McGee knew clear back in 1975: "It is not likely that the source of her contamination will ever be known." He knew that. The AEC had come in and never came to any such conclusion. They investigated it. Morgan Moore said, "All there are are suspicions." Everybody said they can't prove it. "I can't prove it, I can't prove it, I can't prove it." They couldn't prove it. Mr. Paul knew he couldn't prove it when he talked to you the first time, and still he has been willing to make the accusation. Why? Because it is the only defense they have, and they hope to drag you into mud springs.

Like Will Rogers used to say: "If you say it enough, even if it ain't true, folks will get to believing it."

Well, I think it is reckless. I would like to see that kind of stuff stopped. I think a verdict in this case should stop it. It is necessary for people to be honorable, and to tell the truth, and if they can't be honorable and tell the truth, then to not make reckless accusations and destroy and desecrate the good name of a decent, honorable person.

They were more interested, you know, in providing her with attorneys than they were—when she was frightened of dying—with medical help. They brought her attorneys. Doctors, no. Attorneys, yes. "I think I'm going to die." Is she talking to a doctor? No. Is she talking to attorneys? Yes. And, they send her, by their choice, to Voelz: "I'm dying." "You're not dying." Morgan Moore sneered. It was the most inhuman treatment of a human being I've really ever seen, short of physical torture.

Phillip, their own witness, said she was crying and upset. Norwood, their own witness, said that she was crying and upset. I know people who have said, "I wouldn't go through an experience like that for a million and a half dollars." I think that is maybe how you feel about this. Her mother said she was crying—she was nervous, something was wrong—she knew something was wrong: "She wouldn't tell me what was wrong. She was afraid of something at the plant. She was contaminated—she said she thought she was going to die. She wanted to come home. She wanted to get away from it, but there was something wrong." Her sister said: "There is something wrong. Karen wouldn't tell me over the phone. She wanted me to come so I could talk to her. She was afraid to talk to me on the phone. There was something that she knew besides the fact that she was contaminated."

Well, the key question is: "Did she know too much?" "Who contaminated her?" "Did she know too much?" "How much did she know?" "She knew enough to bring this whole mess to an end—the whole Kerr-McGee plant to an end." "What would *The New York Times* information have done to the world had it been published?" The information of the doctored X rays on the first nuclear reactor going on in Congress at that time—the first breeder reactor, that hasn't been built yet—congressional hearings were going on, what would that have done in the newspaper? What would it have done if they had told what she knew about the way they lied to workers, the way they were treating people, the way the plant conditions were? "Was she injured?" Gofman said—and you don't have to get into number-crunching games to believe what he said—Gofman said, "I'm telling you unequivocally that a person like Karen Silkwood exposed to that amount of plutonium is married to lung cancer." Dr. Morgan said: "She got more plutonium in one week than the AEC permitted during a year."

Well, what finally happened to Karen Silkwood? Unfortunately, it is the rule that we can't go past the time when you saw her leave Ms. Jung with the materials. Fifteen minutes after that she was dead. She was on her way. She said to Ms. Jung, "I've got the materials. I've got it here." We know she was there on the thirteenth. That is where it ends, when she walked out of that cafe. She was tied up in the last union negotiation. She was ready to leave. She had already written the numbers down of the forged rods. And, you know, she had a premonition: before she had left, remember, she gave those numbers to Steve Wodka, didn't she? Not the notebook you see but the numbers on them that finally came up in the report, where I read to you those numbers, the same numbers are in that report where I read that they were doctored here, doctored there, this weld here, and that weld, you remember that—those are the numbers that were in her notebook. She gave that before she left. Why? We'll never know. All we know is that her mother said she was afraid of something: "She wouldn't tell me on the phone. She was afraid to talk on the phone." Her sister said she was afraid of something: "She wouldn't talk to me on the phone."

They put her with an escort—that is a fancy name for a "guard"—they took her out of there and put her under guard, and she couldn't walk without a guard. They had taken her house away from her. They wiped her out, took everything down to the Durkee's dressing, and the salt and pepper, and tore the walls down. And, [*union representatives*] Mazzocchi and Wodka said that was so they could find the missing documents that they were looking for. Everybody knew about the documents being missing. It was their way to enter. That is what they say. I'm not saying that it is or isn't—it isn't a part of our proof—but I'm saying to you that it all is there. She knew too much. The conditions, the forty pounds, the numbers game, the doctored evidence, the quality control. The cause of death isn't in issue, but fifteen minutes after she left she was dead. And that is the story of Karen Silkwood.

I will be back with you after the defendants have concluded their arguments. Thank you.

THE COURT: All right, ladies and gentlemen of the jury, we will have the usual fifteen-minute recess.

[*After the defendant's argument, Spence responded. Note: During closing arguments, the plaintiff argues first, then the defense argues, and the plaintiff then gets one last opportunity to be heard.*]

MR. SPENCE: Thank you, Your Honor. Fellow counsel, Mr. Paul, . . . ladies and gentlemen:

I, during the recess, wondered about whether there is enough in all of us to do what we have to do. I'm afraid—I'm afraid of two things: I'm afraid that you have been worn out, and that there may not be enough left in you to hear, even if you try, and I know you will try, but I know you are exhausted; and I've been afraid that there isn't enough left in me, that my mind isn't clear and sharp now, and that I can't say the things quickly that I need to say, and yet it has to be done, and it has to be done well.

I have asked my friends, during the recess—and they are here, I asked my father, my mother, my close friends for strength to do this. I hope that you have been able to do that yourselves, and that you can, with each other, and call upon your own strength and from your own sources, because this is the last time that we, as living, breathing humans, will talk together about this subject. And it is the last time that anybody will speak for Karen Silkwood. And when your verdict comes out, it will be the last time that anybody will have the opportunity that you have, and so it is important that we have the strength and the power to do what we need to do.

You know, history has always at crucial times reached down into the masses and picked ordinary people and gave ordinary people extraordinary power. That is the way it has always been in history, and I have no reason to believe that it is any different now.

Ladies and gentlemen, I need to get to the issues—our time is short. The issue that seems to be one that everyone wants to talk about is not really an issue—it is the only possible defense that Kerr-McGee has, and it is one that they have talked about. We are right back where we started from: "If the lion gets away, Kerr-McGee has to pay." You remember Mr. Paul was critical of me for not trying to explain to you how the lion got away. Do you remember his criticalness, his sort of accusation that somehow we had failed in our obligation? It is like this—listen to the story: "My lion got away. Why is my lion on your property?" That is the question he asked me. "Why is my lion on your property?" "It is on your property." "Tell me why my lion is on your property. Explain it." And, I say: "But, ah hah, ah hah, ah hah." And, he says: "It wasn't there two hours ago. It wasn't there last night." And, he says: "Wait a minute. Your kids don't get along with my kids. That is why my lion is on your property." And, then he says: "Why did you let my lion eat you? You let my lion on your property," he says. "I accuse you—I accuse you—I blame you, and why don't you explain it?" And, I say: "But, it isn't my lion—it is your lion—it is your lion that got away."

Now, the court says—and I want this—I want to put it to rest, because I don't want you jumping in mud springs on this one—there are too many other places for you to jump into mud springs on—please hear it: it is unnecessary for you to decide how plutonium escaped from the plant, how it entered her apartment, or how it caused her contamination, since it is a stipulated fact that the plutonium in Karen Silkwood's apartment was from the defendants' plant.

Now, Mr. Paul, that is why we haven't explained how your lion got on our property. The court says that is not our obligation—it is your lion, Mr. Paul—you must explain it.

Then it goes on to say that it is for the defendants to prove to you, by a preponderance of the evidence, that it was Karen Silkwood who took it. Failing their proof—please hear the word "proof," it is the word "proof"—failing which proof Kerr-McGee has to pay. The lion got away, Karen Silkwood was damaged. Does Karen Silkwood prove how the lion got away? The court says no. You will hear it again tomorrow. Why? Because it is their lion. So if the lion got away, and Kerr-McGee can't prove how, then Kerr-McGee has to pay. Now, that's the law, the law of strict liability, and it is that simple.

Now, I heard Mr. Paul say this: "My heart reaches out praying for answers based upon the evidence." "Praying for answers based upon the evidence." I would think he would pray for answers based upon the evidence, because he hasn't got any. He doesn't have any more now that he ever did. All that you ever heard Mr. Paul say, as he stood up here and pointed his finger toward Karen Silkwood—and I want you to stop and remember, ladies and gentlemen, please, that this is a free country—and the one thing that makes this country different from all the other countries in the world is that when somebody makes the accusation against a citizen of this country, alive or dead, they have to make the proof. Mr. Paul doesn't have the right to come into a court and say: "I think this happened." And: "I think that happened." And: "Maybe this happened." And: "Isn't it probable that that happened." And: "I think the circumstances of this, and the circumstances of that." And to take a whole series of unrelated events and put them together and try to tell you somehow that I have the responsibility that the judge and the law doesn't place upon me, and to mislead you in that fashion. And I'm angry about that. I expect that when a corporation of the size of this one comes into this courtroom that they should bring to you honest, fair, documented evidence—that they shouldn't hide behind little people—and that they should bring you the facts that they know.

Now, listen: I have some problems here in being straight with you, and I want to put them right here on the table. If we want to play guess-um— that is, point the finger, the game of playing, of pointing the finger—I can play that game; but when I do that I become as bad as Mr. Paul. You want me to do that? Is that the way you want to decide the case? Tell me. If that is the way you think the case ought to be decided in a court of American jurisprudence, to see who can make the biggest accusations against the other one, then I'm willing to play that game. But, when I do it, I want you to know it isn't right, because I can't prove that any more than they can prove it. I can give you motive. What was the motive for them to do that? "She was a troublemaker. She was doing union negotiations. She was on her way—she was gathering documents—every day in that union, everybody in that company, everybody in management knew that." Nobody would admit it, but they knew it. . . .

Compare the motive, just for the fun of it. Supposing that you've got to weigh those motives. Here is Karen Silkwood. The motive was she was

furious. We found out that she wasn't furious. Their own witness, Mr.—
what is his name—Phillip, says she was miffed, wasn't that the word?
Their witness, under oath, said she was miffed. "Was she furious?" "No,
she wasn't furious. She was miffed." "She was furious," he said.

Did Karen Silkwood—and you have listened to her voice talking in
private to Steve Wodka—did she sound like a kook to you? Did she
sound nuts? Did she sound like she was acting under some kind of
compulsive behavior that suggested it? There isn't any proof to that. It
comes out of Mr. Paul's mouth. He says it over, and over, and over, and
over, and over again. Compare that motive with the motive of people to
stop her. "She knew too much."

What would she do had she gotten to *The New York Times?* What if
they could show she was a silly woman who contaminated herself? Do
you think she would have done that, and put insoluble urine—strike
that: I'm getting tired already, and you heard it on the tape, and you saw
it in her notes—insoluble plutonium in her urine when she knew that
insoluble plutonium is not excreted through the urine? She knew that,
and yet that is what was there. She was an intelligent woman. You can't
have it both ways, Mr. Paul. You can't say she was an intelligent, scheming woman, and on the other hand a stupid broad who put insoluble
plutonium in her urine, which would have immediately told everybody
that it was spiked.

Who is being silly? These people, if you want to talk about motives,
had a motive to stop her, and she was stopped. We are not to talk about
her—I won't talk about it—but she never got there with her X rays.

Now, I don't think that is the way I want to defend my case. I don't
think that is the way I want to present it to you. I've only brought these
matters out because in the course of this trial it seems too patently
unfair to continually point their finger at a woman who can't defend
herself about matters that they have no proof of, and never had any
proof of to begin with, and knew from the beginning that they would
never have any more proof of, as evidenced by Mr. McGee's initial letter: "It is not likely that the source of her contamination will ever be
known." He knew that. Mr. Paul knew it. It was the only thing available
to them, and I congratulate them for making a lot out of that, but it is
sad to me that they didn't call the witnesses that knew—they didn't give
us the information, and that is sad to me. It is sad to me that one of the
mightiest—you know, in history it will go down, this case, I can see it in
the history books: "One of the mightiest corporations of the United

States of America, a multinational corporation, with two billion dollars in assets, and two billion dollars in annual income, goes down in history, with all that power, with all of those resources, with the only thing that they could do was to accuse, and not prove."

Well, the key—please forgive my raging, but you are listening to a man who is angry—the key, ladies and gentlemen, is simple. I will have to tell you what it is. It is proof. They have the burden of proving that she took it. The judge says they have the burden to proving it. They have to prove it by a preponderance of the evidence. Now, that is something, that phrase "preponderance of the evidence"—which you will hear His Honor use tomorrow—isn't just a phony phrase; it means the greater weight of the evidence. There isn't any evidence here that she did it, not one iota of evidence. There are only the accusations. But, if there was any evidence, it would have to be the greatest weight of evidence, not suspicions, not the greatest weight of suspicions, not the one who can accuse the worst—but the greatest weight of the evidence. The burden of proof is on the defendant Kerr-McGee Nuclear Corporation to establish that Karen Silkwood took the plutonium from work to her apartment where she was injured. That is the court's instruction.

Well, we talk about her wanting to see the high urine sample on the tenth. They forgot to tell you an important fact—one that you already know—one that you will remember the minute I tell it to you: she had urine samples in there in August . . . she was told on October 10 of urine samples that went in on the eighth, in August. . . . They were returned, August urine samples, were returned in October. And, she was told—everybody admits she was told—they had the duty to tell her, and they did tell her, and they wanted to find out about them—she heard they were back, and so they use that information, when she comes in and says, "I want to find out about my hot urine samples," to suggest that she didn't know.

You know, they used the position—I can't believe it, again they use the— they give the ugly connotation that she called up her girlfriend and says—you know, this is on the seventh, now everybody knows it isn't coming from the plant—she comes home, she comes from her house, and she has left from work and she's clean, right? They scrub her, right? So, she knows that she's clean when she goes home. When she comes back the next day, she doesn't go into an area where there is any plutonium, and now she's dirty again. And, they scrub her, and she goes home, and the next day she comes back and she's dirty again. So, she has to know—and everybody has to know, and Mr. Norwood admits that he knew—that there was an off-site contamination some-place. And the first thing she did was what? She says, "Let's find it. Go check my locker." It was her that said, "Go check my locker." And then the next thing she said is, "Go check my car." And when they couldn't find it in her locker, or car, then she knew the only other place she had been was her house. And she calls up her roommate, like one decent human being for another, in front of Mr. Norwood—not hiding, but in front of him—and says: "Sherry, don't go into the kitchen"—that is where she had been—"or the bathroom, or my bedroom."

How do you interpret that? If you want to interpret it ugly, you can say she knew, she knew, and she was such a stupid woman, and she knew she had contaminated herself on purpose, and she said that all in front of Mr. Norwood just so he could come here and testify about it.

And then here's a quotation from Mr. Paul—I hope you heard it like I heard it: "The reason I want to embarrass you"—he's quoting Karen Silkwood. "The reason I want to embarrass you is because I did it." She never said that. There wasn't any showing she wanted to do any such thing. Why would they do that? She already had the goods on them. She really had the goods on them. And she knew it. And that isn't in the evidence. That came out of Mr. Paul's mouth. And he kept saying perhaps it was she that was testing—remember his argument to you: "Maybe she was testing to see if they were checking her samples." "Maybe she was turning in high samples to see if they would catch them." "Maybe this." "Maybe that." "It was possibly this." "She said it could have been that she was using this for leverage." All of it speculation. "I guess this." "I guess that." "Maybe this—maybe that." How would you like to have to defend yourselves, how would you like to be in my shoes trying to defend a dead woman against those kinds of accusations? No proof. All maybe—all accusations. All blame.

What did you hear uncontradicted in this case? First of all, you got the notebook, and you have seen it with your own eyes, of the bad welds, and all of the screaming and hollering of Mr. Paul isn't going to change those facts, and the findings that were made that I read to you, and that you saw. . . . You heard Karen Silkwood talk about it on the tape: "They grind them down, and grind them down until the welds break through, and the occlusions show." . . . Why don't they come and tell you why? I can't understand that. I can't understand. We are dealing with the most dangerous substance in the history of mankind, and [*government inspector*] Barger is locked out of the weld room, out of the X-ray room. The—what are the initials?—the DCAS, that government entity of people who were doing the inspections were locked out. You tell me there isn't a hide-up, a cover-up. They never explained it—never tried to explain it—never came to you with any evidence.

You know, Karen Silkwood was afraid for her life. She wasn't ready to accept the medical care that was offered to her and I don't blame her. And these people that testified, Steve Wodka, said she didn't trust them—she was afraid that they would give her something that wouldn't be right, and she wouldn't take what they gave her, and I don't blame her. And those doctors told her: "You're okay, you don't have any long-term effects." And, she knew they were lying to her—she knew that with the kind of exposure, with the kind of stuff that she had in her nose, the 45,000 DPM in the nostrils, and exposure of hundreds of thousands of DPM in her house, that she probably wasn't all right. She was afraid to go to Los Alamos. She was afraid to go there alone—remember? And the AEC had to shake those people out of enough money to send her, and to send somebody else along with her. But, they used that against her, too.

And the motives, those are all Mr. Paul's assumptions. Not one person said she contaminated herself as a motive to get even, or to help the union. Not one from that witness stand ever established that fact—it was only Mr. Paul. They are all his theories.

You know, if all of the leaks, and all of the spills, and the incidents, and all the rest of the five hundred things—if all of those violations, some seventy-five of them. Violations. All those weeks, from the testimony of all of those people, wouldn't somehow embarrass them enough, if the fact that they were doctoring—one of the world's great corporations doctoring? Now that wouldn't embarrass them enough? She didn't need to embarrass them. She wasn't trying to embarrass them—she was trying to do something that was important to people. Her words were: "Something has to be done about this." Steve Wodka was proud of what they were doing. Sure. He was open and straight with you in saying: "We were using it for our activities, but it was also something that eventually had to be done—the American people had to know." You remember [*union representative*] Mazzocchi saying that? This is an almost direct quotation from him. And, he said, "You know, Mr. Paul, it is despicable what they did to Karen Silkwood." And this is his language. "It is despicable to use her to uncover the worst cover-up in history." You think that is despicable? I think she was a heroine. I think her name will be one of the names that go down in history, along with the great names of women heroines. I think she will be the woman who speaks through you, and may save this industry and this progress and may save, out of that industry, hundreds of thousands of lives. But Mr. Paul calls it "despicable." I think it was the greatest service that was ever conceived. I think she was exactly what the people said she was: "A courageous woman." No wonder Mr. Mazzocchi and Mr. Wodka were proud of her. "That is despicable," Mr. Paul thinks. Mr. Paul thinks I'm despicable. Mr. Paul thinks I try to fool you. He thinks, he points his finger at everybody, and anything that shows the truth, and anything that uncovers the truth of Kerr-McGee, of his client, is "despicable."

Do you remember—I had the witness on the stand—and I was looking at him, and I was trying to figure out what to do, and I said to Mr. Moore: "Mr. Moore, is that the right way for a decent company to do business, to doctor its X rays?" To me it was shocking. Mr. Paul's response was: "That is ridiculous."

Now, the man who did the X ray doctoring was who? Who was he—do you remember? A man by the name of Dotter, wasn't it? Where is he? They say he didn't have anything to do with anything. Why isn't he here? What do you suppose Mr. Dotter would tell you? Do you suppose Mr. Dotter would say to you: "I guess that I doctored those because I was told to because we were behind on production." Do you think his testimony would have fit right in with the testimony of Mr. Hammock, who said, "We were shipping those defective rods because we were behind"? Would it fit in with Karen Silkwood, who you heard say the same thing? What do you think Kerr-McGee said about it? What did this letter show? Where is it? Anyway, they referred to it as a former employee. Do you remember that, in the letter? I can't see it—there it is: "A former employee had made some minor alterations." A former employee. That's the old blame syndrome again, isn't it? You always blame the employee. Always blame the former employee. Always blame the weak. Always blame those that aren't here, and then you don't call them to court, and then you make the argument, and then you take the jury through mud springs. But there it is: a Kerr-McGee investigator determined that "a former employee had made some minor alterations on certain X-ray films used to verify test results, but the established alterations were not made with intent to falsify results." Do you believe that? Blame him. Why are they doing it? Why didn't they come in and explain to us why they are doctoring scores, and scores, and scores of those? Why do they doctor them? I think you know why.

Now, they rest their case on her emotional state. They say—I'm referring to their notes: "This woman was in an emotional state, and therefore because she was in an emotional state she doctored her own urine sample." That is what they said. How did she get in such an emotional state? How was it that she was almost ready to break? How was it that she was nervous and moody? She couldn't find the contamination. How would you like to come home all clean, go to your bed—cleaned up at the plant—go to your own bed, and come back the next day and find you're dirty again, and be cleaned up again, and come back to go to your own bed, and come back the second day and find you're dirty again? How would you like that? Would it upset you? Would it scare you? Would you say to people: "I don't know why they're doing this. Somebody is contaminating me. I don't know where this is coming from. It must be coming out of my body. It is in my nose. It must be coming out of my lungs. I've been cleaned up. It isn't anywhere else. I go home, and I come back the next day. What is going on, Mr. People of the Management, Mr. Morgan Moore—I gave you my samples, they're hot—you're not doing anything about it. It is coming out of my lungs." And you know what they do? They accuse her. They accused her then, and they accuse her now, and they continue to accuse her. They said: "You're unstable. You've lost control." And then Mr. Paul says: "Let's be fair." I heard him say it over and over: "Let's be fair." She thought she was going to die, and they gave her lawyers—"Let's be fair"—not doctors. They put her through a hospital sham. They said: "Let's be fair." They sent her to Los Alamos, where they put her through machines that couldn't register anything and they said: "Let's be fair." And they continued to blame her. They even blamed her because whoever was driving the car took the wrong turn. You remember that? They are still blaming her today.

Mr. Paul not two hours ago, from his own lips, was saying to you: "She didn't appear in time, she was unreliable." Written by Dr. Sternhagen—you know when he wrote that stuff about her—look at the evidence. He wrote that stuff about her about three days after she died—not when she was alive, but after she was dead. And if there is an ugly way to interpret it, Mr. Paul did it in every case. Now, I don't hold that against him—I want you to know that. We all have a free choice to do what we want to with our lives, and to represent the people we want to. That's his client. He has done the best he can. And I'm not saying Mr. Paul is an evil man. I'm not saying his client, the people that work there are evil people. But I'm saying that it shows you how low in the barrel, how bottom in the barrel, they've scraped for a defense in such an important case. I would have thought a lot more of them if they had come in and said: "Yes, we let it go. Yes, we had a sloppy operation. Yes, we did it. We're sorry. We will pay the damages. We'll pay the fiddler." I don't think I would be nearly so angry as when they try to slander. You know what Will Rogers said about slander? Will Rogers said, "Slander is the cheapest defense going." It doesn't cost anything to slander anybody. I can slander you, and if I say it enough, somebody will start believing it. And, it is pretty hard to defend. You remember when you were a kid in high school, and somebody said you did certain things, and you didn't do it, but your mother accused you of something and you couldn't prove you didn't do it, or your daddy said you did something and you couldn't prove it. How about when people slander you like this in the most important case in the world, and base their defense upon it? Now stop and think about what I just said. How about it when the slander is in the most important case of this century—maybe of this nation's history—and all the defense is a slander? What about that—how do you feel? How does it make you feel? How do you feel about the kind of corporation that tells Mr. Paul this is what he has to do?

Now let me ask you this question: When we walk out of here I ain't going to be able to say another word, and you're going to have to make some decisions, and they are going to be made not just about Karen Silkwood, and not just about those people at that plant, but people involved in this industry and the public that is exposed to this industry. That is a frightening obligation. You need to trust somebody. You need not to get in mud springs. If you get in there, you're lost forever. If you get down in there and start dealing with the number crunches, and this exhibit and that exhibit, and all the other junk, you get into mud springs. But you don't need to. You need to trust somebody. Who are you going to trust? Are you going to trust Kerr-McGee? Are you going to leave your kids to them? Do you feel safe in that? Are you going to leave your children and their futures to those people, the men in gray? Do you feel safe about that? I'm not saying they are bad men—I'm saying are you going to leave it on those arguments? Do they satisfy you? Can you do it? Is your verdict going to say something about the number-crunching game—that it's got to stop? Is it going to be heard from here around the world? Can you do it? Do you have the power? Are you afraid? If you are, I don't blame you, because I'm afraid, too. I'm afraid that I haven't the power for you to hear me. I'm afraid that somehow I can't explain my knowledge and my feelings that are in my guts to you. I wish I had the magic to put what I feel in my gut and stomach into the pit of every one of you.

I guess the last thing that I want to talk about is the immense tragedy in this case that most of us haven't thought about verbally. I'm sure you've thought about it when you've gone home at night, but I doubt if any of you have had a chance to talk about it with each other. And I want to talk about it, because I would feel remiss, I would feel like I hadn't done what I was supposed to do, I would have felt that somewhere I didn't do my job if I didn't talk to you about an immense tragedy: I see young [*Kerr-McGee employee*] Bill Apperson at age forty or fifty. Dr. Gofman says that these young men may very well die. That is a horrid secret that nobody has told us. Nobody told them. The only thing that was ever told was that there was a million hours without an off-time accident. And the only thing you were told was that somebody got a plaque. And I can hear them saying to you and to those boys and girls that "there has never been a cancer caused by plutonium, that we know of." I can hear that in my ears, and I can see those young men, and those young women, when they sat on that witness stand, and it was about all I could do to sit in this courtroom and to look at their open faces, and I could hear the man in charge, Norwood, saying to you, and to those poor boys and girls: "There has never been proven cancer from plutonium."

And I look at the green book, and there was nothing there to warn them. And I looked at the article on lungs from the manual, and there was nothing there but the gobbledygook and it is the worst kind of deceit in my career that I have ever seen. Why do I say that? I want to tell you something about me. I have been in courtrooms in Wyoming, little old towns in Wyoming, five thousand here—I grew up in Riverton, Wyoming, five thousand people there—Dubois, Rock Springs, I've been all over. I've been the county attorney, and I've prosecuted murderers—eight years I was a prosecutor—and I prosecuted murderers and thieves, and drunk and crazy people, and I've sued careless corporations in my life, and I want to tell you that I have never seen a company who misrepresented to the workers that the workers were cheated out of their lives. These people that were in charge knew of plutonium.

They knew what alpha particles did. They hid the facts, and they confused the facts, and they tried to confuse you, and they tried to cover it, and they tried to get you in the mud springs. You know and I know what it was all about. It was about a lousy $3.50 an hour job. And if those people knew they were going to die from cancer twenty or forty years later, would they have gone to work? The misrepresentations stole their lives. It's sickening. It's willful, it's callous.

Nobody seriously contends Kerr-McGee told these people about cancer. No one said that they heard about cancer. Even the little girl that was on the stand, the one employee that they called in—they didn't dare ask her: "When you appeared, when you were there over to the uranium plant, honey, did they tell you that plutonium caused cancer?" The question was never presented to her.

No one came in to contradict young Apperson. Karen Silkwood, before she died, before this case was thought of, said that "these young men don't know." You heard her voice: "These young men, eighteen, nineteen, twenty, twenty-one years old don't understand."

A schoolteacher, Noel, surely smart enough, a smart young man, surely he would have understood. He never heard of it. And I had to ask Valentine five times, in your presence, before I could finally get him to use the word "cancer." Do you remember that? They hid it. They hid the fact. It was a trap, surely as deadly as the worst kind of land mines, the worse kind of traps. I tell you, if you were in the army, and your officer said to you to "walk down that road, and that it was safe, and they knew it was full of land mines, and the only reason they told you it was safe was because that was the only way they could get you to go down the road, and that they blew you all to hell," what would your feelings be? It's that kind of misconduct that we are talking about in this case, and it is that kind of misconduct relative to the entire training of these people that this case is about. They blame it on something else after it is all over.

Now, I have a vision. It is not a dream—it's a nightmare. It came to me in the middle of the night, and I got up and wrote it down, and I want you to hear it because I wrote it in the middle of the night about a week ago. Twenty years from now—the men are not old, some say they're just in their prime, they're looking forward to some good things. The men that worked at that plant are good men with families who love them. They are good men, but they are dying—not all of them but they are

dying like men die in a plague. Cancer they say, probably from the plutonium plant. He worked there as a young man. They didn't know much
about it in those days. He isn't suffering much, but it is just a tragedy.
They all loved him. Nobody in top management seemed to care. Those
were the days when nobody in management in the plutonium plant
could be found, even by the AEC, who knew or cared. They worked the
men in respirators. The pipes leaked. The paint dropped from the walls.
The stuff was everywhere. Nobody cared very much. The place was run
by good money men. They were good money men—good managers.
The company, well, it covered things up. Profits were up 83 percent in
'79. One hundred thirty-eight million dollars profit in '79.

I continued to write in the middle of the night. It goes on: what training? More dangerous work than war. It is more dangerous work than
combat, and yet they told them nothing. Put them in the respirators.
And the information was kept from them, or they wouldn't have
worked. And one had the oxygen cut off and gasped, and the plutonium
filled the air, and filled his lungs. And one had the stuff spilled on him
while he was welding. And there wasn't room to weld and to work. And
once it was a foot deep in production on the wet side, and they never
shut it down—never. Production went on as usual. They used up one
hundred gallons of paint on one spill. And the plutonium cracked off
everywhere, off the valves, the table tops in the lunch room, and it was
in the air. The filters. Five hundred forty-three exposures in five years.
That's one hundred a year—one every three days. This, by their own
records, I wrote. Lord knows what they didn't report. Lord knows what
they covered up.

The training. Well, it was as bad as telling children that the Kool-Aid,
laced with poison, is good for them. A hidden danger—they never
knew.

Some read about plutonium and cancer in the paper for the first time
during a trial—the trial called "The Silkwood Case"—but it was too late
for them. Karen Silkwood was dead, the company was trying to convince an Oklahoma jury that she contaminated herself. They took two
and a half months for trial. The company had an excuse for everything.
Blamed it all on the union. Blamed it all on everybody else—on Karen
Silkwood, on the workers, on sabotage, on the AEC. It was a sad time
in the history of our country. They said the AEC was tough. Seventy-
five violations later they hadn't even been fined once.

It was worse than the days of slavery. It was a worse time of infamy than the days of slavery because the owners of the slaves cared about their slaves, and many of them loved their slaves. It was a time of infamy, and a time of deceit, corporate dishonesty. A time when men used men like disposable commodities—like so much expendable property. It was a time when corporations fooled the public, were more concerned with the public image than with the truth.

It was a time when the government held hands with these giants, and played footsie with their greatest scientists. At the disposal of the corporation, to testify, to strike down the claims of people, and it was too late. It was a sad time, the era between '70 and '79—they called it the Cimarron Syndrome.

What is this case about? It is about Karen Silkwood, who was a brave, ordinary woman who did care. And she risked her life, and she lost it. And she had something to tell the world, and she tried to tell the world. What was it that Karen Silkwood had to tell the world? That has been left to us to say now. It is for you, the jury, to say. It is for you, the jury, to say it for her.

What was she trying to tell the world? Ladies and gentlemen of the jury, I wish Karen Silkwood was standing here by me now and could say what she wanted to say. I think she would say, "Brothers and sisters . . ." I don't think she would say ladies and gentlemen. I think she would say, "Brothers and sisters, they were just eighteen- and nineteen-year-olds. They didn't understand. There wasn't any training. They kept the danger a secret. They covered it with word games and number games." And she would say: "Friends, it has to stop here today, here in Oklahoma City today."

Ladies and gentlemen, I've still got half an hour, and I'm not going to use it. I'm going to close my case with you right now. I'm going to tell you a story, a simple story, about a wise old man—and a smart-aleck young boy who wanted to show up the wise old man for a fool. The boy's plan was this: he found a little bird in the forest and captured the little bird. And he had the idea he would go to the wise old man with the bird in his hand and say, "Wise old man, what have I got in my hand?" And the old man would say, "Well, you have a bird, my son." And he would say, "Wise old man, is the bird alive, or is it dead?" And the old man knew if he said, "It is dead" the little boy would open his hand and the bird would fly away. Or if he said, "It is alive," then the boy would take the bird in his hand and crunch it and crunch it, and crunch the life out of it, and then open his hand and say, "See, it *is* dead." And so the boy went up to the wise old man and he said, "Wise old man, what do I have in my hand?" The old man said, "Why it is a bird, my son." He said, "Wise old man, is it alive, or is it dead?" And the wise old man said, "The bird is in your hands, my son."

Thank you very much. It's been my pleasure, my God-given pleasure, to be a part of your lives. I mean that.

Thank you, Your Honor.

CHAPTER FIVE

Leopold and Loeb

"Spare Them, for They Know All Too Well What They Do"

During his long career, Clarence Darrow had defended more than 100 accused murderers by the late spring of 1924, but perhaps none so remorseless, nor so brilliant, as Nathan F. Leopold Jr. and Richard Loeb. In the predawn hours of June 3, Darrow was awakened by visitors carrying grim news: the son of a family friend had confessed to the murder of a young boy, and it appeared that hanging was inevitable. Darrow, sixty-seven, was bitterly opposed to the death penalty, and realized that such a notorious trial would provide him with a public stage upon which he could rail against capital punishment to a national audience. But the odds against acquittal were long; there was a mountain of evidence pointing to their guilt, and the unsympathetic defendants had confessed to the senseless crime. While the press and public demanded a quick march to the gallows for the killers, Darrow worked on a strategy to mitigate the gruesome facts of the case.

On May 21, 1924, Chicago police received a call from Jacob Franks, a wealthy resident of Hyde Park, asking that they search for his fourteen-year-old son Robert, who had failed to come home that evening. Later that night, Mrs. Franks received a telephone call from a "Mr. Johnson," saying that he had kidnapped Robert, who had not been harmed, and that she would receive further information in the morning.

The next day, the Franks received a typewritten letter from a "George Johnson" assuring them that their son was still alive. The letter told the Franks to prepare $10,000 in old, unmarked bills and put them in a box, wrapped in white paper and sealed with wax. The letter stated that the Franks would receive further instructions by telephone on how to deliver the money. If they notified the police or failed to follow the instructions precisely, the letter promised their son would die. That afternoon, Jacob Franks received a telephone call from "Johnson" telling him that a taxi would soon pick him up at home and take him to a drug-store, where Franks would receive further instructions.

That same morning, a railroad maintenance worker made a shocking discovery in a culvert on prairie land south of Chicago: the naked body of a boy. The worker also found a pair of horn-rim glasses near the corpse. Despite the fact that Robert did not wear glasses, the police called Mr. Franks—only minutes after the worried father received his instructions from "Johnson." Ignoring the kidnapper's orders to wait for a taxi, Franks went to examine the body, which he identified as that of his missing son. The boy had been killed by strangulation and blunt trauma to the head, and had probably been dead before Franks received "Johnson"'s first call.

The police began their investigation with only two real pieces of evidence: the typed letter to the Franks and the glasses found with the body. First, the glasses were traced to their maker, a local optician, whose records showed that he had only sold three pairs with the prescription of the glasses found with the body. Of the three buyers, only Nathan Leopold lacked a convincing alibi.

Leopold was the youngest graduate in the history of the University of Chicago, an accomplished ornithologist, and the son of a millionaire businessman. When the police arrived at the Leopold residence, only a few blocks from the Franks's home, to ask him about the glasses, his friend Richard Loeb was visiting. Loeb, the son of a Sears Roebuck vice president, held the distinction of being the youngest graduate of the University of Michigan.

Leopold said that he had studied the birds in the area where the body was discovered. The weekend before the murder, he said that he had trekked across the culvert where the body had been found while taking some photographs. Leopold claimed his glasses were at home, but an intensive search failed to find them. Suspicious, the police took Leopold and Loeb into custody.

Detectives concentrated on Leopold, questioning him about his activities on the day of the kidnapping and murder. At first Leopold said he couldn't recall his whereabouts, then claimed that he and Loeb had driven Leopold's car to the Chicago Loop for lunch, then spent the afternoon studying birds in Lincoln Park. Leopold then said that he and Loeb had become too drunk to return home that evening, and so they picked up some girls and drove out to Jackson Park. Loeb confirmed Leopold's story.

The investigators then focused on the letter, which experts determined had been typed on an Underwood portable typewriter. Police questioned Leopold further, but he denied owning an Underwood. The investigators then learned that Leopold and some classmates had prepared exam outlines on a typewriter belonging to the suspect. A close inspection of these outlines proved that they and the letter from "Johnson" had been typed on the same typewriter. The students told the police that they had used Leopold's typewriter to make the outlines. Even when confronted with this fact, Leopold maintained he didn't own an Underwood; it must have belonged to one of his classmates. However, a servant in the Leopold home confirmed that there had indeed been an Underwood typewriter in the house as recently as two weeks before, although a further search of the home failed to find it.

At this time, the police learned another important fact: Leopold's chauffeur had been cleaning and repairing Leopold's car the day of the murders; Leopold and Loeb could not have driven it that day. When confronted with this new evidence, Loeb confessed that in a carefully planned scheme to commit the perfect crime, he and Leopold had kidnapped and killed Bobby Franks. The two then confessed to the state attorney, agreeing to every detail of the crime, except who had dealt the fatal blows to the victim.

While driving a rented car in search of a victim, Leopold and Loeb spotted Bobby Franks, Loeb's distant cousin. After Franks declined a ride, Loeb managed to lure the boy into the car by telling him that he needed to speak with him about a tennis racket. The killers struck Bobby in the head with a chisel and stuffed a rag in his mouth. Leopold and Loeb both accused the other of being the actual assailant, but agreed the boy died quickly in the backseat.

The two then sped toward Gary, Indiana, to dispose of the body. Having worked up an appetite, they stopped for sandwiches and dined in the car, with the corpse for company. Waiting until dark, they drove to an area Leopold knew well, having often visited while bird-watching. They removed Bobby's clothes, poured acid on the body to hamper identification, and stuffed the corpse into a culvert. Leopold and Loeb then drove back to Chicago, where they burned Bobby's clothing and tried to clean bloodstains from the car.

The next day, Leopold telephoned Franks and instructed him to go immediately by taxi to a drugstore. Leopold told the investigators that after Franks arrived at the store, he intended to call with instructions for

Franks to board a train with the ransom and retrieve a note instructing him to throw the ransom money off the moving train at a point where Leopold and Loeb would be waiting.

Faced with this confession, Darrow felt he had no choice. Both of his clients admitted taking part in the crime, and the traditional insanity defense (requiring that the defendant not know that what he was doing was "wrong") was not appropriate in this case: both defendants were brilliant, well educated, and in fact had tried to commit "the perfect crime."

Chicagoans were stunned when Darrow decided to plead both defendants guilty to the crime of murder; it had been expected that the famed trial lawyer would use his considerable skills to win an acquittal.

By pleading guilty, Darrow—in a masterstroke of trial tactics—put his clients beyond the reach of a vengeful jury pool, one that would have sent the teen killers to the gallows. Darrow knew that under these circumstances, Illinois law gave the judge discretion to fix the penalty in this case at death or life imprisonment. Darrow also knew that he would be allowed to present evidence mitigating the severity of the crime. He would try to show through the testimony of psychiatrists that, like defective machines, Leopold and Loeb were not responsible for their actions. Therefore, the death penalty, always unjust in Darrow's eyes, was especially inappropriate for two teens who could not be held accountable for their actions.

The climax to this "trial of the century" was Clarence Darrow's eloquent closing plea to spare the boys' lives, a plea that moved the judge to tears. After Darrow finished his impassioned summation, Judge Caverly ruled that the two teens should spend the rest of their lives in prison.

One killer ended up spending more than twice as much time behind bars as the other, but likely considered himself lucky by comparison. Richard Loeb was stabbed to death by a fellow inmate after serving only twelve years. Nathan Leopold was more fortunate than his friend. After he spent twenty-five years behind bars, the parole board reduced his sentence in 1949, making him eligible for release in 1953. Leopold left prison in 1958; he died of natural causes in 1971.

Commentary

The dynamic of this closing argument is strikingly different from Darrow's summation in his own defense (see chapter 2), due to the differences between the two proceedings. In his own case, Darrow was arguing to twelve jurors, trying to convince them that there had been no crime, that he was innocent of the charges. In *Leopold and Loeb,* Darrow argued to a judge, admitting that the defendants had in fact committed the killing, but arguing that the punishment should not, must not, be death.

Darrow's quest to save his clients from the gallows faced significant obstacles, including public outrage over the callous nature of the murder and the defendants' lack of remorse; resentment over the killers' wealth and social status; and a constant drumbeat in the press, echoing the overwhelming public support for the execution of Leopold and Loeb.

Early in his summation, Darrow raises the possibility that the wealthy families of the defendants can buy special treatment for their sons. "It was announced that there were millions of dollars to be spent on this case . . . here was to be an effort to save the lives of the two boys by the use of money in fabulous amounts. . . ."

Darrow quickly disposes of the issue, pointing out that his fee and the fee of the psychiatrists hired by the defense would be moderate, set by the Chicago Bar Association, and not the attorneys or doctors. Then in a brilliant example of what is now known as "spin," Darrow takes a liability and turns it into an asset. "If we fail in this defense it will not be for lack of money. It will be on account of money. Money has been the most serious handicap that we have met. There are times when poverty is fortunate." Darrow continues, telling the judge that had the defendants been poor, the prosecutor would have accepted a guilty plea, sent them away for life, and not even asked for a death sentence. Darrow concludes that the only reason for the state's insistence that the killers be put to death is that their parents have money. In a few sentences, he has generated some sympathy for his clients, as well as providing the judge with a compelling point to mull over—that the prosecution's pursuit of a capital verdict may in fact be unjust.

The next challenge facing Darrow was to convince the judge that the so-called lack of remorse exhibited by his clients was reason not for greater punishment, but instead for compassion, because their cold, callous demeanor revealed how deeply sick they were. Darrow argues that because they did not kill for money, nor spite, nor hate, without any motive other than curiosity, they are no more deserving of hatred than a spider for killing a fly. He asks the judge to consider that two men so deeply flawed in their very nature as to be totally remorseless were acting in the only way that could be expected.

In addition to mitigating his clients' seeming lack of remorse, Darrow carefully negates the homosexual issue by helping build the case that these boys were sick. Darrow argues, "He did it, obsessed of an idea, perhaps to some extent influenced by what has not been developed publicly in this case, perversions that were present in the boy. Both signs of insanity, both, together with this act, proving a diseased mind."

Darrow next turns to the task of overcoming the tidal wave of public opinion that the two men should be executed for their crime. Rousing himself to Olympian heights of rhetoric, Darrow draws on a lifetime of impassioned opposition to the death penalty, questioning the very humanity of those who would kill in order to punish killers: "I sometimes wonder if I am dreaming. If in the first quarter of the twentieth century there has come back into the hearts of men the hate and feeling and the lust for blood which possesses the primitive savage of barbarous lands. . . ."

He poses questions to the judge, asking him to consider that if they are hanged, "Wouldn't it be a glorious day for Chicago? Wouldn't it be a glorious triumph for the state's attorney? Wouldn't it be a great triumph for justice in this land? Wouldn't it be a glorious illustration of Christianity and kindness and charity?"

Finally, Darrow was masterful in his manipulation of the judge, cajoling, haranguing, and flattering, until he succeeded in boxing him in. By the time Darrow was done, the choice was a stark one. As Darrow put it, "[Y]our Honor, if these boys hang, you must do it. . . . It must be by your cool, premeditated act, without a chance to shift responsibility. . . . [Y]ou know that I would have been untrue to my clients if I had not concluded to take this chance before this court, instead of submitting it to a poisoned jury in the city of Chicago. I did it knowing that it would be an unheard of thing for any court . . . to sentence these boys to death."

By using the facts, playing to his audience, and tailoring his argument, Darrow overcame insurmountable odds, sparing his clients the hangman's noose.

Closing Argument

The State of Illinois v. *Nathan Leopold & Richard Loeb*
Delivered by Clarence Darrow
Chicago, Illinois, August 22, 1924

Your Honor, it has been almost three months since the great responsibility of this case was assumed by my associates and myself. It has been three months of great anxiety. A burden which I gladly would have been spared excepting for my feelings of affection toward some of the members of one of these unfortunate families.

Our anxiety over this case has not been due to the facts that are connected with this most unfortunate affair, but to the almost unheard of publicity it has received; to the fact that newspapers all over this country have been giving it space such as they have almost never before given to any case. The fact that day after day the people of Chicago have been regaled with stories of all sorts about it, until almost every person has formed an opinion. And when the public is interested and demands a punishment, no matter what the offense, great or small, it thinks of only one punishment, and that is death. It may not be a question that involves the taking of human life; it may be a question of pure prejudice alone; but when the public speaks as one man, it thinks only of killing.

It was announced that there were millions of dollars to be spent on this case. Wild and extravagant stories were freely published as though they were facts. Here was to be an effort to save the lives of two boys by the use of money in fabulous amounts. We announced to the public that no excessive use of money would be made in this case, neither for lawyers nor for psychiatrists, or in any other way. We have faithfully kept that promise. The psychiatrists are receiving a per diem, and only a per diem, which is the same as is paid by the state. The attorneys, at their own request, have agreed to take such amount as the officers of the Chicago Bar Association may think proper in this case. If we fail in this defense it will not be for lack of money. It will be on account of money. Money has been the most serious handicap that we have met. There are times when poverty is fortunate.

I insist, Your Honor, that had this been the case of two boys of these defendants' age, unconnected with families of great wealth, there is not a state's attorney in Illinois who could not have consented at once to a plea of guilty and a punishment in the penitentiary for life. Not one. No lawyer could have justified any other attitude. No prosecution could have justified it.

We are here with the lives of two boys imperiled, with the public aroused. For what? Because, unfortunately, the parents have money. Nothing else.

I have heard in the last six weeks nothing but the cry for blood. I have heard from the office of the state's attorney only ugly hate. I have heard precedents quoted which would be a disgrace to a savage race. I have seen a court urged almost to the point of threats to hang two boys, in the face of science, in the face of philosophy, in the face of humanity, in the face of experience, in the face of all the better and more humane thought of the age.

Why, Mr. Savage [*one of the prosecutors*] says age makes no difference, and that if this court should do what every other court in Illinois has done since its foundation, and refuse to sentence these boys to death, none else would ever be hanged in Illinois.

Well, I can imagine some results worse than that. So long as this terrible tool is to be used for a plaything, without thought or consideration, we ought to get rid of it for the protection of human life.

Now, Your Honor, Mr. Savage, in as cruel a speech as he knew how to make, said to this court that we pled guilty because we are afraid to do anything else.

Your Honor, that is true.

It was not correct that we would have defended these boys in this court; we believe we have been fair to the public. Anyhow, we have tried, and we have tried under terribly hard conditions.

We have said to the public and to this court that neither the parents, nor the friends, nor the attorneys would want these boys released. Unfortunate though it be, it is true, and those the closest to them know perfectly well that they should not be released, and that they should be permanently isolated from society. We are asking this court to save their lives, which is the least and the most that a judge can do.

We did plead guilty before Your Honor because we were afraid to submit our cause to a jury.

I can tell Your Honor why. I have found that years and experience with life tempers one's emotions and makes him more understanding of his fellowman. When my friend Savage is my age, or even yours, he will read his address to this court with horror. I am aware that as one grows older he is less critical. He is not so sure. He is inclined to make some allowance for his fellowman. I am aware that a court has more experience, more judgment, and more kindliness than a jury.

Your Honor, it may be hardly fair to the court, I am aware that I have helped to place a serious burden upon your shoulders. And at that, I have always meant to be your friend, but this was not an act of friendship. I know perfectly well that where responsibility is divided by twelve, it is easy to say: "Away with him."

But, Your Honor, if these boys hang, you must do it. There can be no division of responsibility here. You can never explain that the rest overpowered you. It must be by your deliberate, cool, premeditated act, without a chance to shift responsibility. It was not a kindness to you. We placed this responsibility on your shoulders because we were mindful of the rights of our clients, and we were mindful of the unhappy families who have done no wrong.

Your Honor will never thank me for unloading this responsibility upon you, but you know that I would have been untrue to my clients if I had not concluded to take this chance before court, instead of submitting it to a poisoned jury in the city of Chicago. I did it knowing that it would be an unheard of thing for any court, no matter who, to sentence these boys to death. Your Honor, I must for a moment criticize the arguments that have preceded me. I can sum up the prosecutor's arguments in a minute: cruelly, dastardly, premeditated, fiendish, abandoned, and malignant heart.

Now, that is what I have listened to for three days against two minors, two children, who have no right to sign a note or take a deed. Cowardly? Well, I don't know. Let me tell you something that I think is cowardly, whether their acts were or not. Here is Dickie Loeb, and Nathan Leopold, and the state objects to anybody calling one "Dickie" and the other "Babe" although everybody does, but they think they can hang them easier if their names are Richard and Nathan, so, we will call them Richard and Nathan. Eighteen and nineteen years old at the time of the homicide. Here are three officers watching them. They are led out and in [to] this jail and across the bridge waiting to be hanged. Not a chance to get away. Handcuffed when they get out of this room. Not a chance. Penned like rats in a trap; and for a lawyer with physiological eloquence to wave his fist in front of their faces and shout "Cowardly!" does not appeal to me as a brave act.

Cold-blooded? Why? Because they planned, and schemed. Yes. But here are the officers of justice, so-called, with all the power of the state, with all the influence of the press, to fan this community into a frenzy of hate; with all of that, who for months have been planning and scheming, and contriving, and working to take these two boys' lives. You may stand them up on the trapdoor of the scaffold, and choke them to death, but that act will be infinitely more cold-blooded, whether justified or not, than any act that these boys have committed or can commit.

Cold-blooded! Let the State, who is so anxious to take these boys' lives, set an example in consideration, kindheartedness, and tenderness before they call my clients cold-blooded.

Now, Your Honor, I have been practicing law a good deal longer than I should have, anyhow, for forty-five or forty-six years, and during a part of that time I have tried a good many criminal cases, always defending. I have never yet tried a case where the state's attorney did not say that it was the most cold-blooded, inexcusable, premeditated case that ever occurred. If it was murder, there never was such a murder. If it was robbery, there never was such a robbery. If it was a conspiracy, it was the most terrible conpiracy that ever happened since the star-chamber passed into oblivion. If it was larceny, there never was such a larceny.

I want to give some attention to this cold-blooded murder, Your Honor. Was it a cold-blooded murder? Was it the most terrible murder that ever happened in the state of Illinois? Was it the most dastardly act in the annals of crime? No.

I insist, Your Honor, that under all fair rules and measurements, this was one of the least dastardly and cruel of any that I have known anything about.

Now, let us see how we should measure it. They say that this was a cruel murder, the worst that ever happened. I say that very few murders ever occurred that were as free from cruelty as this. There ought to be some rule to determine whether a murder is exceedingly cruel or not.

Of course, Your Honor, I admit that I hate killing, and hate it no matter how it is done, whether you shoot a man through the heart, or cut his head off with an axe, or kill him with a chisel or tie a rope around his neck, I hate it. I always did. I always shall. But there are degrees, and if I might be permitted to make my own rules I would say that if I were estimating what was the most cruel murder, I might first consider the sufferings of the victim. Poor little Bobby Franks suffered very little. There is no excuse for his killing. If to hang these two boys would bring him back to life, I would say let them go, and I believe their parents would say so, too. But:

Leopold and Loeb

The moving finger writes, and having writ,
Moves on; nor all your piety nor wit
Shall lure it back to cancel half a line,
Nor all your tears wash out a word of it.

Robert Franks is dead, and we cannot call him back to life. It was all over in fifteen minutes after he got into the car, and he probably never knew it or thought of it. That does not justify it. It is the last thing I would do. I am sorry for the poor boy. I am sorry for his parents. But it is done.

Now, what else would stamp a murder as being a most atrocious crime?

First, I put the victim, who ought not to suffer; and next, I would put the attitude of those who kill. What was the attitude of these two boys? It may be that the state's attorney would think that it was particularly cruel to the victim because he was a boy. Well, my clients are boys, too, and if it would make more serious the offense to kill a boy, it should make less serious the offense of the boys who did the killing.

What was there in the conduct of these two boys which showed a wicked, malignant, and abandoned heart beyond that of anybody else, who ever lived?

This is a senseless, useless, purposeless, motiveless act of two boys. Now, let me see if I can prove it. There was not a particle of hate, there was not a grain of malice, there was no opportunity to be cruel except as death is cruel, and death is cruel. There was absolutely no purpose in it all, no reason in it all, and no motive for it all.

In order to make this the most cruel thing that ever happened, of course they must have a motive. And what, do they say, was the motive? Your Honor, if there was ever anything so foolish, so utterly futile as the motive claimed in this case, then I have never listened to it. What did Tom Marshall say? What did Joe Savage say? "The motive was to get $10,000," say they. These two boys, neither one of whom needed a cent, scions of wealthy people, killed this little inoffensive boy to get $10,000? First, let us call your attention to the opening statement of Judge Crowe [*another of the prosecutors*], where we heard for the first time the full details of this homicide after a plea of guilty.

He said these two young men were heavy gamblers, and they needed the money to pay gambling debts. What did he prove? He put on one witness, and one only, who had played bridge with both of them in college, and he said they played for five cents a point. Now, I trust Your Honor knows better than I do how much of a game that would be. At poker I might guess, but I know little about bridge. But what else? He said that in a game one of them lost $90 to the other one. They were playing against each other, and one of them lost $90? Ninety dollars! Their joint money was just the same; and there is not another word of evidence in this case to sustain the statement of Mr. Crowe, who pleads to hang these boys. Your Honor, is it not trifling?

It would be trifling, excepting, Your Honor, that we are dealing in human life. And we are dealing in more than that; we are dealing in the future fate of two families. We are talking of placing a blot upon two houses that do not deserve it. And all that they can get out of their imagination is that there was a game of bridge and one lost $90 to the other, and therefore they went out and committed murder. Your Honor knows that it is utterly absurd. The evidence was absolutely worthless. The statement was made out of whole cloth, and Mr. Crowe felt like that policeman who came in here and perjured himself, as I will show you later on, who said that when he was talking with Nathan Leopold Jr., he told him the public was not satisfied with the motive. I wonder if the public is satisfied with the motive? If there is any person in Chicago who under the evidence in this case would believe that this was the motive, then he is stupid. That is all I have to say for him, just plain stupid.

But let us go further than that. Who were these two boys? And how did it happen?

On a certain day they killed poor little Robert Franks. They were not to get $10,000; they were to get $5,000 if it worked; that is, $5,000 each. Neither one could get more than five, and either one was risking his neck in the job. So each one of my clients was risking his neck for $5,000, if it had anything to do with it, which it did not.

Did they need the money? Why, at this very time, and a few months before, Dickie Loeb had $3,000 [in his] checking account in the bank. Your Honor, I would be ashamed to talk about this except that in all apparent seriousness they are asking to kill these two boys on the strength of this flimsy foolishness. At that time, Richard Loeb had a three-thousand-dollar checking account in the bank. He had three Liberty Bonds, one of which was past due, and the interest on each of them had not been collected for three years. And yet they would ask to hang him on the theory that he committed this murder because he needed money.

How about Leopold? Leopold was in regular receipt of $125 a

month; he had an automobile; paid nothing for board and clothes, and expenses; he got money whenever he wanted it, and he had arranged to go to Europe and had bought his ticket and was going to leave about the time he was arrested in this case. He passed his examination for the Harvard Law School, and was going to take a short trip to Europe before it was time for him to attend the fall term. His ticket had been bought, and his father was to give him $3,000 to make the trip. Your Honor, jurors sometimes make mistakes, and courts do, too. If on this evidence the court is to construe a motive out of this case, then I insist that a motive could be construed out of any set of circumstances and facts that might be imagined.

The boys had been reared in luxury, they had never been denied anything; no want or desire left unsatisfied; no debts; no need of money; nothing. And yet they murdered a little boy, against whom they had nothing in the world, without malice, without reason, to get $5,000 each. All right. All right, Your Honor, if the court believes it, if anyone believes it, I can't help it. That is what this case rests on. It could not stand up a minute without motive. Without it, it was the senseless act of immature and diseased children, as it was; a senseless act of children, wandering around in the dark and moved by some motion, that we still perhaps have not the knowledge or the insight into life to thoroughly understand.

Now, let me go on with it. What else do they claim?

It has been argued to this court that you can do no such thing as to grant the almost divine favor of saving the lives of two boys, that it is against the law, that the penalty for murder is death; and this court, who, in the fiction of the lawyers and the judges, forgets that he is a human being and becomes a court, pulseless, emotionless, devoid of those common feelings which alone make men; that this court as a human machine must hang them because they killed.

Now, let us see. I do not need to ask mercy from this court for these clients, nor for anybody else, nor for myself; though I have never yet found a person who did not need it. But I do not ask mercy for these boys. Your Honor may be as strict in the enforcement of the law as you please and you cannot hang these boys. You can only hang them because back of the law and back of justice and back of the common instincts of man, and back of the human feeling for the young, is the hoarse voice of the mob which says, "Kill." I need ask nothing. What is the law of Illinois? If one is found guilty of murder in the first degree by a jury, or if he pleads guilty before a court, the court or jury may do one of three things: he may hang, he may imprison for life, or he may imprison for a term of not less than fourteen years. Now, why is that the law?

Does it follow from the statute that a court is bound to ascertain the impossible, and must necessarily measure the degrees of guilt? Not at all. He may not be able to do it. A court may act from any reason or from no reason. A jury may fix any one of these penalties as they separate. Why was this law passed? Undoubtedly in recognition of the growing feeling in all the forward-thinking people of the United States against capital punishment. Undoubtedly, through the deep reluctance of courts and juries to take human life.

Without any reason whatever, without any facts whatever, Your Honor must make the choice, and you have the same right to make one choice as another. It is Your Honor's province; you may do it, and I need ask nothing in order to have you do it. There is the statute. But there is more than that in this case.

We have sought to tell this court why he should not hang these boys. We have sought to tell this court, and to make this court believe, that they were diseased of mind, and that they were of tender age. However, before I discuss that, I ought to say another word in reference to the question of motive in this case. If there was no motive, except the senseless act of immature boys, then of course there is taken from this case all of the feeling of deep guilt upon the part of these defendants.

There was neither cruelty to the deceased, beyond taking his life, nor was there any depth of guilt and depravity on the part of the defendants, for it was a truly motiveless act, without the slightest feeling of hatred or revenge, done by a couple of children for no sane reason.

But, Your Honor, we have gone further than that, and we have sought to show you, as I think we have, the condition of these boys' minds. Of course it is not an easy task to find out the condition of another person's mind.

Now, I was about to say that it needs no expert, it needs nothing but a bare recitation of these facts, and a fair consideration of them, to convince any human being that this was the act of diseased brains.

But let's get to something stronger than that. Were these boys in their right minds? Here were two boys with good intellect, one eighteen and one nineteen. They had all the prospects that life could hold out for any of the young; one a graduate of Chicago and another of Ann Arbor; one who had passed his examination for the Harvard Law School and was about to take a trip in Europe, another who had passed at Ann Arbor, the youngest in his class, with $3,000 in the bank. Boys who never knew what it was to want a dollar; boys who could reach any position that was given to boys of that kind to reach; boys of distinguished and honorable families, families of wealth and position, with all the world before them. And they gave it all up for nothing, for nothing! They took a little companion of one of them, on a crowded street, and killed him, for nothing, and sacrificed everything that could be of value in human life upon the crazy scheme of a couple of immature lads.

Now, Your Honor, you have been a boy; I have been a boy. And we have known other boys. The best way to understand somebody else is to put yourself in his place. Is it within the realm of your imagination that a boy who was right, with all the prospects of life before him, who could choose what he wanted, without the slightest reason in the world would lure a young companion to his death, and take his place in the shadow of the gallows?

How insane they are I care not, whether medically or legally. They did not reason; they could not reason; they committed the most foolish, most unprovoked, most purposeless, most causeless act that any two boys ever committed, and they put themselves where the rope is dangling above their heads.

There are not physicians enough in the world to convince any thoughtful, fair-minded man that these boys are right. Was their act one of deliberation, of intellect, or were they driven by some force such as Dr. White and Dr. Glueck and Dr. Healy have told this court?

There are only two theories; one is that their diseased brains drove them to it; the other is the old theory of possession by devils, and my friend Marshall could have read you books on that, too, but it has been pretty well given up in Illinois. That they were intelligent, sane, sound, and reasoning is unthinkable. Let me call Your Honor's attention to another thing.

Why did they kill little Bobby Franks? Not for money, not for spite; not for hate. They killed him as they might kill a spider or a fly, for the experience. They killed him because they were made that way. Because somewhere in the infinite processes that go to the making up of the boy or the man something slipped, and those unfortunate lads sit here hated, despised, outcasts, with the community shouting for their blood.

Mr. Savage, with the immaturity of youth and inexperience, says that if we hang them there will be no more killing. This world has been one long slaughterhouse from the beginning until today, and killing goes on and on and on, and will forever. Why not read something, why not study something, why not think instead of blindly shouting for death?

Kill them. Will that prevent other senseless boys or other vicious men or vicious women from killing? No! It will simply call upon every weak-minded person to do as they have done. I know how easy it is to talk about mothers when you want to do something cruel. But I am thinking of the others, too. I know that any mother might be the mother of little Bobby Franks, who left his home and went to his school, and who never came back. I know that any mother might be the mother of Richard Loeb and Nathan Leopold, just the same. The trouble is this, that if she is the mother of a Nathan Leopold or of a Richard Loeb, she has to ask herself the question: "How come my children came to be what they are? From what ancestry did they get this strain? How far removed was the poison that destroyed their lives? Was I the bearer of the seed that brings them to death?" Any mother might be the mother of any of them. But these two are the victims.

No one knows what will be the fate of the child he gets or the child she bears; the fate of the child is the last thing they consider.

I am sorry for the fathers as well as the mothers, for the fathers who give their strength and their lives for educating and protecting and creating a fortune for the boys that they love; for the mothers who go down into the shadow of death for their children, who nourish them and care for them, and risk their lives, that they may live, who watch them with tenderness and fondness and longing, and who go down into dishonor and disgrace for the children that they love.

All of these are helpless. We are all helpless. But when you are pitying the father and the mother of poor Bobby Franks, what about the fathers and mothers of these two unfortunate boys, and what about the unfortunate boys themselves, and what about all the fathers and all the mothers and all the boys and all the girls who tread a dangerous maze in darkness from birth to death?

Do you think you can cure the hatreds and the maladjustments of the world by hanging them? You simply show your ignorance and your hate when you say it. You may here and there cure hatred with love and understanding, but you can only add fuel to the flames by cruelty and hate.

Your Honor, that no human being could have done what these boys did, excepting through the operation of a diseased brain. I do not propose to go through each step of the terrible deed, it would take too long. But I do want to call the attention of this court to some of the other acts of these two boys, in this distressing and weird homicide; acts which show conclusively that there could be no reason for their conduct.

I want to come down now to the actions on the afternoon of the tragedy.

Without any excuse, without the slightest motive, not moved by money, not moved by passion or hatred, by nothing except the vague wanderings of children, about four o'clock in the afternoon they started out to find somebody to kill. For nothing.

They went over to the Harvard School. Dick's little brother was there, on the playground. Dick went there himself in open daylight, known by all of them; he had been a pupil there himself, the school was near his home, and he looked over the little boys. They first picked out a little boy named Levinson, and Dick trailed him around. Now, of course, that is a hard story. It is a story that shocks one. A boy bent on killing, not knowing where he would go or who he would get, but seeking some victim. Here is a little boy, but the circumstances are not opportune, and so he fails to get him. Dick abandons that lead; Dick and Nathan are in the car, and they see Bobby Franks on the street, and they call to him to get into the car. It is about five o'clock in the afternoon, in the long summer days, on a thickly settled street, built up with homes, the houses of their friends and their companions known to everybody, automobiles appearing and disappearing, and they take him in the car.

If there had been a question of revenge, yes; if there had been a question of hate, where no one cares for his own fate, intent only on accomplishing his end, yes. But without any motive or any reason they picked up this little boy right in sight of their own homes, and surrounded by their neighbors. They hit him over the head with a chisel and killed him, and go on about their business, driving this car within half a block of Loeb's home, within the same distance of the Franks's home, drive it past the neighbors that they knew, in the open highway, in broad daylight. And still men will say that they have a bright intellect.

I say again, whatever madness and hate and frenzy may do to the human mind, there is not a single person who reasons who can believe that one of these acts was the act of men, of brains that were not diseased. There is no other explanation for it. And had it not been for the wealth and the weirdness and the notoriety, they would have been sent to the psychopathic hospital for examination, and been taken care of, instead of the state demanding that this court take the last pound of flesh and the last drop of blood from two irresponsible lads.

They pull the dead boy into the backseat, and wrap him in a blanket, and this funeral car starts on its route. If ever any death car went over the same route or the same kind of a route driven by sane people, I have never heard of it, and I fancy no one else has ever heard of it.

This car is driven for twenty miles. The slightest accident, the slightest misfortune, a bit of curiosity, an arrest for speeding, anything would bring destruction. They go down the Midway, through the park, meeting hundreds of machines, in sight of thousands of eyes, with this dead boy. They go down a thickly populated street through South Chicago, and then for three miles take the longest street to go through this city; built solid with business, buildings, filled with automobiles backed upon the street, with streetcars on the track, with thousands of peering eyes; one boy driving and the other on the backseat, with the corpse of little Bobby Franks, the blood streaming from him, wetting everything in the car.

And yet they tell me that this is sanity; they tell me that the brains of these boys are not diseased. Their conduct shows exactly what it was, and shows that this court has before him two young men who should be examined in a psychopathic hospital and treated kindly and with care. They get through South Chicago, and they take the regular automobile road down toward Hammond. They stop at the forks of the road, and leave little Bobby Franks, soaked with blood, in the machine, and get their dinner, and eat it without an emotion or a qualm.

I repeat, you may search the annals of crime, and you can find no parallel. It is utterly at variance with every motive, and every act and every part of conduct that influences normal people in the commission of crime. There is not a sane thing in all of this from the beginning to the end. There was not a normal act in any of it, from its inception in a diseased brain, until today, when they sit here awaiting their doom.

But we are told that they planned. Well, what does that mean? A maniac plans, an idiot plans, an animal plans; any brain that functions may plan. But their plans were the diseased plans of the diseased mind. Is there any man with an air of intellect and a decent regard for human life, and the slightest bit of heart that does not understand this situation?

And still, Your Honor, on account of its weirdness and its strangeness, and its advertising, we are forced to fight. For what? Forced to plead to this court that two boys, one eighteen and the other nineteen, may be permitted to live in silence and solitude and disgrace and spend all their days in the penitentiary. Asking this court and the state's attorney to be merciful enough to let these two boys be locked up in a prison until they die.

I sometimes wonder if I am dreaming. If in the first quarter of the twentieth century there has come back into the hearts of men the hate and feeling and the lust for blood which possesses the primitive savage of barbarous lands. What do they want? Tell me, is a lifetime for the young boys spent behind prison bars, is that not enough for this mad act? And is there any reason why this great public should be regaled by a hanging? I cannot understand it, Your Honor. It would be past belief, excepting that to the four corners of the earth the news of this weird act has been carried and men have been stirred, and the primitive has come back, and the intellect has been stifled, and men have been controlled by feelings and passions and hatred which should have died centuries ago.

My friend Savage pictured to you the putting of this dead boy in this culvert. Well, no one can minutely describe any killing and not make it shocking. It is shocking. It is shocking because we love life and because we instinctively draw back from death. It is shocking wherever it is and however it is, and perhaps all death is almost equally shocking.

But here is the picture of a dead boy, past pain, when no harm can come to him, put in a culvert, after taking off his clothes so that the evidence would be destroyed; and that is pictured to this court as a reason for hanging. Well, Your Honor, that does not appeal to me as strongly as the hitting over the head of little Robert Franks with a chisel. The boy was dead.

I could say something about the death penalty that, for some mysterious reason, the state wants in this case. Why do they want it? To vindicate the law? Oh, no. The law can be vindicated without killing anyone else. It might shock the fine sensibilities of the state's counsel that this boy was put into a culvert and left after he was dead, but, Your Honor, I can think of a scene that makes this pale into insignificance. I can think, and only think, Your Honor, of taking two boys, one eighteen and the other nineteen, irresponsible, weak, diseased, penning them in a cell, checking off the days and the hours and the minutes, until they will be taken out and hanged. Wouldn't it be a glorious day for Chicago? Wouldn't it be a glorious triumph for the state's attorney? Wouldn't it be a great triumph for justice in this land? Wouldn't it be a glorious illustration of Christianity and kindness and charity? I can picture them, wakened in the gray light of morning, furnished [with a] suit of clothes by the state, led to the scaffold, their feet tied, black caps drawn over their heads, stood on a trapdoor, the hangman pressing a spring, so that it gives way under them; can see them fall through space and stopped by the rope around their necks.

I am always suspicious of righteous indignation. Nothing is more cruel than righteous indignation. To hear young men talk glibly of justice. Who knows what it is? Does Mr. Savage know? Does Mr. Crowe know? Do I know? Does Your Honor know? Is there any human machinery for finding it out? Is there any man can weigh me and say what I deserve? Can Your Honor? Let us be honest. Can Your Honor appraise yourself, and say what you deserve? Can Your Honor appraise these two young men and say what they deserve? Justice must take account of infinite circumstances which a human being cannot understand.

These boys left this body down in the culvert and they came back; telephoned home that they would be too late for supper. Here, surely, was an act of consideration on the part of Leopold, telephoning home that he would be late for supper. Dr. Krohn says he must be able to think and act because he could do this. But the boy who through habit would telephone his home that he would be late for supper had not a tremor or a thought or a shudder at taking the life of little Bobby Franks for nothing, and he has not had one yet. He was in the habit of doing what he did when he telephoned, that was all; but in the presence of life and death, and a cruel death, he had no tremor, and no thought.

They came back. They got their dinner. They parked the bloody automobile in front of Leopold's house. They cleaned it to some extent that night and left it standing in the street in front of their home. They took it into the garage the next day and washed it, and the poor little Dickie Loeb—I shouldn't call him Dickie, and I shouldn't call him poor, because that might be playing for sympathy, and you have no right to ask for sympathy in this world: you should ask for justice, whatever that may be; and only the state's attorneys know.

And then in a day or so we find Dick Loeb with his pockets stuffed with newspapers telling of the Franks's tragedy. We find him consulting with his friends in the club, with the newspaper reporters; and my experience is that the last person that a conscious criminal associates with is a reporter. He even shuns them more than he does a detective, because they are smarter and less merciful. But he picks up a reporter, and he tells him he has read a great many detective stories, and he knows just how this would happen and that the fellow who telephoned must have been down on Sixty-third Street, and the way to find him is to go down on Sixty-third Street and visit the drugstores, and he would go with him.

And Dick Loeb pilots reporters around the drugstores where the telephoning was done, and he talks about it, and he takes the newspapers, and takes them with him, and he is having a glorious time. And yet he is "perfectly oriented," in the language of Dr. Krohn. "Perfectly oriented." Is there any question about the condition of his mind? Why was he doing it? He liked to hear about it. He had done something that he could not boast of directly, but he did want to hear other people talk about it, and he looked around there, and helped them find the place where the telephone message was sent out.

Does not the man who knows what he is doing, who for some reason has been overpowered and commits what is called a crime, keep as far away from it as he can? Does he go to the reporters and help them hunt it out? There is not a single act in this case that is not the act of a diseased mind, not one.

Talk about scheming. Yes, it is the scheme of disease; it is the scheme of infancy; it is the scheme of fools; it is the scheme of irresponsibility from the time it was conceived until the last act in the tragedy.

Now, Your Honor, let me go a little further with this. I have gone over some of the high spots in this tragedy. This tragedy has not claimed all the attention it has had on account of its atrocity. There are two reasons, and only two that I can see. First is the reputed extreme wealth of these families; not only the Loeb and Leopold families, but the Franks family, and of course it is unusual. And next is the fact [that] it is weird and uncanny and motiveless. That is what attracted the attention of the world. Many may say now that they want to hang these boys. But I know that giving the people blood is something like giving them their dinner: when they get it they go to sleep. They may for the time being have an emotion, but they will bitterly regret it. And I undertake to say that if these two boys are sentenced to death, and are hanged on that day, there will be a pall settle over the people of this land that will be dark and deep, and at least cover every humane and intelligent person with its gloom. I wonder if it will do good. I marveled when I heard Mr. Savage talk. Mr. Savage tells this court that if these boys are hanged, there will be no more murder. Mr. Savage is an optimist. He says that if the defendants are hanged there will be no more boys like these. I could give him a sketch of punishment, punishment beginning with the brute which killed something because something hurt it; the punishment of the savage; if a person is injured in the tribe, they must injure somebody in the other tribe; it makes no difference who it is, but somebody. If one is killed his friends or family must kill in return.

You can trace it all down through the history of man. You can trace the burnings, the boilings, the drawings and quarterings, the hangings of people in England at the crossroads, carving them up and hanging them, as examples for all to see.

We can come down to the last century when nearly two hundred crimes were punishable by death, and by death in every form; not only hanging that was too humane, but burning, boiling, cutting into pieces, torturing in all conceivable forms.

I know that every step in the progress of humanity has been met and opposed by prosecutors, and many times by courts. I know that when poaching and petty larceny was punishable by death in England, juries refused to convict. They were too humane to obey the law; and judges refused to sentence. I know that when the delusion of witchcraft was spreading over Europe, claiming its victims by the millions, many a judge so shaped his cases that no crime of witchcraft could be punished in his court. I know that these trials were stopped in America because juries would no longer convict.

Gradually the laws have been changed and modified, and men look back with horror at the hangings and the killings of the past. What did they find in England? That as they got rid of these barbarous statutes, crimes decreased instead of increased; as the criminal law was modified and humanized, there was less crime instead of more. I will undertake to say, Your Honor, that you can scarcely find a single book written by a student, and I will include all the works on criminology of the past, that has not made the statement over and over again that as the penal code was made less terrible, crimes grew less frequent.

If these two boys die on the scaffold, which I can never bring myself to imagine, if they do die on the scaffold, the details of this will be spread over the world. Every newspaper in the United States will carry a full account. Every newspaper of Chicago will be filled with the gruesome details. It will enter every home and every family. Will it make men better or make men worse? I would like to put that to the intelligence of man, at least such intelligence as they have. I would like to appeal to the feelings of human beings so far as they have feelings— would it make the human heart softer or would it make hearts harder?

What influence would it have upon the millions of men who will read it? What influence would it have upon the millions of women who will read it, more sensitive, more impressionable, more imaginative than men? Would it help them if Your Honor should do what the state begs you to do? What influence would it have upon the infinite number of children who will devour its details as Dicky Loeb has enjoyed reading detective stories? Would it make them better or would it make them worse? The question needs no answer. You can answer it from the human heart. What influence, let me ask you, will it have for the unborn babes still sleeping in their mother's womb? Do I need to argue to Your Honor that cruelty only breeds cruelty? That hatred only causes hatred; that if there is any way to soften this human heart which is hard enough at its best, if there is any way to kill evil and hatred and all that goes with it, it is not through evil and hatred and cruelty; it is through charity, and love, and understanding.

I am not pleading so much for these boys as I am for the infinite number of others to follow, those who perhaps cannot be as well defended as these have been, those who may go down in the storm, and the tempest, without aid. It is of them I am thinking, and for them I am begging of this court not to turn backward toward the barbarous and cruel past.

Now, Your Honor, who are these two boys?

Leopold, with a wonderfully brilliant mind; Loeb, with an unusual intelligence; both from their very youth, crowded like hothouse plants, to learn more and more and more. Dr. Krohn says that they are intelligent. But it takes something besides brains to make a human being who can adjust himself to life.

In fact, as Dr. Church and as Dr. Singer regretfully admitted, brains are not the chief essential in human conduct. There is no question about it. The emotions are the urge that make us live; the urge that makes us work or play, or move along the pathways of life. They are the instinctive things. In fact, intellect is a late development of life. Long before it was evolved, the emotional life kept the organism in existence until death. Whatever our action is, it comes from the emotions, and nobody is balanced without them.

The intellect does not count so much. The state put on three alienists and Dr. Krohn. Two of them, Dr. Patrick and Dr. Church, are undoubtedly able men. One of them, Dr. Church, is a man whom I have known for thirty years, and for whom I have the highest regard.

On Sunday, June 1, before any of the friends of these boys or their counsel could see them, while they were in the care of the state's attorney's office, they brought them in to be examined by these alienists. I am not going to discuss that in detail as I may later on. Dr. Patrick said the only thing unnatural he noted about it was that they had no emotional reactions. Dr. Church said the same. These are their alienists, not ours. These boys could tell this gruesome story without a change of countenance, without the slightest feelings. There were no emotional reactions to it. What was the reason? I do not know. How can I tell why? I know what causes the emotional life. I know it comes from the nerves, the muscles, the endocrine glands, the vegetative system. I know it is the most important part of life. I know it is practically left out of some. I know that without it men cannot live. I know that without it they cannot act with the rest. I know they cannot feel what you feel and what I feel; that they cannot feel the moral shocks which come to men who are educated and who have not been deprived of an emotional system or emotional feelings. I know it, and every person who has honestly studied this subject knows it as well.

Is Dickey Loeb to blame because out of the infinite forces that conspired to form him, the infinite forces that were at work producing him ages before he was born, that because out of these infinite combinations he was born without it? If he is, then there should be a new definition for justice. Is he to blame for what he did not have and never had? Is he to blame that his machine is imperfect? Who is to blame? I do not know. I have never in my life been interested so much in fixing blame as I have in relieving people from blame. I am not wise enough to fix it. I know that somewhere in the past that entered into him something missed. It may be defective nerves. It may be a defective heart or liver. It may be defective endocrine glands. I know it is something. I know that nothing happens in this world without a cause.

There are at least two theories of man's responsibility. There may be more. There is the old theory that if a man does something it is because he willfully, purposely, maliciously, and with a malignant heart sees fit to do it. And that goes back to the possession of man by devils. The old indictments used to read that a man being possessed of a devil did so and so. But why was he possessed with the devil? Did he invite him in? Could he help it? Very few half-civilized people believe that doctrine anymore. Science has been at work, humanity has been at work, scholarship has been at work, and intelligent people now know that every human being is the product of the endless heredity back of him and the infinite environment around him. He is made as he is and he is the sport of all that goes before him and is applied to him, and under the same stress and storm, you would act one way and I act another, and poor Dickey Loeb another.

Dr. Church said so and Dr. Singer said so, and it is the truth. Take a normal boy, Your Honor. Do you suppose he could have taken a boy into an automobile without any reason and hit him over the head and killed him? I might just as well ask you whether you thought the sun could shine at midnight in this latitude. It is not a part of normality. Something was wrong. I am asking Your Honor not to visit the grave and dire and terrible misfortunes of Dickey Loeb and Nathan Leopold upon these two boys. I do not know where to place it. I know it is somewhere in the infinite economy of nature, and if I were wise enough I could find it. I know it is there, and to say that because they are as they are you should hang them, is brutality and cruelty, and savors of the fang and claw.

Now, Your Honor is familiar with Chicago the same as I am, and I am willing to admit right here and now that the two ablest alienists in Chicago are Dr. Church and Dr. Patrick. There may be abler ones, but we lawyers do not know them.

And I will go further: if my friend Crowe had not got to them first, I would have tried to get them. There is no question about it at all. And I say that, Your Honor, without casting the slightest reflection on either of them, for I really have a high regard for them, and aside from that a deep friendship for Dr. Church. And I have considerable regard for Dr. Singer.

We could not get them, and Mr. Crowe was very wise, and he deserves a great deal of credit for the industry, the research, and the thoroughness that he and his staff have used in detecting this terrible crime. He worked with intelligence and rapidity. If here and there he trampled on the edges of the Constitution I am not going to talk about it here. If he did it, he is not the first one in that office and probably will not be the last who will do it, so let that go. A great many people in this world believe the end justifies the means. I don't know but that I do myself. And that is the reason I never want to take the side of the prosecution, because I might harm an individual. I am sure the state will live anyhow.

On that Sunday afternoon before we had a chance, he got in two alienists, Church and Patrick, and also called Dr. Krohn, and they sat around hearing these boys tell their stories, and that is all. Your Honor, they were not holding an examination. They were holding an inquest, and nothing else. It has not the slightest reference to, or earmarks of, an examination for sanity. It was just an inquest; a little premature, but still an inquest.

What is the truth about it? What did Patrick say? He said that it was not a good opportunity for examination. What did Church say? I read from his own book what was necessary for an examination, and he said that it was not a good opportunity for an examination. What did Krohn say? "It was a fine opportunity for an examination," the best he had ever heard of, or that ever anybody had, because their souls were stripped naked. Krohn is not an alienist. He is an orator. He said, because their souls were naked to them. Well, if Krohn's was naked, there would not be much to show. But Patrick and Church said that the conditions were unfavorable for an examination, that they never would choose it, that their opportunities were poor. And yet Krohn states the contrary. Krohn, who by his own admissions, for sixteen years has not been a physician, but has used a license for the sake of haunting these courts, civil and criminal, and going up and down the land peddling perjury. He has told Your Honor what he has done, and there is scarcely a child on the street who does not know it, there is not a judge in the court who does not know it; there is not a lawyer at the bar who does not know it; there is not a physician in Chicago who does not know it; and I am willing to stake the lives of these two boys on the court knowing it, and I will throw my own in for good measure. What else did he say, in which the state's alienists dispute him?

Both of them say that these boys showed no adequate emotion. Krohn said they did. One boy fainted. They had been in the hands of the state's attorney for sixty hours. They had been in the hands of policemen, lawyers, detectives, stenographers, inquisitors, and newspapermen for sixty hours, and one of them fainted. Well, the only person who is entirely without emotions is a dead man. You cannot live without breathing and some emotional responses. Krohn says, "Why, Loeb had emotion. He was polite; begged our pardon; got up from his chair"; even Dr. Krohn knows better than that. I fancy if Your Honor goes into an elevator where there is a lady he takes off his hat. Is that out of emotion for the lady or is it habit? You say, "Please," and "thank you," because of habit. Emotions haven't the slightest thing to do with it. Mr. Leopold has good manners. Mr. Loeb has good manners. They have been taught them. They have lived them. That does not mean that they are emotional. It means training. That is all it means. And Dr. Krohn knew it.

Krohn told the story of this interview and he told almost twice as much as the other two men who sat there and heard it. And how he told it, how he told it! When he testified my mind carried me back to the time when I was a kid, which was some years ago, and we used to eat watermelons. I have seen little boys take a rind of watermelon and cover their whole faces with water, eat it, devour it, and have the time of their lives, up to their ears in watermelon. And when I heard Dr. Krohn testify in this case, to take the blood of these two boys, I could see his mouth water with the joy it gave him, and he showed all the delight and pleasure of myself and my young companions when we ate watermelon.

I can imagine a psychiatrist, a real one who knows the mechanism of man, who knows life and its machinery, who knows the misfortunes of youth, who knows the stress and the strain of adolescence which comes to every boy and overpowers so many, who knows the weird fantastic world that hedges around the life of a child; I can imagine a psychiatrist who might honestly think that under the crude definitions of the law the defendants were sane and knew the difference between right and wrong.

Without any consideration of the lives and the trainings of these boys, without any evidence from experts, I have tried to make a plain statement of the facts of this case, and I believe, as I have said repeatedly, that no one can honestly study the facts and conclude that anything but diseased minds was responsible for this terrible act. Let us see how far we can account for it, Your Honor.

The mind, of course, is an illusive thing. Whether it exists or not no one can tell. It cannot be found as you find the brain. Its relation to the brain and the nervous system is uncertain. It simply means the activity of the body, which is coordinated with the brain. But when we do find from human conduct that we believe there is a diseased mind, we naturally speculate on how it came about. And we wish to find always, if possible, the reason why it is so. We may find it, we may not find it; because the unknown is infinitely wider and larger than the known, both as to the human mind and as to almost everything else in the universe.

I have tried to study the lives of these two most unfortunate boys. Three months ago, if their friends and the friends of the family had been asked to pick out the most promising lads of their acquaintance, they probably would have picked these two boys. With every opportunity, with plenty of wealth, they would have said that those two would succeed. In a day, by an act of madness, all this is destroyed, until the best they can hope for now is a life of silence and pain, continuing to the end of their years.

How did it happen?

Let us take Dickie Loeb first.

I do not claim to know how it happened; I have sought to find out. I know that something, or some combination of things, is responsible for his mad act. I know that there are no accidents in nature. I know that effect follows cause. I know that if I were wise enough, and knew enough about this case, I could lay my finger on the cause. I will do the best I can, but it is largely speculation.

The child, of course, is born without knowledge. Impressions are made upon its mind as it goes along. Dickie Loeb was a child of wealth and opportunity. Over and over in this court Your Honor has been asked, and other courts have been asked, to consider boys who have no chance; they have been asked to consider the poor, whose home had been the street, with no education and no opportunity in life, and they have done it, and done it rightfully.

But Your Honor, it is just as often a great misfortune to be the child of the rich as it is to be the child of the poor. Wealth has its misfortunes. Too much, too great opportunity and advantage given to a child has its misfortunes. Can I find what was wrong? I think I can. Here was a boy at a tender age, placed in the hands of a governess, intellectual, vigorous, devoted, with a strong ambition for the welfare of this boy. He was pushed in his studies, as plants are forced in hothouses. He had no pleasures, such as a boy should have, except as they were gained by lying and cheating. Now, I am not criticizing the nurse. I suggest that some day Your Honor look at her picture. It explains her fully. Forceful, brooking no interference, she loved the boy, and her ambition was that he should reach the highest perfection. No time to pause, no time to stop from one book to another, no time to have those pleasures which a boy ought to have to create a normal life. And what happened?

Your Honor, what would happen? Nothing strange or unusual. This nurse was with him all the time, except when he stole out at night, from two to fourteen years of age, and it is instructive to read her letter to show her attitude. It speaks volumes; tells exactly the relation between these two people. He, scheming and planning as healthy boys would do, to get out from under her restraint. She, putting before him the best books, which children generally do not want; and he, when she was not looking, reading detective stories, which he devoured, story after story, in his young life. Of all of this there can be no question. What is the result? Every story he read was a story of crime. We have a statute in this state, passed only last year, if I recall it, which forbids minors reading stories of crime. Why? There is only one reason. Because the legislature in its wisdom felt that it would produce criminal tendencies in the boys who read them. The legislature of this state has given its opinion, and forbidden boys to read these books. He read them day after day. He never stopped. While he was passing through college at Ann Arbor he was still reading them. When he was a senior he read them, and almost nothing else.

Now, these facts are beyond dispute. He early developed the tendency to mix with crime, to be a detective; as a little boy shadowing people on the street; as a little child going out with his fantasy of being the head of a band of criminals and directing them on the street. How did this grow and develop in him? Let us see. It seems to me as natural as the day following the night. Every detective story is a story of a sleuth getting the best of it; trailing some unfortunate individual through devious ways until his victim is finally landed in jail or stands on the gallows. They all show how smart the detective is, and where the criminal himself falls down.

This boy early in his life conceived the idea that there could be a perfect crime, one that nobody could ever detect; that there could be one where the detective did not land his game; a perfect crime. He had been interested in the story of Charley Ross, who was kidnapped. He was interested in these things all his life. He believed in his childish way that a crime could be so carefully planned that there would be no detection, and his idea was to plan and accomplish a perfect crime. It would involve kidnapping, and involve murder.

They wanted to commit a perfect crime. There had been growing in this brain, dwarfed and twisted, not due to any wickedness of Dickie Loeb, for he is a child. It grew as he grew; it grew from those around him; it grew from the lack of the proper training until it possessed him. He believed he could beat the police. He believed he could plan the perfect crime. He had thought of it and talked of it for years. Had talked of it as a child; had worked at it as child, and this sorry act of his, utterly irrational and motiveless, a plan to commit a perfect crime which must contain kidnapping, and there must be ransom, or else it could not be perfect, and they must get the money.

We might as well be honest with ourselves, Your Honor. Before I would tie a noose around the neck of a boy I would try to call back into my mind the emotions of youth. I would try to remember what the world looked like to me when I was a child. I would try to remember how strong were these instinctive, persistent emotions that moved my life. I would try to remember how weak and inefficient was youth in the presence of the surging, controlling feelings of the child.

But, Your Honor, that is not all there is to boyhood. Nature is strong and she is pitiless. She works in her own mysterious way, and we are her victims. We have not much to do with it ourselves. Nature takes this job in hand, and we play our parts. In the words of old Omar Khayyám, we are only

> Impotent pieces in the game He plays
> Upon this checkerboard of nights and days,
> Hither and thither moves, and checks, and slays,
> And one by one back in the closet lays.

What had this boy to do with it? He was not his own father; he was not his own mother; he was not his own grandparents. All of this was handed to him. He did not surround himself with governesses and wealth. He did not make himself. And yet he is to be compelled to pay.

For God's sake, are we crazy? In the face of history, of every line of philosophy, against the teaching of every religionist and seer and prophet the world has ever given us, we are still doing what our barbaric ancestors did when they came out of the caves and the woods.

Your Honor, I am almost ashamed to talk about it. I can hardly imagine that we are in the twentieth century. And yet there are men who seriously say that for what Nature has done, for what life has done, for what training has done, you should hang these boys.

I say this again, without finding fault with his parents, for whom I have the highest regard, and who doubtless did the best they could. They might have done better if they had not had so much money. I do not know. Great wealth often curses all who touch it.

I catch myself many and many a time repeating phrases of my childhood, and I have not quite got into my second childhood yet. I have caught myself doing this while I still could catch myself. It means nothing. We may have all the dreams and visions and build all the castles we wish, but the castles of youth should be discarded with youth, and when they linger to the time when boys should think wiser things, then it indicates a diseased mind. "When I was young I thought as a child, I spoke as a child, I understood as a child; but now I have put off childish things," said the Psalmist twenty centuries ago. It is when these dreams of boyhood, these fantasies of youth still linger, and the growing boy is still a child, a child in emotion, a child in feeling, a child in hallucinations that you can say that it is the dreams and the hallucinations of childhood that are responsible for his conduct. There is not an act in all this horrible tragedy that was not the act of a child, the act of a child wandering around in the morning of life, moved by the new feelings of a boy, moved by the uncontrolled impulses which his teaching was not strong enough to take care of, moved by the dreams and the hallucinations which haunt the brain of a child. I say, Your Honor, that it would be the height of cruelty, of injustice, of wrong and barbarism to visit the penalty upon this poor boy.

This boy needed more of home, more love, more directing. He needed to have his emotions awakened. He needed guiding hands along the serious road that youth must travel. Had these been given him, he would not be here today. Now, Your Honor, I want to speak of the other lad, Babe.

Babe is somewhat older than Dick, and is a boy of remarkable mind, away beyond his years. He is a sort of freak in this direction, as in others; a boy without emotions, a boy obsessed of philosophy, a boy obsessed of learning, busy every minute of his life.

He went through school quickly; he went to college young; he could learn faster than almost everybody else. His emotional life was lacking, as every alienist and witness in this case excepting Dr. Krohn has told you. He was just a half boy, in intellect, an intellectual machine going without balance and without a governor, seeking to find out everything there was in life intellectually; seeking to solve every philosophy, but using his intellect only.

Of course his family did not understand him; few men would. His mother died when he was young; he had plenty of money, everything was given to him that he wanted. Both these boys with unlimited money; both these boys with automobiles; both of these boys with every luxury around them and in front of them. They grew up in this environment.

Babe took to philosophy. I call him Babe, not because I want it to affect Your Honor, but because everybody else does. He is the youngest of the family and I suppose that is why he got his nickname. We will call him a man. Mr. Crowe thinks it is easier to hang a man than a boy, and so I will call him a man if I can think of it.

He grew up in this way. He became enamored of the philosophy of Nietzsche.

Your Honor, I have read almost everything that Nietzsche ever wrote. He was a man of a wonderful intellect; the most original philosopher of the last century. Nietzsche believed that some time the superman would be born, that evolution was working toward the superman.

He wrote one book, *Beyond Good and Evil,* which was a criticism of all moral codes as the world understands them; a treatise holding that the intelligent man is beyond good and evil, that the laws for good and the laws for evil do not apply to those who approach the superman. He wrote on the will to power. Nathan Leopold is not the only boy who has read Nietzsche. He may be the only one who was influenced in the way that he was influenced.

At seventeen, at sixteen, at eighteen, while healthy boys were playing baseball or working on the farm, or doing odd jobs, Babe was reading Nietzsche, a boy who never should have seen it, at that early age.

Nietzsche held a contemptuous, scornful attitude to all those things which the young are taught as important in life; a fixing of new values which are not the values by which any normal child has ever yet been reared. Nietzsche's attitude is but a philosophical dream, containing more or less truth, that was not meant by anyone to be applied to life.

Nietzsche says, "The morality of the master class is irritating to the taste of the present day because of its fundamental principle that a man has obligation only to his equals; that he may act to all of lower rank and to all that are foreign, as he pleases."

In other words, man has no obligations; he may do with all other men and all other boys, and all society, as he pleases. The superman was a creation of Nietzsche.

The supermanlike qualities lie not in their genius, but in their freedom from scruple. They rightly felt themselves to be above the law. What they thought was right, not because sanctioned by any law, beyond themselves, but because they did it. So the superman will be a law unto himself. What he does will come from the will and superabundant power within him.

Here is a boy at sixteen or seventeen becoming obsessed with these doctrines. There isn't any question about the facts. Their own witnesses tell it and every one of our witnesses tell it. It was not a casual bit of philosophy with him; it was his life. He believed in a superman. He and Dickie Loeb were the supermen. There might have been others, but they were two, and two chums. The ordinary commands of society were not for him.

Many of us read this philosophy but know that it has no actual application to life; but not he. It became a part of his being. It was his philosophy. He lived it and practiced it; he thought it applied to him, and he could not have believed it excepting that it either caused a diseased mind or was the result of a diseased mind.

Here is a boy who by day and by night, in season and out, was talking of the superman, owing no obligations to anyone; whatever gave him pleasure he should do, believing it just as another man might believe a religion or any philosophical theory.

You remember that I asked Dr. Church about these religious cases and he said, "Yes, many people go to the insane asylum on account of them," that "they place a literal meaning on parables and believe them thoroughly"? I asked Dr. Church, whom again I say I believe to be an honest man, and an intelligent man, I asked him whether the same thing might be done or might come from a philosophical belief, and he said, "If one believed it strongly enough."

And I asked him about Nietzsche. He said he knew something of Nietzsche, something of his responsibility for the war, for which he perhaps was not responsible. He said he knew something about his doctrines. I asked him what became of him, and he said he was insane for fifteen years just before the time of his death. His very doctrine is a species of insanity.

Here is a man, a wise man, perhaps not wise, but a brilliant, thoughtful man who has made his impress upon the world. Every student of philosophy knows him. His own doctrines made him a maniac. And here is a young boy, in the adolescent age, harassed by everything that harasses children, who takes this philosophy and believes it literally. It is a part of his life. It is his life. Do you suppose this mad act could have been done by him in any other way? What could he have to win from this homicide?

A boy with a beautiful home, with automobiles, a graduate of college, going to Europe, and then to study law at Harvard; as brilliant in intellect as any boy that you could find; a boy with every prospect that life might hold out to him; and yet he goes out and commits this weird, strange, wild, mad act, that he may die on the gallows or live in a prison cell until he dies of old age or disease.

He did it, obsessed of an idea, perhaps to some extent influenced by what has not been developed publicly in this case—perversions that were present in the boy. Both signs of insanity, both, together with this act, proving a diseased mind.

Is there any question about what was responsible for him?

What else could be? A boy in his youth, with every promise that the world could hold out before him, wealth and position and intellect, yes, genius, scholarship, nothing that he could not obtain, and he throws it away, and mounts the gallows or goes into a cell for life. It is too foolish to talk about. Can Your Honor imagine a sane brain doing it? Can you imagine it coming from anything but a diseased mind? Can you imagine it is any part of normality? And yet, Your Honor, you are asked to hang a boy of his age, abnormal, obsessed of dreams and visions, a philosophy that destroyed his life, when there is no sort of question in the world as to what caused his downfall.

I know, Your Honor, that every atom of life in all this universe is bound up together. I know that a pebble cannot be thrown into the ocean without disturbing every drop of water in the sea. I know that every life is inextricably mixed and woven with every other life. I know that every influence, conscious and unconscious, acts and reacts on every living organism, and that no one can fix the blame. I know that all life is a series of infinite chances, which sometimes result one way and sometimes another. I have not the infinite wisdom that can fathom it, neither has any other human brain. But I do know that if back of it is a power that made it, that power alone can tell, and if there is no power, then it is an infinite chance which man cannot solve.

Why should this boy's life be bound up with Frederick Nietzsche, who died thirty years ago, insane, in Germany? I don't know. I only know it is. I know that no man who ever wrote a line that I read failed to influence me to some extent. I know that every life I ever touched influenced me, and I influenced it; and that it is not given to me to unravel the infinite causes and say, "This is I, and this is you." I am responsible for so much; and you are responsible for so much. I know that in the infinite universe everything has its place and that the smallest particle is a part of all. Tell me that you can visit the wrath of fate and chance and life and eternity upon a nineteen-year-old boy! If you could, justice would be a travesty and mercy a fraud.

There is something else in this case, Your Honor, that is stronger still. There is a large element of chance in life. I know I will die. I don't know when; I don't know how; I don't know where; and I don't want to know. I know it will come. I know that it depends on infinite chances. Did I make myself? And control my fate? I cannot fix my death unless I commit suicide, and I cannot do that because the will to live is too strong; I know it depends on infinite chances.

Take the rabbit running through the woods; a fox meets him at a certain fence. If the rabbit had not started when it did, it would not have met the fox and would have lived longer. If the fox had started later or earlier it would not have met the rabbit and its fate would have been different.

My death will depend upon chances. It may be by the taking in of a germ; it may be a pistol; it may be the decaying of my faculties, and all that makes life; it may be a cancer; it may be any one of an indefinite number of things, and where I am at a certain time, and whether I take in that germ, and the condition of my system when I breathe is an accident which is sealed up in the book of fate and which no human being can open.

These boys, neither one of them, could possibly have committed this act excepting by coming together. It was not the act for one; it was the act of two. It was the act of their planning, their conniving, their believing in each other; their thinking themselves supermen. Without it they could not have done it. It would not have happened. Their parents happened to meet, these boys happened to meet; some sort of chemical alchemy operated so that they cared for each other, and poor Bobby Franks's dead body was found in the culvert as a result. Neither of them could have done it alone.

I want to call your attention, Your Honor, to the two letters in this case which settle this matter to my mind conclusively; not only the condition of these boys' minds, but the terrible fate that overtook them.

Your Honor, I am sorry for poor Bobby Franks, and I think anybody who knows me knows that I am not saying it simply to talk. I am sorry for the bereaved father and the bereaved mother, and I would like to know what they would do with these poor unfortunate lads who are here in this court today. I know something of them, of their lives, of their charity, of their ideas, and nobody here sympathizes with them more than I.

On the twenty-first day of May, poor Bobby Franks, stripped and naked, was left in a culvert down near the Indiana line. I know it came through the mad act of mad boys. Mr. Savage told us that Franks, if he had lived, would have been a great man and have accomplished much. I want to leave this thought with Your Honor now. I do not know what Bobby Franks would have been had he grown to be a man. I do not know the laws that control one's growth. Sometimes, Your Honor, a boy of great promise is cut off in his early youth. Sometimes he dies and is placed in a culvert. Sometimes a boy of great promise stands on a trap-door and is hanged by the neck until dead. Sometimes he dies of diphtheria. Death somehow pays no attention to age, sex, prospects, wealth, or intellect.

And I want to say this, that the death of poor little Bobby Franks should not be in vain. Would it mean anything if on account of that death, these two boys were taken out and a rope tied around their necks and they died felons? Would that show that Bobby Franks had a purpose in his life and a purpose in his death? No, Your Honor, the unfortunate and tragic death of this weak young lad should mean something. It should mean an appeal to the fathers and the mothers, an appeal to the teachers, to the religious guides, to society at large. It should mean an appeal to all of them to appraise children, to understand the emotions that control them, to understand the ideas that possess them, to teach them to avoid the pitfalls of life.

I have discussed somewhat in detail these two boys separately. Their coming together was the means of their undoing. Your Honor is familiar with the facts in reference to their association. They had a weird, almost impossible relationship. Leopold, with his obsession of the superman, had repeatedly said that Loeb was his idea of the superman. He had the attitude toward him that one has to his most devoted friend, or that a man has to a lover. Without the combination of these two, nothing of this sort probably could have happened. It is not necessary for us, Your Honor, to rely upon words to prove the condition of these boys' minds, and to prove the effect of this strange and fatal relationship between these two boys.

It is mostly told in a letter which the state itself introduced in this case. Not the whole story, but enough of it is shown, so that no intelligent, thoughtful person could fail to realize what was the relation between them and how they had played upon each other to effect their downfall and their ruin. I want to read this letter once more, a letter which was introduced by the state, a letter dated October 9, a month and three days before their trip to Ann Arbor, and I want the court to say in his own mind whether this letter was anything but the products of a diseased mind, and if it does not show a relationship that was responsible for this terrible homicide. This was written by Leopold to Loeb. They lived close together, only a few blocks from each other; saw each other every day, but Leopold wrote him this letter:

October 9, 1923.

Dear Dick:

In view of our former relations, I take it for granted that its [*sic*] unnecessary to make any excuse for writing you at this time, and still I am going to state my reasons for so doing, as this may turn out to be a long letter, and I don't want to cause you the inconvenience of reading it all to find out what it contains if you are not interested in the subjects dealt with.

First, I am enclosing the document which I mentioned to you today, and which I will explain later. Second, I am going to tell you of a new fact which has come up since our discussion. And third, I am going to put in writing what my attitude toward our present relations, with a view of avoiding future possible misunderstandings, and in the hope (though I think it rather vain) that possibly we may have misunderstood each other, and can yet clear this matter up.

Now, as to the first, I wanted you this afternoon, and still want you, to feel that we are on an equal footing legally, and therefore, I purposely committed the same tort of which you were guilty, the only difference being that in your case the facts would be harder to prove than in mine, should I deny them. The enclosed document should secure you against changing my mind in admitting the facts, if the matter should come up, as it would prove to any court that they were true.

As to the second. On your suggestion I immediately phoned Dick Rubel, and speaking from a paper prepared beforehand (to be sure of the exact wording) said: "Dick, when we were together yesterday, did I tell you that Dick (Loeb) had told me the things which I then told you, or that it was merely my opinion that I believed them to be so?"

I asked this twice to be sure he understood, and on the same answer both times (which I took down as he spoke) felt that he did understand.

He replied: "No, you did not tell me that Dick told you these things, but said that they were in your opinion true."

He further denied telling you subsequently that I had said that they were gleaned from conversation with you, and I then told him that he was quite right, that you never had told me. I further told him that this was merely your suggestion of how to settle a question of fact that he was in no way implicated, and that neither of us would be angry with him at his reply. (I imply your assent to this.)

This of course proves that you were mistaken this afternoon in the question of my having actually and technically broken confidence, and voids my apology, which I made contingent on proof of this matter.

Now, as to the third, last, and most important question. When you came to my home this afternoon I expected either to break friendship with you or attempt to kill you unless you told me why you acted as you did yesterday.

You did, however, tell me, and hence the question shifted to the fact that I would act as before if you persisted in thinking me treacherous, either in act (which you waived if Dick's opinion went with mine) or in intention.

Now, I apprehend, though here I am not quite sure, that you said that you did not think me treacherous in intent, nor ever have, but that you considered me in the wrong and expected such statement from me. This statement I unconditionally refused to make until such time as I may become convinced of its truth.

However, the question of our relation I think must be in your hands (unless the above conceptions are mistaken), inasmuch as you have satisfied first one and then the other requirement, upon which I agreed to refrain from attempting to kill you or refusing to continue our friendship. Hence I have no reason not to continue to be on friendly terms with you, and would under ordinary conditions continue as before.

The only question, then, is with you. You demand me to perform an act, namely, state that I acted wrongly. This I refuse. Now it is up to you to inflict the penalty for this refusal at your discretion, to break friendship, inflict physical punishment, or anything else you like, or on the other hand to continue as before.

The decision, therefore, must rest with you. This is all of my opinion on the right and wrong of the matter.

Now comes a practical question. I think that I would ordinarily be expected to, and in fact do expect to continue my attitude toward you, as before, until I learn either by direct words or by conduct on your part which way your decision has been formed. This I shall do.

Now a word of advice. I do not wish to influence your decision either way, but I do want to warn you that in case you deem it advisable to discontinue our friendship, that in both our interests extreme care must be had. The motif of "A falling out of—" would be sure to be popular, which is patently undesirable and forms an irksome but unavoidable bond between us.

Therefore, it is, in my humble opinion, expedient, though our breech need be no less real in fact, yet to observe the conventionalities, such as salutation on the street and a general appearance of at least not unfriendly relations on all occasions when we may be thrown together in public.

Now, Dick, I am going to make a request to which I have perhaps no right, and yet which I dare to make also for "Auld Lang Syne." Will you, if not too inconvenient, let me know your answer (before I leave tomorrow) on the last count? This, to which I have no right, would greatly help my peace of mind in the next few days when it is most necessary to me. You can if you will merely call up my home before 12 noon and leave a message saying, "Dick says yes," if you wish our relations to continue as before, and "Dick says no," if not.

It is unnecessary to add that your decision will of course have no effect on my keeping to myself our confidences of the past, and that I regret the whole affair more than I can say.

Hoping not to have caused you too much trouble in reading this, I am (for the present), as ever

"BABE."

Now, I undertake to say that under any interpretation of this case, taking into account all the things Your Honor knows, that have not been made public, or leaving them out, nobody can interpret that letter excepting on the theory of a diseased mind, and with it goes this strange document which was referred to in the letter: "I, Nathan F. Leopold Jr., being under no duress or compulsion, do hereby affirm and declare that on this, the ninth day of October, 1923, I for reasons of my own locked the door of the room in which I was with one Richard A. Loeb, with the intent of blocking his only feasible mode of egress, and that I further indicated my intention of applying physical force upon the person of the said Richard A. Loeb if necessary to carry out my design, to wit, to block his only feasible mode of egress."

There is nothing in this case, whether heard alone by the court or heard in public, that can explain these documents, on the theory that the defendants were normal human beings.

I want to call your attention then to an extract from another letter by Babe, if I may be permitted to call him Babe, until you hang him. On October 10, this is written by Leopold on the Twentieth Century train, the day after the other letter was written, and in it he says:

> . . . now, that is all that is in point to our controversy. But I am going to add a little more in an effort to explain my system of the Nietzschean philosophy with regard to you.
>
> It may not have occurred to you why a mere mistake in judgment on your part should be treated as a crime when on the part of another it should not be so considered? Here are the reasons. In formulating a superman he is, on account of certain superior qualities inherent in him, exempted from the ordinary laws which govern ordinary men. He is not liable for anything he may do, whereas others would be, except for the one crime that it is possible for him to commit, to make a mistake.
>
> Now obviously any code which conferred upon an individual or upon a group extraordinary privileges without also putting on him extraordinary responsibility, would be unfair and bad. Therefore, the superman is held to have committed a crime every time he errs in judgment, a mistake excusable in others. But you may say that you have previously made mistakes which did not treat as crimes. This is true. To cite an example, the other night you expressed the opinion, and insisted, that Marcus Aurelius Antonius was practi-

cally the founder of Stoicism. In so doing you committed a crime. But it was a slight crime, and I chose to forgive it. I have, and had before that, forgiven the crime which you committed in committing the error in judgment which caused the whole train of events. I did not and do not wish to charge you with crime, but I feel justified in using any of the consequences of your crime for which you are held responsible, to my advantage. This and only this I did, so you see how careful you must be.

Is that the letter of a normal eighteen-year-old boy, or is it the letter of a diseased brain? Is that the letter of boys acting as boys should, and thinking as boys should, or is it the letter of one whose philosophy has taken possession of him, who understands that what the world calls a crime is something that the superman may do, who believes that the only crime the superman can commit is to make a mistake? He believed it. He was immature. It possessed him. It was manifest in the strange compact that the court already knows about between these two boys, by which each was to yield something and each was to give something. Out of that compact and out of these diseased minds grew this terrible crime.

I submit the facts do not rest on the evidence of these boys alone. It is proven by the writings; it is proven by every act. It is proven by their companions, and there can be no question about it.

We brought into this courtroom a number of their boyfriends, whom they had known day by day, who had associated with them in the club-house, were their constant companions, and they tell the same stories. They tell the story that neither of these two boys was responsible for his conduct.

Maremont, whom the state first called, one of the oldest of the boys, said that Leopold had never had any judgment of any sort. They talked about the superman. Leopold argued his philosophy. It was a religion with him. But as to judgment of things in life he had none. He was developed intellectually, wanting emotionally, developed in those things which a boy does not need and should not have at his age, but absolutely void of the healthy feelings, of the healthy instincts of practical life that are necessary to the child.

We called not less than ten or twelve of their companions and all of them testified the same: Dickie Loeb was not allowed by his companions the privileges of his class because of his childishness and his lack of judgment.

As to the standing of these boys amongst their fellows, that they were irresponsible, that they had no judgment, that they were childish, that their acts were strange, that their beliefs were impossible for boys, is beyond question in this case.

And what did they do on the other side?

It was given out that they had a vast army of witnesses. They called three. A professor who talked with Leopold only upon his law studies, and two others who admitted all that we said, on cross-examination, and the rest were dismissed. So it leaves all of this beyond dispute and admitted in this case.

Now both sides have called alienists and I will refer to that for a few moments. I shall only take a little time with the alienists.

The facts here are plain; when these boys had made the confession on Sunday afternoon before their counsel or their friends had any chance to see them, Mr. Crowe sent out for four men. He sent out for Dr. Patrick, who is an alienist; Dr. Church, who is an alienist; Dr. Krohn, who is a witness, a testifier; and Dr. Singer, who is pretty good, I would not criticize him but would not class him with Patrick and with Church.

I have said to Your Honor that in my opinion he sent for the two ablest men in Chicago as far as the public knows them, Dr. Church and Dr. Patrick. You heard Dr. Church's testimony. Dr. Church is an honest man though an alienist. Under cross-examination he admitted every position which I took. He admitted the failure of emotional life in these boys; he admitted its importance; he admitted the importance of beliefs strongly held in human conduct; he said himself that if he could get at all the facts he would understand what was back of this strange murder. Every single position that we have claimed in this case Dr. Church admitted.

Dr. Singer did the same. The only difference between them was this: it took but one question to get Dr. Church to admit it, and it took ten to a dozen to get Dr. Singer. He objected and hedged and ran and quibbled. There could be no mistake about it, and Your Honor heard it in this courtroom. He sought every way he could to avoid the truth, and when it came to the point that he could not dodge any longer, he admitted every proposition just exactly the same as Dr. Church admitted them: the value of emotional life; its effect on conduct; that it was the ruling thing in conduct, as every person knows who is familiar with psychology and who is familiar with the human system.

Could there be any doubt, Your Honor, but what both those witnesses, Church and Singer, or any doubt but what Patrick would have testified for us? Now what did they do in their examination? What kind of a chance did these alienists have? It is perfectly obvious that they had none. Church, Patrick, Krohn went into a room with these two boys who had been in the possession of the state's attorney's office for sixty hours; they were surrounded by policemen, were surrounded by guards and detectives and state's attorneys; twelve or fifteen of them, and here they told their story. Of course this audience had a friendly attitude toward them. I know my friend Judge Crowe had a friendly attitude because I saw divers, various and sundry pictures of Prosecutor Crowe taken with these boys.

When I first saw them I believed it showed friendship for the boys, but now I am inclined to think that he had them taken just as a lawyer who goes up in the country fishing has his picture taken with his catch. The boys had been led doubtless to believe that these people were friends. They were taken there, in the presence of all this crowd. What was done? The boys told their story, and that was all. Of course, Krohn remembered a lot that did not take place, and we would expect that of him; and he forgot much that did take place and we would expect that of him, too. So far as the honest witnesses were concerned, they said that not a word was spoken excepting a little conversation upon birds and the relation of the story that they had already given to the state's attorney; and from that, and nothing else, both Patrick and Church said they showed no reaction as ordinary persons should show it, and intimated clearly that the commission of the crime itself would put them on inquiry as to whether these boys were mentally right; both admitted that the conditions surrounding them made the right kind of examination impossible; both admitted that they needed a better chance to form a reliable opinion.

The most they said was that at this time they saw no evidence of insanity.

Now, Your Honor, no experts, and no alienists with any chance to examine, have testified that these boys were normal.

Singer did a thing more marvelous still. He never saw these boys until he came into this court, excepting when they were brought down in violation of their constitutional rights to the office of Judge Crowe, after they had been turned over to the jailer, and there various questions were asked them, and to all of these the boys replied that they respectfully refused to answer on advice of counsel. And yet that was enough for Singer.

Your Honor, if these boys had gone to the office of any one of these eminent gentlemen, had been taken by their parents or gone by themselves, and the doctors had seriously tried to find out whether there was anything wrong about their minds, how would they have done it? They would have taken them patiently and carefully. They would have sought to get their confidence. They would have listened to their story. They would have listened to it in the attitude of a father listening to his child. You know it. Every doctor knows it. In no other way could they find out their mental condition. And the men who are honest with this question have admitted it.

And yet Dr. Krohn will testify that they had the best chance in the world, when his own associates, sitting where they were, said that they did not.

Your Honor, nobody's life or liberty or property should be taken from them upon an examination like that. It was not an examination. It was simply an effort to get witnesses, regardless of facts, who might at some time come into court and give their testimony, to take these boys' lives.

Now, I imagine that in closing this case Judge Crowe will say that our witnesses mainly came from the East. That is true. And he is responsible for it. I am not blaming him, but he is responsible for it. There are other alienists in Chicago, and the evidence shows that we had the boys examined by numerous ones in Chicago. We wanted to get the best. Did we get them?

Your Honor knows that the place where a man lives does not affect his truthfulness or his ability. We brought the man who stands probably above all of them, and who certainly is far superior to anybody called upon the other side. First of all, we called Dr. William A. White. And who is he? For many years he has been superintendent of the Government Hospital for the Insane in Washington; a man who has written more books, delivered more lectures, and had more honors, and knows this subject better than all of their alienists put together; a man who plainly came here not for money, and who receives for his testimony the same per diem as is paid by the other side; a man who knows his subject, and whose ability and truthfulness must have impressed this court.

It will not do, Your Honor, to say that because Dr. White is not a resident of Chicago that he lies. No man stands higher in the United States, no man is better known than Dr. White, his learning and intelligence was obvious from his evidence in this case.

Who else did we get? Do I need to say anything about Dr. Healy? Is there any question about his integrity? A man who seldom goes into court except upon the order of the court.

Your Honor was connected with the Municipal Court. You know that Dr. Healy was the first man who operated with the courts in the city of Chicago to give aid to the unfortunate youths whose minds were afflicted and who were the victims of the law. His books are known wherever men study boys. His reputation is known all over the United States and in Europe. Compare him and his reputation with Dr. Krohn. Compare it with any other witness that the state called in this case.

Dr. Glueck, who was for years the alienist at Sing Sing, and connected with the penal institutions in the state of New York; a man of eminent attainments and ripe scholarship. No one is his superior.

And Dr. Hulbert, a young man who spent nineteen days in the examination of these boys, together with Dr. Bowen, an eminent doctor in his line from Boston. These two physicians spent all this time getting every detail of these boys' lives, and structures; each one of these alienists took all the time they needed for a thorough examination, without the presence of lawyers, detectives, and policemen. Each one of these psychiatrists tells this court the story, the sad, pitiful story, of the unfortunate minds of these two young lads.

I submit, Your Honor, that there can be no question about the relative value of these two sets of alienists; there can be no question of their means of understanding; there can be no question but that White, Glueck, Hulbert, and Healy knew what they were talking about, for they had every chance to find out. They are either lying to this court, or their opinions good.

On the other hand, not one single man called by the state had any chance to know. He was called in to see these boys, the same as the state would call a hangman: "Here are the boys; officer, do your duty." And that is all there was of it.

Now, Your Honor, I shall pass that subject. I think all of the facts of this extraordinary case, all of the testimony of the alienists, all that Your Honor has seen and heard, all their friends and acquaintances who have come here to enlighten this court, I think all of it shows that this terrible act was the act of immature and diseased brains, the act of children. Nobody can explain it in any other way. No one can imagine it in any other way. It is not possible that it could have happened in any other way. And I submit, Your Honor, that by every law of humanity, by every law of justice, by every feeling of righteousness, by every instinct of pity, mercy, and charity, Your Honor should say that because of the condition of these boys' minds, it would be monstrous to visit upon them the vengeance that is asked by the state.

I want to discuss now another thing which this court must consider and which to my mind is absolutely conclusive in this case. That is, the age of these boys.

I shall discuss it more in detail than I have discussed it before, and I submit, Your Honor, that it is not possible for any court to hang these two boys if he pays any attention whatever to the modern attitude toward the young, if he pays any attention whatever to the precedents in this county, if he pays any attention to the humane instincts which move ordinary men.

I have a list of executions in Cook County beginning in 1840, which I presume covers the first one, because I asked to have it go to the beginning. Ninety poor unfortunate men have given up their lives to stop murder in Chicago. Ninety men have been hanged by the neck until dead, because of the ancient superstition that in some way hanging one man keeps another from committing a crime. The ancient superstition, I say, because I defy the state to point to a criminologist, a scientist, student, who has ever said it. Still we go on, as if human conduct was not influenced and controlled by natural laws the same as all the rest of the universe is the subject of law. We treat crime as if it had no cause. We go on saying, "Hang the unfortunates, and it will end." Was there ever a murder without a cause? Was there ever a crime without a cause? And yet all punishment proceeds upon the theory that there is no cause; and the only way to treat crime is to intimidate every one into goodness and obedience to law. We lawyers are a long way behind.

Crime has its cause. Perhaps all crimes do not have the same cause, but they all have some cause. And people today are seeking to find out the cause. We lawyers never try to find out. Scientists are studying it; criminologists are investigating it; but we lawyers go on and on and on, punishing and hanging and thinking that by general terror we can stamp out crime.

It never occurs to the lawyer that crime has a cause as certainly as disease, and that the way to rationally treat any abnormal condition is to remove the cause.

If a doctor were called on to treat typhoid fever he would probably try to find out what kind of milk or water the patient drank, and perhaps clean out the well so that no one else could get typhoid from the same source. But if a lawyer was called on to treat a typhoid patient, he would give him thirty days in jail, and then he would think that nobody else would ever dare to take it. If the patient got well in fifteen days, he would be kept until his time was up; if the disease was worse at the end of thirty days, the patient would be released because his time was out.

As a rule, lawyers are not scientists. They have learned the doctrine of hate and fear, and they think that there is only one way to make men good, and that is to put them in such terror that they do not dare to be bad. They act unmindful of history, and science, and all the experience of the past.

Still, we are making some progress. Courts give attention to some things that they did not give attention to before.

Once in England they hanged children seven years of age; not necessarily hanged them, because hanging was never meant for punishment; it was meant for an exhibition. If somebody committed a crime, he would be hanged by the head or the heels, it didn't matter much which, at the four crossroads, so that everybody could look at him until his bones were bare, and so that people would be good because they had seen the gruesome result of crime and hate.

Hanging was not necessarily meant for punishment. The culprit might be killed in any other way, and then hanged. Hanging was an exhibition. They were hanged on the highest hill, and hanged at the crossways, and hanged in public places, so that all men could see. If there is any virtue in hanging, that was the logical way, because you cannot awe men into goodness unless they know about the hanging. We have not grown better than the ancients. We have grown more squeamish; we do not like to look at it, that is all. They hanged them at seven years; they hanged them again at eleven and fourteen.

We have raised the age of hanging. We have raised it by the humanity of courts, by the understanding of courts, by the progress in science which at last is reaching the law; and in ninety men hanged in Illinois from its beginning, not one single person under twenty-three was ever hanged upon a plea of guilty, not one. If Your Honor should do this, you would violate every precedent that had been set in Illinois for almost a century. There can be no excuse for it, and no justification for it, because this is the policy of the law which is rooted in the feelings of humanity, which are deep in every human being that thinks and feels. There have been two or three cases where juries have convicted boys younger than this, and where courts on convictions have refused to set aside the sentence because a jury had found it.

Your Honor, what excuse could you possibly have for putting these boys to death? You would have to turn your back on every precedent of the past. You would have to turn your back on the progress of the world. You would have to ignore all human sentiment and feeling, of which I know the court has his full share. You would have to do all this if you would hang boys of eighteen and nineteen years of age who have come into this court and thrown themselves upon your mercy.

Your Honor, I must hasten along, for I will close tonight. I know I should have closed before. Still there seems so much that I would like to say. I do not know whether Your Honor, humane and considerate as I believe you to be, would have disturbed a jury's verdict in his case, but I know that no judge in Cook County ever himself upon a plea of guilty passed judgment of death in a case below the age of twenty-three, and only one at the age of twenty-three was ever hanged on a plea of guilty.

Your Honor, if in this court a boy of eighteen and a boy of nineteen should be hanged on a plea of guilty, in violation of every precedent of the past, in violation of the policy of the law to take care of the young, in violation of all the progress that has been made and of the humanity that has been shown in the care of the young; in violation of the law that places boys in reformatories instead of prisons, if Your Honor in violation of all that and in the face of all the past should stand here in Chicago alone to hang a boy on a plea of guilty, then we are turning our faces backward, toward the barbarism which once possessed the world. If Your Honor can hang a boy at eighteen, some other judge can hang him at seventeen, or sixteen, or fourteen. Someday, if there is any such thing as progress in the world, if there is any spirit of humanity that is working in the hearts of men, someday men would look back upon this as a barbarous age which deliberately set itself in the way of progress, humanity, and sympathy, and committed an unforgivable act.

I do not know how much salvage there is in these two boys, hate to say it in their presence, but what is there to look forward to? I do not know but what Your Honor would be merciful if you tied a rope around their necks and let them die; merciful to them, but not merciful to civilization, and not merciful to those who would be left behind. To spend the balance of their days in prison is mighty little to look forward to, if anything. Is it anything? They may have the hope that as the years roll around they might be released. I do not know. I will be honest with this court as I have tried to be from the beginning. I know that these boys are not fit to be at large. I believe they will not be until they pass through the next stage of life, at forty-five or fifty. Whether they will be then, I cannot tell. I am sure of this; that I will not be here to help them. So far as I am concerned, it is over.

I would not tell this court that I do not hope that some time, when life and age has changed their bodies, as it does, and has changed their emotions, as it does, that they may once more return to life. I would be the last person on earth to close the door of hope to any human being that lives, and least of all to my clients. But what have they to look forward to? Nothing. And I think here of the stanzas of Housman:

> *Now hollow fires burn out to black,*
> *And lights are fluttering low:*
> *Square your shoulders, lift your pack*
> *And leave your friends and go.*
> *O never fear, lads, naught's to dread,*
> *Look not left nor right:*
> *In all the endless road you tread*
> *There's nothing but the night.*

I care not, Your Honor, whether the march begins at the gallows or when the gates of Joliet close upon them, there is nothing but the night, and that is little for any human being to expect. But there are others to be considered. Here are these two families, who have led honest lives, who will bear the name that they bear, and future generations must carry it on. Here is Leopold's father, and this boy was the pride of his life. He watched him, he cared for him, he worked for him; the boy was brilliant and accomplished, he educated him, and he thought that fame and position awaited him, as it should have awaited. It is a hard thing for a father to see his life's hopes crumble into dust.

Should he be considered? Should his brothers be considered? Will it do society any good or make your life safer, or any human being's life safer, if it should be handed down from generation to generation, that this boy, their kin, died upon the scaffold?

And Loeb's, the same. Here is the faithful uncle and brother, who have watched here day by day, while Dickie's father and his mother are too ill to stand this terrific strain, and shall be waiting for a message which means more to them than it can mean to you or me. Shall these be taken into account in this general bereavement?

Now, I must say a word more and then I will leave this with you where I should have left it long ago. None of us are unmindful of the public; courts are not, and juries are not. We placed our fate in the hands of a trained court, thinking that he would be more mindful and considerate than a jury. I cannot say how people feel. I have stood here for three months as one might stand at the ocean trying to sweep back the tide. I hope the seas are subsiding and the wind is falling, and I believe they are, but I wish to make no false pretense to this court. The easy thing and the popular thing to do is to hang my clients. I know it. Men and women who do not think will applaud. The cruel and the thoughtless will approve. It will be easy today; but in Chicago, and reaching out over the length and breadth of the land, more and more fathers and mothers, the humane, the kind, and the hopeful, who are gaining an understanding and asking questions not only about these poor boys but about their own, these will join in no acclaim at the death of my clients. But, Your Honor, what they shall ask may not count. I know the easy way. I know Your Honor stands between the future and the past. I know the future is with me, and what I stand for here; not merely for the lives of these two unfortunate lads, but for all boys and all girls; for all of the young, and as far as possible, for all of the old. I am pleading for life, understanding, charity, kindness, and the infinite mercy that considers all. I am pleading that we overcome cruelty with kindness and hatred with love. I know the future is on my side. Your Honor stands between the past and the future. You may hang these boys; you may hang them by the neck until they are dead. But in doing it you will turn your face toward the past. In doing it you are making it harder for every other boy who in ignorance and darkness must grope his way through the mazes which only childhood knows. In doing it you will make it harder for unborn children. You may save them and make it easier for every child that some time may stand where these boys stand. You will make it easier for every human being with an aspiration and a vision and a hope and a fate. I am pleading for the future; I am pleading for a time when hatred and cruelty will not control the hearts of men. When we can learn by reason and judgment and understanding and faith that all life is worth saving, and that mercy is the highest attribute of man.

I feel that I should apologize for the length of time I have taken. This case may not be as important as I think it is, and I am sure I do not need to tell this court, or to tell my friends, that I would fight just as hard for the poor as for the rich. If I should succeed in saving these boys' lives and do nothing for the progress of the law, I should feel sad, indeed. If I can succeed, my greatest reward and my greatest hope will be that I have done something for the tens of thousands of other boys, or the countless unfortunates who must tread the same road in blind childhood that these poor boys have trod, that I have done something to help human understanding, to temper justice with mercy, to overcome hate with love.

I was reading last night of the aspiration of the old Persian poet, Omar Khayyám. It appealed to me as the highest that can vision. I wish it was in my heart, and I wish it was in the hearts of all:

> *So I be written in the Book of Love,*
> *Do not care about that Book above.*
> *Erase my name or write it as you will,*
> *So I be written in the Book of Love.*

CHAPTER SIX

A Man's World No More

Clara Shortridge Foltz Sends Shockwaves
Through the Turn-of-the-Century Legal Establishment
When She Becomes the First Woman to Do Battle
in California's Courts

In the latter half of the nineteenth century, the idea of women becoming attorneys was beyond foolish to American men, and more than a few women. Lawyers were thought of as bold, brilliant, aggressive, incisive, and ruthless in pursuit of justice and the interests of the client. In the United States of the 1870s, nothing could have been further from the popular conception of what a woman should be. The chief judge of Wisconsin spoke for many when he said that "[r]everence for all womanhood would suffer in the public spectacle" of women practicing law

The numbers speak for themselves. In the 1880 national Census there were only seventy-five women lawyers in the entire country. It took an 1879 act of Congress—sponsored by the senator from California (an attorney)—to allow the first woman to argue before the United States Supreme Court.

It was in this hostile atmosphere that Clara Shortridge Foltz stepped into the breech and forever changed the practice of law. Foltz, married at fifteen, followed her husband on a trek that led from Iowa to Oregon and then to San Jose, California, where they and their four children arrived in time for an economic depression featuring spectacular bank and crop failures. Within a few short years they had a fifth child, and Jeremiah Foltz was gone, abandoning his family and leaving his wife to support the youngsters. In 1878, Foltz, twenty-nine, turned to public lecturing to support herself, filling auditoriums with her rhetoric in support of the women's suffrage movement.

Foltz soon set her sights on becoming an attorney. She wrote to a renowned California trial attorney, seeking a position with his firm, so that she might study the law with an expert. His reply was succinct:

> My dear young friend:
> Excuse my delay in answering your letter asking for permission to enter my law office as a student. My high regard for your parents, and for you, who seem to have no right understanding of what you say you want to undertake, forbids encouraging you in so foolish a pursuit—when you would invite nothing but ridicule if not contempt.
> A woman's place is at home, unless it [is] as a teacher. If you would like a position in our public schools I will be glad to recommend you, for I think you are well qualified.

Not one to be easily discouraged, Foltz went to work in the office of an early male feminist with whom her father had practiced law before becoming a minister. Foltz knew from the beginning that once her studies were completed she would have an even more formidable hurdle to overcome.

The state of California did not allow women to practice law. A law school education or passing a statewide examination was not required to be a member of the bar; the only qualifications were that the applicant be a twenty-one-year-old white male citizen of good moral character, and possess the necessary "learning and ability." Prospective lawyers also had to pass local bar examinations.

Clara convinced a young state senator from her area to introduce a legislative bill she had drafted, "The Women Lawyer's Bill," substituting the word "person" for "white male" in the law. Most observers gave the bill little or no chance of passing the all-male state legislature. But they had not reckoned with Foltz's determination to fulfill her ambition to become an attorney. With no previous experience as a lobbyist, she threw herself into the fight for passage of the new law. She organized other women around the state who collected hundreds of signatures on petitions in support of the legislation.

The critics of the bill argued that women would use their seductive powers to unfairly sway juries. They said that women could not take the emotional strains of practicing law. Working themselves into an indignant lather, they made the slippery-slope argument: if women became lawyers, next they might become jurors and then perhaps even judges.

Foltz persisted despite the strong objections of the bar and the press. The bill managed to pass the state senate, but appeared doomed in the state assembly. But Foltz worked the halls of the legislature, forming alliances with progressive male legislators. The bill eventually passed, thirty-seven to thirty-five.

Foltz and her allies then went to work to secure the governor's signature. On the last possible day, the governor signed the Women Lawyer's Bill into law. Foltz wasted no time, and began studying for the bar. The press made note of how she managed to keep house for her children and prepare for the examination. A Chicago paper wrote that "young men who moan and groan because they have not the means to acquire an education . . . it is not money they need—it is pluck and energy of a woman like Mrs. Foltz."

Foltz faced a rigorous three-hour oral examination before a committee of three prominent attorneys, including the man who had advised her in his letter that she was inviting ridicule in her quest. Foltz received a unanimous recommendation, and on the very next day, September 5, 1878, Clara Foltz became California's first female lawyer.

Aided by her friendships throughout the state, as well as the publicity from the numerous "first woman" stories in the press, Foltz quickly amassed a clientele. But she remained insecure, self-conscious about her lack of formal schooling. It was not uncommon for practicing attorneys to attend law school, and so Foltz reasoned that as she was the first female attorney in California, it made sense for her to attend California's first law school, Hastings. She paid her ten-dollar registration fee on January 9, 1879, and received a note the next day from the registrar stating that the directors of the school had decided that women should not be admitted.

Foltz's efforts at negotiating a settlement were rebuffed, and so she turned to litigation. When she went to appear in a San Francisco court, the judge refused to honor her bar admission certificate. Foltz then requested that he appoint a committee to examine her for admission. In late January she underwent a second bar examination and passed.

Foltz began her fight. The attorneys for the law school began by requesting delays as a means of harassing Foltz. As it became clear that Hastings intended to fight Foltz at every turn, she gained an important new weapon. The delegates to the state constitutional convention, aware of the ongoing legal battle, adopted without debate or change a section providing that "no person shall, on account of sex, be disqualified from entering upon or pursuing any lawful business, vocation or profession." This was the first time women had gained constitutionally protected equal rights outside the home. Acting again to support Foltz, the convention adopted a provision that "no person shall be barred admission to any of the collegiate departments of the university on account of sex."

When it came time for oral argument before the court, Foltz spoke first. Limiting herself to thirty minutes, she used a three-prong attack: First, that she met the requirements for admission to Hastings; second, that Hastings was a part of the University of California, which admitted women; and finally, that given the passage of the Women Lawyer's Bill, it defied common sense that the state should give women the right to practice law while creating a law school to which they were denied admission.

The attorneys for the school argued that "[L]aw has essentially and habitually to do with all that is selfish and extortionate, knavish and criminal, coarse and brutal, repulsive and obscene, in human life. It would be revolting . . . that woman should be permitted to mix professionally in all the nastiness of the world which finds its way into courts of justice; all the unclean issues, all the collateral questions of sodomy, incest, rape, seduction, fornication, adultery, pregnancy, bastardy, legitimacy, prostitution, lascivious cohabitation, abortion, infanticide, obscene publication, libel and slander of sex, impotence, divorce—all the nameless catalogue of indecencies. Reverence for all womanhood would suffer in the public spectacle of women so engaged. . . ."

When Foltz replied, she made quick work of her opponents' claims that, as she put it, "broader education would make woman less womanly" and thus "destroy our homes." Foltz replied, "That is not the legitimate effect of knowledge of any kind. On the contrary, a knowledge of the law of our land will make women better mothers, better wives, and better citizens."

Ten days after the close of argument, the judge issued a writ directing that Hastings College admit Foltz. Attorneys for the law school filed an appeal of the order with the California Supreme Court. Foltz, much disappointed, wrote later that "they knew that though I had much law, I had little money, and they hoped . . . to wear out my courage or cool my ardor." The school obtained a stay in the case, so that Foltz was denied admission pending the appeal.

Exhausted and broke, Foltz returned to San Jose to practice law and prepare her appellate argument. In yet another obstacle she was forced to overcome, the California Supreme Court required Foltz to take another bar examination before they would allow her to argue her own case before the high court. Foltz passed the exam, her third in two years.

Foltz eventually won her appeal, prompting one observer to say of her performance before the justices, "I have never heard a better argument . . . made by anyone." Now that she had finally won the right to attend law school, Foltz's career prevented her from enrolling. She was leaving in January 1880 to become counsel to the Assembly Judiciary Committee, the first woman to occupy the position.

Her fifty-year career was nothing if not varied. Foltz moved to San Diego in the late 1880s, where she opened a real estate law practice and started a daily newspaper. In 1896, Foltz joined the New York bar, attracting the attention of the national press in the process. Refusing to adhere to social custom, she sued a restaurant after she and her daughter were refused service because they had not been escorted by a man. By the turn of the century, Foltz was back in San Francisco, practicing oil and gas law while publishing a trade and technical magazine devoted to the field. The 1906 earthquake destroyed her home and office, so Foltz moved to Los Angeles, where she was appointed the first woman deputy district attorney in 1911.

Perhaps Foltz's most lasting contribution to the modern practice of criminal law was the public defender's office. Foltz attended the 1893 Chicago World's Fair as a representative of the California bar, where she presented a compelling argument in favor of the then-radical notion that the government should pay for attorneys to represent indigent defendants. She wrote well-crafted law review papers on the subject, and lobbied so successfully that California soon passed legislation mandating the creation of a public defender's office.

Throughout her career, Foltz was the subject of ridicule, suspicion, and condescension, but her humor and rapier wit served her well. On one occasion, Foltz parried her opponent's scorn during trial with "Counsel intimates with a curl on his lip that I am called the lady lawyer. I am sorry I cannot return the compliment, but I cannot. I never heard anybody call him any kind of a lawyer at all." When another attorney attacked her very presence in the courtroom, Foltz replied, "A woman would better be almost any place than home raising men like you."

Foltz delivered the following closing argument in a trial set in either 1889 or 1890; the exact date is unknown. A San Francisco judge had appointed Foltz, by this time an experienced lawyer with a decade of practice behind her, to defend a young Italian immigrant accused of arson. Squaring off against her was Col. Thetas Stonehill, a captain in the Confederate army, referred to by all as "Colonel." The combat veteran did not relish the idea of clashing with a member of the "fairer sex," one who lacked the intellectual abilities of men, considering it an unfair fight. Stonehill's dismay at trying a case against a woman found its expression when the time came to deliver his summation.

Foltz described Stonehill's closing argument in her memoirs, praising his skill while parenthetically commenting on his attacks upon her: [Stonehill] "had 'no use for women at the bar,' (unless she was a defendant). . . . [H]e flayed 'ambitious women who have no sense of the fitness of things . . . women who have no child (I had five), no husband (I was a widow), no home,' (I had the dearest, cleanest little home in San Francisco). . . . 'SHE IS A WOMAN,' bellowed this learned limb of the law, 'she cannot be expected to reason; God Almighty decreed her limitations, but you can reason, and you must use your reasoning faculties against this young woman. . . .' "

The criticism was painful to endure. Foltz was able to recall the details years later, so vivid was the scene in her memory. "My time had come at last," she recalled. "The courtroom was crowded. I rose all trembling and ashamed. I felt as though my clothes had all slipped off of me and that I stood there nude before the court and the jury."

Foltz began her summation, responding eloquently and passionately, admitting that, yes, she was indeed a woman lawyer, and chastising opposing counsel for trying to use whatever prejudice the jury might have against her to harm her client.

The jury returned a verdict of "not guilty" without even leaving the jury box to deliberate.

Unfortunately, Ms. Foltz's entire closing argument has not been preserved. However, enough of it has been found to give a sense of the remarkable oratorical abilities of this amazing woman.

Closing Argument

The State of California v. Unknown Defendant
Delivered by Clara Shortridge Foltz
San Francisco, California, 1890

If Your Honor please and gentlemen of the jury:
You well know that I am not before you by my own choice! That in

obedience to a time-honored rule I am here by order of this court trying as best I can to represent this despairing man. Is it not strange then
that the district attorney should make me an object of his displeasure
and challenge my presence at this bar because only that I am a woman?
The kind indulgence of the court has permitted counsel to range over
much matter that is neither of record nor part of the evidence in this
case. I would rather the immaterial and irrelevant part of his speech had
remained unspoken, for I take no pleasure in the wanton abuse of a
jury's patience nor in burdening them with matter wholly foreign to the
case. Besides, when the ingenuity of counsel has entangled the true with
the false, the relevant with the irrelevant, it is sometimes a wearisome
task both to opposing counsel and to the jury to separate the woof of fact
from the warp of fiction with which it has been woven, and enable one
to arrive at the true measure of justice in the matter. I regret it all the
more because I shall in some degree be obliged to follow counsel
through the labyrinth of his immaterialities. In referring to them, I trust
that to me the court will not be less indulgent in permitting me to speak,
nor the jury in disposition to patiently listen.

Allow me to say, I have been pleased with much of the speech of the
counsel on the other side. He has made of the testimony all there was in
it. He has lost no effort in throwing upon it the strongest light in the
state's behalf; he has marshaled it with all the skill and ingenuity of a subtle lawyer, a skilled debater, and a practiced dialectician; he has spared no
pains in the coloring of the testimony to produce the highest effect.
When he had finished, you saw the state's case in its most advantageous
light and there was indeed nothing more to be said. And yet, I do not
think the legitimate results of his reasoning are at all alarming to the
defendant or to his inexperienced counsel. I have seen higher monuments
of sophistry than his crumble before the magic touch of truth. I have seen
verdicts rendered contrary to more finished logic than his. Indeed, I am
very sure that verdicts are rendered more on evidence than on oratory;
that it is oftener the good heart and the sound sense of the jury, the
innate spirit of right and appreciation of justice that renders a verdict than
the seeming logic of a prosecuting officer, who too often moved by a selfish ambition to win, overlooks the real issue, forgets the principle
involved in every criminal case, that the accused is presumed to be innocent until proven guilty and that this presumption obtains at every stage
of the case and remains with him until the verdict is rendered.

We could not be so cruel to this feeble child of a brilliant brain as to let it die unhonored and unsung. In the kindness of my heart I would herald its advent with drums and tin horns like a Democratic victory; I would let it grow and flourish "in immortal youth unhurt amid the war of elements, the wreck of matter, and the crash of worlds."

Counsel tells you that I am a woman. I wonder that the planets did not stand still in their courses and rivers cease to run to the sea at the announcement of this startling discovery. I am amazed that His Honor did not faint upon the bench and that you gentlemen of the jury have survived this awful shock to your nervous systems.

Let me kindly admonish the learned counsel that in a matter of great pith and moment like this he should break the news gently and not plunge such an original thought upon an unprepared jury. A few more such thoughtless revelations and your nervous forces will be destroyed and your reason dethroned. Counsel should beware how he heedlessly enlightens an unprepared jury on such a vital topic.

Again he tells you that I am a woman. By a natural antithesis I presume he would have you infer that he is not. I suppose he wants me to tell you that he is a man and he takes this hurried opportunity and adroit method of testifying to the fact. Though nobody yet has denied it, he seems to be in a fever of anxiety to emphasize that he is a man. I don't know why he should make such unseemly haste in announcing it. He should remember that a swift and willing witness to a point not controverted is a herald of suspicion. Useless denial has caught more criminals than has silence a long way.

He reminds me of one of my boys who went in swimming long before I had dreamed that swimming time had come. Guilt hurried the little rebel to my side to explain: "Momma, I didn't go in swimming; it was only Davy went in." The denial was a dead giveaway. I examined the wet and stringy hair and the reversed shirt and found a verdict of guilty against Sammy. I suggest that these premature denials create a strong suspicion against counsel and I call attention of the officers to the male attire ordinances and to his extraordinary conduct and statements in this matter.

I am that formidable and terrifying object known as a woman—while he is only a poor, helpless, defenseless man, and he wants you to take pity on him and give him a verdict in this case. I sympathize with counsel in his unhappy condition. True, the world is open to him. He is the peer of all men—he can aspire to the highest offices, he can carry a torch over our streets during a political campaign and sell his vote for a dollar and a half on election day, and yet he isn't satisfied. Like Alexander, who wanted more worlds to conquer, he wants verdicts, and in order to awaken your sympathy for him, he tells you that I am a woman and he is only a man.

I confess I do not clearly see the relevancy of the statement to this case. The logic is, I am a woman; therefore you should find this defendant guilty. The conclusion is rather sudden. We are hurried across the river of dispute without bridge or ferry or fording place. In the chain of his logic an important link seems wanting. There is a weakness somewhere, but mothers are always weak after such extraordinary births, and we presume we ought to be lenient. "Be to his faults a little blind, be to his virtues very kind."

But counsel insists that I am a woman. Gentlemen of the jury, of the atrocious crime I plead guilty. Into this world I have brought five healthy children. By my industry I have supported them till some are even now stepping from youth and maidenhood into the broader estate of manhood and womanhood. And I repel the covert slur and innuendo that came with the words, "She is a woman," words intended to depreciate me and my efforts before you in this cause, words none the less obnoxious because spoken under the cloak of a honeyed compliment. In the name of the mothers who nursed you, and of the wives and maidens who look love into your eyes, I resent this hidden appeal to a supposed prejudice of this jury. I resent this ill-concealed slur and covert innuendo that the presence of woman in a lawsuit contaminates her and that her sex must militate against her client. And I resent for you gentlemen, whose mouths are closed, the implication that you are small enough and narrow enough to bring prejudice into the jury box, and the insulting inference that you could be induced to visit punishment upon this defendant in violation of your solemn oaths.

The speech of the district attorney was neither complimentary to this body who are sworn to decide according to the law and the evidence, nor honorable to the profession he should strive to adorn. If he hoped to draw your attention from the real merits of the case, let me say it was a course obnoxious to his official oath and foreign to his professional duty. But perhaps it was the woman lawyer that has troubled him. I think myself that the fact of being a lawyer has been a good deal more troublesome than the fact of being a woman. Counsel intimates with a curl on his lip that I am called the lady lawyer. I am sorry I cannot return the compliment, but I cannot. I never heard anybody call him any kind of a lawyer at all.

And now let us take it altogether. I am a woman and I am a lawyer— and what of it? It is not so new or wonderful a thing. I am practicing law in this city; I have offices in one of its largest buildings, and I go daily to and from those offices sober and in my right mind. I am certainly not unknown to the bench and bar of California. And gentlemen, I came into the practice of my profession under the laws of this state, regularly and honestly, and not by the certificate of another state that required no learning to secure, and I have come to stay. I am neither to be bullied out or worn out. I ask no special privileges and expect no favors, but I think it only fair that those who have had better opportunities than I, who have had fewer obstacles to surmount and fewer difficulties to contend with should meet me on even ground, upon the merits of law and fact without this everlasting and incessant reference to sex—reference that in its very nature is uncalled for and which is as unprofessional as it is unmanly.

If Your Honor please, I fear that I have trespassed too largely upon your time and patience. To you I owe an excuse and gladly give it. I believe I have as much friendship and kindly feeling from the bench and bar of this city as any attorney of it. But there is a class of counsel that makes it a point to harangue the court and jury often in the cold-bloodedness and malice of a set speech upon my sex. Such counsel sets out with the remarkable statement that I am a woman. To this I am precluded from retorting that he is a man. I am precluded from retorting that he is a man. I would not libel the human race. I have borne this many times with patience. This is the first time I have taken occasion to rebuke the effrontery or to chastise the offender. It is the first mutterings of retaliation and I earnestly hope that I may not hereafter have to proceed further or say more. This controversy was not of my seeking. I would have avoided it as I have innumerable others, but the day of avoidance was past; the idea that it was an effective weapon against me and against other women who enter the profession of law must grow to the hurt of their business and to their clients' damage, or it must cease. I prefer that it cease—and it shall cease.

Counsel thought I was too timid to resent this miserable inference against women in courts of justice. I am descended from the heroic stock of Daniel Boone, and never shrunk from contest nor knew a fear. I inherit no drop of craven blood. If I have remained silent when others would have retorted, it is because of my respect for the courts and halls of justice, which I grieve to see become the arena of personal encounter. But the patience which at first may have been a virtue would become criminal by longer exercise. This controversy was not of my seeking— a long series of abuses have forced it upon me.

When I so far forget the dignity of my profession, when I so trample upon its courtesy, when I so shut my eyes to the honor and respect due this bench as to introduce such irrelevant matter, I hope that I may be barred the profession and banished the country.

CHAPTER SEVEN

Peace, Love, and Murder

Manson Family Mastermind Sentenced to Die for Followers' Murderous Rampage

Two random homes, two consecutive days, and seven gruesome murders. The nights of August 9 and 10, 1969, seemed typical, peaceful Southern California nights. The houses were ordinary to the naked eye. But what happened in Los Angeles over those two days terrorized Americans. The violence seemed so random; the question on everyone's mind, "Why?"

The scene that greeted police at the bloodstained home of film director Roman Polanski and his wife, actress Sharon Tate, on August 9 was horrific. Officers first spotted the body of Steven Earl Parent, nineteen. Parent, a young hi-fi enthusiast working two jobs in order to save money for college, just happened to be in the wrong place at the wrong time. He had been shot five times and was found slumped in his car near the gate. Crossing the front lawn, the officers found the bodies of Voytek Frykowski, thirty-two, and his lover, coffee heiress Abigail Folger, twenty-five, lying on the grass. Frykowski had been stabbed fifty-one times, repeatedly beaten over the head with a blunt object, and shot twice. Folger had been stabbed twenty-eight times. Moving toward the house, police spotted the word "Pig," written on the front door—they would later learn it had been scrawled using Sharon Tate's blood. Inside, the bodies of Tate and her former fiancé, hairstylist Jay Sebring, thirty-five, lay in the living room, connected by a piece of rope. Tate, whose blood was found all around the property, had been stabbed sixteen times. Sebring, a towel tied around his neck and covering his head, had been stabbed seven times and shot once.

Testimony would later show that the twenty-six-year-old actress, eight months pregnant, had pleaded for her life and the life of her baby before she was murdered. She begged her killers, "Please don't kill me. Please don't kill me. I don't want to die. I want to live. I want to have my baby. I want to have my baby."

The police found no evidence that anything had been stolen from the house or the victims.

Angelenos barely had time to digest the madness that was in their midst before the killers struck again. The next night, August 10, the killers paid a visit to the home of Leno and Rosemary LaBianca. Leno, fourty-four, the owner of a chain of grocery stores, had been sitting on a couch reading the Sunday paper when he was attacked. Rosemary, thirty-eight, hearing the screams of her husband, struggled to come to his aid but fell victim to an even more frenzied attack. Rosemary's killer kept stabbing her, long after she was dead. Police found Leno in his living room, his hands tied behind his back, his head covered with a blood-soaked pillowcase and an electrical cord knotted around his neck. He had been stabbed thirteen times and had fourteen puncture wounds caused by a carving fork. Police did not have to search far for the murder weapons; the fork was found stuck in his stomach, the knife protruding from his neck. The word "War" had been scratched on his stomach. Rosemary was found in the couple's bedroom, facedown in a large pool of blood. As with her husband, Rosemary's killers had covered her head with a pillowcase and had knotted an electrical cord around her neck. She had been stabbed so many times it was difficult to count the individual wounds. The words "Death to pigs" and "Rise" decorated the living room walls, painted with the victims' blood. On the refrigerator door in the kitchen there were two words, the first of which was misspelled: "Healter Skelter." Again, nothing had been stolen from the house or the victims.

Fear spread quickly among Angelenos. In two days, a Beverly Hills sporting goods store sold 200 firearms, up from the three or four a day they averaged before the murders. Private security forces doubled, then tripled their personnel. Guard dogs, once priced at $200, quickly jumped to $1,500 and those who supplied them ran out. Locksmiths quoted two-week delays on orders. There was a dramatic increase in accidental shootings and suspicious persons reports. Hollywood was in a panic. Reports quickly surfaced that stars were canceling engagements and going into hiding for fear they would be next.

It took only days for Hollywood gossips to solve the murders. The general consensus was that somehow the victims had brought the murders upon themselves. Headlines read everything from "Ritual Murders" to "Bloody Orgy." Some believed the murders cult-related because Polanski had directed *Rosemary's Baby,* wherein actress Mia Far-row was impregnated by the devil, and because of the manner in which the victims were killed. Speculations of hard-core drug use and flamboyant lifestyles gone out of control added to the notoriety of the crimes. Polanski and friends of the Polanski family offered to pay a $25,000 reward to the person or persons who would furnish information leading to the arrest and conviction of the killer of Sharon Tate, her unborn child, and the other four victims. Peter Sellers, Warren Beatty, and Yul Brynner all contributed to the reward.

The Los Angeles Police Department assigned a team of investigators and officers to each murder scene. After over two months of investigation and hundreds of interviews, the police were still no closer to finding the killers. Unable to find any connection between the murders, the LAPD concluded that they were unrelated. In November the police got a break in the case through a jailhouse confession—or rather, a boast.

A young woman, Susan Denise Atkins, who had been arrested on unrelated murder charges, began talking to a jail mate about a man called "Charlie." Atkins, a high school dropout and topless dancer, had met Charlie in Haight-Ashbury, the famed "hippie district" of San Francisco. "He was the strongest man alive," Atkins bragged. "[We] followed his orders without question, all the kids who lived with him." And on his orders she, and three others, dressed in black, had chosen a house at random (the Polanski house) and slaughtered everyone in sight. Atkins told of Tate pleading for the life of her baby and her responding, "Look, bitch . . . I don't care if you're going to have a baby. . . . You're going to die, and I don't feel anything about it."

Charles Manson, the man who inspired such devotion, was born the illegitimate son of sixteen-year-old Kathleen Maddox. Maddox married a much older man, William Manson, who was around just long enough to provide a surname for the boy. Manson spent his childhood going from one boys' home to another. He didn't adjust well and eventually turned to crime. In his early teens, Manson began burglarizing stores, stealing cars, and by age thirteen had committed armed robberies. From this point on Manson spent his life in and out of jail, committing crimes shortly after being paroled. He was noted for being intelligent, having an IQ of 121, and possessing musical and theatrical abilities, as well as a criminal sophistication. At the age of thirty-two, he was released, having spent more than seventeen years of his life in institutions.

Manson went to "The Haight." In San Francisco, he soon amassed a harem of adoring women whom he called "young loves" through the use of drugs and hypnotic messages. Manson then used the women to draw males into his "Family." The Family soon grew to include twenty-five hard-core members and sixty "associates." Manson and his followers migrated south to the Los Angeles area.

Coincidentally, Manson, Atkins, and twenty-two others had been rounded up in mid-October, two months after the murders, at Spahn Ranch, an isolated location outside Los Angeles, and booked for arson and auto thefts all completely unrelated to the murders. All, except Atkins, were released within forty-eight hours because the warrants had been misdated. Atkins was being held as a suspect in the Malibu torture-murder of musician Gary Hinman a few days before the Tate-LaBianca slayings. The jail mate who had heard Atkins's stories told police, indicating that she knew who had committed the Tate and LaBianca murders; that the person who had told her had been involved and was now in custody; but that the other killers were on the loose and unless they were apprehended soon there would be more murders.

On December 1, 1969, Police Chief Ed Davis announced that after 8,750 hours of police work they had solved the Tate and LaBianca murders. Warrants were issued for the arrest of Charles D. "Tex" Watson, Patricia Krenwinkel, Linda Kasabian, Susan Atkins, Leslie Van Houten, and Charles Manson.

June 15, 1970, found Judge Charles Older's courtroom already crowded before the first panel of sixty jurors was escorted in. The prospective jurors saw for the first time who they might sit in judgment of. One juror gasped, loud enough for those around him to hear, "My God, it's the Manson trial!"

Security in the courtroom was very tight—there were rumors that the judge had received several death threats. Judge Older requested a bodyguard, a personal driver, and security for his home on a twenty-four-hour basis. During jury selection Manson and the girls caused no disruptions and the jury panel was finally selected on July 14, 1970. The panel of twelve jurors was chosen from 205 people and consisted of seven men and five women ranging in age from twenty-five to seventy-three. They and six alternates were sworn and sequestered.

Spectators began lining up outside the courtroom at 6:00 A.M., hoping to get a seat and a glimpse of Manson. When Manson entered the courtroom, gasps were heard as members of the audience spotted the bloody X on his forehead. The previous night Manson had carved the mark, explaining, "I have X'd myself from your world . . . You have created the monster. I am not of you, from you, nor do I condone your unjust attitude toward things, animals, and people that you do not try to understand . . . I stand opposed to what you do and have done in the past . . . You make fun of God and have murdered the world in the name of Jesus Christ . . . My faith in me is stronger than all of your armies, governments, gas chambers, or anything you may want to do to me. I know what I have done. Your courtroom is a man's game. Love is my judge . . ."

Following his lead, Manson's fellow defendants carved their foreheads, just like Charlie. When Manson later changed his *X* into a swastika, they followed suit. During the trial, those Manson Family members not under indictment conducted vigils outside the courthouse, exclaiming, "We're waiting for our father to be set free." The Manson trial was front-page news every day. Underground newspapers presented Manson as a savior, declaring him "Man of the Year." Manson posters and sweatshirts appeared in psychedelic shops, along with "Free Manson" buttons. In a press conference, President Richard Nixon railed against all the publicity Manson was getting.

Deputy District Attorney Vincent Bugliosi was assigned the case. His first task would be to discover the motive for the murders. Bugliosi interviewed Atkins, who said the reason for the murders ". . . was to instill fear in the establishment and cause paranoia. Also show the black man how to take over the white man. This would be the start of 'Helter Skelter.' " Manson interpreted the lyrics in the Beatles song "Helter Skelter" to mean there was going to be a violent black uprising against whites. So he planned the murders to look like hate crimes with the intent of causing an uprising between the races. Manson also looked to the lyrics in the Beatles song "Revolution 9," which he convinced his Family paralleled the Bible's Revelation 9. The two songs explained the words "pig," "war," "rise," "death to pigs," and "Helter Skelter," found at the murder scene. Manson then expected to flee the uprising by leading his followers into the California desert.

At a pretrial hearing before Judge Dell, Manson requested that he be released because the sheriff was depriving him of his constitutional liberties. Manson questioned the judge and asked, ". . . like sometimes I wonder if you know what is going on." Manson continued, "[w]ell, I was going to ask him [*the sheriff*] to call the whole thing off. It would save a lot of trouble." Judge Dell responded, "Disappoint all these people? Never, Mr. Manson."

At yet another pretrial hearing, Manson appeared in front of Judge Keene, who declared himself "appalled" at Manson's requests. Keene revoked Manson's right to represent himself, causing Manson to respond, "You can kill me, but you can't give me an attorney. I won't take one." Toward the end of the proceeding, Manson shouted, "There is no God in this courtroom!" In response to this, a number of Family members jumped up and yelled at Judge Keene, "You are a mockery of justice! You are a joke!" The judge found three of them in contempt.

Bugliosi entertained doubts about the strength of the people's case against Manson in the Tate-LaBianca murders. Bugliosi went so far as to have charges of arson, which were dropped after Manson was indicted for the murders, reinstated against Manson for fear he might be set free.

The strangest element in the case was that no one placed Manson at the murder scenes; he was instead the driving force behind the deaths. Bugliosi had one witness who defected from the Manson Family to testify about the Tate and LaBianca murders: Linda Kasabian. She testified that Manson had instructed her to get a knife and change clothes so she could accompany the others to Polanski's house. Kasabian, twenty-one, the mother of two, went with the other Family members to the Polanski home but took no part in the killings. She further testified that she drove Manson and the others to the LaBianca home the following night.

In a surprise move, the defense rested without calling any witnesses. The judge called counsel into his chambers and demanded to know exactly what was going on. In chambers it was disclosed that there was a split between the defense attorneys and their clients. The three female defendants wanted to testify that they had planned and committed the murders and that Manson was not involved. Manson also indicated that he wanted to testify. The court recessed and the next day Manson was allowed to testify outside the presence of the jury.

Once on the stand Manson spoke for over an hour. He began in an almost apologetic manner, speaking so low that listeners had to lean forward to hear him. But as he continued his voice grew strong and more animated. He lectured: "These children that come at you with knives, they are your children. You taught them. I didn't teach them. I just tried to help them stand up. . . . I have eaten out of your garbage cans to stay out of jail. I have worn your secondhand clothes. . . . I have done my best to get along in your world and now you want to kill me, and I look at you, and then I say to myself, You want to kill me? Ha! I'm already dead, have been all my life. I've spent twenty-three years in tombs that you built."

Throughout the trial the four defendants were often removed from the courtroom for creating disturbances. During closing arguments the judge had allowed the three female defendants to return to the courtroom. Manson had no desire to return and remained in the lockup. Arguments had just resumed when Van Houten created a disturbance, causing her codefendants to follow suit. The judge ordered them removed and as they walked by the lectern one kicked a female deputy and grabbed Bugliosi's notes. Under his breath he muttered, "You little bitch!" as she tore the notes in half.

Exactly seven months after the start of the trial, on January 15, 1971, the trial concluded and the jury began its deliberations. During deliberations, the jury requested a record player to play the Beatles' White Album (which included the song "Helter Skelter"), the letter from Susan Atkins to her former cell mates to be reread, and permission to visit the Tate and LaBianca residences. The latter was denied. After deliberating for forty-two hours and forty minutes over nine days, they reached a verdict. Manson was found guilty of murder. The three female defendants had been found guilty of conspiracy to commit murder and seven counts of murder in the first degree.

Biography

Vincent Bugliosi Jr. was born in Hibbing, Minnesota, the son of Vincent and Ida Bugliosi. Bugliosi's father, who immigrated from Italy at the age of thirteen, ran a grocery store and later worked as a conductor for the Great Northern Railroad from the early 1940s to the mid-1960s.

Bugliosi moved to California in his senior year of high school. After college, he attended law school at the University of California, Los Angeles, where he was voted president of the class of 1964. After graduation, Bugliosi passed the California bar and joined the Los Angeles County District Attorney's Office.

After only five years as a prosecutor, Bugliosi became the lead attorney in the state of California's case against Charles Manson. Before that trial began, an attorney representing one of the defendants told the *Los Angeles Times,* "There's no case against Manson and the other defendants. All the prosecution has are two fingerprints and Vince Bugliosi."

Although Manson was not at the murder scene, Bugliosi won convictions and the trial made Bugliosi one of the most famous lawyers in America. He went on to chronicle the case in *Helter Skelter,* which sold more copies than any true-crime book in publishing history.

Bugliosi's years in the DA's office brought him other memorable cases, one of which was documented in his book *Till Death Us Do Part,* about the trial of a former Los Angeles police officer and his paramour, who murdered their spouses for insurance money—a case eerily similar to the one in the movie classic *Double Indemnity.* The case was so circumstantial, and Bugliosi's investigation and prosecution so exceptional, that F. Lee Bailey said, "Bugliosi, the quintessential prosecutor, has written a crime book that should be read by every lawyer and judge in America." The book has indeed become a staple on reading lists in law schools.

During his eight years as prosecutor, he won 105 of the 106 felony jury cases he tried. Of the twenty-one that were murder cases, not one defendant was acquitted.

After losing the Los Angeles County district attorney's race in 1972, he returned to private practice to pursue a career as an author and defense attorney.

The pugnacious ex-DA has earned the respect of his peers. The editor of *Courtwatcher's Newsletter,* recalling a summation he saw Bugliosi give in 1981 for the defense, said "Having seen the likes of F. Lee Bailey, James Neal, etc., Bugliosi's performance today in Judge Crowley's courtroom was the finest I have ever seen, and I have been a courtwatcher in Chicago since 1960." Harry Weiss, a veteran criminal defense attorney who has gone up against Bugliosi in court, told *Los Angeles* magazine, "I've seen all the great trial lawyers of the past thirty years and none of them are in Vince's class."

Bugliosi has continued his record in the courtroom, winning all three murder trials he has handled for the defense, making a total of twenty-four consecutive murder trials without a loss.

In 1985, British television decided to stage a "docutrial" of Lee Harvey Oswald (in front of a real federal judge and Dallas jury, with the original key law witnesses in the Kennedy assassination and no script or actors). Bugliosi appeared for the prosecution, and criminal defense attorney Gerry Spence, who had not lost a jury trial in seventeen years, represented Oswald. Bugliosi and Spence worked on the case for five months, and the twenty-one-hour trial took place in London in a replica of a Dallas federal courtroom. When the jury returned with a guilty verdict, Spence said, "No lawyer in America could have done what Vince did in this case."

Bugliosi has said that he won't defend someone unless he believes they are innocent. That's why he declined to take the case of Dr. Jeffrey MacDonald, the Princeton-educated U.S. Army Green Beret who was charged (and later convicted) in the murder of his wife and two children in North Carolina in 1970. For the same reason, he passed on defending Dan White, charged and found guilty in the murder of San Francisco Mayor George Moscone and Supervisor Harvey Milk in 1978.

Bugliosi's book detailing the mistakes made by the prosecution team in the criminal trial of O. J. Simpson, *Outrage,* spent months on the bestseller list, and was well received by the legal community.

Commentary

In evaluating any closing argument, it is impossible to divorce that assessment from the surrounding circumstances in which it was rendered. The circumstances encountered by Deputy District Attorney Vincent Bugliosi in the prosecution of Charles Manson, Leslie Van Houten, Patricia Krenwinkel, and Susan Atkins for the Tate-LaBianca murders were most daunting. First, in multiple-defendant cases, the prosecutor has to continually assess the state of the evidence as it relates to each of the defendants. Keeping track of the evidence and its relevance to each defendant, especially in a complicated trial, is no mean feat. Additionally, multiple-defendant cases feature multiple defense lawyers, all working to foil the prosecutor. Manson's defense lawyer, Irving Kanarek, was a true obstructionist, in that he continually engaged in dilatory tactics in the form of motions and objections intended to slow and confuse the proceedings. While certainly a number of Kanarek's motions and objections had merit, most did not and served solely to delay and confuse. Additionally, Kanarek never felt the need to confine himself to the facts of the case, frequently casting accusations of intrigue and conspiracy well beyond the boundaries of the trial at hand.

A third complicating factor was the defendants themselves. All four continually engaged in confrontational outbursts typically directed at Bugliosi. Even through closing arguments, Manson, Atkins, Van Houten, and Krenwinkel would not miss an opportunity to distract

Bugliosi. The continuing nature of the outbursts was a source of great distraction as Bugliosi worked through literally volumes of testimony in delivering this closing argument.

A fourth complicating factor was the sheer complexity of the trial, with voluminous pages of testimony to be reviewed and eighty witnesses to be corralled. Bugliosi, with his considerable commitment and stamina, was undaunted.

The final complicating factor was the horrific nature of the crimes, with the attendant massive press coverage and public interest. The pressure on Bugliosi to perform had to be intense. Yet through it all, he was able to successfully conclude the prosecution.

Given the arduous circumstances under which Bugliosi toiled, his closing argument becomes even more impressive. There are two aspects of this close that bear particular attention. First is his effective use of Linda Kasabian's testimony, which truly constituted the core of the prosecution case, and second was his ability to effectively re-create the mindset of "the Family" to successfully implicate Manson himself. Bear in mind, Manson was not present during any of the seven murders.

Linda Kasabian, one of the Manson "girls," agreed to testify for the prosecution in return for immunity. Obviously, testimony from such a witness is going to be viewed with a great deal of skepticism, yet Bugliosi, because of the nature of the case, had no choice but to make her the centerpiece of the argument, as well as at the trial itself. Bugliosi essentially worked through both nights of murder using Kasabian's testimony as the focal point. At key points of the Kasabian testimony, he weaved in corroborative testimony from other witnesses. This technique effectively lent credibility to Kasabian's account of the events. For instance, following the Tate murders, Kasabian testified that Charles "Tex" Watson pulled the car over so that he and the "girls" could wash off using a garden hose at the front of a house. Subsequent investigation established that the house belonged to Rudolph Weber. Bugliosi argues, "the testimony of Rudolph Weber, all by itself, without anything more, proves that Linda Kasabian was telling the truth on that witness stand. Her testimony concerning this hose incident is very, very closely corresponding. It is almost identical to the testimony of Rudolph Weber. And there is no way in the world, no way under the stars, that she could have known what happened in the hose incident unless she was one of the persons Weber saw in front of his home. She was the small girl. Weber's testimony alone proves that Linda Kasabian was with the defendants on the night of the Tate murders."

Also noteworthy was Bugliosi's ability to re-create the mind-set within "the Family" that essentially permitted Manson to so thoroughly control his minions that they would murder for him. Given that Manson was not present during any of the killings, it was crucial for Bugliosi to establish that Charlie wielded that kind of control over his "robots." Bugliosi went to considerable lengths to establish the atmosphere that was so pervasive that summer at the Spahn Ranch.

Closing Argument

The State of California v. Charles Manson, et al.
Delivered by Vincent Bugliosi
Los Angeles, California, January 15, 1971

Your Honor, defense counsel, ladies, and gentlemen:

As you know, the defendants Charles Manson, Susan Atkins, and Patricia Krenwinkel are charged with the five Tate murders occurring on August the ninth, 1969, and they are charged with the murders of Leno and Rosemary LaBianca, on August 10, 1969. They are also charged with the crime of conspiracy to commit murder.

The defendant Leslie Van Houten is not charged with the five Tate murders. She is charged with the murder of Leno and Rosemary LaBianca, and with the crime of conspiracy to commit murder.

When the prosecution finally called its last witness to the stand a few weeks ago and rested, the defense also rested.

DEFENDANT MANSON: The defense never rested. The lawyers, the judge's lawyers, rested. [*There were a number of outbursts by Manson and the other defendants during Bugliosi's closing argument. They have been included so that the reader may fully understand the circumstances under which the closing argument was delivered.*]

MR. BUGLIOSI: I am sure all of you heaved a sigh of relief. It has been an incredibly long, grueling trial and an enormous imposition on all of you. Before I discuss the evidence and the testimony in this case, I would like to briefly go over the law that you are going to be dealing with during your deliberations.

In my discussion with you on the law of murder, I am only going to address myself at this particular point to the issue of whether these crimes were committed. The far more important issue of who committed the crimes I will discuss later on in my argument.

The crime of murder is not a simple crime to understand. Fortunately, the California penal code has given us a helping hand. Murder is the unlawful killing of a human being with malice aforethought. I will discuss the last word first.

As His Honor will instruct you, "aforethought" does not mean that the intent to kill was formed as a result of any deliberation or premeditation. Aforethought does not mean deliberation or premeditation. The key word here is "malice"; that is the key word. Malice refers to the state of mind of the killer.

Now, obviously we cannot open up the top of a person's head, peek in and say, "Ah hah, so that is what you were thinking." Rather, we have to look at the person's conduct and the surrounding circumstances, and from that person's conduct and from the surrounding circumstances we have to draw inferences as to what his state of mind was at the time he engaged in the act in question. In other words, we prove state of mind by circumstantial evidence.

Express malice is an intent to kill, a specific intent to kill. Unquestionably, in all seven murders the killer had the specific intent to kill, and hence expressed malice. If the unbelievably savage murders in this case do not show an intent to kill, I don't know what in the world would. For instance, with respect to the victim Voytyek Frykowski, you don't stab a person forty-nine times, strike him over the head thirteen times with a hard object, and shoot him twice if you are just trying to frighten or injure him. You do it to kill him. So, there is no question in this case [that] we are dealing with express malice, specific intent to kill. So, in this case, then, the seven killings were unlawful, unquestionably, and they also were with malice aforethought; therefore you have a murder.

The next question is, were these murders in the first or second degree. There are three types of first-degree murder. The prosecution is alleging in this case that these were willful, deliberate, and premeditated killings. With respect to the willful, deliberate, and premeditated type of first-degree murder, the word "willful" simply means that the act of killing was intentional as opposed to unintentional. The word "deliberate" merely means that the intent to kill was formed in the killer's mind as the result of careful thought and weighing of considerations for and against the killing. In other words, the killer realized what he intended to do; he knew it would undoubtedly result in death, but he decided to do it anyway.

The key word and most important requirement of first-degree murder is that the killing be "premeditated"—premeditation. Premeditation refers to the time element.

In a premeditated murder, not only must the intent to kill precede the act of killing, but the intent to kill must have been formed as a result of some pre-existing reflection. In other words, an instantaneous spur-of-the-moment decision to kill is not a premeditated murder. However, as His Honor will instruct you, the law does not undertake to measure in specific units of time the length of period that the intent to kill has to be pondered in a killer's mind before it will ripen, as it were, into an intent to kill that is truly premeditated. The decision to kill may be arrived at in a very short period of time, perhaps one minute; one minute might suffice. But a spur-of-the-moment, instantaneous decision to kill is not a premeditated murder. Unquestionably, the seven murders in this case were premeditated murders. The killers, armed with deadly weapons, went into the homes of the victims, in the dead of night, and mercilessly stabbed them to death.

We will talk a little about conspiracy. As you know, all of these defendants are charged with the crime of conspiracy to commit murder. A conspiracy is nothing more, ladies and gentlemen, than an agreement between two or more persons to commit a crime, just an agreement; they get together and agree to commit a crime, followed by an overt act, in carrying out the object of the conspiracy. They form an agreement, then one or more of them commits some overt act to carry out the object of the conspiracy.

Now, how do we prove the existence of a conspiracy? Normally we prove it in the same way, the same way that we prove the state of mind of a killer, by circumstantial evidence. That is, we look at the conduct of the parties, and from that conduct we infer that the parties were acting together in concert; that they had a meeting of the minds, a common goal, a common objective.

For example, I like to give examples because I think they are very illustrative of what I am trying to prove.

Let us assume that A and B are charged with committing a robbery. Let's call it the robbery of the Gotham Bank—that's going back to the days of Robin and the Batman. In any event, A and B are charged with robbing the Gotham Bank. The evidence at the trial shows that A and B were seen by witnesses entering the Gotham Bank together, armed with guns. They held up the bank together and they fled together in the same car. Now, under those facts, ladies and gentlemen, to believe that A and B did not even know each other, and they just coincidentally decided to rob the same bank at the same time and coincidentally found it convenient to flee in the same car, simply would not be reasonable. It would be extremely unreasonable.

Even though there was no evidence of any statement at the trial, no evidence of any statement made by A to B or B to A, and no evidence showing A's and B's preparation for this robbery, the inference is unmistakable, it is unavoidable that at some time prior to A and B entering that Gotham Bank, they must have gotten together and agreed to rob the bank, i.e., they must have entered into a conspiracy to commit robbery. In other words, we can prove the existence of a conspiracy to commit robbery by circumstantial evidence, circumstantial evidence being they were seen entering the bank together and they perpetrated the robbery together and they fled together in the same car.

The prosecution would not have the burden of putting on a witness who was with A and B two hours earlier at the Ajax pool room and overheard A and B agreeing to rob this bank. We don't have that burden. No, in the case you have just witnessed, ladies and gentlemen, we have proved the existence of a conspiracy to commit murder, not just by circumstantial evidence which is a typical way, but by direct evidence. Linda Kasabian, ladies and gentlemen, was present with these defendants on these two nights of murder. That is direct evidence. Her testimony, which I will review in depth very shortly, clearly shows that on both nights these defendants were acting together in concert, had a meeting of the minds, a common purpose, a common goal. Their mission on both nights was murder. In other words, on both nights there was an agreement, a conspiracy to commit murder.

Once a conspiracy is formed, each member of the conspiracy is criminally responsible for it and equally guilty of the crimes committed by his coconspirators which were in furtherance of the object of the conspiracy. For example, A and B conspired to murder X. Pursuant to the agreement, B actually murders X. A, although he is not the party that actually murdered X, is equally guilty of that murder even if he was not present at the scene. He could have been playing badminton somewhere. It wouldn't make any difference. If he was a member of that conspiracy, he is guilty of that murder.

Although the evidence at this trial shows that Charles Manson was the leader of the conspiracy to commit these murders, there is no evidence that he actually personally killed any of the seven victims in this case. However, the joint responsibility rule of conspiracy makes him guilty of all seven murders.

DEFENDANT MANSON: Even if I have never been in the Gotham Bank!

MR. BUGLIOSI: Now that you have had a little legal background, I would like to discuss with you the evidence and the facts of this case.

In a very general fashion I am going to start out summarizing the testimony of the witnesses on the Tate murders; then summarize the testimony of witnesses on the LaBianca murders, and then finally the testimony of witnesses who testified to both the Tate and the LaBianca murders.

Ruby Pearl—Ruby Pearl testified that she has worked at Spahn Ranch for twenty years, and in recent years had been the manager of the ranch working for Mr. Spahn who is some eighty-three years old.

She first saw Manson in midsummer of 1968 when Manson came to the ranch with "one or two men and several girls." Some of the girls were Mary Brunner, Lynette "Squeaky" Fromme, Susan Atkins, Sandra Good, Ruth Morehouse, Helen Bailey, and Brenda McCann. She said the group called themselves the Family. In return for room and board, the girls in the Family cooked, cleaned, helped with the office work. The men took care of the trucks. They did not tend to the horses. Ranch hands working for Mr. Spahn did that. She said she never saw Charles Manson ever do any work at the ranch. She said Charles "Tex" Watson was always working on trucks and dune buggies, and was a good mechanic. She said the original group grew to between twenty and thirty. She recalls Leslie Van Houten started living there in the late summer of 1968.

Shahrokh Hatami. Mr. Hatami was a very close personal friend of Sharon Tate, and her director husband Roman Polanski. Shahrokh is a photographer and he photographed Sharon and filmed her on many occasions. Mr. Hatami testified that in late March 1969, he was at Sharon's residence one day at 10050 Cielo Drive. Sharon was packing to go to Rome the following day, and Hatami was taking some film of her. Abigail Folger, Voytyek Frykowski, and Jay Sebring were also present.

Sometime in the afternoon Hatami, who was in the living room of the Tate residence, looked out of the window and saw a man walking toward the residence; the man was by himself.

Now, we learned that this man was Charles Manson; the person that

Manson was looking for was Terry Melcher. [*Melcher was involved in the music industry and was an acquaintance of Manson. Manson hoped that he could interest Melcher in his music.*] But Hatami had never heard the name Terry Melcher before. I asked him whether he was angry about the fact that this man had walked upon the premises, and he answered: "Yes, because he was entering on property of a friend of mine, which I was concerned about because Roman isn't there and Sharon is there."

This is how he said he spoke to the man: "He was coming in; I went toward him. He stopped and I asked him who is he looking for. . . . He mentioned the name, and then I angrily, of course, I wasn't happy that he was coming to that property, and looking at the people he doesn't know, so I angrily pointed out, 'This is not the place. The people you want is back there and you have to take the back alley.' "

Hatami said then that he spoke loudly to the man and he demonstrated. He came off the witness stand and he demonstrated the manner in which he spoke with him. And when he demonstrated he indicated that he pointed with his finger when he said, "Take the back alley."

Hatami testified that near the end of this conversation with the man, Sharon Tate came out of the front door of the residence and said, "Who is it, Hatami?" And Hatami told Sharon that the man was looking for someone and he, Hatami, told the man to go to the rear. Hatami testified that Sharon could see the man and the man could see Sharon as they were relatively close to each other, and there were no obstacles between them. Moreover, when the man later turned around and walked away he walked in the dirt pathway, inasmuch as the dirt pathway was right in front of the Tate residence, and Sharon was standing at the front door. At that time she also would have the opportunity to look directly at him and him at her.

So, it appears, ladies and gentlemen, that Charles Manson saw Sharon Tate and Sharon Tate saw Charles Manson on the date of March the twenty-third, 1969, when Manson was on the Tate premises.

A very beautiful honey blonde, Sharon Tate, looked into the eyes of the man who the evidence shows just four and a half months later would order her tragic and violent death.

Now, the back alley may be an alley to Hatami, a foreigner from Iran, but to Charles Manson, a back alley is a place where they have garbage cans, it is the habitat of rats and cats and dogs. So I am sure he wasn't too happy when Hatami says to take the back alley. One doesn't have to stretch the imagination to realize that the Tate residence was symbolic to Charles Manson, and particularly the establishment's rejection of him.

Now, with an overall motive for these murders, an overall motive of Helter Skelter, the victims who Charles Manson ordered murdered really didn't make too much difference to him. As long as they were white and members of the establishment they were qualified, as it were.

On the evening of August the eighth, 1969, when Charles Manson sent his robots out on a mission of murder, since the only qualifications the victims had to have was that they be white and members of the establishment, obviously, it made immense sense to Charles Manson, so he may just as well select a residence that he was familiar with, particularly one where he had been treated rather shabbily and whose former occupant, Terry Melcher, had rejected him. If the Tate premises, ladies and gentlemen, did not symbolize the establishment to Charles Manson, no residence, no premises, ever would.

Linda Kasabian.

As you know, of course, Linda Kasabian originally was a defendant with these defendants and was charged with these murders in the grand jury indictment. Now, you heard the term "star witness for the prosecution" on television and in movies. However, independent and in addition to Linda Kasabian's testimony, the prosecution offered a massive amount of evidence connecting each defendant with these murders, completely apart from Linda's testimony. But Linda obviously was the single most important witness whom the prosecution called to the witness stand. At the start of Linda's testimony, I asked her why she was going to tell everything she knew about these seven murders, and she replied, "I strongly believe in truth, and I feel that truth should be spoken."

Linda was on that witness stand, ladies and gentlemen, for eighteen days. An extraordinarily long period of time for any witness to testify in any case. I think you will all agree with me that during that eighteen days Linda Kasabian and the truth were companions. Linda testified that she was born on June the twenty-first, 1949, in Bitteford, Maine. That would make her twenty-one years old now, twenty years old at the time of these murders. Her first marriage was at the age of sixteen and quickly ended in divorce. Then she married her second husband, Bob Kasabian, in September of '67. They had two children, a girl Tanya, and a boy Angel.

On July the fourth, 1969, a girl named Gypsy—her true name is

Katherine Share—a member of the Family, came to visit Charles Melton [*an acquaintance of Linda Kasabian*]. Linda had never met Gypsy before, nor had Linda ever been out to the Spahn Ranch. They got to talking to each other, and Gypsy told her that there was a beautiful man that they had all been waiting for. Gypsy told her that they were living there like a family, and that she would be accepted. Pursuant to Gypsy's invitation, and in view of the fact that she had been, in her words, rejected by Bob, Linda left her husband on July the fourth, 1969, and went to Spahn Ranch and started to live with the Family.

The first day she was at Spahn Ranch, July 4, she did not meet Charles Manson, but she did meet Charles "Tex" Watson and she had sex with him that night. The next day, July the fifth, 1969, she and Gypsy and Mary Brunner left the Spahn Ranch to go to Charles Melton's truck for the purpose of having Linda steal $5,000 of Melton's money, which Linda did. When she returned to Spahn Ranch, she believes she gave the $5,000 to Leslie Van Houten, although she did not know for sure Leslie was the person whom she gave the money to. In any event, she never saw the $5,000 again, and she did not receive any benefit from the $5,000. Now, let's face it. Linda stole $5,000. But let's also face the fact that the theft of the $5,000 took place after Linda had been exposed to the members of Charles Manson's Family.

DEFENDANT MANSON: At least a day and a half.

MR. BUGLIOSI: Also, let's face the fact that her state of mind—and I am not covering up for the fact that she stole the $5,000—let's face the fact that her state of mind was not the state of mind typically of someone stealing money, because she didn't steal it for herself. She gave the entire $5,000 to other members of the Family and did not profit in any fashion from it. She testified that she took the $5,000 to help Charlie Manson go to the desert. I don't know why they needed $5,000 to get there, but apparently Linda felt they did, or the Family felt they did.

The first time Linda met Manson, Charlie was with several girls, Gypsy, Brenda McCann, and Snake.

DEFENDANT MANSON: They were not allowed to testify either.

MR. BUGLIOSI: Manson asked Linda why she came to live at the ranch. She told him that her husband had rejected her and that Gypsy told her he would welcome her as part of the Family. Manson then felt Linda's legs, and she testified that she got the impression he thought they were okay. The next day Manson made love to Linda in a cove in back of the ranch, and he told her she had a father hang-up. Linda was impressed by this because no one ever told her this before, and she said she did have a hang-up. She disliked her stepfather very much.

Linda testified to life at the ranch. She said that the group that lived there was called the Family, and that she became a member of the Family. When I asked her what she meant when she said she was a member of the Family, she replied, "Well, we live together as one Family, as a Family who is living together, a mother and a father and children, but we were all just one and Charlie was the head." She said there were about twenty members of the Family, most of whom were young girls.

Manson told her about Helter Skelter and the revolution between the blacks and whites, and all nonblacks, including brown people, would be killed by the black men. Linda testified that Helter Skelter was a daily word in the Family, an everyday word used constantly. She said she even saw the word "Helter Skelter" painted on a jug in the parachute room.

Linda testified that she and all the girls worshiped Manson, that she loved him and thought he was Jesus Christ. She said Manson had a power over her and "I just wanted to do anything and everything for him because I loved him and he made me feel good, and it was just beautiful."

When I asked Linda this question: Did you ever see or observe any members of the Family refuse to do anything that Manson told him or her to do? She replied: No, nobody did. We always wanted to do anything and everything for him. The girls used to tell Linda, the girls in the Family, used to tell Linda, "We never question Charlie. We know that what he is doing is right." In fact, Manson told Linda, when Linda joined the Family, "Never ask why."

It is rather obvious, ladies and gentlemen. It is rather obvious that when the sun set at Spahn Ranch on the night of August the eighth, 1969, the atmosphere at the ranch, the climate at the ranch, was such that neither Linda nor anyone else would have dared or even wanted to disobey any instructions given to them by Charles Manson. Linda testified that on the afternoon of August the eighth, 1969, the afternoon of the Tate murders, "he," referring to Manson "was telling us, that the people were not really together, they were just off on their little trips and getting together. So he came out and said, 'Now is the time for Helter Skelter.' "

Now, mind you, ladies and gentlemen, this is several hours, just a few hours before the Tate murders. Manson is saying, "Now is the time for Helter Skelter."

Let's look at the transcript of what happened that particular night. This is extremely important testimony in evidence:

"The night of the afternoon that Mr. Manson said 'Now is the time for Helter Skelter,' were you still at the ranch that night?"

"Yes."

"Was this the evening of August the eighth, 1969?"

"I believe so."

"What took place that evening, Linda, at the ranch?"

"I remember I was standing out front at this one point and Charlie came up to me and pulled me off the porch, and I was standing at the very end of the porch, closest to George Spahn's house, and he told me that—"

"He told you what?"

"He told me to get a change of clothing, a knife, and my driver's license."

"Did Mr. Manson tell you to change the clothing you already had on or to bring an additional change of clothing?"

"To bring an additional."

"To bring an additional change of clothing?"

"Yes."

"Now, when you walked up to the car, you say Katie and Sadie— that is Patricia and Susan—were inside the car. Where was Tex?"

"He was standing over by the driver's side."

"Was he talking to anyone?"

"I think he was talking to Charlie."

"What is the next thing that happened?"

"Tex got in the car, and we started—"

"What happened at that point?"

"We got about to the middle of the driveway, you know, and Charlie called us and told us to stop, and he came to the car to my side of the window, stuck his head in, and told us to leave a sign. He said, 'You girls know what I mean, something witchy,' and that was it."

Much of the evidence, of course, I haven't got into yet. There is no question at all that Manson was sending Tex, Sadie, Katie, and Linda out on his mission of murder. Linda testified that they were all wearing dark clothing, Sadie a black T-shirt, Katie a dark T-shirt, Tex with a black turtleneck, sort of a velour velvet shirt. She said all three were wearing dark Levi's.

Linda testified that [when] they drove off from Spahn Ranch she did not know where they were going, although Tex did say he had been to the place before. Linda said she also did not know what Tex, Sadie, and Katie were going to do. In other words, Linda thought she was going out to steal that night. She apparently did not know that the mission was going to be murder.

As they were proceeding toward their destination, Tex told Linda to wrap the three knives and a gun in a piece of clothing, and if they were stopped, to throw them out of the window, whereupon Linda did wrap the three knives and the gun in a skirt of hers which was part of her change of clothing. Linda testified that Tex drove all the way to their ultimate destination. She said Tex drove directly to the Tate residence. The significance of this is that apparently this night as opposed to the following night when they were roaming the city, this particular night the killers knew exactly where they were going to go from the moment they left the Spahn Ranch.

She said that it took Tex between a half hour and an hour to drive to the Tate residence, and she guessed they arrived roughly around midnight. Tex turned the car around at the top of the hill, outside the gate of the Tate residence, and parked the car next to a telephone pole. And you will recall that Linda testified that eventually she, Tex, Katie, and Sadie climbed over the front gate.

She said Tex got out of the car, climbed the telephone pole, and although she doesn't remember hearing Tex cut the telephone pole wire, she did see a few wires fall onto the ground. Tex got back in the car, drove to the bottom of the hill, and parked the car. All four got out of the car at that particular point and started to walk up the hill. Tex was carrying a rope. Let's pick up her testimony at this point: "We climbed over a fence and then a light started coming toward us and Tex told us to get back and sit down."

At this point Linda began to cry on the witness stand and I asked her if we could go on, and she said yes, she's okay.

"A car pulled up," she said, "in front of us and Tex leaped forward with a gun in his hand and stuck his hand with the gun at this man's head. And the man said, 'Please don't hurt me, I won't say anything.' And Tex shot him four times."

"Did you actually see Tex point the gun inside the window of the car and shoot the man?"

"Yes, I saw it clearly."

"About how far away were you from Tex at the time that he shot the driver of the car?"

"Just a few feet."

"After Tex shot the driver four times what happened next?"

"The man just slumped over. I saw that, and then Tex put his head in the car and turned the ignition off. He may have taken the keys out, I don't know, and then he pushed the car back a few feet and then we all proceeded toward the house and Tex told me to go in back of the house and see if there were open windows and doors, which I did."

"Did you find any open doors or windows in the back of the house?"

"No, there was no open windows or doors."

"What is the next thing that happened, Linda?"

"I came around from the back, and Tex was standing at a window, cutting the screen, and he told me to go back and wait at the car, and he may have told me to listen for sounds, but I don't remember him saying it."

"While you were down by the car do you know where Tex, Sadie, and Katie were?"

"No, I didn't see them."

"Did either of those three come down to the car?"

"Yes, Katie came down at one point."

"Did Katie say anything to you?"

"Yes, she asked for my knife, and I gave it to her, and she told me to stay there and listen for sounds, and I did, and she left."

"When she left, did she walk in the direction of the residence?"

"Yes."

"Did you see either Patricia Krenwinkel or Susan Atkins or Tex walk into the residence?"

"No, I didn't."

"Were you all alone by the car?"

"Yes."

Linda testified that a few minutes after Katie left she started hearing these horrifying screams coming from the direction of the Tate residence. She said, "I heard a man scream out 'No. No.' Then I just heard screams."

She said, "I just heard screams at that point. I don't have any words to describe how a scream is. I never heard it before."

"How long did the screaming continue?"

"Oh, it seemed like forever, infinite. I don't know."

"Was the screaming constant or was it in intervals?"

"It seemed constant, I don't know."

"Now, what did you do when you heard these screams?"

"I started to run toward the house."

"Why did you do that?"

"Because I wanted them to stop."

"What happened after you ran toward the house?"

"There was a man just coming out of the door and he had blood all over his face and he was standing by a post, and we looked into each other's eyes for a minute, and I said, 'Oh, God, I am so sorry. Please make it stop.' And then he just fell to the ground into the bushes.

"And then Sadie came running out of the house, and I said, 'Sadie, please make it stop.'

"And then I said, 'I hear people coming.'

"And she said, 'It is too late.'

"And then she told me that she left her knife and she couldn't find it, and I believe she started to run back into the house.

"While this was going on the man had gotten up, and I saw Tex on top of him, hitting him on the head and stabbing him, and the man was struggling, and then I saw Katie in the background with the girl, chasing after her with an upraised knife, and I just turned and ran to the car down at the bottom of the hill."

"Now, when you told Sadie that people were coming, was that the truth?"

"No."

"Why did you tell her that?"

"Because I just wanted them to stop."

"You said you saw Katie. That is Patricia Krenwinkel?"

"Yes."

"Was she chasing someone?"

"Yes."

"Was it a man or a woman?"

"It was a woman in a white gown."

Linda later testified that she though the woman had long dark hair, possibly brown, "I'm not positive." And you will note later from a photograph of Abigail Folger that she does have long dark hair. You recall that Linda Kasabian was crying on the witness stand when she related her observations of these horrible murders. After Linda observed Tex stabbing Frykowski, she testified that she ran down to the car at the bottom of the hill. She got down on the ground and tried to collect her thoughts. She said her first thought was to go to the police and get help but, "I had a vision."

"What sort of a vision?"
"Charlie entered my head again. Tanya was there and I was just afraid for Tanya's life."
"Where did you think Tanya was?"
"I knew she was back at the ranch."
"Where did you think Charlie was?"
"I knew he was back at the ranch."

A few minutes after Linda got in the car, she said Tex, Katie, and Sadie arrived back in the car. She testified Tex drove off and Tex, Katie, and Sadie started to change their clothing.

She said there were only two knives and a revolver in the car at that point—the buck knife was left inside the Tate residence. There were two knives left still inside the car.

Now, we don't know for sure, ladies and gentlemen, whether this is the knife [*holding the knife*] that Susan Atkins left inside the Tate residence. We cannot be positive of that, but it would seem like it was because Susan Atkins did tell Linda that she left her knife inside the residence, and this knife was found on a sofa inside the Tate residence.

With respect to the revolver, I showed her the revolver again, and I asked her if the right hand grip was on the revolver earlier in the evening. She said yes it was, and she believes it was not on the revolver when Tex brought it back to the car. I asked Linda if Tex said anything about the grip of the gun after he returned it to the car, and she answered, "I am not positive but I think he said something to the effect that when he hit the man over the head that it shattered the gun and it didn't work any more."

"Did Katie and Sadie say anything as you were driving off from the residence?"

"What did they say?"

"They complained about their heads, that the people were pulling their hair, and that their heads hurt. And Sadie even came out and said that when she was struggling with a big man, that he hit her in the head. And also Katie complained of her hand, that it hurt."

"Did she say why her hand hurt?"

"Yes."

"What did she say?"

"She said when she stabbed, that there were bones in the way, and she couldn't get the knife through all the way, and that it took too much energy or whatever, I don't know her exact words, but it hurt her hand."

The poor little sweetheart, her hands hurt, could you imagine that? If ever there was a sweet little innocent girl, it's Patricia Krenwinkel.

Linda testified that after they drove away from the Tate residence Tex started to look for a place to hose the blood off their bodies.

"Did Tex eventually stop the car?"

"Yes, he did."

"Do you know where he stopped the car?"

"I don't know the names or anything, but it was a street—we had spotted a hose coming out from a house, and we went up the hill and turned around and parked and walked up to the house."

As you recall, later Rudolph Weber testified that this was his house. He said he came out, he observed the three people—four people actually, three of them apparently had been hosing themselves off.

"Would you relate what happened, Linda?"

"An older woman came running out of the house."

"This is the house where the hose was?"

"Yes."

"All right, what happened next?"

"And I don't remember her exact words, but she said, 'Who is there?' or 'Who is that, what are you doing?' And Tex said, 'We are getting a drink of water.'

"Then she got sort of hysterical and she said, 'My husband is a policeman; he is a deputy,' or something like that. And then her husband came out and he said, 'Is that your car?' And Tex said, 'No, we are walking.'"

"What is the next thing that happened?"

"And we started to walk toward the car."

"All four of you?"

"Yes. And the man was behind us."

"Did the man follow you all the way to the car?"

"Yes, he did."

"Do you recall what the man looked like?"

"I just remember he was old and he had white hair, that is all I remember."

Of course, Mr. Weber has white hair and he is approximately sixty-five years of age. And I asked her what happened at the bottom of the hill. She said they all got into the car. I said:

"What is the next thing that happened?"

She said, "The man was right behind us and he came to the driver's seat and he started to put his hand in the car to reach for the keys and Tex blocked him, grabbed his hand and just jammed, you know."

"What is the next thing that happened?"

"I remember we came to sort of a level part of the road and through a dirt shoulder, and he pulled off"—referring to Tex—"and handed me the clothing and told me to throw them out, which I did."

"What clothing are you talking about?"

"The clothing that the three, Tex, Katie, and Sadie had changed from."

At this point in Linda's testimony she identified the black T-shirt Katie wore, the dark blue T-shirt Sadie wore. The only article of clothing Linda could not identify, as you recall, was the white T-shirt. She said she doesn't recall seeing it at that time.

I think that is understandable, the mission this night, ladies and gentlemen, was murder. The reason, of course, why Tex, Katie, and Sadie and Linda were all dressed in black, obviously, was to avoid detection.

After Linda threw the clothing over the side of the hill, Tex drove off and told Linda to wipe the fingerprints off the two knives and throw them out of the window. Linda testified she wiped the prints off with a rag, and while the car was still in motion, threw the first knife out, a few seconds thereafter the second knife was thrown out, bounced into the curb off the side of the road. She testified she threw the knives out of the window shortly after throwing the clothing over the side of the hill.

She said she did not remember whether or not she threw the revolver out of the car. Now, if Linda didn't, surely one of these defendants must have, probably Tex. The revolver was found very close to where the clothing was found. Obviously Tex or Manson did not drive back to this area a day or two later and throw the revolver over the side of the hill, it must have been thrown on that particular night by either Katie, Sadie, or, probably, Tex, because Linda just does not simply recall the revolver being thrown out of the car.

Linda testified that after the clothing and the knives and undoubtedly the revolver were thrown out of the car, Tex stopped at a gas station where Sadie and Katie and Tex went into a restroom and washed off. Linda then became the driver and she drove back to Spahn Ranch.

Was Charlie Manson sleeping, ladies and gentlemen? Was he sleeping when Tex, Sadie, Katie, and Linda arrived back at Spahn Ranch? After successfully completing his mission of murder, was he sleeping? After all, Linda testified that they arrived back at the ranch about an hour to an hour and a half after the murders, which would place their arrival back at the ranch somewhere around one-thirty or two A.M. in the morning, when only the goblins are out. But no, Charlie Manson was up; he was up around two o'clock all by himself, and in fact almost in the same place in the parking area of Spahn Ranch where he had seen them off a couple—several hours earlier. Charlie was not going to go to sleep that night, when he sent his robots off on a mission like that he wanted to know what happened, obviously. I asked Linda:

"Was there anyone in the parking area at Spahn Ranch as you drove in the Spahn Ranch area?"
"Yes."
"Who was there?"
"Charlie."
"Was there anyone there other than Charlie?"
"Not that I know of."

"Where was Charlie when you arrived at the premises?"

"About the same spot he was in when he first drove away."

"What happened after you pulled the car onto the parking area and parked the car?"

"Sadie said she saw a spot of blood on the outside of the car when we were at the gas station."

"Who was present at that time when she said that?"

"The four of us and Charlie."

"What is the next thing that happened?"

"Well, Charlie told us to go into the kitchen, get a sponge, wipe the blood off, and he also instructed Katie and I to go all through the car and wipe off the blood spots."

"What is the next thing that happened after Mr. Manson told you and Katie to check out the car and remove the blood?"

"He told us to go into the bunk room and wait, which we did."

Once inside the bunk room, Tex told Manson and the group that when he arrived at the residence where the murders took place he told the people at the residence: "I am the devil here, to do the devil's work."

Tex also told Manson that "there was a lot of panic and it was real messy and bodies were laying all over the place but they were all dead."

In other words, Tex was reporting; Tex was giving his report to Charlie, mission accomplished, sir. But even the mission being accomplished was not enough for Charlie Manson. That wasn't enough. That wasn't enough that his robots had just viciously cut down and slaughtered five human beings at the Tate residence, their blood probably still trickling out of their dead bodies when Tex reported to Manson; that wasn't enough for Charlie. Charlie wanted assurances from all of them that they had no remorse. He was not just satisfied with the murders; he wanted to make sure that all of them had absolutely no remorse for what they had done. Of course, why should they have remorse? All they had done was kill five human beings. But human beings are pigs, and pigs don't deserve to live. Of course, they all told Charlie that they had no remorse. But even then Manson was not satisfied because his savages had caused fear and panic in the victims, and it was too messy. Charlie did not quarrel with the fact that five people had been brutally slain, but he wanted them to be slain in such a way where they didn't panic, I mean he is a considerate guy.

Before I discuss Linda's testimony with respect to the LaBianca murders, I am going to discuss the remaining witnesses whose testimony solely or essentially pertains to the Tate murders; then I will pick Linda up again on the second night.

[*At this point Bugliosi discusses the testimony of Rudolph Weber. At approximately 1 A.M. on August 9, Weber was awakened by one man and three women who were using his garden hose. Weber confronted the group and they drove away in a Chevrolet with a license plate number that was traced back to Spahn Ranch and the Family.*]

Officer DeRosa. He was the first police officer to arrive at the scene, arriving at about 9:05 A.M. on August the ninth, in response to a possible homicide radio call.

He testified to observing Mr. Parent dead behind the driver's seat of the Rambler. He testified to examining the premises and discovering the dead bodies of the five victims.

[*Bugliosi shows the jury photographs.*]

These are the five victims, ladies and gentlemen, as they appeared in life. That is Sharon Tate, Jay Sebring, Voytek Frykowski, shown here with Abigail Folger; and here is Steven Parent.

This is the way the beautiful Sharon Tate looked in life, ladies and gentlemen. This is the ghastly, horrifying way she looked after Susan Atkins and Tex Watson and Patricia Krenwinkel savagely murdered her.

Likewise, with the other victims, Voytek Frykowski and Abigail Folger. Here is Abigail Folger lying dead on the front lawn of the Tate residence. You will notice she does have long dark hair like Linda Kasabian testified, and she is wearing a white gown. You recall that Linda testified that Patricia Krenwinkel was chasing a woman with an upraised knife, and that the woman had on a white gown and had long dark hair.

That is Abigail Folger. This is Voytek Frykowski in death on the front lawn of the residence.

DEFENDANT MANSON: In color, too.

MR. BUGLIOSI: Here is a picture.

DEFENDANT MANSON: He wouldn't want to influence your mind.

MR. BUGLIOSI: Here is a picture of Jay Sebring alive, and in death.

Dr. Noguchi, the coroner of Los Angeles County, conducted the autopsy on the body of Sharon Tate and supervised and directed the autopsies on the bodies of the other four Tate victims, Frykowski, Folger, Sebring, and Parent.

He found sixteen stab wounds on Sharon Tate's body, all of which were penetration wounds. Four of the stab wounds were found in the chest, one stab wound to the abdomen, eight stab wounds in the back, one stab wound in the right upper arm, one stab wound in the left upper arm, and one stab wound in the right thigh. He also testified that he observed two rope burn abrasions to Sharon's left cheek. Two rope burn abrasions to Sharon's left cheek. And he concluded that these rope burn abrasions were caused when Sharon was hanged. Sharon was hanged at the scene. Maybe the correct grammar is hung.

The rope connected Sharon Tate's neck with Jay Sebring's neck, and it was also flung over a wood beam, and then it fell back onto the floor. If one were to pull the rope, it would have tightened around Sharon's neck, not Jay Sebring's neck. So, although we cannot be sure, it is entirely possible that Sharon received these two rope burn abrasions when either Tex, Katie, or Sadie—probably Tex—pulled on the rope, perhaps temporarily suspending Sharon in the air. But the cause of her death was not hanging.

The doctor's autopsy discovered an eight-month-old fetus, [an] unborn baby, in Sharon's uterus. The doctor estimated that the unborn baby could not have lived in Sharon's womb more than fifteen or twenty minutes after Sharon died. Now, although from a legal stand-point an unborn baby cannot be the subject of a homicide, I think you will all agree with me that in a very, very real sense, six human beings lost their lives.

Miss Folger's cause of death was "stab wound of the aorta." That is the large blood vessel. Miss Folger had twenty-eight stab wounds. All of which, however, were penetration wounds, and five or six of which were fatal in and of themselves.

Jay Sebring's cause of death was exsanguination due to multiple stab wounds. The doctor said by exsanguination that Jay Sebring simply bled to death. Mr. Sebring had seven stab wounds, all of which were pene-tration wounds, and three of which were fatal in and of themselves. Sebring also had one gunshot wound which the doctor also felt would have been fatal. Dr. Noguchi recovered the bullet inside the back of Mr. Sebring's shirt. It entered Sebring's body and passed all the way through and was lodged between his back and his shirt, where Dr. Noguchi found the bullet. This bullet definitely and unequivocally was fired from this revolver here, *People*'s 40. That is the revolver which has been connected with Charles Manson and the Spahn Ranch.

I will go into this in much more detail later.

Mr. Frykowski had fifty-one stab wounds. Fifty-one stab wounds. All of which were penetration wounds. Seven of which were fatal in and of themselves. Five of the stab wounds were to Mr. Frykowski's back. Now, you will recall that Linda testified that Frykowski was on his knees in front of the Tate residence, and she saw Tex stab Frykowski in the back. That was Linda's testimony. Now, Dr. Noguchi comes along and, lo and behold, Voytek Frykowski does have five stab wounds on his back. Again, completely corroborating Linda Kasabian's testimony.

Steven Parent's autopsy determined that the cause of death was multiple gunshot wounds. Mr. Parent had five gunshot wounds, two of which were fatal in and of themselves. Note, Dr. Noguchi said that Steven Parent had five gunshot wounds, however he testified that Parent was only shot four times, inasmuch as two of the gunshot wounds, gunshot wounds two and four, were caused by the same bullet. So Parent, according to Dr. Noguchi, was only shot four times. This is completely consistent, of course, with the testimony of Linda Kasabian who testified that Tex Watson shot Steven Parent four times.

The total number of stab wounds to the five victims was 102.

Ladies and gentlemen, 102 stab wounds!

[*At this point, Bugliosi explains that a fingerprint belonging to Tex Watson was found on one of the doors at the Tate home, and that a fingerprint matching Patricia Krenwinkel was also found in the house. Bugliosi also discusses testimony revealing the discovery of a bundle of bloodstained clothing, the clothes thrown from a car by Kasabian following the murders. The prosecutor then told the jurors of the discovery of a revolver, linked by expert testimony to the Tate murders.*]

Barbara Hoyt. The eighteen-year-old girl who is a member of the Family, who was a member and lived with the Family at Spahn Ranch, and at the desert between April and September of 1969.

She testified that Manson spoke to the Family at dinnertime. Among other things, Manson spoke about Helter Skelter, and he told the Family that Helter Skelter meant that the "blacks would rise up against the whites and everyone would die except the Family." Manson said—this is Barbara Hoyt's testimony now—that he would like to see Helter Skelter come down and that he would like to show the blacks how to do it.

She said the first time she heard about the Tate murders was on TV the day after the murders. She said she was watching television when Susan Atkins came into the trailer and wanted to watch the news. Susan asked Barbara to turn the channel, and Barbara turned it to Channel 2 for the six o'clock news. She said Sadie called Tex and Patricia Krenwinkel into the trailer, and she is pretty sure that Tex and Katie actually came into the trailer to watch the news. She said the group watched the

TV account of the Tate murders. At one point a couple of the group watching TV laughed.

Unbelievable! Unbelievable! Watching the TV account of the Tate murders, and they are laughing, ladies and gentlemen. Can you believe it? Stop to think about it for a moment. Yes, five people being brutally slain and butchered like animals is a rather amusing event.

Right after the news, Sadie and Tex and Katie left the trailer.

Barbara testified that in late August she went to the desert in Inyo County, California, with Manson, Tex, and several of the girls in the Family, and they lived at Barker Ranch, Meyer's Ranch, and Lotus Mine, moving from place to place.

She said that Manson would always be the one to make the decision when they would move from one location to another location, not anyone else in the Family, just Charlie.

She recalled one incident at Meyer's Ranch in September—

DEFENDANT ATKINS: Ladies and gentlemen of the jury, Barbara Hoyt was supposed to have had LSD—

THE COURT: Remove Miss Atkins from the courtroom. [*As Atkins was being escorted from the courtroom, she pushed Bugliosi's notes to the floor.*]

MR. BUGLIOSI: (sotto voce) You little bitch!

THE COURT: Sit down, Mr. Kanarek.

MR. KANAREK: May we approach the bench?

THE COURT: You may not.

MR. KANAREK: May the record reflect—

THE COURT: Proceed, Mr. Bugliosi.

MR. KANAREK: Your Honor, just to preserve what Mr. Bugliosi said, that's all.

THE COURT: You may make your record during the recess. Let's proceed.

MR. KANAREK: Thank you, Your Honor, also to make a motion, Your Honor.

MR. BUGLIOSI: She recalls this incident when Manson told Tex to go to the bottom of the wash area and fix the dune buggy. She testified that Tex left shortly thereafter.

"Do you recall any sleeping incident at Meyer's Ranch involving Mr. Manson and yourself and Tex and Kitty Lutesinger?"

"Yes."

"When did the sleeping incident take place at Meyer's Ranch?"

"Early September or late August."

"Of '69—"

DEFENDANT KRENWINKEL: Tell the truth—

THE COURT: Remove Miss Krenwinkel from the courtroom.

DEFENDANT KRENWINKEL: And you are going to be eaten up by your own lie.

THE COURT: The jury is admonished to disregard the statements of the defendants.

THE COURT: You may proceed, Mr. Bugliosi.

MR. BUGLIOSI: Thank you, Your Honor. I will go on. We had a slight little interruption, as you saw.

I asked Hoyt, "Did you ever, at any time during your living with the Family, ever hear Tex Watson tell Charles Manson to do anything?" And she answered, "No."

How complete was Manson's control over this Family? Tex Watson can't even go to sleep at night before Charlie. He couldn't even go to sleep and lie down on the good earth without Charlie complaining and telling him to get up.

Barbara also testified that in September of '69, while at Meyer's Ranch, she heard Sadie tell Ruth Morehouse that "Sharon Tate came out and she said, 'What is going on here,' or something like that, and Sadie said, 'Shut up, woman.'" She said Sadie also told Ruth Morehouse that Sharon Tate was the last to die because she had to see everybody else go first. If there ever was a little sweetheart on the face of this earth, it was Susan Atkins. This statement by Susan Atkins, standing alone, without anything else, is enough to convict her of all five counts of murder, ladies and gentlemen.

Virginia Castro. Mrs. Castro also goes by the name of Virginia Graham, and I will be referring to her as Virginia Graham.

She testified that in October and November of '69, she was incarcerated at Sybil Brand Institute for Women in East Los Angeles, and while there she met Susan Atkins, whom she knew as Sadie Glutz.

She said that the other girls used to make fun of Sadie because Sadie would do exercises without any underclothing underneath, and she would sing and dance to go-go all the time, and this type of behavior just simply didn't seem to fit the environment out at Sybil Brand. After all, that is a jail out there.

She said the other girls used to laugh at Sadie and every time Sadie would come by, or frequently, they would say, "There goes Sadie Glutz." She said, by and large, other girls used to ignore Sadie. This caused Virginia Graham to feel somewhat sorry for Sadie, and she tried to befriend her and become friendly with her. She testified that on or about November the sixth, 1969, she had a conversation with Sadie about the Tate murders. The conversation took place around 4:45 P.M., on Virginia Graham's bed.

"What were the circumstances leading up to the conversation about the Tate murders?"

"Well, we started talking, we were talking about many things, and then the conversation drifted on to LSD, which I, myself, had taken one time, and we discussed LSD for a while. And then I warned Sadie that she talked entirely too much. I told her that I didn't care particularly what she had done, but I didn't think it was advisable for her to talk so much. She told me that she wasn't really worried about it. And she also told me that she could tell by looking at me, my eyes, that I was a kind person; and that she wasn't worried about it anyway. And that the police were on the wrong track about some murders. And I said, 'What do you mean?' And she said to me, 'The murders at Benedict Canyon.' And just for a moment I didn't quite snap to what she meant, and I said, 'Benedict Canyon?' And she said, 'Yes. The Tate murders.' And she said, 'You know who did it, don't you?' And I said, 'No, I don't.' And she said, 'Well, you are looking at her.' "

"When she told you this, I take it you were probably somewhat shocked, is that correct?"

"Yes."

"Well, what did Susan Atkins tell you with respect to the Tate murders, taking it from the very beginning?"

"She said that after she entered the house, the Tate house, she proceeded toward the bedroom. She noticed a girl sitting in a chair reading a book; the girl didn't look up and notice her. She continued toward the bedroom and she reached the bedroom door. Sharon Tate was sitting in bed with a pillow propped up behind her and Jay Sebring was sitting at the side of the bed and they were engrossed in conversation, and at first she wasn't noticed."

"Did you ask her how Sharon Tate was dressed?"

"Yes, I did. She said she had a bikini bra and pants on."

"Did she identify the person who was seated at the bed with Sharon?"

"Yes, she did."

"What name did she give?"

"Jay Sebring."

"Did she say whether or not Sharon Tate and Jay Sebring eventually entered the living room of the Tate residence?"

"Yes, she did."

"After Sharon Tate and Jay Sebring entered the living room, what did Susan Atkins say took place?"

"She said that the other man—"

"Now, when you say 'other man,' did she indicate that this was a man other than Jay Sebring?"

"Yes, sir, she did."

"What did she say about this other man?"

"She said that the other man ran past her, and as he ran past her she stabbed him four or five times. He got to the door and he started screaming for help. He got out onto the front lawn and he was screaming, 'Help, help, somebody please help!' And with this she put her hand on her hip and she said to me, 'And would you believe that he was screaming "Help, help," and nobody came?' "

"This is what Susan Atkins told you?"

"That's right."

"What else did Sadie say she did?"

"She said she was holding Sharon Tate's arms behind her, and that Sharon Tate looked at her and she said she was crying and said to her, 'Please, please don't kill me, I don't want to die. I just want to have my baby.' She said, 'And I looked Sharon straight in the eye and I said to her, "Look, bitch, you might as well face it right now, you're going to die, and I don't feel a thing behind it," and in a few minutes she was dead.' "

"Did Susan Atkins say whether she in fact killed Sharon Tate?"

"Yes, she did."

"What did she say?"

"She said, 'I killed her.' "

"Did Miss Atkins say anything about blood at that point?"

"Yes, she did."

"What did she say?"

"She said that she had blood in her hand and she looked at her hand and she took her hand and she put it up to her mouth and she said, 'To taste death and yet give life, wow, what a trick.' "

Not just a robot, but a bloodthirsty robot. Bloodthirsty robots. Can you believe that? Susan Atkins is tasting Sharon Tate's blood. Unbelievable.

"Did Miss Atkins ask you if you had ever had that type of experience with blood?"

"Yes, she did. She asked me if I was interested in blood, and I said that I had seen it, and she said that it was really beautiful; that it was warm and sticky."

"Did she say anything about the eyes of the people there at the Tate residence?"

"Yes, she did. She told me that she wanted to take their eyes out and squash them against the wall, and cut their fingers off, but that she didn't have time."

Susan, of course, is just a cloistered nun type, ladies and gentlemen. She is as innocent, of course, as a newborn baby, a little darling.

"Did Miss Atkins tell you anything about who was the last to die at the Tate residence?"

"Yes, she did."

"What did she say?"

"She told me Sharon was the last to die."

"Did she say anything about a knife of hers?"

"Yes, she did. She told me that she lost her knife up there; that she looked for it for a few minutes but could not find it, and then she said she thought the dog had taken it outside and buried it."

"As Miss Atkins was discussing these murders with you, did she say anything about how it felt to stab a human being with a knife?"

"Yes, she did."

"What did she say?"

"She said that when the knife went in, it felt soft and that it was quite a thrill."

"Did you ask Miss Atkins if she knew the people who lived at the Tate residence?"

"Yes, I did."

"What did she say?"

"She said no, that she did not know the people that lived there, but that it did not matter who was there because they would all die."

"Did you ask Miss Atkins how she felt after these murders?"

"Yes, I did."

"What did she say, if anything?"

"She said that she was tired but she felt elated and at peace with herself."

It is too bad that Sadie was tired. What right did these victims have to cause Sadie to be tired?

"During your conversation with Miss Atkins did you again remind her that she should not tell people about what she was telling you?"

"Yes, I did."

"What did she say, if anything?"

"She smiled and she told me that she wasn't worried about it; that she knew how to play crazy and how to act like a little girl, and besides that, she had an alibi anyway."

"Would you describe for the judge and the jury in your own words Sadie's demeanor, Susan Atkins's demeanor, when she spoke to you about these murders?"

"Well, I would say she was highly excited about it, and was very intense about it, almost to the point of reliving it again and enjoying it."

"Did she speak to you loudly when she told you about these murders?"

"Yes, she did, she raised her voice quite a bit. In fact, a few times I told her to lower her voice."

"Did Miss Atkins say that she was sorry or had any remorse for these murders?"

"Absolutely no remorse, nothing."

Now, we must discuss the testimony of witnesses whose testimony primarily pertained to the LaBianca murders.

Harold True testified that he lived at 3267 Waverly Drive in Los Angeles, from the early part of '67 until September of '68, the next door to where True lived was the LaBianca residence.

True testified that in March of '68, Manson, Krenwinkel, Susan Atkins, and several other people who were with Manson, mostly girls, stayed overnight at the True residence. True also testified that in the summer of 1968, Linda Kasabian and her husband visited him at his home once. Linda and her husband were not with Mr. Manson and his group. True testified that on four or five other occasions after the March '68 incident, Manson visited him at his residence. On one of those occasions Manson again stayed overnight. Now, note the tremendous significance, ladies and gentlemen, of this testimony. This testimony by Harold True places Charles Manson, Patricia Krenwinkel, and Susan Atkins right next door to the LaBianca residence, right next door, on occasions prior to the LaBianca murders.

Manson and the others probably never even knew the LaBiancas; in fact, True indicated that when he was living there it was his impression that the home next door was vacant.

The evidence in this trial showed that Charles Manson was on the Tate premises twice, and right next door to the LaBianca residence on several occasions prior to these murders. Now, that is not just a coincidence, ladies and gentlemen, it can't be.

Linda testified that the night after the Tate murders, that is the night of August 9, 1969, she had dinner with the Family in the saloon. We are getting back to Linda again now. This is the night of the LaBianca murders, ladies and gentlemen, the next night after the Tate murders, the very next night of the La Bianca murders.

I asked Linda whether she recalled what time she finished dinner with the Family that night and she said, "Usually an hour after we started."

"After dinner what did you do, if you recall?"

"Charlie came in and called Katie and Leslie and myself aside and told us to get a change of clothes and meet him at the bunk room, which we did."

"Did Mr. Manson say anything to you and the others, once you were all together in the bunk house?"

"Yes, he did."

"What did he say?"

"He said we were going to go out again tonight. Last night was too messy and that he was going to show us how to do it."

"Now, Linda, you testified that the first night you had the idea that you were going on a creepy-crawly mission; you did not know there was going to be any killing, is that correct?"

"Yes, that's right."

"The second night did you know what was going to happen?"

"Yes."

"Did you want to go along with Mr. Manson and the others on the second night?"

"No."

"Why did you go along if you didn't want to?"

"Because Charlie asked me and I was afraid to say no."

Linda testified that after Manson stopped for gas, a mile or two from Spahn Ranch, Manson instructed her to take over the driver's seat. Manson sat beside her and gave Linda instructions where to go. Nobody else in the car during the entire evening other than Charles Manson gave Linda Kasabian any instructions or directions whatsoever on where to drive that car. Manson directed her to get on the freeway. Eventually she got off the freeway at the Fair Oaks turnoff in Pasadena. Once in Pasadena, Manson continued to give Linda directions, but there did not appear to be any specific house Manson had in mind. She testified his directions were, "A left here, a right here, turn around and go back, et cetera." Almost a half hour or so after arriving in Pasadena, Manson instructed Linda to stop the car in front of a home in a residential area. It was a middle-class one-story home that appeared to be in a Caucasian area.

"What happened after you stopped in front of this house?"

"Charlie got out of the car and told me to drive around the block."

"Did he get out of the car by himself?"

"Yes, he did."

"Did you in fact drive around the block?"

"Yes, I did."

"With the other people?"

"Yes."

"Did you come back to the front of the house?"

"Charlie was standing in approximately the same spot I left him, and he got back in the car."

Linda testified that after Manson got back in the car, they noticed a man and a woman a few houses away getting in or out of their car.

Manson remarked that the man was too big. He told Linda to drive off. As they drove off, she testified:

"Charlie told us that when he had walked up to the house and looked into the window that he saw pictures of children on the wall, and he said he couldn't do it, he couldn't go in, but he said later on that we shouldn't let children stop us for the sake of the children of the future."

"Was Mr. Manson continuing to give you directions?"

"Yes, he was."

"Where did he direct you to drive at that point?"

"I don't know the district or the areas, but residential areas, houses, and we came to one point, I remember I was really tired, I just could not drive anymore, so he just took over the driving and then I remember we started driving up a hill with lots of houses, nice houses, rich houses, and trees. We got to the top of the hill and turned around and stopped in front of a certain house and we all looked at the house."

Linda testified that when they were parked in front of this house, Manson said that the houses were too close together; that was the reason that he gave for driving off.

Then he drove to a church in Pasadena. She said he pulled into the parking area of the church and remarked, she recalls, there were a lot of trees nearby. Linda said she was not positive, but she thinks Manson said something to the effect that he was going to go into the church and get a minister, a preacher or priest or whoever was in there. Manson got out of the car alone, walked to the door of the church, came back to the car, and said the doors were locked, so he drove off. After Manson drove off from the church, he then got onto the freeway. He eventually got off the freeway, and ended up on Sunset Boulevard in a residential area beyond the Sunset Strip. At that point, Manson instructed Linda to take over the driving.

"Did anything unusual happen while you were driving east on Sunset Boulevard in the residential area?"

"Yes, after I had been driving for a few minutes there was a small white sports car in front of us and there [were] stoplights here and there, and Charlie—"

"Do you know who was in the car?"

"I believe it was a man, one person."

"No one else was in the car with him?"

"No, I don't think so."

"Did Mr. Manson say anything to you with respect to that car?"

"Yes, he did."

"What did he say to you?"

"He told me to follow it and at the next stoplight when it was green to pull up beside it."

"When the stop light was green?"

"I mean, excuse me, red, I get my colors mixed up. So that we were stopped. It would have been red, excuse me. Charlie wanted me to pull up beside the car, and Charlie was going to get out and kill the man, shoot the man, whatever."

"Did you in fact pull up next to this white sports car at a red light?"

"Yes, I did."

"Did Mr. Manson get out of the car or start to get out of the car?"

"He proceeded to get out of the car, yes."

"And what happened at that point?"

"The light turned green, so the car left."

And I think one point is abundantly clear, ladies and gentlemen, the only reasonable inference that can be drawn from Linda Kasabian's testimony, that up until the time of the white sports car incident, up until that point in time, Manson was looking for his victims totally at random.

You remember Harold True testified that Linda had been to the residence, to his residence the summer of 1968 with her husband.

"When had you been parked in front of that home prior to this occasion?"

"A year before, approximately, in July of 1968."

"What was the occasion for your being in that particular location a year earlier?"

"My husband and I and friends were on our way down from Seattle, Washington, to New Mexico and we stopped off in Los Angeles, and this one particular person knew Harold True, so we went to his house and had a party."

"Is this the house in front of which Manson told you to stop the car?"

"Yes, it is."

"Now, when Manson directed you to stop in front of Harold True's place, did you recognize the spot?"

"Yes, I did right away."

"Did you say anything to Manson with respect to this?"

"Yes."

"What did you say to him?"

"Charlie, you are not going into that house, are you?"

"Did he say anything to you when you said that to him?"

"Yes, he did, he said, 'No, I'm going next door.' "

"What was the next thing that happened?"

"He got out of the car alone."

"Did all of you remain in the car?"

"Yes, we did."

"What is the next thing that happened?"

"I saw him put something in his pants, an object, I don't know what it was."

"What is the next thing that he did?"

"He disappeared up the walkway, the driveway leading toward Harold's house, and I could not follow him any longer. He just disappeared."

"Several minutes?"

"Yes."

"What happened after Mr. Manson returned to the car?"

"He called Leslie and Katie and Tex out of the car."

"Was he out of the car at that point, too?"

"Yes."

"What happened next?"

"Sadie—excuse me—Clem [Tufts] jumped in the backseat with Sadie and I pushed over on the passenger side, and I heard bits and pieces of the conversation that he had with Tex and Katie."

"What did you hear him say?"

"I heard him say that there was a man and a woman up in the house, and that he had tied their hands and that he told them not to be afraid; that he was not going to hurt them."

"Did he say anything else to Leslie, Katie, and Tex?"

"Yes, at one point he instructed them, for Leslie and Tex, to hitchhike back to the ranch, and for Katie to go to the waterfall."

In addition to those instructions, ladies and gentlemen, Linda also recalls hearing Manson telling Tex, Katie, and Leslie not to cause fear and panic to the people. He was concerned about the people.

And although she is not positive, she testified: "It keeps ringing in my head that he said, 'Don't let them know you are going to kill them.' "

Now, wasn't that considerate, wasn't that considerate of Charles Manson?

Since Manson was able to leave Mr. and Mrs. LaBianca in their home all by themselves while he walked back to the car, we can assume that Mr. and Mrs. LaBianca believed Charles Manson when he told them that everything was going to be all right and he was not going to hurt them. If they didn't believe him, right after he left, it seems to me that one thing they could have done would be to run out of the house, to get help. There is evidence that Leno's wrists were tied. There is no evidence that Leno and Rosemary had their feet tied. So if they did not fall for Charles Manson's lies when he left the house, they could have ran out of the house for help, or they could have locked the door.

Manson probably left them still alive with pillowcases over their heads, and they probably thought he was just some freaked-out hippie, and if they did everything he told them to do and did not resist him, no harm would come to them. To fool the LaBiancas, ladies and gentlemen, Charles Manson had to wear the same mask that he is wearing in this court, just a peace-loving individual. In assuring them everything was going to be all right, and not to be afraid, obviously Manson had to talk to Mr. and Mrs. LaBianca. Can't you just picture the scene, ladies and gentlemen, Leno and Rosemary with pillowcases over their heads, Manson saying to them: "You two piggies just stay put, now, and everything is going to be all right."

And then silently snaking, snaking out of that residence to go down and get his bloodthirsty robots. Mr. and Mrs. LaBianca had no way of knowing that Charles Manson and his soft voice, his soft demeanor, was preparing them for their horrible death.

Linda testified that she did not hear all of the instructions Manson gave to Tex, Katie, and Leslie. Outside of the car, you recall, she said she heard bits and pieces. She testified that when Tex, Katie, and Leslie left the car, she thinks each of them were carrying a change of clothing in a bundle. Manson then got back in the car and handed Linda a wallet. Linda testified that she did not see the wallet in the car before Manson got out of the car. She also said it was the only thing that Manson appeared to have brought back to the car with him.

"Did he tell you to do anything with respect to this wallet after he handed it to you?"

"Yes, he did."

"What did he tell you?"

"He told me to take the change out of the wallet and to wipe off the fingerprints, and then—this is while we were driving off—and we drove a few blocks, and he told me that he would stop, and he wanted me to throw it out on the sidewalk."

"Well, when he gave you those instructions about wiping the fingerprints off the wallet, did you do that?"

"Yes, I did."

"Did you remove the change from the wallet?"

"Yes, I did."

"What did you do with the change?"

"I believe I put it in the glove compartment."

I then showed Linda this wallet, and Linda identified this as being the wallet which Charles Manson gave her on the night of the LaBianca murders, and she said she wiped the fingerprints off of it.

With respect to Manson telling her to throw the wallet out of the window, I asked Linda: "Did he tell you why he wanted you to throw the wallet out of the window?"

She answered: "Yes, he did. He said he wanted a black person to pick it up and use the credit cards so that the people, the establishment would think it was some sort of an organized group that killed these people."

Presumably, the Black Panthers.

However, Manson changed his mind and told Linda not to throw it out of the window of the car. He changed his mind at that point.

Manson then got on a freeway which Linda said did not appear to be too far from the LaBianca residence. As they were driving Manson said that he wanted to show "Blackie" how to do it. Driving on a freeway Manson says, "I want to show Blackie how to do it."

Linda doesn't recall what town or near what town she stopped. She testified she really didn't know where they were.

"What happened after you stopped the car?"

"We all got out of the car, started walking toward the beach, we got down to the beach, walked on the sand, and Charlie told Clem and Sadie to stay a little bit behind us. And Charlie and I started walking hand in hand on the beach, and it was sort of nice, you know, we were just talking, and I gave him some peanuts, and he just [sort] of made me forget about everything, just made me feel good.

"I told him I was pregnant and started walking. We got to a side street, a corner, and a police car came by and stopped and asked what we were doing. And Charlie said, 'We are just going for a walk.' Charlie said something like, 'Don't you know who I am?' or 'Don't you remember my name?' They just said no. It was a friendly conversation. It just lasted for a minute. Then they walked back to the car."

"With respect to this conversation with the policemen, did they write your names down?"

"Not that I saw, no."

Charlie wanted to pay a social visit, apparently, at five in the morning to say hello to someone and ask them how they were feeling and maybe have a cup of coffee and then drive off.

They all told Charlie they did not know anyone at the beach.

"Then he looked at me and he said, 'What about that man you and Sandy met?' He said, 'Isn't he a piggy?' I said, 'Yes, he is an actor.'

"And then he further questioned me and he asked me if the man would let him in. And I said, 'Yes.'

"And he asked me if the man would let my friends in, Sadie and Clem. And I said, 'Yes.'

"And he said, 'Okay. I want you to kill him,' and he gave me a small pocket knife. And at this point I said, 'Charlie, I am not you, I cannot kill anybody.' And I don't know what took place at that moment, but I was very much afraid. And then he started to tell me how to go about doing it, and I remember I had the knife in my hand, and I asked him, 'With this?'

"And he said, 'Yes,' and he showed me how to do it."

"He said, 'As soon as you enter the residence, the house, as soon as you see the man, slit his throat right away.' And he told Clem to shoot him. And then, also, he said if anything went wrong, you know, not to do it."

"What happened after you arrived at this man's apartment?"

"Charlie wanted me to show him where he lived."

"Did you do that?"

"Yes, I did."

"Did you get out of the car with Charlie?"

"Yes."

"What about Sadie and Clem?"

"No, they stayed behind."

"What is the next thing that happened?"

"We entered the building and we walked up the stairs. I am not sure if I took him to the top floor—I am not sure exactly what floor I took him to. Then I pointed out a door which was not his door."

"Which was not the actor's door?"

"Yes."

"What is the next thing that happened?"

"Then we walked back downstairs to the car, and he gave Clem a gun."

"Charlie Manson gave him a gun?"

"Yes. At this point he said something—"

"When you say 'he,' you are talking about Charles Manson?"

"Yes. He said that if anything went wrong, you know, don't do it; and of course, to hitchhike back to the ranch, and for Sadie to go to the waterfall."

Manson told Clem and Sadie that while Linda knocked on the door, for them to wait around the corner until she entered and asked the man if they could come in.

"Did either Clem or Sadie say anything to Mr. Manson at this point?"

"No, not that I know of."

"Then you say Charlie drove off?"

"Yes."

"What is the next thing that happened?"

"Clem, Sadie, and myself walked up—I believe I took them to the fourth floor, because I know I didn't go all the way to the top, and I went—as I entered the hallway, whatever it is, where all the doors are, I went straight to—to the first door, and I knocked. They hid behind the corner."

"When you say 'they,' you are referring to whom?"

"Sadie and Clem. And I knocked on the door, which I knew wasn't the door, and a man said, 'Who is it?' And I said, 'Linda.' And he sort of opened the door and peeked around the corner, and I just said, 'Oh, excuse me. Wrong door.' "

"And that was it? How long did you look at this man who opened the door?"

"Just for a split second."

Linda identified a photograph of the actor, and we learned his name as being Saladin Nader. She said the beach house had five floors, and Nader lived on the top floor. Linda said that the actor lived on the top floor. So, there is just obviously no question in the world that the actor whom Linda was testifying about lived on the top floor.

Now assuming—of course, we don't know, because Nader has not been able to be located—assuming that Nader was in his apartment house that night—we don't know, but if he was—but for Linda's deliberately knocking on the wrong door, the probabilities are great there would have been eight murders, not seven, on these two nights of horrendous murder.

Recall that Clem Tufts had a gun which Manson had given him, and Sadie was with Clem, waiting around the corner. Now, I am not saying, ladies and gentlemen, that Linda Kasabian deserves any medal, any award from the Kiwanis Club or anything like that; all I am saying is that there is a distinct possibility that she saved the life of a human being on the night of the LaBianca murders, and this act by Linda in deliberately knocking on the wrong door shows, along with all the other evidence in this case about her, that although she is not an angel—and we have never said she was; and she would be the first one to admit that she is not an angel—she is not cut out of the same cloth that these defendants are.

Keep one further point in mind. Linda was not a hard-core member of this Family. She had just joined the Family a little over one month before these two nights of murder; whereas, Sadie had been with Manson for over two years, and Katie and Leslie for over one year.

I asked Linda why she knocked on the wrong door.

"Why did you knock on the wrong door, Linda? When you knocked on the door of this apartment, did you know it was the wrong door?"

"Yes, I did."

"Why did you knock on the wrong door, Linda?"

"Because I didn't want to kill anybody."

[*Bugliosi discusses Kasabian's escape from Spahn Ranch and her eventual reunification with her daughter.*]

Linda told her mother about everything. Her mother went to the police; they arrested her. She did not resist extradition, and came back to Los Angeles the following day, December 3, 1969, and, as you know, pursuant to a request by the prosecution, on August 10, 1970, Judge Older granted Linda Kasabian immunity from prosecution for these murders.

And, as we saw, ladies and gentlemen, the testimony of the other witnesses in this case was 101 percent consistent with Linda's testimony. Linda's testimony about these two nights of murder, ladies and gentlemen, all by itself, without anything else, all by itself, I think convinced each and every one of you that these defendants committed these murders, just her testimony alone.

The LaBiancas. While Manson, ladies and gentlemen, and his killers were roaming the Pasadena area indiscriminately looking for their victims, Leno and Rosemary LaBianca were driving toward Los Angeles, their home, and violent death.

Officer Rodriguez, the first officer to arrive at the scene around 10:35 P.M., on August 10, 1969. He entered through the front door. Although the front door was closed, it wasn't locked. He observed Leno LaBianca lying on his back in the living room, a fork stuck into his stomach, papers all over, pillowcase over his head.

After Rodriguez observed Leno, he said he ran out of the house to his radio car and called for an ambulance and a backup police unit. Sgt. Edward Cline arrived around 10:45 P.M. He testified to discovering Rosemary dead in her bedroom. He also testified to observing the writings "Death to pigs" and "Rise" on the walls in the living room, and

"Helter Skelter" on the refrigerator door, and he identified photos of these things. "Death to pigs" on the living room wall in the LaBianca residence, the word "Rise" printed in blood in the LaBianca residence.

[Bugliosi shows the jurors a photograph.]

Here is "Helter Skelter." It looks like it is misspelled, H-e-a-l-t-e-r S-k-e-l-t-e-r, printed in blood on the refrigerator door at the LaBianca residence.

When the pillow was removed he observed a blood-soaked pillowcase covering Leno's head. Around the pillowcase was an electrical cord which was attached to a lamp around four or five feet from Leno's body. He observed the fork, of course.

And he also observed Leno's wrists to be tied with leather thongs, and he observed the word "War" to be carved on Leno LaBianca's stomach, "War."

He said he observed no evidence of a struggle in the living room, and he testified that Rosemary also had a pillowcase over her head, an electrical cord from a nearby lamp was also tied around her neck, very much like that of her husband.

He testified he found several items of value, such as several diamond rings, one of which was marked "14 karat," wristwatches, expensive camera equipment, many rifles and guns, a jar of coins, a coin collection, and other matters of value, personal property, all of which he said were inside the residence and easily accessible to anyone if their intent had been to steal.

Dr. Katsuyama. He is the deputy medical examiner for the Coroner's Office. He performed the autopsies on Leno and Rosemary on August eleventh in the Coroner's Office. With respect to Leno, the cause of death was multiple stab wounds to the neck and abdomen, causing massive hemorrhage.

The doctor said that when he removed the pillowcase he observed the knife, lodged in Leno's throat, and he gave it to a representative of the Los Angeles Police Department. He said Leno had twelve stab wounds in his body, all of which were penetration wounds, and six of which were fatal in and of themselves.

In addition to the twelve stab wounds, there were seven pairs of double-tined fork wounds, in other words, fourteen puncture wounds, for a total of twenty-six wounds in Leno LaBianca's stomach and body. The doctor also observed the word "War" scratched on Leno's abdomen. There were no defense wounds on Leno. And, of course, there wouldn't be. Leno's hands had been tied up around his wrists and obviously he was helpless, helpless to defend himself.

With respect to Rosemary, her cause of death was multiple stab wounds to the neck and trunk causing massive hemorrhage. When Rosemary's body arrived at the Coroner's Office, the pillowcase was still over her head, and the electrical cord was wrapped over the pillowcase around Rosemary's neck. Rosemary, ladies and gentlemen, had forty-one stab wounds, all of which were penetration wounds, eight of which were fatal in and of themselves. Dr. Katsuyama also found three linear abrasions on Mrs. LaBianca's back, which he felt were caused by an instrument such as a screwdriver, or the metal prongs on the plug to the electric cord. He ruled out a sharp knife. Rosemary had one defense wound to her right jawbone.

Dr. Katsuyama testified that several of Rosemary's stab wounds to her buttocks were definitely inflicted after Rosemary had already died, and he even circled these areas in black here, because you will notice that the wounds within the circle are [of a] very, very light color, very, very light colored, as opposed to the darkness around the wounds up above.

He found blood at various places at the LaBianca scene, took samples of the blood, and determined what the blood type was. The words "Helter Skelter" were B-type blood, Leno LaBianca's type blood.

The testimony of the following witnesses, basically, apply to both the Tate and the LaBianca murders. We are starting to get into an area now of Manson's state of mind, his philosophy on life.

First, we will discuss briefly Sergeant Gutierrez's testimony. He testified on the morning session of the second day that Linda Kasabian testified, he was seated in front of the rail here in court. He observed [that] Mr. Manson's and Mrs. Kasabian's eyes meet, and observed Mr. Manson make a slitting-of-the-throat motion to Mrs. Kasabian, by taking his right index finger and moving it across his throat from right to left. This act alone, of course, by Manson, is indicative of guilt. The motion by Manson was a threatening motion, the obvious purpose of which was to silence Mrs. Kasabian. He certainly does not want her to tell you folks what happened on these two nights of murder. You twelve people are the last people in the world he wants to know about these two nights of murder.

Gutierrez also testified that one day in August 1970, during the trial, he observed Mr. Manson came to court with an X scratched on his forehead. The very next day he observed the three female defendants, Atkins, Krenwinkel, and Van Houten with X's on their foreheads. This clearly and vividly illustrates the power and the control this man has over these three female codefendants. They follow whatever he does.

Incidentally, Revelation 9, you will be reading it back in the jury room, speaks of locusts going out into the world and destroying everything, including men who do who not have a mark on their foreheads. So maybe Charlie put that *X* on his forehead to save himself from the locusts.

Deputy Dunlop. He testified he was among the forty or so armed deputy sheriffs who raided the Spahn Ranch on August the sixteenth, 1969. He testified that when he first saw Mr. Manson, Manson was in a little hole beneath the floorboards of one of the buildings on the ranch. Manson refused to come out, and Dunlop had to crawl under the building and pull Manson out by his hair. So, just one week after the seven Tate-LaBianca murders he ordered, Manson is hiding out under a building at the Spahn Ranch. It certainly shows a consciousness of guilt on his part.

Of course, Manson had no idea why the sheriffs came to the ranch. He could have easily thought they were coming out there to arrest him for these murders. He was probably extremely relieved to find out that they were just making a bust at the ranch for the grand theft auto ring. Everyone at the ranch was arrested, and shortly thereafter released, on the grand theft auto charges.

Out of the twenty-seven adults at the ranch who were arrested, nineteen were girls.

Paul Watkins, Mr. Watkins as you know, is a young lad, twenty years of age, also a member of Charles Manson's Family, who knew Mr. Manson rather intimately. Paul is not a bad-looking young man, and Manson apparently realized this because he told Paul to go out and get young women and bring these women in to him.

Manson was sure to add, parenthetically, however, that he didn't want Paul to touch these girls before Paul brought them in to him. Watkins, in reflecting back, observed, "That was a pretty good trip on Charlie's part." Charlie liked young love, and he wanted them to be untainted; he wanted to taint them himself. He had this discussion with Watkins about Helter Skelter.

"During your association with Charles Manson, did he frequently discuss Helter Skelter with you?"

"Constantly."

"He used the word 'Helter Skelter' constantly?"

273

"I wouldn't go so far as to say constantly. He did not say, 'Helter Skelter, Helter Skelter, Helter Skelter.' But he did quite a bit, yes, it seemed to be the main topic."

Manson told Watkins, in January of 1969, the reason Helter Skelter hadn't started yet was because the black man could release his frustrations by going up to Haight-Ashbury and having the white man's young daughters. He said when the young white love left Haight-Ashbury, "Blackie" would have to release his frustrations elsewhere, and that elsewhere would be Helter Skelter. He said it was going to start that summer, that is, the summer of 1969. Manson told Watkins how Helter Skelter was going to start.

I believe that now it is clear to each and every one of you that Helter Skelter was the principal and main motive for these savage murders. Here is what Manson told Watkins how Helter Skelter was going to start:

"There would be some atrocious murders; that some of the spades from Watts would come up into the Bel-Air and Beverly Hills district and just really wipe some people out, just cut bodies up and smear blood and write things on the wall in blood, and cut little boys up and make parents watch.

"So, in retaliation—this would scare; in other words, all the other white people would be afraid that this would happen to them, so out of their fear they would go into the ghetto and just start shooting black people like crazy. But all they would shoot would be the garbage man and Uncle Toms, and all the ones that were with Whitey in the first place. And underneath it all, the Black Muslims would—he would know that it was coming down."

"Helter Skelter was coming down?"

"Yes. So, after Whitey goes in the ghettoes and shoots all the Uncle Toms, then the Black Muslims come out and appeal to the people by saying, 'Look what you have done to my people.' And this would split Whitey down the middle, between all the hippies and the liberals and all the up-tight piggies. This would split them in the middle and a big civil war would start and really split them up in all these different factions, and they would just kill each other off in the meantime through their war. And after they killed each other off, then there would be a few of them left who supposedly won."

"A few of who left?"

"A few white people left who supposedly won. Then the Black Muslims would come out of hiding and wipe them all out."

"Wipe the white people out?"

"Yes. By sneaking around and slitting their throats."

"Did Charlie say anything about where he and the Family would be during this Helter Skelter?"

"Yes. When we was [*sic*] in the desert the first time, Charlie used to walk around in the desert and say—you see, there are places where water would come up to the top of the ground and then it would go down and there wouldn't be no more water, and then it would come up again and go down again. He would look at that and say, 'There has got to be a hole somewhere, somewhere here, a big old lake.' And it just really got far out, that there was a hole underneath there somewhere where you could drive a speedboat across it, a big underground city. Then we started from the 'Revolution 9' song on the Beatles album which was interpreted by Charlie to mean the Revelation 9. So—"

"The last book of the New Testament?"

"Just the book of Revelation and the song would be 'Revelations 9.' So, in this book it says, there is a part about, in Revelations 9, it talks of the bottomless pit. Then later on, I believe it is in 10."

"Revelation 10?"

"Yes. It talks about there will be a city where there will be no sun and there will be no moon."

"Manson spoke about this?"

"Yes, many times. That there would be a city of gold, but there would be no life, and there would be a tree there that bears twelve different kinds of fruit that changed every month. And this was interpreted to mean—this was the hole down under Death Valley."

"Did he talk about the twelve tribes of Israel?"

"Yes. That was in there, too. It was supposed to get back to the 144,000 people. The Family was to grow to this number."

"The twelve tribes of Israel being 144,000 people?"

"Yes."

"And Manson said that the Family would eventually increase to 144,000 people?"

"Yes."

"Did he say when this would take place?"

"Oh, yes. See, it was all happening simultaneously. In other words, as we are making the music and it is drawing all the young love to the desert, the Family increases in ranks, and at the same time this sets off Helter Skelter. So then the Family finds the hole in the meantime and gets down in the hole and lives there until the whole thing comes down."

"Until Helter Skelter comes down?"

"Yes."

"Did he say who would win this Helter Skelter?"

"The karma would have completely reversed, meaning that the black men would be on top and the white race would be wiped out; there would be none except for the Family."

"Except for Manson and the Family?"

"Yes."

"Did he say what the black man would do once he was all by himself?"

"Well, according to Charlie, he would clean up the mess, just like he always has done. He is supposed to be the servant, see. He will clean up the mess that he made, that the white man made, and build the world back up a little bit, build the cities back up, but then he wouldn't know what to do with it, he couldn't handle it."

"Blackie couldn't handle it?"

"Yes, and this is when the Family would come out of the hole, and being that he would have completed the white man's karma, then he would no longer have this vicious want to kill."

"When you say 'he,' you mean Blackie?"

"Blackie then would come to Charlie and say, you know, 'I did my thing, I killed them all and, you know, I am tired of killing now. It is all over.' And Charlie would scratch his fuzzy head and kick him in the butt and tell him to go pick the cotton and go be a good nigger, and he would live happily ever after."

Watkins did not appear to be any dummy, but he testified that he actually and sincerely believed that Charles Manson was Jesus Christ when he was a member of the Family. Of course he doesn't believe that anymore. He recognizes Manson for the complete and total fraud that he is. When he was a member of the Family he actually believed that Manson was Jesus Christ. Watkins recalled one experience with Manson in which Manson almost killed him. He said,

"We was sitting around on acid, and I was getting kind of—I was feeling really weird, getting really stoned, and I was reacting quite a bit. And Charlie was telling me to die. He was just saying 'Die,' just 'Die.' And I didn't just die. So he jumped up and started choking me. At first I sort of fought it. I mean, I was going to physically fight it. Then I knew there was something else going on, so I didn't. I just laid there. But I was emotionally fighting it. In other words, I was scared, and really, really afraid. He was laying on top of me, looking into my eyes, and he was actually overpowering me. My throat wasn't strong enough to overcome the strength in his hands, and I noticed that there was a relationship between my fear and how strong his hands were on my throat, because it puzzled me that he could overcome me like this. So then it was going on for quite a while, in other words I was really running out of air, and then he smiled and looked in my eyes and he says, 'I'm going to kill you now.'

"And at that point I thought I was dead anyway so I just says—well, I couldn't talk, but I just sort of mentally said, 'Okay, I give up, go ahead.' And he jumped off and he sat back and smiled and said, 'Then if you are willing to die, then you don't have to die.' Then he said, 'Come on and make love with me.' "

Watkins testified, of course, to Manson's control, absolute and complete control over his Family. He said that one time Manson told him to hang on a cross near Spahn Ranch and be crucified, and Watkins agreed to do it. Watkins said he was willing to die for Charlie. He testified he never disobeyed Charles Manson.

Charlie once told Sadie to go to Rio de Janeiro to get a half a coconut—and Sadie headed out the door, at which time Charlie told her she didn't have to go, he wasn't that hungry for coconuts.

At this time, I would like to tie all the evidence together in a concluding summary. I will separate the wheat from the chaff and tie everything together.

In all murder cases, ladies and gentlemen, evidence of motive is extremely powerful and extremely important evidence. Motive points toward the killer. There is always a motive for every murder; for instance, revenge, hatred, money, fear, passion, escape. People simply do not go around killing other human beings for no reason whatsoever. There is always a reason, there is always a motive.

Likewise, there was a motive for these murders. The fact that the motive for these murders was not a typical motive does not make it any less of a motive. Charles Manson and Charles Manson alone had a motive for these barbaric murders. It was an incredibly bizarre motive. The motives that the codefendants, the actual killers, had, on the other hand, was a very simple motive. It was not bizarre. They killed the people "Because Charlie told us to."

One thing is abundantly clear. That the motive for these seven horrendous murders was not money, it was not burglary or robbery. These savage murders were not committed to effectuate a robbery. If that had been the motive, there wouldn't have been any need to stab Voytek Frykowski fifty-one times, to hit him thirteen times over the head and shoot him twice. There would have been no need to stab Rosemary LaBianca so many times. There wouldn't have been any need for any of these victims to have been murdered so mercilessly. One gunshot would have sufficed. And if robbery or burglary had been the motive, there wouldn't have been any need to print the words in the victims' blood at the scene of both residences.

In view of the unbelievably savage nature of these murders, and in view of the fact that hardly anything at all was taken from either the Tate or the LaBianca residences, and in view of all the other evidence in this case, including the statements of Manson, Watson, and Atkins that I have just referred to, a conclusion that these seven murders were perpetrated to help carry out some burglary or robbery would not seem to be consistent with the evidence in this case. The mission, ladies and gentlemen, the mission of these defendants on both nights, was murder. Clear and simple, murder. No other reason.

Now, why were these murders committed? Well, this trial answered that question. There appears to be three motives for these murders. There was Manson's hatred, his hatred for human beings, and his passion and lust for their violent death.

Anyone who could order these seven savage, horrendous murders had to have a lust, a passion for violent death. The evidence at this trial amply showed Manson's complete immersion and engrossment and preoccupation with death, blood, and murder.

Another motive—another motive—was Manson's extreme anti-establishment hatred. Unquestionably, on both nights, Charles Manson was viciously striking out at the establishment; and with respect to the Tate residence particularly, the establishment's rejection and repudiation of him. Of course, the principal motive for these murders, the main motive, was Helter Skelter, Manson's fanatical obsession, his mania with Helter Skelter. Helter Skelter was Charlie's religion, a religion that he lived by. To Manson, Helter Skelter was the black man rising up against the white man, and then the black-white war.

Keep this in mind, ladies and gentlemen, that murders as extremely bizarre as these murders were, almost by definition—by definition—are not going to have a simple, common, everyday type of motive. Just imagining the incredible barbarism and senselessness of these murders would leave one to conclude that the person who masterminded them had a wild, twisted, bizarre reason for ordering them.

The evidence at this trial shows that Charles Manson is that person who had that motive, and the trial showed what that motive was.

I, as a prosecutor, and you folks as members of the jury, cannot help it, we cannot help it if Manson had this wild, crazy idea about Helter Skelter. It is not our fault. Manson is the one that made the evidence, not we. We can only deal with the evidence that presents itself.

That evidence was that he wanted to start this black-white war out in the streets. That is what the evidence was that came from that witness stand.

On the very day of the Tate murders, a matter of hours before these five murders, Linda Kasabian testified that Manson said: "Now is the time for Helter Skelter."

After dropping Tex, Katie, and Leslie off at the LaBianca residence, as they were driving away on the freeway, Manson told Linda: "I have to show Blackie how to do it."

Of course, he then gives Linda the wallet and tells her to hide the wallet, and says, I hope a black person finds it and uses the credit cards, thereby leading the white community to believe that black people had committed these murders. On the refrigerator door at the LaBianca residence we find the words "Helter Skelter" printed in blood. We know the killers printed those words, "Rise," and "Death to pigs," printed in blood on the living room wall of the LaBianca residence. "War" was carved on Leno's stomach. "Rise," "Death to pigs," "War," all of these terms are tied in with Manson's fanatical obsession with Helter Skelter.

The Family at Spahn Ranch was Charlie Manson's Family, ladies and gentlemen. He controlled every single facet of their daily existence.

Manson and the Family used the term "Helter Skelter" constantly. It was an everyday word with them. Even a song composed by Charles Manson had the words "Helter Skelter" in there. The song "Helter

Skelter," as recorded by the Beatles, was played over and over again by Manson and the Family.

When these defendants and Charles "Tex" Watson printed the word "Pig" at the Tate residence and the words "Death to pigs," "Rise," and "Helter Skelter," and "War" at the LaBianca residence, instead of those words, ladies and gentlemen, they may just as well have printed the name Charles Manson. It is that obvious. Those words and Charles Manson are synonymous.

The prosecution at this trial put on some very, very powerful evidence of motive. All of it—all of it—unerringly and irresistibly pointed in one direction, toward these defendants, and particularly Charles Manson, and His Honor will instruct you—His Honor will instruct you that you may consider evidence of motive, you may consider motive evidence as evidence of the guilt of these defendants.

Very briefly summarizing the main and principal items of evidence against each defendant, including coconspirator "Tex" Watson, and without repeating many other items of evidence that I have already gone over, these are the highlights against each particular defendant.

Against Watson, coconspirator in count number eight of the indictment, in addition to Linda Kasabian's testimony, which, of course, proves that Watson was one of the Tate and the LaBianca killers, we have his fingerprints found at the scene. This is conclusive proof that he was one of the Tate killers.

Now, since Watson was a member of the Family living with Manson and the others at Spahn Ranch, and since Linda Kasabian testified that Watson was at the Tate residence on the night of the Tate murders, murdering the people with Katie and Sadie, and since his fingerprints were found at the scene, evidence proving that Watson was at the scene can be used by you as circumstantial evidence against his coconspirators. In other words, these defendants.

The fact that Watson was at the scene is circumstantial evidence against his coconspirators, these defendants.

Against Krenwinkel—and I am omitting many, many peripheral items of evidence against all of these defendants, I am just giving you the main ones—against Krenwinkel, in addition to Linda's testimony, which proves beyond all doubt that Patricia Krenwinkel was one of the murderers at the Tate and LaBianca residences, her fingerprint was found at the Tate residence, right inside Sharon Tate's bedroom. When you leave your fingerprints at the scene, ladies and gentlemen, you leave your calling card. You leave your calling card. It is positive, conclusive, scientific evidence.

Susan Atkins, in addition to Linda's testimony which clearly ties Miss Atkins in with the Tate and LaBianca murders, confessed to three people of her involvement in the Tate murders.

Leslie Van Houten. Of course, we have Linda Kasabian's testimony which irrevocably ties Miss Van Houten in with the LaBianca murders. In addition to that, Leslie Van Houten confessed of her involvement in the LaBianca murders.

Charles Manson. Of course, Linda Kasabian's testimony proves beyond all doubt that Charles Manson and Charles Manson alone ordered the seven Tate-LaBianca murders. In addition to Linda Kasabian's testimony, there was a massive amount of other evidence against Charles Manson. There was very, very strong evidence of his motive for committing these murders, and that is very powerful evidence, evidence of motive.

The .22 caliber revolver that was used to murder Steven Parent and shoot Jay Sebring and Voytek Frykowski was obtained by Manson on a trade for a truck. Witnesses saw Manson fire that gun at Spahn Ranch, carry it in a holster. It was Manson's favorite firearm.

Manson had been to the Tate premises and had been treated brusquely by Shahrokh Hatami and had been rejected by the former resident of the Tate premises, Terry Melcher. Certainly the Tate residence represented the establishment to Charles Manson.

Was there any other evidence against Charles Manson? Yes, of course there was. The Family, the Family that lived at Spahn Ranch in the very, very last analysis, was nothing more than a closely knit band of vagabond robots who were slavishly obedient to one man and one man only, their master, their leader, their god, Charles Manson. Within his domain, his authority and power were unlimited. He was the dictatorial maharajah, if you will, of a tribe of bootlicking slaves who were only too happy to do his bidding for him.

Charlie Manson's Family preached love but practiced cold-blooded, savage murder. Why was that so? Because Charles Manson, their boss, ordained it. If Manson had wanted his Family to be singers in a church choir, that is what they would have been.

On the other hand, if Charlie wanted the girls in his Family to be streetwalkers and the boys to pimp for them, again, that is what they would have been. But, churches and whoredom, ladies and gentlemen, were not Charles Manson's business. Charlie's trip was violent death. And since that was his trip, we have these seven Tate-LaBianca murders. He controlled everything that they did on a day-to-day basis. He even controlled their sex lives.

Manson's total and complete domination over his Family, including the actual killers, "Tex" Watson, Krenwinkel, Atkins, Leslie Van Houten, is extremely powerful circumstantial evidence that on the two nights in question he was also dominating them and directing everything that they did. He dominated Watkins, Atkins, Krenwinkel, and Van Houten before the Tate-LaBianca murders, during the Tate-LaBianca murders, and after the Tate-LaBianca murders, right up until the time of the Family's arrest in October of 1969 at Barker Ranch.

There is a very powerful item of evidence, circumstantial evidence, that you may consider against Manson, Atkins, and Krenwinkel on the LaBianca murders—not on the Tate murders—but on the LaBianca murders, and not against Van Houten, just Manson, Atkins, and Krenwinkel on the LaBianca murders.

Now, remember we discussed during voir dire, we went over it ad nauseam, that from circumstantial evidence of one fact we infer the existence of another fact.

Now, the testimony that I am referring to is this, it is rather clear, ladies and gentlemen, even without Linda Kasabian's testimony, in fact, without the testimony of any witnesses in this case, other than the testimony of the coroners [and] the testimony of the officers who testified of their observations of the murder scene, just by looking at their testimony without any other evidence, it is obvious, ladies and gentlemen, that the people who murdered the Tate victims also murdered Leno and Rosemary LaBianca.

Now, I say this because of the very, very substantial and unique similarities between the Tate murders and the LaBianca murders.

These murders happened on consecutive nights; both murders apparently were committed in the depth of night. The Tate-LaBianca victims were all Caucasians, and I think they would be considered or described to be members of the establishment.

Certainly, Sharon Tate, Abigail Folger, and Jay Sebring were rather prominent people. Mr. LaBianca was the chief stockholder in Gateway Markets.

Getting into the murders themselves, the main murder weapon in both the Tate and LaBianca murders was a knife; not only was the murder weapon a knife, ladies and gentlemen, but four out of the five of the Tate victims and Mr. and Mrs. LaBianca received a great number of stab wounds. The five Tate victims were stabbed 102 times. Mr. and Mrs. LaBianca were stabbed sixty-seven times for a total of 169 stab wounds! In fact, the cause of death of six out of seven of the Tate-LaBianca victims was multiple stab wounds. This multiplicity of stab wounds certainly is a strong similarity between the Tate and the LaBianca murders, and somewhat related to what I just said, both murders were marked by incredible savagery.

There was a literal orgy of murder at both places.

Also, both murders were marked by a lack, an absence of a conventional motive. Neither the Tate nor the LaBianca residences had been ransacked, and many items of very valuable personal property were found all over the residence and had not been stolen. These were not murders committed to carry out any burglary or robbery.

At the Tate residence, the killers placed a towel over Jay Sebring's head. That is kind of unusual, very unusual, and yet at the LaBianca residence Mr. and Mrs. LaBianca had pillowcases over their heads.

Sharon Tate and Jay Sebring had ropes tied around their necks. Leno and Rosemary LaBianca had electrical cords tied around their necks.

Perhaps the most unique and conclusive similarity between the Tate and the LaBianca murders is that not only did the killers print words in the victims' blood at the scene of both residences, which in and of itself was extremely unusual—extremely unusual by itself, but some of the words they printed were the same.

"Pig" at the Tate residence. "Death to pigs" at the LaBianca residence.

Now, what is the legal relevance? What is the legal relevance of these similarities to you? The legal relevance is simply this:

If you ladies and gentlemen of the jury believe beyond a reasonable doubt that Manson, Watson, Atkins, and Krenwinkel are the Tate killers, you are convinced of this fact, inasmuch as there are a remarkable number of unique similarities between the Tate murders and the LaBianca murders, the fact that Manson, Watson, Atkins, and Krenwinkel were the Tate killers is circumstantial evidence that they were also the LaBianca killers.

When you go back to that jury room you may consider this as circumstantial evidence against Manson, Atkins, and Krenwinkel on the LaBianca murders.

Briefly discussing the rules of law under which these defendants are guilty of these murders, you will recall my earlier discussion, beginning with my opening argument regarding the law which you are going to be dealing with during your deliberations, all of these defendants are charged in count eight of the indictment with the crime of conspiracy to commit murder.

Conspiracy is nothing more than an agreement, getting together, agreeing to commit a crime, followed by an overt act to carry out the object of the conspiracy. Conspiracies can be and normally are proven by circumstantial evidence.

In this case, we proved the conspiracy by direct evidence; Linda Kasabian, ladies and gentlemen, was present with these defendants and she told you everything that happened in her presence. To have a conspiracy it is not necessary that the conspirators enter into any formal agreement. All that is necessary is that there be a meeting of the minds; that they be working together toward a common goal.

There couldn't possibly be a more obvious conspiracy than this case, ladies and gentlemen. To say that on these two nights these defendants did not have a meeting of the minds and they were not working together toward the common goal would just be totally preposterous.

The object of the conspiracy on both nights was murder, and these defendants, working together with deadly and savage precision, carried out that mission of murder by mercilessly cutting down their victims. All defendants are guilty of count eight of the indictment, the count of conspiracy to commit murder.

What about the first seven counts of murder, what about those counts?

Patricia Krenwinkel is guilty of all seven counts of murder because it is obvious from the evidence that she was one of the actual killers of the Tate and LaBianca victims.

Susan Atkins is guilty of the five Tate murders because she was one of the actual killers of the Tate victims.

Leslie Van Houten is guilty of the two LaBianca murders because it is obvious from the evidence that she was one of the actual killers of Mr. and Mrs. LaBianca.

Since Charles Manson was not one of the actual killers of the seven victims, and since Susan Atkins was not one of the killers of Mr. and Mrs. LaBianca, under what rule of law are they guilty of these murders?

Manson is guilty of all seven counts of murder under the vicarious liability rule of conspiracy. It is also called the joint responsibility rule of conspiracy.

And likewise, Susan Atkins is guilty of the two LaBianca murders because of the vicarious liability rule, the joint liability rule of conspiracy.

The law is clear then that once a conspiracy is formed, each member of the conspiracy is criminally responsible for and equally guilty of crimes committed by his coconspirators which were in furtherance of the object of the conspiracy.

As I stated in my opening argument, if A and B conspired to murder X, and pursuant to that agreement B murders X, A, even though he was not the actual killer, is equally guilty of that murder. I don't care where he was; he could have been playing tennis, badminton, anywhere; he was [a] member of that conspiracy. He was guilty of that murder. That is the law of conspiracy, and there just are no ifs, ands, or buts about it.

Even if Charles Manson was merely a member, just a member of this conspiracy to commit these murders, and never killed anyone, he would still be guilty of all seven murders, but here he is not only a member, he is a leader, the leading force behind all of these conspiracies.

Charles Manson is a clever fellow all right. He is clever all right.

In Manson's world, he probably felt if he never himself killed anyone but had someone else murder for him, he was thereby immunized or insulated, as it were, from all criminal responsibility. Well, it is not quite that easy, and when you folks come back into this courtroom with your verdict of first-degree murder against Charles Manson, you are going to tell him it's not quite that easy. In the offbeat world of Charles Manson he probably never heard of this rule of law. Well, he is learning about it right now.

The law of this state, ladies and gentlemen, has trapped and subdued these defendants just as they trapped and subdued these seven helpless, defenseless victims whom they so mercilessly murdered.

His Honor will instruct you that Linda Kasabian is an accomplice to these seven murders. This simply means that in the court's judgment, Linda Kasabian's testimony concerning her involvement with these defendants on these nights of murder makes her an accomplice as a matter of law.

His Honor will go on to instruct you that you cannot convict any defendant on the uncorroborated testimony of an accomplice. If Linda's testimony has been corroborated as to each defendant, then of course you can convict each defendant.

If, on the other hand, her testimony has only been corroborated as to certain defendants and not as to others, you can only convict those defendants against whom Linda Kasabian's testimony has been corroborated.

However, the prosecution's burden under the law, ladies and gentlemen, is that we only have to offer slight evidence to corroborate the testimony of an accomplice, and this slight evidence, which has to be independent of Linda's testimony, can be any type of evidence, direct or circumstantial. Of course, ladies and gentlemen, we offered an enormous amount of evidence, not just slight evidence, which is our only burden, we only have to offer slight evidence to corroborate the testimony of an accomplice.

We offered a massive and enormous amount of evidence corroborating the testimony of Linda Kasabian. There is no question whatsoever that her testimony has been corroborated as to each defendant. Just for instance, Linda testified that three people were with her on the night of the Tate murders. What could possibly corroborate Linda Kasabian's testimony more than the fact that two out of the three people who she said she was with, Tex Watson and Patricia Krenwinkel, were proven to be there by positive scientific, conclusive evidence. In other words, their fingerprints were found at the scene. This evidence is totally independent of Linda's testimony.

And the third person, the third person she says was with her on that night, Susan Atkins, confesses to three people of her involvement in the Tate murders.

Of course, the confessions of Manson, Krenwinkel, and Van Houten also of course corroborate Linda's testimony.

And all of the other—many other items of evidence, all of the other many items of evidence I have just enumerated a short while back against each defendant on that Tate-LaBianca murders, of course, constitute corroboration of Linda's testimony. The evidence connecting these defendants with these murders was monumental.

The world's leading skeptic, I don't know where he comes from, whether it's supposed to be Missouri or some place else; wherever he comes from, the world's leading skeptic would have to concede that the prosecution clearly, unquestionably proved the guilt of these defendants beyond all reasonable doubt.

I feel confident; I feel very confident that Linda Kasabian's testimony alone without any other evidence satisfied each and every one of you that these defendants committed these murders. She was on that witness stand for eighteen days, ladies and gentlemen. Each one of you watched her very, very closely. If any witness was ever placed under a microscope, it was Linda Kasabian, and I am convinced that each and every one of you saw the same thing under that microscope, a young hippie girl whose aimless drug-oriented life tragically led her to Spahn Ranch, Charles Manson, and two nights of murder—two nights of horror.

You saw a witness who took that witness stand with one and only one purpose in mind, to tell you everything she knew about these two nights of murder. Although she testified for eighteen days, I am convinced that long, long before she was through testifying, long before that, it was obvious to each and every one of you that Linda was telling the truth.

The defense did everything possible during fourteen days of cross-examination to crack Linda's testimony. They never even caused a sub-microscopic dent in her testimony. It was ridiculous. If they were wise they would have let her alone. Not only was she an excellent witness, answering all questions in an honest, forthright, unevasive attitude, but the testimony of all of the other witnesses in this case was completely consistent with her testimony. Moreover, there was no way under the moon, no way under the stars, for Linda Kasabian to have known all of the details about these two nights of murder unless she was with these defendants.

All that can be expected of you as reasonable men and women is that you conscientiously evaluate the evidence in this case and apply your logic and your common sense and your reasoning powers and the law given to you by Judge Older to that evidence, and thereby reach a just and a fair verdict.

When you apply the law and your logic and your common sense and your reasoning powers to the evidence in this case, you won't have any difficulty whatsoever coming to the conclusion that the prosecution proved the guilt of these defendants beyond all reasonable doubt.

Under the laws of this state and nation these defendants were entitled to have their day in court. They got that. They were also entitled to have a fair trial by an impartial jury. They also got that. That is all that they are entitled to. Since they committed these seven savage, senseless murders, the people of the state of California are entitled to a guilty verdict.

Thank you very much.

CHAPTER EIGHT

Justice Delayed but Not Denied

Three Trials and Thirty Years Later, Medgar Evers's Assassin Pays the Piper

A bullet "aimed by prejudice, propelled by hatred, fired by a coward" exploded into his back and killed one of America's last great civil rights leaders. As Medgar Evers lay bleeding to death in his own garage, his three young children who had heard the explosion begged, "Daddy, Daddy, please get up."

Evers was a giant in the civil rights movement at the time of his death, as influential as peers Martin Luther King Jr. and Malcolm X. As a field secretary for the NAACP, he was determined to bring racial equality to Mississippi. His work included leading black voter registration drives and petitioning the federal government on civil rights abuses. Evers was a man committed to the goals of an integrated society. He wanted blacks and whites to go to school together, work together, and play together. Perhaps the most unique aspect of Evers's work was that he was not motivated by the need for public recognition. He was motivated by a desire to live in a prejudice-free America where blacks and whites could simply live together.

Medgar Evers knew that the fight for equality would be a momentous struggle. He acknowledged to family and friends that the struggle might cost him his life and maybe even the lives of others. Nonetheless, he continued to work day in and day out to fight for what he considered to be the most "basic" of all civil rights—equality. While living on the perimeters of death, Evers held fast to his goal and only allowed fear to serve as his greatest motivator.

While the 1960s was a time of positive change in America, it was also a time when the forces of segregation would dig in their heels and fight the fresh winds of integration. Byron De La Beckwith was one of those forces of segregation, who viewed blacks as "beasts of the field, who should remain unseen and unheard." De La Beckwith believed that in order to "preserve" the American way of life, the leadership of the NAACP must be exterminated.

De La Beckwith, an orphan, grew up in one of the most racist states in the Old South—Mississippi. This environment allowed him to develop his character as a well-known, outspoken, and opinionated bigot. He truly believed that his ideals paralleled the true intentions of our American forefathers.

After returning home from World War II, De La Beckwith was enraged with the direction in which "his" state was turning. The same events that enraged De La Beckwith served to motivate and inspire Evers. While Evers was on a mission to make changes, De La Beckwith was on a mission to turn back history.

De La Beckwith solidified his mission to end the heretical ideas of a civil rights leader on June 12, 1963. On that same night, Evers attended a meeting where he watched a televised speech on civil rights given by President John F. Kennedy. Just after midnight on June 12, De La Beckwith lay hidden, waiting for Evers to come home. Evers pulled up to the driveway, got out of his car, and, as his children ran to greet him, a shot rang out from behind and Evers was pounded to the ground. He died with his children and his wife standing over his body.

De La Beckwith was charged with the murder. Witnesses testified to seeing De La Beckwith's car parked near Evers's house and his fingerprints were found on a gun that had been discarded in the same vicinity.

A bullet, a cause, a white man, a black man, a murder. Simple. But the difficult part of this scenario was yet to come. The hurdle would come with trying to convict a white man for murder of a black man in the South in 1964.

In 1964, the fundamental question was not whether or not there was a murder but rather, whether it was a crime for a white man to kill a "nigger." Six months after the murder, on February 6, this question was posed to the all-white, all-male jury. With society awaiting an acquittal, a deadlocked jury was not only a surprise, it was the catalyst for change in the civil rights movement. After eleven days of trial, fifty-six witnesses' testimony, more that fifty pieces of evidence, and a 200,000 word transcript, six men held fast to their conviction that De La Beckwith was the assassin. This led to one of the most surprising deadlocks in Mississippi history. These six men kept the flame alive. Without them, there would never have been a second trial, a third trial, or the eventual conviction.

Even though the first trial did not end in a conviction for the prosecution, this deadlock was recognized as a clear victory. Byron De La Beckwith raised doubt even among a jury comprised of his true peers, all white men. It was this victory that gave the prosecutors a second opportunity to show that Byron De La Beckwith was guilty of the murder of Medgar Evers.

The second trial began on April 7, 1964. It was a trial that would be markedly different from the first. According to the *Clarion Ledger,* "The two principle differences were 1) the considerable dimming of the glare of publicity that surrounded the first, and 2) a businesslike, no-fooling-around speeding up of the tedious job of picking a jury."

The second trial was also a chance for a different defense strategy, which involved streamlining the jury. From the onset of jury selection, they first excused five members of the police force, one attorney, one engineer, and one fireman.

Even though the defense called this a change of strategy, these were really subtle differences. The second jury would still sit in the same seats, in the same room, and listen to the same lawyers argue the same facts as they did in the first trial.

Again, twelve white men were selected as jurors and they, too, listened to the white segregationist defend his story that he did not kill Medgar Evers. This despite the overwhelming evidence to the contrary. Again, in the minds of the jurors, the question may not have really been whether he murdered Evers or not. Rather, they were still contemplating whether or not this murder was really a crime.

Despite the prosecution's efforts and despite the evidence, the jury was again unable to reach a verdict. De La Beckwith went home with a second mistrial. A decision of eight to four for acquittal still left the state with the option to prosecute again. But, according to the prosecutor's office, they couldn't "see any way of doing it better than they already have."

The passage of considerable time allowed new evidence to surface. Decisively and most importantly, Deputy District Attorney Bobby DeLaughter and his investigator came in contact with FBI informant and ex-Klan member Delmar Davis. Davis was willing to testify that De La Beckwith had boasted of getting away with murder.

To Myrlie Evers, Medgar's wife, this was a last chance to find long-overdue justice. Her motivation, coupled with the newly found evidence, sparked the prosecution to once again try Beckwith some thirty years after the first trial.

Many were quick to criticize the re-opening of the De La Beckwith case. After all, the pitfalls of prosecuting old cases are no secret. "People die, memories fade, and documents disappear," said Paul Rothstein, criminal law and evidence expert. Indeed, as the third trial unfolded, several key witnesses were dead and the fatal bullet and rifle had been lost. DeLaughter knew the trial was "meant to be" when he found the murder weapon at his ex-father-in-law's among a vast gun collection.

DeLaughter fought back the problems and was able to get the third trial of Byron De La Beckwith under way. With a jury transplanted from various parts of Mississippi, the prosecutor's goal was to cover the case as quickly and as effectively as possible. After ten days of trial, the prosecution was wrapping up when breaking news came to the attention of DeLaughter: a new witness had appeared. On the day before closing arguments, Mark Reily had contacted the Jackson district attorney's office after seeing a picture of Byron De La Beckwith on CNN. Reily, a former prison guard, recognized De La Beckwith from his days working in the penitentiary. He remembered discussions with De La Beckwith when he was incarcerated at Angola Penitentiary for another crime. Apparently, De La Beckwith had a loose mouth and couldn't help bragging about murdering Medgar Evers. This evidence corroborated testimony of Davis's and other witnesses and according to DeLaughter was the "final nail in the coffin."

After ten days of trial and five and a half hours of deliberation, the jury on February 4, 1994, convicted Byron De La Beckwith for the assassination of Medgar Evers.

Biography

When Byron De La Beckwith first stood trial in 1966 for the murder of Medgar Evers, Bobby DeLaughter was more interested in playing Little League baseball than in the criminal justice system. Little did he realize that some thirty years later he would be the prosecutor who successfully convicted De La Beckwith for the assassination of Medgar Evers.

DeLaughter, as a law student at "Ole Miss"—the University of Mississippi—did not plan for a career in criminal prosecution. After graduating with his law degree, DeLaughter went into private practice. It was not until ten years later that he would join the district attorney's office. This was not the usual pattern for prosecutors. Typically, young lawyers fresh from law school come into the district attorney's office to gain trial experience before leaving for the lure of high salaries in the

private sector. For DeLaughter, it was different. After successfully practicing in the private sector, he left that career and became a deputy district attorney for what he believed to be the right reasons—to fulfill a
sense of professional responsibility, to do the right thing, to help enforce
the law equally regardless of race.

Prior to the De La Beckwith trial, DeLaughter had become one of the
senior trial attorneys in the Jackson County District Attorney's Office.
His skill and expertise made it only logical to assign him on one of the
most noteworthy trials in American history—the third trial of suspected
assassin Byron De La Beckwith.

From the onset, DeLaughter felt that he had a tie with Evers, one that
went beyond this as just another murder, just another trial. When the case
was reopened for investigation, DeLaughter, then thirty-seven, was the
same age as Evers when he was gunned down, and had three children, as
did the slain civil rights leader. But the sense of connection, of kindred
spirit, transcended age and offspring. DeLaughter greatly admired the life
of Evers, a life of unflinching passion for basic dignity and struggle
against the old ways of midnight raids and lynchings.

DeLaughter wanted to approach this case as what it really was—
murder—the intentional killing of another with malice aforethought.
As DeLaughter said, "This isn't about black versus white or white versus black. This case is about a man being gunned down and shot
down, in the back, in the dark from ambush, not being able to face his
self-appointed accuser, his judge, his executioner."

Commentary

Prosecutor Bobby DeLaughter confronted nearly insurmountable
obstacles in his prosecution of Byron De La Beckwith. Beckwith had
twice previously been tried for the assassination of Medgar Evers and
both times the jury had deadlocked, unable to reach a verdict. Retrying
a case that has ended with a "hung" jury presents several problems:
memories fade, witnesses disappear, and—even when still available—
seldom testify exactly as they had before, making them vulnerable at
cross-examination. Add to the mix that there had been not one but *two*
mistrials and the case becomes even more difficult.

DeLaughter faced another, more significant problem in his 1994
prosecution of Beckwith: the passage of thirty-one years since the assassination. Taking jurors back a generation, to a different time, presented
a problem for the prosecutor. The killing seemed like ancient history;

how do you make twelve jurors feel like this trial is not a day late and a dollar short? DeLaughter dealt with it straight up: "If you believe from the evidence that he (De La Beckwith) did it on June twelfth of 1963, he's guilty and its your duty to find him guilty. Because, you see, ladies and gentlemen, what we're talking about here, this type of offense, this type of murder, this assassination by a sniper from ambush, is something that's timeless."

DeLaughter began by recognizing that there is no substitute for a powerful and gripping introduction. His vivid description of a dying man crawling through his own blood to reach his family as his children plead, "Daddy, Daddy, please get up," is high drama, sure to grab the jurors.

DeLaughter made sure his description of the act, his revulsion, was shared by the jurors, putting them in the position of having to agree; who among them was willing to say they disagreed with the D.A. that this killing "spans the races. It is something that every decent human being should absolutely be sickened by, whether you be black, white, Hispanic; it doesn't matter. Murder by ambush is the most vile, savage, reprehensible type of murder that one can imagine. And that's what you've got here."

DeLaughter backed the jury into a corner, because he correctly guessed that we all think of ourselves as "good" people. When he says that this trial "isn't about black versus white or white versus black," DeLaughter is putting the jury smack dab in the middle. When he says that "this is about something that is reprehensible to decent minds," he is saying to the jurors that he believes they are reasonable, decent people. And when DeLaughter says that this case "is about society, civilized society, versus the vile, society versus the reprehensible, society versus the shocking. This, ladies and gentlemen, is about the state of Mississippi versus this defendant, Byron De La Beckwith," he has put the jurors in the position of identifying either with the good people of Mississippi, or with the villain who escaped justice for so long.

DeLaughter made it impossible for the jury to identify with the defendant, quoting vile passages from Beckwith's racist writings, passages that may have been unobjectionable in the early sixties, but that leaves a foul aftertaste in today's courtroom.

DeLaughter repeated a mantra, one that ties the defendant to the crime: "His gun. His scope. His fingerprint. His car."

DeLaughter gives the jury the motive for the killing, why Beckwith pulled the trigger. "And why did this happen? Why did any of this happen? For what reason was Medgar Evers assassinated? For what he believed. Not in necessary self-defense was this done. Medgar Evers didn't do anything of a violent nature to this defendant. What he did was to have the gall, the 'uppityness' to want for his people things like what? To be called by name, instead of 'boy.' To go in a restaurant, to go in a department store, to vote, and for your children to get a decent education in decent school. For wanting some degree of equality for himself, his family, and his fellowman, and for them to be accepted as human beings with some dignity."

When DeLaughter finishes his summation by telling the jurors, "in effect, you are Mississippi," and then asks them, "So what is Mississippi justice in this case, ladies and gentlemen? What is Mississippi justice for this defendant's hate-inspired assassination; assassination of a man that just desired to be free and equal?" there can be only one answer.

Bobby DeLaughter Reflects on the De La Beckwith Trial

In his novel *The Daybreakers,* Louis L'Amour wrote that "[t]he words a man speaks today live on in his thoughts or the memories of others, and the shot fired, the blow struck, the thing done today is like a stone tossed into a pool and the ripples keep widening out until they touch lives far from ours."

Some things are timeless. A single blast from a 1917 Enfield 30.06 caliber rifle, fired shortly after midnight in the early-morning hours of Wednesday, June 12, 1963, from a thicket of honeysuckle and sweet gum in Jackson, Mississippi, had—and is still having—just such an effect. It ended the life of Medgar Evers, field secretary of the NAACP in Mississippi. It followed his assassin, Byron De La Beckwith, who was tried unsuccessfully twice in 1964 by all-white juries, juries that ended up "hanging," unable to agree on a verdict.

A quarter-century later, the ripples emanating from that shot touched the state of Mississippi once again, as well as the lives of many individuals, including my own; on February 5, 1994, thirty-one-years later, a racially mixed Mississippi jury pronounced the long-elusive words, "We, the jury, find the defendant guilty as charged."

The verdict of the jury brought some degree of closure to the Evers family, and was a landmark event both in my personal reckoning and growth in my faith. There was a "bigger picture" involved, though it was for the state of Mississippi a crucial act of validation (to itself and to the world) that things had truly changed there over the past thirty years, in a positive way, for all races. Neither Mississippi nor I was attempting to relive the 1960s, but we could not, in my opinion, move ahead and realize our full potential unless and until we freed ourselves of the shackles of our past.

The jury's verdict in the Beckwith case was a significant stage in that catharsis. Mississippi, with the eyes of the world watching, was "called to the plate" to see how it would handle one heck of a curveball thrown at it. Mississippi not only hit a home run, it slammed one in the upper deck. We not only cast aside the shackles that had inexorably bound us to our past, we exorcized some of the ghosts of racism that had haunted us.

The case of *The State of Mississippi* v. *Byron De La Beckwith* illustrates that the system can work. While there is still racism everywhere, including Mississippi (though probably less there than in many places in the North), it is not going unchecked. This case reveals that human decency and simple justice are things that span both the gulf between the races as well as time—even if it takes thirty years to realize. It is never too late to do the right thing, for each of us personally, nor collectively as a nation.

No matter what our race or background, there are at least two common grounds of humanity—decency and simple justice—that may be shared by all, if we try. It is, I think, a noble message that began with a shot fired in the driveway of a modest home in Jackson, Mississippi, more than three decades ago, and its ripples are ever-widening.

One of the most crucial stages of any trial is the closing arguments—or summations—of the lawyers to the jury. This was especially so, I thought, in the Beckwith case. Four years passed from the time I began re-investigating the case in October of 1989 and the time we finally commenced the trial in January of 1994. Throughout that time, there were numerous negative comments made to me about my pursuit of this case, none of which had anything to do with the evidence or the law. Beckwith's guilt, to these people, was a given fact, but that was of no consequence to them. Some felt that it was wrong to prosecute a man of his age (early seventies). Some felt that it was a waste of taxpayers' money. Others thought it had just been too long since the murder happened. In other words, "Who cares?"

Four years of my life had gone into this case, and I barely had an hour to convince twelve total strangers not only that Beckwith was guilty, but *why* they should care, *why* they should take a stand, *why* they should vote to convict him.

I had made note over the years every time someone made a negative comment, asked a question, or expressed any doubt about the case. If the average person "on the street" had those kinds of feelings or questions, it was a safe bet that at least one person on the jury would have them as well. If that one juror, at the end of my summation, retained any of those feelings or questions, we were sunk. At best, there would in that event be another hung jury, just like the two in 1964. Such a result would have been erroneously perceived by many that nothing had changed in Mississippi in thirty years.

Thus, long before the trial began, I retrieved my notes and used them as an outline and a checklist for the things I had to say before passing the mantle in the case that I had shepherded for so long. I had one brief chance and second-guessing would have driven me insane, later wishing that I had said this, that, or the other.

The result is contained in this text. I make no claim of being a great orator—I can only attest that this summation was crafted from notes spanning a four-year period, and was delivered from the heart and with the passion of a man pleading with each man and woman on the jury, in a one-on-one soliloquy, to validate the previous four years of my life and the future of the state I love so much. Mississippi pulled through, and I am both proud and honored to share these words and feelings with the reader.

Closing Argument

The State of Mississippi v. *Byron De La Beckwith*
Delivered by Bobby DeLaughter
Jackson, Mississippi, January 25, 1994

When we started the testimony a little over a week ago now, I stood before you and I told you what the evidence would show in this case. I told you then that when all the evidence was in, you would see what this case was about; you would see what this case was not about; it is about an unarmed man, arriving home [in] the late hours of the night, having been working, coming home to his family, his wife, three small children that were staying up, waiting on him to get home inside the home there, getting out of his automobile with his back turned, and being shot down by a bushwacker from ambush. And that he dropped T-shirts in his arms, and he crawled from that automobile where he was gunned down, down the side of that carport, into the carport, trying to make it to his door, in this puddle of blood, with his keys in his hand, and his wife and children coming out when they hear the shot, and his three children pleading over and over, "Daddy, Daddy, please get up." And that's what the case is about. This man being gunned down and shot down in the back in the dark from ambush, not able to face his self-appointed accuser, his judge, and his executioner.

And the court has given you several instructions. And this instruction here tells you what the case is about legally. Legally, it's about whether or not this defendant killed and murdered Medgar Evers on June the twelfth, 1963. And you've taken an oath to make that determination, not on speculation, not on conjecture, and not on guesswork, and not "what if" and not "what maybe," but on the evidence. And this doesn't say unless the defendant is of a certain age, because no man, ladies and gentlemen, is above the law. And if we start making decisions like that, that doesn't have anything to do with the law, eventually, where do we draw the line? Do we say in this case, "We're gonna draw the line when the person is seventy-something," and in another case if they're sixty-five. No man, regardless of his age, is above the law. And it doesn't say, "Unless you find that this offense was committed thirty year ago." It says, "If you believe from the evidence that he did it on June 12 of 1963, he's guilty, and it's your duty to find him guilty."

Because you see, ladies and gentlemen, what we're talking about here, this type of offense, this type of murder, this assassination by a sniper from ambush is something that's timeless. This is something that spans the races. It is something that every decent human being should absolutely be sickened by, whether you be black, white, Hispanic; it doesn't matter. Murder by ambush is the most vile, savage, reprehensible type of murder that one can imagine. And that's what you've got here.

This isn't about black versus white or white versus black. This is about something that is reprehensible to decent minds. This is about society, civilized society, versus the vile, society versus the reprehensible, society versus the shocking. This, ladies and gentlemen, is about the state of Mississippi versus this defendant, Byron De La Beckwith.

Now, who could do such a thing? I'll tell you. [*Reading*] "The foul, contemptible, selfish person who continually tells the Negro that America is equally his; that he's as good as anybody; that he has the right to govern this land should be ashamed to lie like that. Believing such a lie has put many a darkie in the river late at night, some at the end of a rope, stirring others of their race to unrest. The Negro in our country is as helpful as a boll weevil to cotton. Some of these weevils are puny little runts and can't create the volume of damage that others can. Some are powerful, becoming mad monsters, snapping and snarling and biting the cotton. They must be destroyed with their wretched remains burned, lest the pure white cotton bolls be destroyed."

Well, in Medgar Evers, the field secretary for the NAACP, the focal point of integration in 1963, the boll weevil that fit the scope of this defendant's rifle was done exactly, what this defendant said in Exhibit 7, should be done. Eliminated, lest the pure white cotton bolls be destroyed.

Exhibit 69, submitted by this defendant, [*reading*] "Believe it or not, the NAACP, under the direction of its leaders, is doing a first-class job of getting itself in a position to be exterminated." So who could do such a shocking thing? And his opinion has not changed one iota from those words up until 1963.

How do we know that? Exhibit 71, written in November of 1976, [*reading*] "as much involved in Klan activity as a person can be." He hadn't mellowed one bit. That is what the words are that this defendant submitted, and whosoever—whatsoever a man thinks in his heart, so shall he become. And that's exactly what he became. He was on a one-man mission to exterminate what he considered to be the most important, in his words, "boll weevil" of that time. Lest the pure white bolls be destroyed.

And so we know from the evidence that on Saturday before Medgar Evers was gunned down, this defendant was in Jackson, Mississippi; couldn't find his prey's residence. Why? Because Medgar Evers, by that time, had to get an unlisted phone number. He couldn't just go to a phone book and look up his number and his address. And so he was down there at the Continental Trailways bus station trying to find out where he lived. And we know from the evidence that he went up to some cab drivers trying to find out. And then, we know after that his car was seen parked on the north side of Pittman's grocery, right there in the area. And so we know he was here on Saturday trying to find where Medgar Evers lived; drove to the location; walked into that vacant lot, getting things ready and set up. And then we know he went back to Greenwood; got this rifle; went out; target practiced; getting those crosshairs, those sights, set in for his target; got that scar over his right eye when the recoil of that rifle, when that scope jammed his eyeball there; went to work on Monday; worked all day; but what was on his mind? What did John Book tell you? All he wanted to do was talk about integration and guns. Couldn't even keep his mind on his business that day.

And so the next day was the day. The next day was the day, and his car is seen by those then-teenage boys in that area again. His car is seen by Barbara Holder who worked at times at Joe's Drive-In. This car, his car, is seen parked in that corner with the rear end backed into it, where all he's got to do is get out of that car right here in the corner where [it] was parked, walk down that path as shown in the pictures, get to this clump of trees, and wait. And he waited, and while he's waiting, he takes his hand and he breaks off this branch here, and what does he have? He has a hole. And what do you see in that hole? His perfect view of the driveway of Medgar Evers, and he waits.

And after midnight that night, Medgar Evers, unsuspecting, gets out; gets his T-shirts out of the car; and this rifle was propped up against this sweet gum tree that we know from the testimony of Officer Luke and the other detectives that were in the area that described the scratch mark in the bark there. And so he takes this rifle, and he braces it up against a tree, and he finds Medgar Evers, his prey, in this scope, and he pulls the trigger, and ends his life in one fatal shot.

He gets in his car. On the way out, he cannot be found holding that weapon in his car. No matter what his planning, no matter his effort— remember what Barbara Holder told you of when he pulled into this area, instead of driving up in here, instead of coming around the front, the car came from around the back. And so after he does his dirty work and he's on the way back to his car, perchance if he's seen or stopped, he can't afford to have this rifle with him in that automobile. And so he takes it, and he sticks it in the honeysuckle vines right here behind this hedge row. Gets in his car, and leaves directly, and he's heading north on Delta Drive, Highway 49, back to his home in Greenwood.

And so the gun is found in the search the next day. His gun. The same gun that he had traded, had obtained from Ennis Thorn McIntyre. We know that how? Several ways. The serial number on this gun matches the serial number on the invoice where Mr. McIntyre first purchased it from International Firearms. We also know from the testimony of that FBI agent at the crime lab, Richard Poppleton. Remember when he told you that he compared the cartridges that had been removed from this weapon with cartridges that McIntyre had provided to the FBI, and from comparing the individual microscopic characteristics that would be caused by that firing pin, and that breech face, and that firing pin and that breech face alone matched. Those cartridges came from one and the same gun, and you're looking at it. Exhibit 36. This defendant's gun. This defendant's scope. His gun. His fingerprint. His car.

We're not just talking about some 1960s model. We're talking about a 1962 white Valiant that witnesses say, what? It also had a long aerial on it. And we're not even talking about a car that witnesses say was a 1960s white Valiant with a long aerial. What did they say? What did they say, not only in this courtroom, but in the courtroom thirty years ago and to the police, it was a white Valiant—Ronald Pittman said it was a white Valiant, a 1962 white Valiant, long antenna on it, long aerial, and what else? "The thing I remember most about it, when we got up close was that emblem on the rearview mirror."

And so what did the police do? What did we have the police do? What did we have the FBI do in recent years? To go back and get this photograph, the negative from this photograph, enlarge this area here, and let's see if it has any type of emblem hanging from it. And so, lo and behold, there she is. Now a person's words may be one thing, but a picture speaks a thousand words.

His gun. His scope. His fingerprint. His car. And lastly, but certainly not least, his mouth. When he thought he had beat the system thirty years ago, he couldn't keep his mouth shut with people that he thought were gonna be impressed by him, and that he thought were his buddies and comrades, two of them from the Klan, one in Florida, one from Mississippi, testified. At least six people have given you sworn testimony that at various times in different locations, none of whom knew each other or came across each other at any time, told you what he has said about this. He wants to take credit for what he has claimed should be done, but he just don't want to pay the price for it. And so he hasn't been able to keep his mouth shut.

And so not only do we have his car, his gun, his scope, his fingerprint, his mouth, we've got his own venom. His venom has come back to poison him just as effectively as anything else.

And why did this happen? Why did any of this happen? For what reason was Medgar Evers assassinated? For what he believed. Not in necessary self-defense was this done. Medgar Evers didn't do anything of a violent nature to this defendant. What he did was to have the gall, the "uppityness" to want for his people things like what? To be called by name, instead of "boy."

To go in a restaurant, to go in a department store, to vote, and for your children to get a decent education in a decent school. For wanting some degree of equality for himself, his family, and his fellowman, and for them to be accepted as human beings with some dignity. This kind of murder, ladies and gentlemen, no matter who the victim, no matter what his race; this kind of murder, when you're talking about somebody that's assassinated, shot down in the back for what they believe, for such meager things as wanting some dignity, when that kind of murder happens, there is just a gaping wound laid open on society as a whole. And even where justice is fulfilled, that kind of murder, that kind of wound will always leave a scar that won't ever go away. We have to learn from the past, folks, that where justice is never fulfilled—justice has sometimes been referred to as that soothing balm to be applied on the wounds inflicted on society—where justice is never fulfilled and that wound can never be cleansed, all it does is just fester and fester and fester over the years.

And so it is up to the system; it's up to the law-abiding citizens, and the law of the state of Mississippi that the perpetrator of such an assassination be brought to justice. This defendant. So that the decent law-abiding people of this state will maintain a new respect for the value of human life, and that our state will truly be one that is of the people, for the people, and by the people, no matter what you race, color, or creed is.

One of the defense attorneys early on in the jury selection process asked whether or not any of you had heard something to the effect of the eyes being on Mississippi; Mississippi on trial. Mississippi is not on trial. And I'm not sure what eyes are on Mississippi, but this I do know. Justice in this case, in whatever case, is what the jury says it is. Justice in this case is what you twelve ladies and gentlemen say it is. So in this case, in effect, you are Mississippi. So what is Mississippi justice in this case, ladies and gentlemen? What is Mississippi justice for this defendant's hate-inspired assassination; assassination of a man that just desired to be free and equal?

If you analyze the evidence, use your common sense that God gave you, examine your heart, your consciences, and base your verdict on the evidence and the law, then you will have done the right thing. If you base it on the law and the evidence, and in the spirit of human dignity, there's no question in my mind that whatever you come out with, it'll be the right thing, because I have faith that it will be to hold him accountable. And the only way to do that is to find him guilty.

Remember the words of the Psalms, as I have over the past four years: "Commit your way to the Lord, trust in Him, and He will act. He will make your vindication shine like the light, and the justice of your cause as the noon day." From the evidence in this case, the law that you've sworn to apply, it can't be but one way if justice is truly going to be done.

And so on behalf of the state of Mississippi, I'm gonna do what I told you I was gonna do in the very beginning. I'm gonna ask you to hold this defendant accountable. You have no part in sentencing. That's something that the law will take care of. It's up to the court.

But to hold him accountable, find him guilty, simply because it's right, it's just, and Lord knows, it's just time. He has danced to the music for thirty years. Isn't it time that he pay the piper? Is it ever too late to do the right thing? For the sake of justice and the hope of us as a civilized society, I sincerely hope and pray that it's not.

CHAPTER NINE

Coke, Lies, and Videotape

The DeLorean Defense Team Convinces Jurors
They Can't Trust Their Eyes—Or the Feds

In 1982, John DeLorean had it all. Ten years after leaving General Motors, the youngest man to ever lead Chevrolet was running DeLorean Motor Company, building his high-tech stainless-steel car in a factory in Northern Ireland. A handsome man, at fifty-eight he was married to a woman twenty-five years his junior, former top fashion model Christina Ferrare. They led an opulent lifestyle with their two children, shuttling between their three multimillion-dollar homes in Manhattan, New Jersey, and California. But all was not well.

The automotive press was not impressed by the DeLorean; the English government's $155 million investment had produced an overpriced gull-winged "sports car" with poor acceleration and unimpressive handling. The company was on the brink of bankruptcy, and DeLorean was looking for a way to raise $20 million.

DeLorean learned of an opportunity to make some quick cash from a neighbor, James Timothy Hoffman. What he didn't know was that Hoffman was a drug smuggler turned government informant. A series of meetings was arranged between DeLorean and federal agents posing as drug smugglers, all but the first recorded on audio and videotape. Hoffman claimed that at the first meeting, DeLorean said he wanted to invest up to $2 million in "China white," a form of heroin.

On October 19, 1982, the players met in a hotel room near Los Angeles International Airport to finalize their plans. According to the feds, DeLorean was going to finance the importation of $24 million of Colombian cocaine. DeLorean was arrested after undercover agents presented him with a suitcase filled with fifty-five pounds of the drugs. The indictment charged him with eight felony counts involving the alleged importation of 220 pounds of coke. Released on $5 million bail, DeLorean was facing sixty-seven years in a federal prison.

U.S. District Court Judge Robert Takasugi refused media requests to release the surveillance tapes, saying that broadcast of the tapes would have a "devastating" effect on DeLorean's chances for a fair trial. Takasugi's efforts were wasted. Larry Flynt, the publisher of *Hustler* magazine, paid a law clerk $5,000 for duplicate copies which he then passed on to *CBS News*. They were broadcast on national television in October 1983. The pool of potential jurors saw DeLorean inspect the suitcase filled with cocaine, proclaim it "better than gold," then lift a glass of champagne in a toast for "a lot of success for everyone." Viewers watched as a man entered the room and told the bewildered DeLorean, "Hi, John. I'm Jerry West from the FBI. You're under arrest for narcotics smuggling violations." In an attempt to limit the potential damage, Takasugi delayed the trial for six months, a move that legal commentators felt helped the defense. Finally, in March 1984, after six delays, jury selection was set to begin. Representing DeLorean were two experienced trial attorneys: Howard Weitzman and Donald Re. The government brought in two career prosecutors with a talent for winning narcotics cases, James Walsh Jr. and Robert Perry. Jury selection began with Takasugi asking the 177 potential jurors to fill out a forty-two-page questionnaire. The 110 questions ranged from "Have you or has any member of your family or any acquaintance ever owned a DeLorean gull-winged sports car?" to "Have you or any member of your family used cocaine?"

It was clear that the broadcast of the tape showing DeLorean fondling the cocaine had heavily influenced the panelists. Weitzman and Re watched with dismay as prospective jurors told the court that DeLorean would have to explain that damning tape before they'd believe him to be innocent. One prospective juror said, "A picture is worth a thousand words. It's kind of hard to put that aside." Weitzman questioned another panelist about the tapes. The man said he'd seen them, but had no opinion about DeLorean's guilt. Weitzman asked whether he thought DeLorean was "more likely guilty than innocent." The man answered, "If I can say so, I would assume that he's probably guilty. But other than that, I have no opinion." So many prospective jurors were dismissed for bias that Judge Takasugi changed the selection process. He began instructing the panelists about the presumption of innocence before allowing any questioning by the attorneys. Even after explaining that they must presume DeLorean to be innocent until—and if—the government had proven his guilt beyond a reasonable doubt, the panelists remained skeptical. Two prospective jurors said that they could not presume DeLorean innocent, not after seeing those tapes. Re was discouraged, commenting, "I have very serious concerns about whether an impartial jury, to which John is entitled, can be found." It took weeks to seat a panel, instead of the usual two days for a federal trial, but the defense and prosecution finally found six men and six women to sit in judgment. The defense team defied conventional wisdom by keeping a former California Highway Patrol officer on the jury, despite the belief of many attorneys that law enforcement personnel are hostile to defendants. If there was anything to cheer the defense, they could take some solace in Judge Takasugi's ruling that the jury would not hear of the results of DeLorean's polygraph tests (he passed the defense's test and failed the prosecution's).

The trial began on Monday, March 5, 1984, in a packed Los Angeles courtroom. Forty-four seats were reserved for U.S. and foreign reporters, with an additional sixty seats in an adjoining room for the rest of the press contingent.

Opening statements began with Walsh laying out the government's case in cool, deliberate tones. He used flow charts and posters filled with excerpts from the taped conversations. The prosecution told the jurors that it was DeLorean's "driving desire to succeed" and threat of financial ruin that drove him to seek out the coke-for-cash deal. The prosecution screened a videotape of an undercover FBI agent, masquerading as a banker, telling DeLorean how money can be laundered. DeLorean, off camera, can be heard: "It looks like a good opportunity." The prosecution told the jurors they were seeing DeLorean "caught in the act of being himself."

Weitzman got to his feet and laid out a tale of moral outrage, declaring that the feds had used DeLorean's financial problems to ruthlessly set him up, setting in motion a scheme he compared to that used in the film *The Sting*. "This is the big guy, and they smell blood, blood," Weitzman told the jurors. "There is no stopping them now. It is like sharks in a feeding frenzy." Weitzman explained that DeLorean had been framed by a convicted drug dealer and admitted perjurer, the prosecution's star witness James Hoffman. According to the defense, the videotapes were easily explained: "Produced, choreographed, and directed to make DeLorean look guilty." And guilty he looked. In a meeting videotaped by government agents, Hoffman told DeLorean that if he wanted out of the deal, "I mean if you don't want to do it, if you want to stop, you're not compelled to, I won't be mad, I won't be hurt, I won't be anything." DeLorean replied, "Well, I want to proceed."

Because the prosecution's case appeared to be almost "airtight" as a result of the tapes, the defense honed in on the prosecution's flaws. Government witnesses admitting backdating documents, destroying original notes, and withholding embarrassing information from the defense. Donald Re subjected DEA agent John Valestra to a withering cross-examination, in which the witness admitted that he had lied when he backdated official documents so that he "wouldn't look bad."

Prosecutors were further embarrassed when Judge Takasugi castigated the government for not providing the defense with relevant information concerning the motives of its star witness. According to a teletype, Hoffman had demanded a percentage of the money seized in the case. "I find that quite offensive, especially in light of the fact that Mr. Hoffman testified he continued to help the government and was motivated by his effort to do good," Takasugi said. "The evidence certainly is that he was a gun for hire." The judge added that he could only wonder whether or not the prosecution was withholding other documents from the defense.

The defense called former DEA agent Gerald Scotti to testify for DeLorean. Moved to tears by Weitzman's questioning, Scotti testified, "I knew from a long way back the government would go to any lengths to prosecute Mr. DeLorean. But I thought there was a limit to it—a bottom to it. Now, I'm not so sure of that anymore." Weitzman asked him if the agents thought DeLorean was guilty at the time of the arrest. Scotti answered that they "wanted to believe an individual of Mr. DeLorean's stature and notoriety—we all wanted to believe that he was guilty, that we had him." Scotti testified that Hoffman had told him during the investigation that he was "setting up an innocent man."

After three weeks of testimony, the defense rested without calling DeLorean to the stand. The pundits were flabbergasted. The only way to mount a viable entrapment defense is to let the defendant explain his state of mind to the jury, to tell what was said by the government to induce him to break the law. The only version the jury heard was that told by Hoffman: that DeLorean initiated the contact, brought up drugs, was the moving force behind the deal. Only DeLorean could tell them what really happened. Only DeLorean wasn't talking. The defense relied instead on testimony that Hoffman had bragged to federal agents,

"I'm going to get John DeLorean for you guys . . . The problems he's got, I can get him to do anything I want."

After fifty days of testimony, the prosecution began its closing argument. Perry pointed out what he called a "defense of diversion" steering the jury back to the prosecution's strongest evidence: the videotapes. Perry spent four hours undercutting defense claims that DeLorean believed he was part of a legitimate business deal. Perry reminded jurors that DeLorean used code words that appeared to refer to narcotics, and of an incident wherein they watched DeLorean discuss financial details written on a scrap of paper, after which the paper was burned. "They put the details on a piece of paper and then they burned it." Perry said. "This is not a legitimate deal."

Re's summation began with a calm reading of all the lies and inconsistencies contained in the prosecution's case. Re told the jury that by the time DeLorean realized that this was a drug deal, he was too frightened to pull out. He finished by telling the jury that "all of us deserve apologies from the government for what happened here."

The jury agreed. On August 16, 1984, the jury acquitted DeLorean, after twenty-nine hours of deliberations. The jurors were split on whether or not DeLorean had actually taken part in a criminal conspiracy, but were unanimous in their belief that even if he had, the government's actions had crossed the line into entrapment. It took only one ballot for the panel to reach its decision.

A free man, DeLorean was without a job and in dire financial straits. The British government had shuttered his factory the day of his arrest, and production of the stainless-steel car was never to resume. But the gull-wing was to go on to lasting fame, a featured player in the three *Back to the Future* films, providing the kind of positive publicity DeLorean so desperately needed in the immutable past.

Biography

Born in 1946, Donald M. Re was raised in New Jersey, graduated from high school in 1963, and attended Princeton University. After earning his bachelor's degree in 1967, he headed west, attending law school at the University of California at Los Angeles; he graduated in 1970 with a law degree and began his career as a trial attorney.

Re went into private practice as a criminal defense attorney in 1971, and taught constitutional law at UCLA for three years in the mid-seventies. In 1982, he formed a law partnership with another prominent criminal defense attorney, Howard Weitzman. Their defense of John DeLorean was the highlight of their association; they dissolved their practice in 1985. Re formed his own Los Angeles law firm in 1985, where he continues to practice with Mona Soo Hoo, the third, unsung member of the DeLorean trial team. Re has participated in many noteworthy trials over his three decades of practice, including his defense of Andrew Daulton Lee on espionage charges. Lee was convicted, along with Christopher Boyce, of selling military secrets to the Soviet Union. The story of the two spies was popularized in the film *The Falcon and the Snowman*. Re had another notable success with his defense of Eddie Nash, a nightclub owner who had been charged with operating an arson-for-profit scheme. Re has also represented the Church of Scientology in cases involving the seizure of court documents.

Re also won an acquittal for his client in *The People* v. *McKinley Lee,* better known to the public as the Snoop Doggy Dogg murder trial. He represented O. J. Simpson confidant Al "A. C." Cowlings, and in 1997 worked out a plea bargain for actor Charlie Sheen on a battery charge.

Commentary

It is an axiom among trial attorneys that the very first thing a lawyer does is write his closing argument, for his entire trial strategy is built upon what he'll say to the jury at the close. As the trial progresses, the attorney adds to the close, using evidence that comes to light during the trial, pruning bits that are ruled inadmissible.

Defense attorney Donald Re set about the daunting task of designing a blueprint for his defense of John DeLorean, hoping that the summation that emerged would not be a house of cards, tumbling down on his client. Re and his co-counsel had to convince a jury that had seen a videotape of DeLorean fondling an attaché case packed with cocaine and hoisting a champagne flute to "success" that things were not as they appeared. What emerged was a two-part strategy: first, shift the battleground from DeLorean's actions to the misdeeds of the government; and second, pick apart and explain each of the numerous contacts between DeLorean and the undercover agents.

Much like Darrow in chapter 2 and Kunstler in chapter 3, Re understood that he must fight the battle on his terms—to allow the prosecution to set the agenda would be fatal. The prosecution's intention would be to focus its efforts on DeLorean's actions and motivations, and, given the facts, the federal government appeared to present an overwhelming case of a man so desperate for money to save his ailing company that he finally turned to the high-risk, high-profit world of narcotics for that cash. Re knew that DeLorean's only hope lay in demonizing the federal agents, turning the trial into a scathing damnation of the actions and motivations of the investigators, in their blind quest for fame and glory at the expense of their victim: John DeLorean. Deep into his argument, Re said: "The agents weren't concerned with the facts. They weren't concerned with intent. They were on a headlong rush to glory because they thought they could nail this man."

Later Re said:

> After September 28, we have heard about a little party the agents had. We hear a toast about *Time* magazine, "We will all be in *Time* magazine." Toasting at the cost of John DeLorean's reputation.
>
> The sad part, ladies and gentlemen, while these people are toasting and partying, no one asked, "What does this man really want to do?" Who was it among them that bothered to listen to these tapes closely, who bothered to listen to what DeLorean was talking about? None of them did because none of them really cared, not the agents, not the informants, not the supervisor; no one cared. What they cared about was that they had a tape that they could play to the jury from which they could argue that DeLorean was guilty, whether or not he was.

Re put the FBI and the DEA on trial, emphasized their every lie and every embarrassing admission by the government's witnesses, and incorporated them into a summation that he hoped would inflame the jurors, and make them mad as hell at the government's conduct. Re became a prosecutor of governmental arrogance, of law enforcement gone mad. In light of the jury's prompt decision to acquit DeLorean, Re had won not just an acquittal for his client, but a moral "guilty" verdict against the government.

The second part of Re's overall strategy was somehow to minimize the devastating impact of that last videotape, where DeLorean appears to be accepting more than fifty pounds of cocaine as a fait accompli of this complicated dope deal. If the prosecutor's insistence that the jury look at the totality of the circumstances prevailed, DeLorean would be convicted. Re therefore had to become an incrementalist. Re went back to the beginning and painstakingly analyzed every contact, every meeting, and to the extent possible, explained it away by putting it into a context more favorable to DeLorean. By going back to the beginning and chronologically explaining and viewing events from his client's point of view, Re systematically knocked the prosecution's case to pieces. At one point, he said:

> If you take the deal that the government has at this point and remove the part about the [DeLorean] investment, you have a straightforward narcotics deal. John Valestra, over here, he's going to buy the dope from Hetrick over here. Valestra is going to sell the dope and get the money, and then he can do with that money as he pleases. That's what dope dealers do. What Valestra chose to do is to invest the money. He could have bought cars with it. He could have bought houses with it. . . . He decided that he was going to buy shares of stock in DeLorean's company. DeLorean is not involved with the drug deal. We have Valestra, Hetrick, and Hoffman over here, and that is a completed drug deal; and over here we have DMCI, which is a corporation, and DeLorean is way over here as an officer, and the deal between DMCI and Vicenza is a normal investment situation.

By the time he reached that last contact, the one broadcast from coast to coast on the nightly news, where DeLorean accepts the cocaine, the impact of that damning scene had dissipated. Re told the jurors:

> Ladies and gentlemen, you listen to that tape, and you tell me if John DeLorean isn't nervous at the time the cocaine is brought up and if that isn't a nervous laugh and a nervous reaction of a man who is feeling like a trapped animal. They put that cocaine in his hand, and they were happy they did because it made him look guilty.
> It is a pathetic, sick performance. The events of the nineteenth don't show anything about DeLorean's intent, but they do show the depths to which the government will go to try and get material that they can put in front of you to inflame you.

Re then moved on to his hard-hitting attack on the government's key informant, James Hoffman. Much of the government's case depended on Hoffman, because they had no tapes of the first meeting between their star witness and the defendant; his credibility had to be erased. Re began his attack on Hoffman by pointing out inconsistencies in his testimony, the differences between what he told the agents and what he testified to before the grand jury, and how his testimony in front of the grand jury differed from what he had testified to at the trial. Re reminded the jurors that Hoffman was a convicted felon, and that Hoffman not only was a paid informant but was also receiving a favorable disposition on a pending criminal charge. Re methodically and systematically destroyed the credibility of the key government witness. By the time Re was done, he had made a convincing argument that the jurors could not believe anything Hoffman said, and with Hoffman's credibility went the government's case.

Finally, the cornerstone of the defense, the mantra of Re's close, was the repetition of the defense's theory of the case. Early in the argument, Re said, ". . . DeLorean was manipulated, DeLorean was maneuvered, DeLorean was conned, John DeLorean is a victim." Re repeated it over and over, after each segment of his closing argument. When the jurors spoke with the press after the verdict, it became apparent that they agreed.

Closing Argument

The State of California v. *John DeLorean*
Delivered by Donald Re
Los Angeles, California, 1984

Good afternoon, ladies and gentlemen.

This part of the argument, as I think you know, gives the defense a chance to say a few words to you. Now, before I get into the argument itself, I want to thank all of you on behalf of the defense. We know this case has gone on longer than you thought it would. We know that all of you have had to come here at an early hour. You have had to inconvenience yourselves personally. I'm sure you have had financial inconvenience. Some of you have had problems with business.

We also have noticed, however, how attentive you have all been and conscientious, and we very much appreciate that. It is very important that you are attentive and conscientious. I think you can understand the importance of this case to John DeLorean and to the system as a whole.

We have been accused this morning of trying to drag the case out in some fashion to I guess divert attention from what the issues are. I can assure you that there is no defense strategy involved in trying to get you so angry at us for making the case long that you go into that jury room holding a grudge.

I think what we have done here is something that you would want done if you were charged with a crime or if a loved one or friend were charged with a crime. I think you would expect nothing less, and certainly we don't expect to do anything less on behalf of our client.

Ladies and gentlemen, the way you defend a case like this is on the facts. The facts demonstrate unequivocally that John DeLorean didn't commit any crime, and John DeLorean should be acquitted of every charge with which he is charged.

You have heard the principles of reasonable doubt and burden of proof tossed around since the very beginning of this case. Not only does the prosecution have the burden, they have the burden of proof beyond a reasonable doubt. That's because our system cannot tolerate the thought that a man who under any reasonable set of facts could be innocent would be convicted. As a result, if there is any reasonable way, any set of facts that you have heard that this man is not guilty, you are required by your oath to find him not guilty.

Your responsibility in this regard is an enormous one because you people stand as the buffer. Without that kind of buffer we'd all be in a lot of trouble. So it's important that jurors, particularly important in serious cases, give the case the attention that it deserves and that you apply a standard of proof beyond a reasonable doubt. I'm not going to talk to you about reasonable doubt for a while. I am going to ask you to put it in the back of your head, lock it up, and when we get toward the end, I will ask you to bring it back out.

I am going to talk to you now about what the case on the facts is all about, what the facts are that you heard.

The prosecution tells you that John DeLorean was a man who was so desperate to hold on to his car company that he was willing to do a heroin deal. They tell you that John DeLorean went to James Hoffman without any hesitation and set up a heroin deal.

What the evidence in the case has shown, however, is that DeLorean was manipulated, DeLorean was maneuvered, DeLorean was conned, and that John DeLorean is a victim. John DeLorean, unfortunately for all of us, was the victim of the very people whose oath it was, whose purpose it was to protect him from criminal activity.

It was the duty of each and every one of the government personnel involved in this case to make sure that John DeLorean intended, actually intended to do a drug deal. It was their duty to make sure that his motives were unambiguous and plain. It was their duty to make sure that he was not manipulated either by the events or by the informant.

Time after time no care was used to determine whether he actually intended to do the deal, to insure that his motives were plain. There was no effort made by any of these agents to make sure that Hoffman the informant didn't manipulate the situation.

What I will do, in order to give you our view of this case, is to break it down into various periods, and I think it is easier, because each one of these periods is a little different. It shows a little difference about how the case was treated. And it shows a little difference about the motivation of the people involved.

We will first be talking about 1980. Those are the conversations between DeLorean and Hoffman when they were neighbors at Pauma Valley. Then there is the period between June 29 and July 11. That's the period before the first meeting at the Marriott, before the first telephone calls. We then have the July eleventh Marriott meeting. Then there's the period between July fourth and September fourth, when there are recorded audio conversations.

Then we have September fourth. That's the videotape which you have been treated to on a wide variety of occasions, which is a classic example of manipulation and deceit by Mr. Hoffman.

Then the period of September fourth to September fifteenth, when John DeLorean withdraws, wants to get out, and was not allowed to. And then the period from September fifteenth to October eighteenth, and then finally the date of arrest on October nineteenth.

Each one of those episodes has areas of inconsistency. Each one of these episodes is critical because it serves to point out exactly how John DeLorean was manipulated.

Turning first to 1980, what Mr. Hoffman tried to get across to the agents at that time was that he lived across the street from John DeLorean, that they became social friends over a nine-month period, that they spoke to each other, that they socialized together, that they came over to one another's house, and that during the course of these relaxed, friendly, and social conversations it came up that, yes, indeed, Mr. Hoffman allegedly said, "I was involved with drug smuggling." That story in and of itself makes very little sense. Mr. Hoffman told you in his own words that drug smugglers don't go about telling people that they are drug smugglers. By the time of the grand jury, Mr. Hoffman elaborated on his story a little bit, and he says that, as a matter of fact, DeLorean told him he started his car company with a cocaine transaction. Now, by the time of the grand jury, of course, Mr. Hoffman is a little more sophisticated, and so what we find is that, "I didn't talk to some person who was a novice in drug dealing; I spoke to a person who actually started his car company with a narcotic transaction."

And now, a couple years after the event, James Hoffman tells you from the witness stand under oath, that, in fact, he only talked to DeLorean over Easter vacation. Not nine months, it's about nine days. Well, of course, there is not much time for socializing in nine days. Mr. Hoffman tells you, "I didn't see Christina DeLorean in the house at all." What happened to the socializing over this nine-month period? Now there is a small problem, you see, because here we have relaxed people talking about their background and confiding in one another as friends that they have some kind of narcotics background.

Well, what Mr. Hoffman has to do now is cook up a new story. He talks about purchasing the Pauma Valley house from DeLorean. There is no mention of that in his earlier statements. Why not? Because he didn't make it up until he got to trial, because he didn't make it up until after the grand jury.

According to Hoffman's testimony to you people, the whole reason that he and DeLorean were talking in 1980 was because Hoffman was interested in buying the house for what I think he said 1.75 or 1.8 million dollars when he couldn't pay the rent on his house across the street.

The government knew that John DeLorean was not at Pauma Valley for a nine-month period. John DeLorean was working in his company in New York, was traveling around, was doing all kinds of things in 1980. He wasn't spending his time relaxing down in Pauma Valley, so a different story had to be made up to give you people, to explain to you, how it was that John DeLorean could have any understanding that Hoffman was involved in narcotics.

That testimony, ladies and gentlemen, is unabashedly put forward to you by the government despite the fact that they have in their possession Hoffman's grand jury statement of July 12, and there is no mention of that in any of those statements.

What you have seen from Hoffman, then, is a lie created on the spur of the moment by a con man. What it should show you is that DeLorean has no reason to ask Jim Hoffman about drugs because DeLorean and Hoffman had never talked about drugs back in 1980. There had been no discussion about heroin, and what you heard fits in exactly with the testimony that you heard from Gerald Scotti [*a government agent*]. Remember what he said? He asked Hoffman about this and Hoffman told him, "I can't mention drugs to DeLorean because it would scare him away." Hoffman shows himself, very early in the game, to be a master at manipulating the agents.

It also shows that the agents were particularly unconcerned with the facts they were getting, with the inconsistencies which were developed in the case, and what they were primarily concerned about was not what happened, but what evidence they could get to make it look like John DeLorean was guilty, and there is one little incident which has been bandied about here, which I think helps to point that up. Agent Valestra told you about the information from Johnny Carson. It's not in his statement, but he recalls that Johnny Carson's name was brought up particularly. What did Agent Valestra testify to concerning that? "I wasn't interested in that because Hoffman never told me he could make a case on Carson." He didn't say, "This is ridiculous." He didn't say to himself, "Maybe I should check this out." His reaction was, "I can't make a case there, so why should I bother. I don't care about the truth or untruth. I just can't make a case."

What happened when Hoffman came to these agents with John DeLorean? Their own interest was "Can we make a case," not "Does he want to do the deal, what is his interest in a deal, is there a conspiracy," but rather, "Can we get some evidence to make it look like John DeLorean was involved."

Now let's move to the time between June 29 and July 11, in which again there are major inconsistencies in Mr. Hoffman's story. During that period of time, DeLorean supposedly tries to set up the meeting with Hoffman so they can discuss the drug deal, and supposedly during this period Mr. DeLorean arranges to meet Hoffman out here in California.

According to what the government would have you believe, Mr. DeLorean was anxious, was very willing to come out here to talk about this drug deal. However, because it's all unrecorded, because the agents told you that they never surveilled the July eleventh meeting, the only person that you have to rely on as to what happened between June twenty-ninth and July eleventh is James Hoffman.

The judge will read you some instructions, and I expect one of his instructions is about the testimony of a perjurer. Mr. Hoffman is an admitted perjurer. He lied. He lied under oath, and he lied under oath with a reason. That's what the government kept telling you; he had a reason, and I have been dying to hear what that reason was, and the reason was if he didn't lie under oath, Mr. Hetrick [*a suspected drug supplier*] wouldn't fly a load for him. So that shows you that James Hoffman not only is a perjurer but he is a man who is willing to perjure himself to further his own illegal narcotic activities. The instructions that you will hear are that the testimony of a perjurer, that is, the person who has knowingly told that untruth under oath, must be viewed with the utmost caution and weighed with great care. You are informed, for the purposes of those instructions, that James Timothy Hoffman is an admitted perjurer.

On that instruction alone you have a basis to discredit and disbelieve everything that Mr. Hoffman has told you.

However, we have more. Mr. Hoffman told you that he has been convicted of a felony. He was convicted of selling narcotics, a serious felony. He was convicted of a felony regarding cocaine at a time when he was under investigation for heroin. He was convicted of a felony as a result of making a deal because he was trying to get out early. Not only was he convicted of a felony, he was convicted of a felony in circumstances again where he was trying to help himself, and the court will instruct you that the testimony of a witness may be discredited or impeached if there is a showing that the witness has been convicted of a felony, that is, of a crime punishable by imprisonment.

So you have two factors: Mr. Hoffman is an admitted perjurer and a convicted felon.

Mr. Hoffman is something else, though, isn't he? He is an informant. That means he is somebody who is working off a crime, doing something for value, and you are going to get an instruction on that; I won't read the entire instruction to you, but a portion of that instruction is that the testimony of an informant must be examined and weighed by the jury with greater care and caution than the testimony of an ordinary witness. The court tells you certain factors that you should consider in looking at the testimony of an informant; whether or not the informant provided testimony for the following reasons: for money, $180,000; for financial consideration, such as medical bills, cars, living expenses— that's Mr. Hoffman; for nonprosecution of other offenses. Remember the tax cases that weren't going to be prosecuted, the heroin case that wasn't going to be prosecuted, includes all of the cocaine counts on the case where he ultimately entered his pleas, for leniency with regard to any sentence imposed. Yes, there is leniency. He got straight probation. He didn't spend a day in jail. The court will instruct you that James Timothy Hoffman is an informant within the meaning of these instructions.

The court also is going to tell you that if a witness makes inconsistent statements, you are to consider the use of those inconsistent statements as a method of determining the witness's credibility, and I have only started with Mr. Hoffman, and you can hear already the inconsistencies in his statements with regard to the critical key elements in this case.

The court will further instruct you that if a witness has shown knowingly to have testified falsely concerning any material matter, you have a right to distrust such witness's testimony and other particulars, and you may reject all the testimony of that witness or give it such credibility as you may think it deserves. So you have the fact that he is a perjurer, he is a felon, and informant, he has made inconsistent statements, and the fact that you can reject his entire testimony because, ladies and gentlemen, there is no doubt that he lied to you on that stand at least about what happened in 1980, and as we go through this, you will see he lied about a lot of other things.

Now, interestingly enough, Mr. Perry [*the prosecutor*] came to you at the beginning of the case and told you about some of these things. Interestingly enough, however, he didn't tell you about Mr. Hoffman's demand for money made on September 3, 1982.

The teletype that was placed in evidence specifically lays out a demand made by Mr. Hoffman when he wanted a piece of the action. It's not characterized in the teletype as a request. It was teletyped to Washington as a demand.

Hoffman has made constant demands for money during the course of this case. He has misrepresented a situation to the government, and yet the government and Mr. Hoffman come before you and say that he is a man who is to be believed. And yet he is not to be believed, ladies and gentlemen, and he is particularly not to be believed in those situations in which he is the only one who was giving the information.

Hoffman was willing to lie, he is a con man. Con men tell you the story that fits at the time.

We then move to the meeting of July 11. Mr. Hoffman tells you that John DeLorean called him. Why does he tell you that? Because John DeLorean was interested in meeting with him, according to Hoffman.

Agent Valestra tells you that he checked the telephone toll records and, lo and behold, there is no toll record from Pauma Valley at John DeLorean's house in Pauma Valley to Jim Hoffman at eight o'clock in the morning or whatever time it was that Hoffman says the call was made.

We know who set up that meeting and who made the phone call.

The meetings weren't recorded. The reason for that, ladies and gentlemen, is that Hoffman had no interest in recording that call.

Now, look at it from Mr. DeLorean's point of view. He shows up at that meeting with brochures, and you saw those brochures. They are in evidence. Those brochures are brochures looking toward investment in the car company. They are offering a portion of that company for sale to someone for an amount of money. The government would have you believe, however, that John DeLorean walks into a meeting, that he has set up for the purpose of discussing a heroin deal, and he starts handing out brochures about the company.

Think about something else. That particular brochure, a copy of that brochure, had already been sent to his office back before John DeLorean ever left New York to come out to California. Why would John DeLorean do that if he thought he was going to meet Mr. Hoffman? If he was sure he was going to meet with Mr. Hoffman, why would he send the brochures, if it was supposed to be a discussion of a heroin deal. Remember, at this point, the deal is supposed to be John DeLorean had $2 million which he wants to invest. The government wants us to believe that Hoffman is going to set up the buy for DeLorean and somehow they are going to split the proceeds. The company is then going to be the main recipient under the government's theory.

The result is that the meeting on July 11 is unrecorded, and Hoffman is left in a position to do or say whatever he wants with regard to John DeLorean, and he is in a position to tell the agents whatever he wants to about that meeting.

Now, again, we have the situation where the contents of the meeting are subject to different stories by Mr. Hoffman. Was cocaine mentioned? Hoffman told Agent Valestra after the meeting, "Well, no, cocaine wasn't mentioned, DeLorean talked about heroin." Cocaine, according to Mr. Hoffman's testimony in front of the grand jury, was only mentioned in September, but now Mr. Hoffman comes to you and says, "Yes, we did talk about cocaine," and the reason he has to say this is that in a later meeting on September 4 there were conversations about cocaine and he would have you believe, and he wants you to believe, that John DeLorean had been aware of those previous conversations.

Mr. Hoffman acknowledges, however, that in the course of that meeting Mr. DeLorean spoke about investments. He said that in his statement. He acknowledges Mr. DeLorean arrived with brochures. He doesn't say that Mr. DeLorean sent brochures.

MR. WEITZMAN: Your Honor, may we approach side bar?

[*Side bar discussion, as follows:*]

MR. WEITZMAN: I think Christina [*DeLorean's wife*] is going to faint, so I don't want to walk her out in front of the jury.

[*End of side bar discussion.*]

THE COURT: We will recess for ten minutes. Please remember the admonition.

[*Recess taken at 2 P.M.*]

THE COURT: All jurors are present and properly seated. Mr. Re, please.

MR. RE: Ladies and gentlemen, before the recess I was talking about the July 11 meeting and what I think you should take away from the evidence concerning that meeting is this: John DeLorean went to a meeting, obviously to talk about an investment. He brought his brochures, the story that Hoffman tells about why he is there is unbelievable. DeLorean shows up with the brochures. He is on a business trip. He is looking for money for the company, and he shows up with brochures which clearly refer to the sale of the company.

Now, what was it that was going on in that meeting? You can from the evidence in front of you understand a few things. Number one, Mr. Hoffman is going to be thinking about himself. "What is in it for me?" is what Hoffman is going to say, and what is going to be in it for Hoffman is the commission. The question is posed to him about a commission, and a commission is something, as I'm sure you know, that is routinely paid to somebody who is able to set up an investment. I think that it is clear that Hoffman went to see DeLorean—DeLorean was looking for money—that our friend, Mr. Hoffman, would have demanded a commission, and I think from what you have heard on the tapes and the evidence in this case, it is very clear Hoffman demanded a commission of $1.8 million.

Take that in context with what the government has said concerning the bank reference. The government is telling you that Mr. Hoffman gave a bank reference to John DeLorean so that John DeLorean can assure himself that Mr. Hoffman isn't going to run away with his investment in a dope deal, and what Mr. Hoffman apparently has Mr. Tisa [*another government agent posing as a banker*] say is that, yes, Hoffman keeps $1 million in the bank.

The bank reference is significant, ladies and gentlemen, because it is a financial institution. John DeLorean could call, and you can see that the relationship between DeLorean and Hoffman at this point in the case, at this point of the investigation, is one based on an investment in the company.

The government says to you, "Look for corroboration. What happened on July 11? Look for corroboration."

First of all, I want to point out to you the reason you have to look for corroboration is because the agents didn't record it. The agents didn't surveil it. The agents didn't do anything with regard to that meeting to try to find out from somebody other than a liar like James Hoffman what happened, and why didn't they do it? From Mr. Valestra's mouth it comes [that] they didn't do it because they didn't know anything was going to be happening there of an illegal nature. If Hoffman told you the truth about what the conversations were, then Mr. Valestra is not telling you the truth. Somebody is lying. The one who is quite clearly lying is James Hoffman.

The government then goes on and says, "Look at the following conversations. Look at the conversations between the twelfth and fourth." Mr. Valestra at one point says the conversation, the first recorded conversation on the thirteenth, is the first bit of corroboration we have. Ladies and gentlemen, what does this conversation corroborate? It corroborates that DeLorean and Hoffman had talked. It doesn't corroborate that they talked about narcotics. You can't tell from that conversation whether they are talking about narcotics or if they are talking about an investment or whether they are talking about something completely different. It all comes from Hoffman. Mr. Hoffman tells the agents it's about narcotics, and the agents choose to believe it in the face of the fact that Hoffman's story about 1980 makes no sense, that his story about June 19 makes no sense.

You have heard every agent involved in the investigation of this case: Tisa, Valestra, Waters, even Hoffman, have told you that the conversations between July 12 and September 4, those telephone conversations, have no indication of criminal activity, unless you take Hoffman's input and put it in. The agents were more than willing to accept Hoffman's input. They were more than willing to believe that it had to do with drugs, because they weren't concerned about the true state of affairs. They were concerned [about] whether they had evidence.

John DeLorean says, "I want to go ahead with our proposition." The government, the agents, say, "We can put that out as evidence that he wanted to do a dope deal," but there is no corroboration of that. If the government is coming out and saying, "Ladies and gentlemen, look for corroboration," why wasn't the government going to the agents back in July, in August, clear up to September fourth and saying to them, "Go get me corroboration"?

It is during this period of time when the government formulated the idea of combining John DeLorean's case with somebody else's case. Now, I will have to admit I was startled to hear that as early as July that they were planning to take John DeLorean, this person they had Hoffman's word wanted to do a drug deal, and link him up with some heroin dealer from the Orient.

What is the government thinking? "We're going to take this man and put him together with a known heroin dealer because maybe Hoffman is telling us the truth." The government wanted to make a case. They were so anxious to make a case on a heroin dealer, that they weren't looking at John DeLorean's intent. They were looking at their own investigative purposes to make cases and make it look like this man was doing something wrong.

Then we have the combination with Hetrick. Now, here is a real way that you can see how James Timothy Hoffman is the master manipulator. Agent Tisa tells us, "I had this great idea. My great idea was we would take Hetrick and DeLorean and put them together, and we could get Hetrick's money in and Hetrick could supply the cocaine, and we could merge the two investigations. I talked to James Hoffman about it to get his input."

Agent Waters tells you, "I had this great idea. We could merge Hetrick and DeLorean."

Hoffman tells you he comes to a meeting to discuss this combination, and, lo and behold, he is surprised to find out everybody else has the same idea, and everybody talked to James Hoffman.

What James Timothy Hoffman did was implant in their minds getting those two together for his own purposes and make the sophisticated drug agents believe it was their idea. Agent Tisa was offended. It was his idea. He took credit for the idea. Look at his notes. To him it is a fabulous notion that he had come up with. He had a stake in that idea, and he believed it was his.

Agent Waters was offended. "We didn't need the FBI. This was our investigation."

Now, Mr. Perry has talked to you about a statement made during the July twelfth to September fourth period about "the full forty." What "full forty" is he talking about? Forty kilos? Hoffman tells you he is talking about $40 million, the money for the investment. The purchase of what? Look at the brochures. Half of the company could be purchased. That's what that's all about. Hoffman is able to introduce language which is vague so he can tell the agents one thing, and he can make DeLorean think he is talking about something else.

We then get to September 3 and Hoffman's demand. Hoffman didn't tell you about that demand when he testified. Waters didn't tell you about that demand or the money received by Hoffman when he testified. Nobody told you about that demand until we got into the defense case and you saw that teletype.

What the prosecution was doing there was trying to make Hoffman look like something other than what he was. Hoffman was the man who would do anything for money. He wanted his money. He wanted that money on September 3. He wanted that money throughout the case.

September 4 rolls around. What Hoffman is able to do is present a situation in which a conversation means one thing to DeLorean, and it will mean another thing to the agents, but remember the agents in the other room. They are not being critical about this. Agent Valestra told you that they just looked at the whole thing. Did DeLorean want to do it? Didn't he want to do it? Doesn't it look like he is involved? It doesn't look like he is involved? They don't care that Hoffman was talking about money to John DeLorean as an investment when as far as they could tell nobody had instructed him to do that.

I recall again what Agent Scotti said, that when drugs had to be brought up they had to be brought up in a way they could get it by John DeLorean, and Hoffman had to put up or shut up because somebody in the government said, "Mention drugs by name."

Now, why would they say, "Mention drugs by name"? Ladies and gentlemen, if before that time they had a clear indication that these people were talking about drugs and that was their intent, the reason Hoffman was told to mention drugs by name is because there was no evidence as to what these people were talking about. Look at Mr. Hoffman. What is Hoffman's motivation in all this? The money. You can see that on September 3, the day before, the day before the videotape meeting, he demands money, the day before he tries to get a percentage of the action.

Mr. Waters says that he told Mr. Valestra, "Disabuse Mr. Hoffman of that thought." We don't know what Mr. Valestra told Mr. Hoffman. We don't know if Mr. Hoffman went through the September fourth meeting thinking whatever he arranged, whatever he could get, he could get a percentage of.

The agents sitting in on the videotape, in the surveillance room, are again looking for evidence, and to make their point of view clear remember the series of questions about outs? What did Mr. Valestra say? He said, "We were going to give John DeLorean an out," and what did he have to do to take the out? He had to be unequivocal. He had to say, "I want out of the deal."

Ladies and gentlemen, what did he have to do to be in the deal? He could say, according to the agents anything equivocal that he wanted, and, as you will see, as we go through the transcripts, he did say something, conditional, highly conditional. Unequivocally indicated very clearly that he really didn't want to be in the deal.

That was okay as far as the government was concerned to say he was in, but they wanted him to unambiguously say he was out. They wanted John DeLorean to go to a meeting with a man who has contacts in the Orient, Colombian contacts for cocaine, has a banker on the payroll, is described as a big-time organized crime person, and they wanted John DeLorean to pick up and leave in order for him to say he was out, and you heard Mr. Valestra tell you that, yes, very likely Colombians have been known to wipe out a family or two, and he expected John DeLorean in those circumstances, where he knew the identity of the banker, he knew the identity of the bank, he knew James Hoffman, that he would simply say to these people, "Well, sorry, I don't want to play ball. Good-bye."

The September fourth meeting starts off with a discussion about Camembert cheese, and then Mr. Hoffman gets into a discussion with DeLorean in which Hoffman asked, "Tell me where you stand with the company."

The first thing that Hoffman talks about in that meeting, after he gets done talking about food is, "Where do you stand with the company?"

Why is it that James Hoffman, the drug dealer, is going to this man, saying, "Where do you stand with the company?" when supposedly John DeLorean is showing up at that meeting to say, "How is your drug deal going? When do I get the profits from the heroin?"

No, Hoffman talks about the company because he knows that he has to talk about things to keep John DeLorean there, to keep John DeLorean happy. We are going to keep him around, and then Hoffman goes on, and says, "I ran into a few delays of my own." Remember, Hoffman has been told to use drug words. Why didn't Hoffman say, "I ran into a few delays of my own in the heroin deal"? He doesn't say that because he knows that's not what John DeLorean thinks he means.

It means to John DeLorean, "I ran into a few delays getting the financing that I talked to you about," and then Hoffman brings up interim deals.

Now, at that point there is a clear indication as to what Hoffman was doing and how he did it. You heard Jim Hoffman testify when he's talking about an interim deal that he is talking about money. He is talking about this money that's going to come from South America. He is talking about investment money, and that's what John DeLorean thinks he is talking about.

John Valestra, who is sitting in the next room, the chief case agent on this case, who supposedly knows what's going on in this case, testifies he thinks that Hoffman is talking about cocaine. Well, how on earth is John Valestra to decide what John DeLorean's intent is if he can't even figure out what Hoffman is talking about, and the reason he can't figure it out is that Hoffman is using words interchangeably. He uses "interim deal" here to talk about money. He testifies he uses "interim deal" later to talk about cocaine. He uses the word "alternatives," a "couple alternatives that I think we've got in the case now." He would have you believe that the alternatives related to the two cocaine deals.

Ladies and gentlemen, I think that, based upon what we have seen so far, there was no discussion about drugs on July 11, and what Hoffman was saying at this point, although DeLorean doesn't at this point understand it, is "I've got alternatives, namely, heroin and cocaine."

I will get back to that later, but remember he says, "I brought up these alternatives because there's something within my control." And what is it that's within Mr. Hoffman's control? The heroin deal which he has been paid for and the cocaine which he says Mr. Vicenza [*fictitious name for agent Valestra, who is playing a narcotics dealer*] is going to be involved in.

What about the fact that Hoffman brings up money at this point? Where does this come from?

Well, the government says, "The defense is sitting here making so much of these unrecorded calls." Well, ladies and gentlemen, where did the money come from? Hoffman's explanation is that unrecorded call of the third of August, that's where it came from. Well, ladies and gentlemen, how come John Valestra didn't know about that call? How come nobody knew about that call? How come nobody knew about the contents of that call until sometime after mid-1983? Because what's happening here is that James Hoffman is making it up as he goes along, and then we get John DeLorean's response.

Now, you may remember we [*the defense lawyers*] asked a series of questions, "Why didn't you wait to see what John DeLorean and I were talking about?" They didn't do that. What did John DeLorean say? Hoffman is talking about interim deals and alternatives, and what is DeLorean's response? "Well, what magnitude are we talking about?" and Hoffman says, "All right, let me show you what," and DeLorean says, "What can they come up with in terms of interim financing? I guess that's the question."

John DeLorean, according to the government, came to this meeting to talk about a drug deal, and the first thing out of his mouth of any substantive nature, any importance, is what can he come up with in terms of interim money. John DeLorean is talking about money. What does Hoffman say? Hoffman goes back and forth and says, "I've done two things. We have a group now that can come up with virtually anything, and for sure $30 million and upward of that."

What is that about? What Hoffman is doing, is he is saying to John DeLorean, "I've got people who can invest $30 million or more into your company. Talk to me." That's what it is about. "You're going to talk to me. I know you need the money. I have these investors who can do the job for you." And then the discussion about whether they have interest, and Hoffman was not willing to let it drop. Hoffman says, "Yeah, more than that," and DeLorean says, "obviously very substantial," and the conversation up to this point has been, "How's your company," and "I've got somebody who can invest $30 million," and DeLorean clearly asked questions about that. He doesn't ask one question about the dope deal, and then Hoffman starts talking about a flow sheet, and he brings out the flow sheet.

Let's consider first that flow sheet for a minute. You have seen a couple of versions of the flow sheet. One of them has John Valestra's initials on it, and another Hoffman's, another didn't have anything on it. It's for you to decide what was shown to John DeLorean, but let's assume for the moment that it was a flow sheet, and let's even assume that it was the same flow sheet that you have seen in court; although, of course, it was Hoffman's idea to do the flow sheet and Hoffman's idea to bring it up.

You saw and heard this morning a portion of that September fourth tape. If you were looking at what Mr. Hoffman was doing, he was pointing to the right-hand side of the flow sheet, pointing to the place where the money was, the amount of money. What he was saying to John DeLorean is, "This is the amount of money you were talking about," so the agents sitting back in the room there, not knowing what Hoffman was talking about, were thinking Hoffman talked about drugs. Ladies and gentlemen, that's the same thing they would like you to believe, that they were talking about drugs, but, just look where he was pointing on the flow sheet.

Now, what is the deal of September 4? What Hoffman tells DeLorean is, "We've paid for part of the heroin." Why is Hoffman telling DeLorean that he and presumably this guy Vicenza had paid for the heroin? This is supposed to be John DeLorean's. The clock doesn't start until the money arrives, but they have gone out and they have already bought the heroin for John DeLorean, taken him on good faith that he will come up with the money. Remember he doesn't give any money, and then you see on the flow sheet that John DeLorean was supposed to be involved with, what, $1.9 million, $2 million in a cocaine transaction. It has nothing to do with John DeLorean. What Hoffman has done here is created a situation in which he was saying to John DeLorean, "Look, I had trouble getting the investment. I had a few delays of my own. Now, I'm supposed to get a commission, $1.8 million commissioned out of that deal, and if I use that 1.8 commission I can generate money from my people. You can then use the money that I generate for your company."

Now, of course, that's why the clock doesn't start until the money arrives. That's why they have already gone out and bought it because they are in the business of doing a dope deal. That's why it's not John DeLorean's dope deal and that's why they said to John DeLorean, "You are in this dope deal if and only if you give us the money."

Now, if there is any doubt about that, just look at what Hoffman says.

"We're going to, assuming that you want to do that—we still want to go along and do this because normally my boss is only involved in the first level of distribution. We don't normally go beyond that. That's where our participation ends."

It is their deal. It is not John DeLorean's deal.

All the statements made by Hoffman are that he and Vicenza are going to be involved with a deal, that it is their deal, and what he is saying is, "We will do the deal, and then this will take the place of the investment. We will be the investors rather than these other people."

What is Hoffman saying to John DeLorean? What is John DeLorean's intent here? Hoffman is saying, "There are two ways to do it," this either referring to dope or interim financing, and John DeLorean's reaction is, "Yeah, that's a better solution. Interim financing is a better solution." The first thing DeLorean says is about interim financing, not about dope.

Now, we have had several indications of DeLorean's intent at that time. The first is that he talks about financing. The second is that later on in the meeting, he says financing is a better way. The third indication is John DeLorean saying, "Look, you've told me you have had this interim financing upwards of $30 million." The next and perhaps clearest indication of his intent is that he conditions what he can do. DeLorean said, "I'm not so sure I can come up with this money that you are talking about, this money that has to do with the IRA [Irish Republican Army]. I have to check with them." Eventually it gets down to the point were John DeLorean says, "Well, I want to proceed. What I've got to do now is get a hold of them."

The government keeps reading the part saying, "I want to proceed," and sloughs off the part saying, "I want to get a hold of them. I want to make sure you understand I have to confirm it with the IRA."

Why does John DeLorean say that? John DeLorean says he made up this story so he can say to these other people that want to do this deal, "I can't do it without consent, but what about the financing?"

We then have John DeLorean's out: "I want to do it, but I have to get a hold of them." I want you to note, that out is given immediately after John Valestra threatened him and says something to the effect, "There won't be any noncompliance; better have a good remedy associated with it."

So was John DeLorean given an out? No. Does he respond to Mr. Hoffman's statements? Answer: Yes.

Whatever, his responses are very clearly an indication, "I don't want to do this deal"; and making excuses, "I'd rather do the interim financing. That's what I'm here to talk about."

What then happens is the situation in which these two people are talking about these deals. DeLorean is stalling on the drug situation, and he is told that the money for the investment can be available in three to four days, and he immediately says to Hoffman, "Well, you couldn't get me that money in three to four days. I will have to check with the IRA. They won't be available for a week," so what he has done is structured a situation which goes on for the rest of this case in which he is saying to them, "Look, your money is coming in first. If I have to do a drug deal, that money comes in later," and he is stalling them, not because he wants to do the drug deal, [but] because he wants the investment. He sets up a situation where he will get an investment. If he gets the investment, he doesn't need to do the drug deal. There is no reason to do the drug deal. There is no reason to do anything because that's what he wanted.

You have a situation in which at the end of this meeting John DeLorean has indicated on at least three or four occasions that he is not interested in a drug deal, that he wants the investment money, and he is put in a situation by a very manipulative informant in which the man says, "I will get your investment, but behind that is a situation regarding drugs."

Now, September 7, there is a meeting with Mr. Tisa. DeLorean is now seeing and meeting the people who are supposedly talking about money laundering.

I want you to consider with regard to money laundering several things. First of all, you have an instruction. John DeLorean is not charged with any crime related to money laundering. The judge will read an instruction to that effect.

Second of all, when John DeLorean talks to these people, he constantly refers to things that are legitimate tax breaks: "Our accountants use every method known to man to avoid payments of taxes, but they are all legitimate."

He talks about methods that are used by Apple Computer. Certainly they are not claiming Apple Computer somehow was involved in illegal narcotic transactions. He talks options and capital gains, which the agents don't know, but they say that it has something to do with illegal activity. He's talking about these things, and maybe he is leading them on, but remember, ladies and gentlemen, the company overseas was in the hands of the receivers in the British government. It was an audited company. Do you really think there would be any way to go into a strictly regulated, audited company and start laundering money?

We then move on to September 14 and 15. During this period of time, the government is supposedly trying to get money out of John DeLorean for the drug deal. John DeLorean is trying to get money out of these investors for his company. On September 14, Hetrick and Tisa talk. Tisa is thinking it is his plan to try and combine Hetrick with DeLorean, and the key to getting Hetrick with DeLorean is because Hetrick expresses an interest in meeting DeLorean and being involved with DeLorean. Now, what Hetrick says to Tisa is, "That man's got to have his money in the bank."

Now, you've heard some conversations about fronting. What Hetrick was saying he would do was he would go down and pick up the cocaine, but he wanted to be paid for it when he got back here, not that he was going to give these people the cocaine and wait however long it took for them to get his money.

The government is trying to say that Tisa in his conversation with DeLorean on the fifteenth made a mistake and talked about fronting the deal, and, ladies and gentlemen, I would ask you to view that transcript and listen to that tape. What Tisa says to John DeLorean on September 15 is, "I want to see the color of the man's [Hetrick's] money." Then Tisa says, "I've gotta have your end in my bank and I gotta see it for real."

Now, the government would have you believe that those statements made by Tisa to DeLorean on the fifteenth indicated to DeLorean that he didn't have to come up with any money. Those statements, specifically, unequivocally, and unambiguously told John DeLorean, "No money, no deal," and any statement, any suggestion that the contrary is true simply flies in the face of the evidence and is an attempt to slip one by you.

So what does DeLorean say in that conversation? He says, "Well, I'm going to have to call you back." DeLorean has been put on the spot now. He has been stalling these people; Can I get the investment without going ahead with this money that they want? Can I do it?

They finally say to him, "John DeLorean, you've gotta come up with the money."

What is it DeLorean says? When he calls back, he says, "The IRA and

Robin Bailie deposited the money." We all know that's a lie. The government never bothered to find out whether it was a lie, but you know it was a lie, and why would he say that? There is no IRA money. There is no deposit. There is no connection with Bailey. He says it, ladies and gentlemen, because he is trying to tell these people, "I want to come up with the money that you are talking about. I want to do it, but it is not my fault. It is the IRA's fault." He doesn't want to say to these people, "Forget it guys. I don't want to do that," because he was trying to protect himself from people who supposedly had connections with Colombia or Orient drug dealers and all kinds of other heavy criminals.

Agent Tisa's response is very interesting. This is an FBI agent. He told you he was trying to sound angry. What on earth is this man doing sounding angry when John DeLorean tells him he doesn't want to come up with the money for a drug deal? Agent Tisa says to John DeLorean on two occasions during the course of that conversation of the fifteenth, "You really put me in a bad spot." Then he says, "This is going to make us look extremely, extremely bad, and it's put me and Jim [*Hoffman*] in a very bad position because we committed ourselves, and you know, on your, on your behalf."

Why is this FBI agent saying to John DeLorean at this time, "You put me," his associate of organized crime, "you put me in a bad spot, John DeLorean." What does he expect John DeLorean to do, say, "Tough luck"?

What does John DeLorean do? DeLorean says, Well, I just can't do it, and then he says things like alternatives.

Ladies and gentlemen, go through that conversation. John DeLorean: "That's where it is, and we can only free it up by replacing it, you know, with ah, with an actual investment in the company. . . . He doesn't think there's any way to get it back until the investment comes in."

Throughout this conversation, DeLorean says to Tisa, "If you have an alternative, mainly, this investment that I have been looking for, the investment that I was looking for since July eleventh," the investment that he still wants, "then we have a chance." What is Tisa's response? Does Tisa say, "No, there is not going to be any investment"? What Tisa says [is], "Hey, you just screwed up a heck of a deal." He keeps filling DeLorean with the notion [that] you can get your investment. You just have to deal with us. If you deal with us, if you do anything, if you show your good faith, you can get your investment.

That's not only improper for an FBI agent to do, it shows quite blatantly the agents were not concerned with what John DeLorean wanted. The agents were only concerned with getting evidence against John DeLorean.

Mr. Perry told you this morning that John DeLorean was a man of means who had $30 or $40 million worth of assets. Why couldn't he use $2 million of that to do the dope deal?

And the government would have you believe that this man, who was so desperate to do a dope deal, so he could save his company, was willing to risk his company by not coming up with the money for the deal. The man who set up this whole thing in motion on June 29 and July 11, who supposedly, according to Hoffman, was offering $2 million to do the dope deal, suddenly doesn't want to do it anymore.

The agents weren't concerned with John DeLorean's true intent. All the agents were concerned about is whether they could make it look as if he was involved.

The next day DeLorean is told that he can give a phony note, to make things look good. He's told by Tisa, "It's between you and whoever." They don't care who this is between. It is a bogus loan. No money was ever involved. DeLorean clearly knew that. It was after they had told DeLorean, "You screwed up a heck of a deal; you can get this money from Hetrick." It is after Tisa says, "You put us in a bad position several times, and it is going to make us look extremely, extremely bad." It is after Hoffman said, "We can't fool around with the people we deal with," and it's after DeLorean knows about the association of these people with Colombians and heroin dealers and people in the Orient.

What does DeLorean give them? Documents to a corporation with no assets. Nothing. This is supposed to be his investment. He doesn't give them anything. It is a corporation with no assets.

You heard the assistant United States attorney, Mr. Rubin, testify to that. It was a shell corporation. The government got no assets. The corporation didn't have any assets.

DeLorean gave them that document to appease them after the statements they made and because he wanted the investment. It does not show an intent to be involved in a dope deal. It shows that he was trying to get the investment, and if he got the investment he did not need the dope deal.

What they are offering DeLorean at that point is nonsense. That's at the point where they are saying, "They will loan you the money; we will do all the work; we will buy all the dope. We will collect all the money, and we will give you the profits."

Do you think that John DeLorean, who they keep referring to as a sophisticated businessman, didn't know that deal was nonsense?

Now, we come to September 20. This is the trip that John DeLorean came three thousand miles for, why did he come? He came because Benedict J. Tisa said to him several days before, "John, I've talked to this man about making the investment, and you're the best one to sell it to him." That's why John DeLorean shows up at that meeting, for the same reason he showed up at every meeting, because of the investment, and what does John DeLorean show up with? He shows up with his brochures once again, and you can see it on the tape, and when he gets done talking about his investment he packs up his little brochures.

What was the conversation about? The first thing they talk about is an investment. DeLorean talks about tax deals, all legitimate. He then talks about investment.

Tisa then makes a reference obliquely to dope. DeLorean runs right over that and keeps talking about investments. Hetrick then says he could possible have $15 million in thirty days. There is another reference by Tisa to dope, which is run over by DeLorean, and he keeps talking about an investment, and then there is a discussion about narcotic activity, and, ladies and gentlemen, John DeLorean's participation is to ask questions about, "Do you really fly that far? How much fuel does it take?"

When they start talking about the prices or the deal, John DeLorean doesn't participate. He is sitting there nodding his head a little. It doesn't mean, "Oh, I agree with everything you are saying." It means, "I hear you. I hear what you are saying."

Now, this man is supposed to be desperate for this dope money, and what he is doing to indicate his assent to this deal, he slowly nods his head. John DeLorean isn't bashful. When John DeLorean wants to talk about an investment, he goes on for pages talking about Bache and Oppenheimer. He can talk. The man can talk.

If he wants to say, "Yes, I want to do that dope deal," he is purely capable of saying, "Yes, I want to do this dope deal."

He doesn't say that, ladies and gentlemen. There is no agreement. One of the reasons there is no agreement is because John DeLorean couldn't agree. John DeLorean didn't have money that he was going to put into a dope deal. It was Valestra's money. Valestra testified that Tisa was his agent at that meeting, that Tisa gave his approval, and that Tisa had the say-so, so any agreement was between Tisa and Hetrick, not with DeLorean. Additionally you will remember that before that meeting Tisa and Hetrick without DeLorean even being present talked about the deal, and reached an agreement at that time. That wasn't even communicated to John DeLorean.

It didn't matter if John DeLorean had said yes because he couldn't spend Valestra's money. DeLorean's agreement, if any, if there was any, was irrelevant, and it would be naive to think that John DeLorean would think that he could go into that deal as the novice in drug deals and negotiate something from this expert, this organized crime figure, and that this fellow would say, "Sure, that's the deal. Let's go ahead with the deal."

Remember what Tisa said: "There was no meeting of the minds."

Well, the bottom line of the September twentieth meeting is that DeLorean doesn't agree to anything. DeLorean is there for his investment. Hetrick is lied to because he is told DeLorean does have the money. DeLorean is lied to because he's told Hetrick does want to invest. They both are lied to. There is no meeting of the minds. There is no agreement, and, again, as Agent Scotti said, they were very upset. They were concerned. They were not satisfied at that meeting.

The upshot of the September 28 meeting, was that Valestra was going to take his money, he was going to do a narcotics deal, and he was going to invest money into the DeLorean company. It doesn't make John DeLorean a coconspirator in a drug deal. It doesn't make John DeLorean guilty of any crime that's before you or any crime at all. That means that John DeLorean was willing to take the money. You may not like that. You may not approve of that. You may think it is a question of morality, but it's not a crime. This meeting was brought about, as you may remember, because the government was concerned that the plant was going to close. The investigation was accelerating. They knew DeLorean [w]as vulnerable. They knew he needed the money very quickly.

They had that article saying that the plant was going to close on the twenty-ninth. They were rushing to get Hetrick and DeLorean. The agents weren't concerned with the facts. They weren't concerned with intent. They were on a headlong rush to glory because they thought they could nail this man.

The first thing DeLorean says in that meeting, by the way, is nothing to do with drugs. Again, it's important what he says first because it's an indication of what he thinks and what he believes.

The first thing he says to these people is, "I need to understand your objectives." What he is telling Valestra is, "Look, you want to invest your money in the company; I have to understand what your objectives are with regard to that investment."

What is it DeLorean talked about? He talked about Bache, how he got the money originally, the investment money he got originally. He talks about capital gains. He talks about what advantage Valestra and any other investor would have in investing in the company. There are a lot of advantages to your investing thirty, forty, fifty, sixty million dollars. There are tax advantages you can have, and John DeLorean was trying to sell those.

The government ignores, once again, DeLorean's first comments. Valestra goes on and says, "I want a piece of that company." He then talks about infusions of capital.

Ladies and gentlemen, please look at the exhibit. Look at those exhibits and brochures. We went over that during the trial, but you will see that those exhibits talk about infusion of $50 million. Do you think that John Valestra, the man who doesn't know what capital gains is and thinks it's some kind of illegal activity, is going to be using words like "infusion" and "capital"?

He got it out of the brochures and he knew that company was for sale.

Then DeLorean goes into investment talk again. He mentions Arthur Anderson and the audit, good business practices. He is telling these people that this company is a legitimate company. "We can do things for you, but we are not going to be doing anything illegal."

Valestra then becomes concerned about his investment, and DeLorean is concerned about how the money is going to come in. All of this is done in an atmosphere where the government would like you to believe there is a conversation about a drug deal. It is not, ladies and gentlemen. It is a conversation about an investment.

If you want to find out who it was, who was involved, just look at the transcript and you will see, ladies and gentlemen, that Hoffman starts talking about drugs. He is the one who brings it up. He says, "We have gone ahead with the Thailand heroin deal." We, who is that? Hoffman and Valestra have gone ahead with the Thailand heroin deal, not DeLorean. These are the people who are the drug dealers.

DeLorean doesn't even respond during this conversation. Hoffman says, "We're going to have approximately thirty-six to thrity-seven million dollars available." That's Hoffman and Valestra. DeLorean doesn't even respond to this part of the conversation.

The most DeLorean is saying during this conversation is "uh-huh" or "right." He's not agreeing. He's not saying anything. He's not taking part because it doesn't have to do with him, ladies and gentlemen.

DeLorean has no participation in that discussion because it has nothing to do with him. DeLorean's participation is to talk about capital gains and Apple Computer because this is what he is concerned about. If they put their money into the company what advantages are there for them.

In DeLorean's mind, in their mind, it is not DeLorean's deal. It is their deal.

After September 28, we have heard about a little party the agents had. We hear a toast about *Time* magazine, "We will all be in *Time* magazine," toasting at the cost of John DeLorean's reputation.

The sad part, ladies and gentlemen, while these people are toasting and partying, no one asked, "What does this man really want to do?" Who was it among them that bothered to listen to these tapes closely, who bothered to listen to what DeLorean was talking about? None of them did because none of them really cared, not the agents, not the informants, not the supervisor, no one cared. What they cared about was that they had a tape that they could play to the jury from which they could argue that DeLorean was guilty, whether or not he was.

Now, what goes on after September 28? The money that the government is going to be making from John Valestra's deal is the money that was offered to John DeLorean for the company. DeLorean is not told it's his deal. In fact, he's told it's their deal.

DeLorean is told, "We're going to put up the money. We're going to do the deal. We're going to make the money, and then we're going to invest the money."

If you take the deal that the government has at that point and remove the part about the [DeLorean] investment, you have a straightforward narcotics deal. John Valestra, over here, he's going to buy the dope from Hetrick over here. Valestra is going to sell the dope and get the money, and then he can do with that money as he pleases. That's what dope dealers do. What Valestra chose to do is to invest the money. He could have bought cars with it. He could have bought houses with it. He could have bought other companies. He could have bought planes. He could have bought whatever he wanted. He decided that he was going to buy shares of stock in DeLorean's company.

DeLorean is not involved with the drug deal. We have Valestra, Hetrick, Hoffman over here, and that is a completed drug deal; and over here we have DMCI, which is a corporation, and DeLorean is way over here as an officer, and the deal between DMCI and between Valestra and those people is a normal investment situation.

Now, throughout this, DeLorean insisted that the money come through the bank so it's traceable. Throughout this, DeLorean was looking for an investment. Throughout this, DeLorean did not commit a crime. He didn't specifically intend to violate the law. He didn't intend to distribute cocaine. He didn't intend to sell cocaine, and he didn't. He didn't intend to possess cocaine, and he didn't. What he intended to do was to get money from these people.

That's not the prosecution's theory. The prosecution's theory is that this man invested in a cocaine deal by putting up collateral. That collateral was from a shell corporation. The collateral wasn't owned by that corporation. It's as if I were to put up the collateral on everything I own in IBM. I don't own anything in IBM. It's not very valuable collateral.

So what we have is a situation where John DeLorean is committing no crime. He wasn't doing a dope deal. He was taking money from these people. But, ladies and gentlemen, even at that, John DeLorean distanced himself from these people. He separated himself, look at that trust agreement. John DeLorean separated himself because he didn't want to be in a position to do anything for these people. He didn't want these people to have a hold over him, he was willing to give up control of that company, rather than deal with these people.

DeLorean's car company was a shell corporation. The $10 million would go into the working capital in the company overseas. This company, this corporation, would have the ability to manufacture the cars. It would have a value only after money was put in, after the investor put in the money.

It had something of value, though, only if the money were put in. John DeLorean's only way to manufacture those cars was through that corporation and through the exercise of that contract. Yes, that was John DeLorean's dream, if that company had worked, if that company had been funded, if that company had made its investment overseas. It would have been a valuable thing to John DeLorean.

However, the company had no assets before the money was put in. That's why we can say that the collateral was valueless, because the company simply had no assets until the $10 to $60 million was put in.

The bottom line of this trust agreement is that John DeLorean did give up the control of the company. If these people were who they claim to be, as Mr. Perry discussed, and if they put in their money, and if John DeLorean were willing to deal with these people to manufacture his car, he could have given them less than 50 percent.

He could have given them no percent of the voting stock. John DeLorean gave them 100 percent of the voting stock. It was totally his idea. It was totally his construction, and John DeLorean could have made this trust agreement last for a period of much less than five years because all the money is supposed to be paid in six months. He could have had the trust in six months.

If John DeLorean had wanted to control this company under the situation that was offered to him, he could have done it any number of ways, but what he chose to do because his back was against the wall was to say to these people, "If you are going to put your money in this company, if you are going to do it under this trust agreement, it's yours. You can't do anything to me, folks, because it's your company. You control it."

He hoped to get an investment which would be a proper investment. He didn't want to deal with these people at this point. He didn't want them to have a hold over his head. He didn't want them coming to him asking him to do things. He gave them 100 percent control of the voting stock.

You may ask what happens in five years. If you were in his position and you had a company, would you think that five years after John Valestra and James Hoffman took it over it would be worth a dime? Because these people were posing as crooks, robbers; they were cheating each other. They certainly were going to cheat John DeLorean.

The theory of the government's case is that DeLorean would do this heroin deal to hold on to his car company, and that's absolutely not true. He wanted an investment, and when that didn't come through, he was willing to give up his right to manufacture the car that bore his name.

The government, however, never bothered to find out what was in this trust agreement. John Valestra never knew about this 100 percent interest until he was right up there on the stand in front of you. Nobody checked it out because nobody cared. Ladies and gentlemen, there is no explanation consistent with the government's theory of John DeLorean's involvement in this case. Why would he give up 100 percent control of that corporation? He didn't have to do that. It was in his power not to do it. The only reason he did it is because he didn't want to deal with these people. He did not have the intent to commit any crime.

What it does show is his inability to walk away. John DeLorean is a man that can be recognized anywhere anytime. He and his family were in an awkward position of him having dealt with these people. Was it a mistake? Sure it was a mistake. Was it a crime? No.

You will hear from the judge an instruction on mere presence. You can talk to people. You can talk to them about things of interest. You can talk to them about crimes. It doesn't make you guilty of a crime.

That trust agreement is probably the clearest indication that DeLorean was not part of the drug deal and had no intent to be part of the drug deal.

Ladies and gentlemen, I suppose that under some theory it's possible that one or more of you may think that DeLorean was involved, even though I don't think it's justified by the evidence. But in the event you do, I think that you would agree that he was manipulated; he was tricked, and he was lied to.

You saw the way these conversations were rigged to keep him involved, constantly talking to him about the investment, constantly luring him, constantly getting him to go to meetings about the investment, and then slipping in the narcotics language. He was pushed and manipulated in every direction by the government.

Mr. Perry says that entrapment is an offense you use when you are caught red-handed. Well, ladies and gentlemen, John DeLorean wasn't caught red-handed; John DeLorean was caught trying to get an investment. He wasn't caught doing any crime. If you listen to what the court says to you, the first part of the instruction reads, "John DeLorean asserts that the government has not proved beyond a reasonable doubt that he is guilty of committing the acts with which he is charged."

That's our position. He didn't commit a crime. He had no intent. He wasn't involved. There was no agreement.

However, if you believe the government has so proved, then John DeLorean maintains that he is a victim of entrapment.

One of the things, one of the primary things you are supposed to look to with regard to entrapment is his reluctance. He was reluctant. Look to the lies, threats, and the actions of the government agents. Remember Tisa's statement, "You put me in a bad position." Remember Hoffman's statement, "We have to be careful with the people that we deal with."

Remember his reluctance on September 4 when he said, "Financing is a better way." Remember his reluctance, "I have to get it from the IRA. I have to check with them." Remember his reluctance on the twenty-eighth when he is talking about, "I don't understand what you want."

Remember his reluctance when he prepares that trust agreement or has it prepared, and remember, ladies and gentlemen, the testimony of Agent Scotti that on June 29, before the first telephone call was ever made. James Hoffman told Scotti he was going to get John DeLorean. Remember that when you think about entrapment and whether John DeLorean was induced.

We finally get to October 18. Hetrick still doesn't know what the deal is. That conversation shows that there is utter confusion and the lack of any kind of agreement or understanding between DeLorean and Hetrick. These people are on totally different wavelengths.

We then move to the mysterious unrecorded call to DeLorean from Hoffman. What was John DeLorean told in that call as far as his reason for coming out to Los Angeles? Based upon everything that has happened in this case, I think you have to conclude that John DeLorean was told that the investment money was ready for him.

We then move to October 19. The reason that John DeLorean is brought out to Los Angeles, is dragged out here, is because the government wanted to tape him one more time and wanted to take a caseful of cocaine and push it in front of him.

The government decided to do that, although the chief case agent on this case, John Valestra, thought it was a bad idea. You heard that there was squabbling and fighting between the New York office and the L.A. office as to where he was going to be arrested. There was no reason for John DeLorean to travel out here except the government wanted to put that cocaine in front of his face.

In the New York office and the L.A. office, they were fighting over this man's carcass. According to what Mr. Scotti said, the decision as to where to arrest him in this simple narcotics case was made by a representative of the [Reagan] White House.

The government didn't evidence any concern about John DeLorean's intent. What they were concerned about was their own ego and the publicity, what they could get and how good this would look in *Time* magazine. They wanted to influence you through this staged and misleading

Hollywood performance and make you believe that DeLorean was guilty.

What did they expect John DeLorean to do, bolt out of the room? You've heard those questions. He had no choice. He had to sit there.

Ladies and gentlemen, you listen to that tape, and you tell me if John DeLorean isn't nervous at the time that cocaine is brought up and if that isn't a nervous laugh and a nervous reaction of a man who is feeling like a trapped animal. They put that cocaine in his hand, and they were happy that they did because it made him look guilty.

It is a pathetic, sick performance. The events of the nineteenth don't show anything about DeLorean's intent, but they do show the depths to which the government will go to try and get material that they can put in front of you to inflame you.

You heard the agent testify about the press conference that he attended. He brought the cocaine up there so the press could see the cocaine, and at the press conference he told the media that John DeLorean was arrested in a room with twenty-five kilos of cocaine.

What the government did at that point, they made it seem to the whole world that John DeLorean was guilty before he was even charged. He had just been arrested moments before, and now, finally, two years later, although it's come out in little dribs and drabs in court, and it had to be yanked out like teeth, you have heard about the manipulation. You have heard about the lies. You have learned about the back-dating, the cover-ups, the demands for money, and the sick story of deceptions.

Ladies and gentlemen, the evidence in this case demonstrates I think unequivocally that John DeLorean did not have an intent to participate in a drug deal. He didn't have an agreement to participate in a drug deal. He did not participate in a drug deal. He was lured, lied to, pushed into the acts which he did do but which did not rise to a level of crime, and this was all done to satisfy the competitive urges of various government agents and agencies. But do you know something, ladies and gentlemen? We don't have to prove that. Remember, at the beginning of this I said toward the end I was going to ask you to unlock that door and bring back reasonable doubt, and I am going to ask you to do that right now.

The instruction which you will hear about reasonable doubt from this court talks in terms of a hesitancy to act.

You, of course, must apply the reasonable doubt standards to the entrapment issue. Was he induced; was he predisposed? You heard about the lies. You heard about the threats. You heard about the lures. You heard about the offers of money. You heard about his reluctance. I explained that to you before about the IRA, about the September fifteenth backing out with the worthless collateral, about the trust agreement.

Ladies and gentlemen, the bottom line is there was no conspiracy in this case. There was no offense in this case.

This case has been described by these agents as the biggest case in their career. I would seem to think if it were, they would have crossed every *t* and dotted every *i*. These agents didn't bother to record the July eleventh meeting. They didn't bother to check out inconsistencies of Mr. Hoffman's statements or find out about unrecorded calls or the contents of those calls until later. They didn't bother to write reports about much of the case, didn't bother to write reports about what Hoffman told them, didn't bother to check out the IRA statements. They didn't bother to check out the value of the collateral to find out if it was worthless, didn't bother to find out the nature of DHCI and DCML, and didn't know the difference. They allowed Hoffman to talk with DeLorean alone to determine his intent.

They didn't bother to get a good recording of DeLorean on the fifteenth, didn't bother to listen to the tape recording that was made until after DeLorean's arrest. They didn't bother to lock tapes in evidence at the appropriate times. All those tapes that were talked about with Mr. Waters, until after John DeLorean's arrest they weren't listened to. They didn't bother to read and analyze the trust agreement to find out about the 100 percent.

Ladies and gentlemen, they didn't even bother to listen to the truth in this case, but they did have time to backdate documents so they could look good. So they could walk into court and say, "We didn't do anything wrong here."

They did apologize for lying to you, but they want you to believe that now they are telling the truth. They toast to *Time* magazine, but they want you to believe they are not motivated by fame. They did fight over participation in the story about the buy/bust in the New York and Los Angeles squabble on the eighteenth, but they want you to believe that had nothing to do with this investigation.

The government in this case wasn't concerned with the truth. They just wanted to make it look like John DeLorean was guilty. As Agent

Scotti said, it was a steamroller in which they were all caught up. The government is now asking that you drive the steamroller right over John DeLorean.

I don't believe you are going to do that, and I don't believe the evidence permits you to do that. On the state of the evidence, I am confident that you can find John DeLorean not guilty on every count.

Before I go, I want to give you one last thought. During the course of the last couple of weeks, I guess like a lot of people in this town, I have been sort of blasé about the Olympics [*1984 Olympics, held in Los Angeles*]. I figured we are sort of in our own Olympics event here and didn't have time for any others.

A friend encouraged me to watch the Olympics, and I'm glad because all of us, every one of us, has a right to be proud of what goes on in this country. We don't have a right to be blasé. With that pride, we have an obligation to do whatever we can to make sure that this country lives up to its reputation, to encourage people to protect people, not to victimize people. The government undoubtedly has tried and will continue to try to justify what happened in this case. They will try to tell you it was unimportant and it didn't affect the case.

Ladies and gentlemen, all of you deserve more than excuses or apologies from the government as to what happened here. All of us are entitled to better than that. We are entitled to better than the lies, changed testimony, inconsistent testimony, contradictory testimony, withheld documents, cover-ups, backdated documents, repeated violations of policy.

John DeLorean is entitled to all of that and much more. He is entitled, particularly under the state of the facts of this record, to be found not guilty. You people are the only people who can do that. You people are the only people who can right the wrong that has been done in this case. You people are the only people who can set this system straight, and we in the defense are confident that you are going to do just that in finding John DeLorean on each and every count not guilty. Thank you very much.

CHAPTER TEN

Baseball, Hot Dogs, Apple Pie, and My Lai

A Generation After Nüremberg, Home-Grown War Criminals Claim They Were Just Following Orders When They Murdered an Entire Village

It was 1969, the Vietnam War was raging, and word started filtering back to the United States of a horrific massacre of civilians by American troops the year before. Thanks to the efforts of outraged GIs like Ron Ridenhour and journalist Seymour Hersh, the story came to light, despite efforts by the Nixon administration, the army, and a congressional commission to bury the ugly truth. American soldiers had systematically executed as many as 504 Vietnamese women, children, and elderly farmers at an obscure village called My Lai.

On March 15, 1968, U.S. Army Capt. Ernest L. Medina informed the soldiers under his command that the Forty-eighth Vietcong Battalion was in My Lai, known as "Pinkville." Intelligence reports predicted that the hamlet's women and children would be on their way to the weekly markets by 7 A.M. and would not be in the village. Charlie Company, Eleventh Light Infantry Brigade, under the command of Lieutenant William Calley, Jr. was ordered to burn houses, blow up bunkers and tunnels, and kill all livestock.

There were sharply conflicting opinions amongst the company over exactly what Medina ordered. One GI later testified that Medina ordered the company to "kill everything in the village." Another GI said that Medina ordered the company not to take any prisoners. However, several men were sure that Medina did not order the killing of women and children. When someone asked Medina, "Who is the enemy?" he responded, "The enemy is anybody that is running from us, hiding from us, or who appears to us to be the enemy."

On March 16, Lieutenant Calley led the first platoon on a search and destroy mission, and at 7:22 A.M. Charlie Company set out for My Lai.

The first platoon's mission was to secure the landing zone and eliminate enemy fire for the second wave of troops. One helicopter pilot reported the area was "hot," meaning Vietcong were waiting below. Calley and his men hit the ground firing; however, there was no return fire and the only people they encountered were the women, children, and old men of My Lai.

The killings began without warning. A group of fifteen or twenty women and children praying at a temple were executed with rifle shots to the back of the head. A GI with an M-16 fired at two young boys walking along a road. The older boy fell on top of the other to protect him; the GI kept firing until both lay dead. Eighty villagers were taken to a plaza area in the hamlet. Calley left several men in charge of guarding the group. "You know what I want you to do with them," he told one GI. Ten minutes later, Lieutenant Calley returned and asked, "Haven't you got rid of them yet? I want them dead." A GI watched as Calley took his rifle and pushed a monk into a rice paddy and shot him point-blank. Another group of women and children were lined up at an irrigation ditch where Calley led his men in shooting them down. A two-year-old boy covered in blood crawled out of the ditch. The child began to run and Calley chased him down, threw him back in the ditch, and shot him.

Helicopter pilot Chief Warrant Officer Hugh C. Thompson could not believe what he was seeing. He flew over a ditch filled with bodies. "I remember that we remarked at the time about the old biblical story of Jesus turning water into wine. The trench had a gray color to it, with the red blood of the individuals lying in it." Part of Thompson's task that day was to mark the location of wounded Vietnamese civilians with smoke so that medical attention could be provided. However, every time he dropped a smoke marker, GIs responded by killing the injured person.

Thompson tried unsuccessfully to radio troops on the ground to find out what was going on. He then radioed headquarters and reported that the troops were shooting down civilians. Thompson landed his helicopter several times to pick up Vietnamese civilians and fly them to a safe area. The second time he landed, he watched as Lieutenant Calley and a group of GIs prepared to destroy a bunker with women and children inside. "I asked him [Calley] if he could get the women and kids out of there before they tore it up, and he said the only way he could get them out was to use hand grenades." Thompson told Calley to hold his men, and he called in two helicopter gunships to rescue the civilians. While waiting for them to arrive, Thompson stood between the American troops and the bunker. Thompson left instructions with his helicopter crew chief while he got the women and children out: "If any of the Americans open up on the Vietnamese, you should open up on the Americans." Calley was visibly angry, but he did nothing to stop Thompson. Later, Calley complained that "The pilot doesn't like the way I'm running the show, but I'm the boss." Thompson was awarded the Distinguished Flying Cross for his heroism—perhaps the first time an American was honored for threatening to kill fellow GIs.

Some, too few, refused to join in the mayhem. Harry Stanley, a machine gunner with Charley Company, refused to open fire with his M-60. "I wasn't firing because I was waiting for some resistance," Stanley said. "There was no resistance. There was no reason for me to shoot. It was just a bunch of . . . craziness to me. I wasn't a murderer." Calley ordered Stanley to mow down the villagers he had brought to the edge of the ditch; Stanley refused. Calley threatened to court-martial the GI, and when that failed, grabbed an M-16 and shoved it in Stanley's gut. Stanley responded by cocking his .45 automatic and shoving it in Calley's stomach. Stanley later said he was thinking, "I'm gonna die here anyway. So, hey, if you're talking about shooting me, we might just as well shoot each other. As far as doing what you're talking about doing, I'm not going to do that because that's wrong to me." Calley backed down, gathered twenty to thirty GIs, and began slaughtering the villagers.

One witness said that he stopped for a lunch break by the ditch where Calley had been supervising the machine gunning of the civilians. By this time the ditch held hundreds of wounded and dying villagers. Two GIs roamed back and forth, picking off the noisemakers, until the ditch fell silent. Another witness told of seeing Captain Medina shoot a young girl at close range, then turn around and grin.

The sadistic nature of the attacks undermined any pretense of a military purpose to the carnage. Women were raped, sodomized, and mutilated. One woman was killed when a GI inserted his M-16 in her vagina and pulled the trigger.

In the aftermath of the slaughter, the headline in *Stars and Stripes,* the official newspaper of the U.S. Army, read "U.S. Troops Surround Reds, Kill 128."

The story of My Lai and photographs taken by an army photographer who accompanied Charlie Company began to reach U.S. newspapers in the fall of 1969, more than a year after the massacre. Americans were divided in their reactions to reports of the atrocity. Some refused to believe that the incident ever occurred, claiming the story was planted by Communist sympathizers. Others believed that such things are to be expected in times of war. Many were outraged.

Calley was charged with the premeditated murder of 102 Vietnamese civilians. The trial was set for November 1970, before a military court at Fort Benning, Georgia. An army judge presided, and the jury consisted of six army officers. The trial lasted four months. Jury selection alone took three days, primarily because most prospective jurors admitted that they supported Calley and were prejudiced against the government. One prospective juror stated, "It seemed to me, somebody was out to railroad somebody." Another said he didn't think prosecuting Calley was right. A colonel said, "Over there, we never knew who was the enemy, really." Twenty-five officers were dismissed because they indicated sympathy for Calley and animosity toward the government for prosecuting him.

Before the trial began, Calley sarcastically commented, "It's true: I sat up with sergeants in the wee hours of March 16, 1968, and I plotted to kill those people in My Lai. I filled up the cartridge clips, and God, how premeditated can you get? Of course, in Vietnam we called it a combat assault."

There were sixty-two witnesses for the government and forty-four for the defense. The jury did not hear from any of the people of My Lai. The prosecution called witness after witness to describe the brutal acts committed by Calley at My Lai. The defense argued that Calley was an army scapegoat and the responsibility for the massacre should have been placed on Captain Medina. Several GIs testified on behalf of Calley, telling the court that Medina ordered the killing of Vietnamese civilians.

The defense also called two psychiatrists, who testified that Calley lacked the mental ability to premeditate murder of Vietnamese civilians. Both doctors testified that Calley was under great mental stress, and that, combined with his limited intellectual background and psychological makeup, made it impossible for him to grasp the enormity of the killings. Subsequently, one of the doctors was dismissed as a witness because the presiding judge expressed doubt as to the truth of his sworn testimony.

Calley took the stand in his own defense. He admitted on direct examination that he shot several Vietnamese civilian prisoners at My Lai. However, he maintained that he was under direct orders from Captain Medina. He also denied that he could have killed 102 civilians that day. However, Calley did testify that he "had no regrets." He stated that Medina told him on at least five different occasions that all inhabitants of My Lai were to be killed, and he followed those orders. Calley stated that he never questioned the legality of Medina's orders and, further, that he was and would always be proud to have served under Captain Medina.

One of the most damaging witnesses to the defense was Captain Medina. As he entered the courtroom, Medina exchanged nods and a tense "Hello, how are you" with Calley. Medina testified that he never ordered the killing of Vietnamese civilians. He further testified that when asked if civilians should be killed, he responded, "No, you do not kill women and children. You use common sense. Shoot back, but you must use common sense." In addition, Medina claimed to have issued an order to the troops on the ground once the massacre had begun not to shoot any unarmed civilians. Medina stated that two days after the massacre, he confronted Calley and asked him if any atrocities took place. Medina quoted Calley as saying, "My God, I can still hear the screaming." This statement was stricken from the record as an inadmissible confession. As Medina stepped down from the witness box, he turned and saluted the judge. He then walked out of the courtroom without glancing at Calley.

Immediately before the jury retired for deliberations, Calley made his final plea. He urged them to understand that the army had never told him his enemies were human.

Three years and two weeks after the My Lai massacre, a military jury found Lt. William L. Calley Jr. guilty of the premeditated murder of the 102 Vietnamese civilians. He was sentenced to life at hard labor. In 1974, Calley's life sentence was reduced to ten years. Originally, the Military Court of Appeal ordered that Calley be taken into custody by the military stockade at Fort Benning. President Richard Nixon vacated that order and demanded that Calley be confined under house arrest in a civilian apartment. Calley spent three years in his apartment and was released.

Today, Calley manages a jewelry store, V. V. Vick Jewelers, in Columbus, Georgia. He is married to the store owner's daughter. Columbus is a military town, and the townspeople have closed ranks around a man they consider a hero. He doesn't deny My Lai, he just doesn't believe that he did anything wrong.

More than thirty men were investigated in connection with the massacre. Some of them, including Medina, were court-martialed. Medina was originally charged with the murder of 102 Vietnamese civilians. However, that charge was reduced to only one count of murder for the death of one Vietnamese woman, and Medina was acquitted. Calley remains the only man who was jailed for the massacre.

The actual number of Vietnamese civilians killed varies according to the source. Official U.S. military reports claimed the dead totaled 268, only 20 percent of which were Vietnamese civilians. Vietnamese officials in My Lai report that 568 of the 900 civilians living in the hamlet were killed. According to a *New York Times* source, both governments agree off the record that the number killed was somewhere between 400 and 500.

Six miles from the spot of the massacre, there is a memorial to My Lai. Visitors walk down a cobblestone path lined with three-foot statues. Each statue is a woman. Some are bent over with their arms wrapped around their waists. Others cross their chest or block their faces with their hands. All are screaming or weeping. The path leads to the My Lai museum which is home to many giant black-and-white photographs depicting the brutality of the massacre. One of the most disturbing photographs is of Calley boarding a helicopter after the slaughter, flashing the "V" sign to the photographer. The caption to the picture reads "Calley Flashes the Peace Sign." But below the display, the museum curators added their own caption: "Calley Flashes the Sign for Victory."

Biography

Aubrey M. Daniel III was born May 15, 1941, in Monk's Corner, South Carolina. Daniel graduated from the University of Virginia in 1963, then continued his studies at the University of Richmond, receiving his law degree in 1966.

Daniel joined the army after graduation, becoming a military lawyer in the army's J.A.G. Corps. Promoted in short order to captain, Daniel gathered experience as both a defense attorney and prosecutor in more than fifty felony cases.

In 1971, the twenty-nine-year-old attorney was selected to prosecute William Calley for the massacre of Vietnamese civilians at My Lai. Daniel gave a bravura performance, despite the glare of constant media attention, capping what had become the longest trial in army history, involving more than 100 witnesses, with a three-hour closing argument.

Despite public opinion favoring the defendant and a strong strain of sympathy among the officer corps, Daniel's painstaking presentation of the evidence convinced the jury of army officers that Calley was guilty as charged.

When President Nixon ordered Calley released from prison and placed under house arrest, Daniel wrote a letter of protest to the commander in chief. Daniel told the president that he had not only damaged the military's judicial process, but "helped enhance the image of Calley as a national hero," giving credence to those who believed that Calley and his troops were merely "killing the enemy." Daniel told Nixon, "I would expect that the president of the United States, a man who I believed should and would provide the moral leadership for this nation, would stand fully behind the law of this land on a moral issue about which there can be no compromise."

Daniel is now a partner with the Washington, D.C., firm of Williams & Connolly, specializing in complex civil and criminal litigation. He has represented *The National Inquirer* in libel actions brought by celebrities ranging from Frank Sinatra to Carol Burnett.

Commentary

Aubrey Daniel presented his argument as if he were conducting a military exercise, each piece precisely placed to be followed up by the next interlocking piece. There was no throwaway or unnecessary windup; Daniel got right down to the business of orienting his jury. He began with a brief overview of the four separate incidents that made up the charges. He then followed up with a more detailed account in which he fleshed out the incidents with a fairly fine brush to establish the compelling nature of the prosecution's case. Interlocking with this more detailed account, Daniel established the corroborating links and witnesses from charge to charge. Having solidly locked up the facts, Daniel then turned his attention to the law of premeditation and how it related to Lieutenant Calley. From there his closing naturally flowed to the prosecution's evidence of Calley's premeditation. The logical and methodical manner in which Daniel organized this close allowed the jurors to more easily follow the argument. Any audience is more apt to remain focused if the "presentation" follows a logical and consistent format.

Daniel faced significant obstacles in the prosecution of Lt. William Calley; perhaps the most troublesome was the perception that Calley was the army's scapegoat, his trial an attempt by the Nixon administration to lay all of the army's sins on Calley and thus purge itself of blame. Daniel recognized this perception and disposed of it, limiting the court's focus to Calley's personal actions at My Lai. The evidence was overwhelming, Daniel said, charging that Calley deliberately murdered 102 Vietnamese civilians, including a man in white robes who might well have been a monk, and a two-year-old child trying to climb from a pile of more than seventy corpses in a ditch. Daniel argued to the court that "By this slaughter of innocent civilians . . . [Calley] prostituted all the humanitarian principles for which this country stands." Daniel rejected the defense's attempt to claim that Calley had been following orders, reminding the court of the lessons learned at the Nüremberg trials a mere twenty years earlier. Daniel argued that the "obedience of a soldier to orders is not the obedience of an automaton. When a man wears a soldier's uniform, he is still required to think, to make moral decisions, to know what is right and wrong."

A third aspect of Daniel's close was his recognition of the flawed nature of the defense theory. In essence, the defense was "We didn't do it and even if we did it was justified." First, the defense claimed that Calley was not involved in murdering innocent civilians or in ordering anyone else to do so. However, as the evidence against Calley mounted, the defense moved to a justification theory, discarding the previous defense.

Another maxim of brilliant litigators is to keep the focus on the strengths of the case. It frequently occurs that during the course of a complex trial brimming with intricacy and nuance, the basics are overlooked. More precisely, during murder trials, the lawyers become so caught up in proving or disproving theories and justifications that the victims are somehow relegated to a distant memory. When that occurs, the prosecution has lost one of its strong cards. It is a sound prosecution theory to make the jurors confront the hard reality of death and if they are inclined to favor the defense, they must take a very deliberate step over the bodies of the victims. Daniel did not forget the victims. In discussing the baby at the ditch, Daniel described how Calley ". . . picked up the child, threw it in the ditch, and without hesitation, gentlemen, without hesitation, he raised his weapon and he fired . . . he just pulled that weapon up and squeezed that trigger, and that baby was at the end of that barrel." In describing the people being shot in the ditch, Daniel said, "Mothers trying to protect their children. People screaming, crying, falling on top of each other as they were shot."

After listening to the defense summation, Daniel delivered his final close to the jurors. The passion, disgust, and disdain for the defendant's actions had been steadily building within the prosecutor throughout the course of the trial; he finally had an opportunity to give voice to his outrage:

> The accused was a commissioned officer of the armed forces of this United States when he slaughtered his innocent victims in My Lai. He has attempted to absolve himself of responsibility by saying that he had his duty there, that he acted in the name of this country and the law of this nation, . . . to make that assertion, is to prostitute all of the humanitarian principles for which this nation stands. It is to prostitute the true mission of the United States soldier. It has been said the soldier be he friend or foe is charged with the protection of the weak and unarmed. It is the very essence and reason for his being. When he violates this sacred trust, he not only profanes his entire cult but threatens the very fabric of international society.

The jury agreed.

Closing Argument

The Court Martial of William L. Calley, Jr.
Delivered by Captain Aubrey Daniel
Fort Benning, Georgia, August 27, 1971

If it please the court, counsel for the accused, president, and gentlemen of the jury: First of all, I'd like to take this opportunity to thank you on behalf of the United States government, Captain Partin, myself, and I'm sure for the court, and counsel for the defense for the patience which you've shown us throughout this long trial.

You have a job, gentlemen, a job which you took an oath to do, to take all this evidence and judge the credibility of each one of those witnesses, and then make a determination in your own mind as to what happened in the village of My Lai on 16 March 1968.

At the beginning of this case, I outlined for you what we expected to prove, to give you the government's theory under which we expected and intended and have in fact established that the accused is guilty of the offenses with which he was charged. At that time, I related to you that we would show that with respect to specification one of the charge that on 16 March 1968, when Charlie Company landed in My Lai on the western side of the village, they didn't receive any fire; they only found unresisting, unarmed men, women, children, and babies. And I told you at that time with respect to specification one that Paul Meadlo and Dennis Conti and other members of the accused's platoon gathered up a group of not less than thirty individuals on the south side of the village, and that the accused came to Paul Meadlo and Dennis Conti and said, "Take care of them." And he left and he returned a few minutes later and he said, "Why haven't you taken care of them?" In the meantime, Dennis Conti and Paul Meadlo had that group of people, unarmed, unresisting men, women, children, and babies, squatting there on that trail, and when Calley came back, they hadn't taken care of them, and he ordered Paul Meadlo to kill those people on that trail, and he in fact participated in the murder of those people. This was the first offense.

We told you that they then moved to an irrigation ditch on the eastern side of the village of My Lai, and there, the accused, along with members of his platoon did as the accused directed, gathered up more people, this time unarmed men, women, children, and babies, and put them in that irrigation ditch and shot them, and that he [*indicating defendant*] participated; and he caused their deaths and that they died.

After the accused, along with other members of his platoon, had killed the people in the ditch, he moved north and he came to a man that was dressed in white, a man that was described as a monk. The accused began to question this individual, and then the accused butt-stroked this man in the mouth, and then he blew half of his head off.

Shortly thereafter, the accused heard someone yell, "A child is getting away!" He ran back to that area, picked the child up, approximately two years old, threw the child in the ditch, shot, and killed him.

Those were the time sequences which I told you we would prove, those are the facts upon which these charges and specification are based, and now you must resolve whether or not we have in fact established what we told you that we would prove to you when this trial began.

First of all, I would like to give you in summary form what the government submits that we have proved happened in the village of My Lai on 16 March 1968. Keep in mind that it is not your function to resolve the guilt or innocence of any other person who may have committed any other offense in the village of My Lai on 16 March 1968. Your function is solely to judge the guilt or innocence of the accused with respect to specific charges and specifications for which he is being tried.

Now, we have shown that when C Company landed on 16 March 1968, they did in fact land on the western side of the village of My Lai. All of the testimony is in agreement on that fact. We have also shown that the accused was in the platoon, a headquarters group, and a mortar platoon. We showed that when they landed, the accused's platoon assumed the position on the south side of the village. He had two squads and a platoon and a headquarters element for this operation. One squad was commanded by Sergeant Mitchell, and the other squad was commanded by Sergeant Bacon. The first lift arrived at 0730 hours and it carried, as you will recall from the testimony, the First Platoon, Captain Medina's headquarters element, and perhaps part of the Second Platoon. As you will recall, after the first lift landed, elements of the First Platoon then secured portions of the LZ [*landing zone*] for the second lift to come in. Before the second lift landed, the First Platoon moved into the village. They received no fire from that village. None. The witnesses are in agreement on that fact.

Now, the accused's platoon had Sergeant Mitchell's squad on the south side of the village, and it had Sergeant Bacon's squad on the north side of the village. And when they entered the village, the platoon, as you will recall, found no armed VC [*Vietcong*]. All they found were old men, women, children, and babies. They began to gather up these thirty to forty unarmed, unresisting men, women, children, and babies because they weren't receiving any fire. Meadlo and Conti moved them out on the trail, and they made them squat down on the north-south trail.

Lieutenant Calley returned fifteen minutes later and said to Meadlo, "Why haven't you taken care of this group?" "Waste them." "I want them dead." "Kill them." The versions differ here slightly between the testimony of Sledge, Conti, and Meadlo regarding the actual words that Lieutenant Calley spoke. But nonetheless, Lieutenant Calley then issued an order to Meadlo, and in fact Calley and Meadlo shot those people on the north-south trail.

Jim Dursi had gathered another group of people and he moved this other group of civilians along the southern edge of the village until he came to an irrigation ditch. And when he arrived at the irrigation ditch with his people, he was joined by Lieutenant Calley. And what happened there? Lieutenant Calley directed that those individuals, those groups of people, be placed into that irrigation ditch, and that they would be shot by Meadlo and Dursi.

You recall the testimony of Paul Meadlo to Jim Dursi, "Why don't you shoot?" "Why don't you fire?" "I can't." "I won't." Dennis Conti approached from the south and came up and observed Calley and Meadlo and Mitchell firing into that ditch and killing those people. And Conti moved north and set up a position. Robert Maples was in the area. He observed ten to fifteen people being put in that irrigation ditch by Lieutenant Calley. He observed Lieutenant Calley and Meadlo place the people in the irrigation ditch and fire into the people, but he didn't see the people come out.

Thomas Turner, you recall, testified that he, while he assumed the position to the north of the ditch, observed over a hundred people placed in that ditch during an hour to an hour-and-a-half period. These people were screaming and crying and that he passed Meadlo and Calley firing into that ditch as he moved forward.

And then you recall the testimony of Charles Sledge, that after that they moved north of the ditch where there was a man dressed in white, a fact which the accused admits, that Calley interrogated this individual; when the man refused to speak, Calley butt-stroked him with his rifle and then shot him. And then Charles Sledge testified that when he returned someone yelled out, "There's a child getting away, a child getting away!" Lieutenant Calley returned to that area, picked up the child, threw the child in the ditch, and shot him.

Many of the facts which we have related to you as having been proved by this evidence beyond any reasonable doubt have not in fact been disputed by the defense and were in many cases supported by the defense's own evidence, including the testimony of the accused.

We stipulated that the operation took place on the sixteenth of March 1968. It has not in fact been disputed that the operation was preceded by an artillery preparation. It was stipulated as to the landing times. There is no dispute by the accused or any other witness that the accused was not in fact present, and that he participated in the operation as platoon leader for the First Platoon. There was also no dispute about the fact that he had under his command a headquarters element and two squads, the First Squad under Sergeant Mitchell and the Second Squad under Sergeant Bacon. Nor has the defense contested the actual presence at My Lai of any of the government's witnesses. There is also no dispute between defense and prosecution as to the formation that the company assumed when it conducted the operation. There is also no dispute about the fact that the First Platoon had the responsibility for clearing the southern portion of the village of My Lai. Further, there can be no dispute about the fact that once the First Platoon entered that village, all they found were unarmed men, women, children, and babies, and that these individuals were in fact gathered up by the members of the accused's platoon. This has been verified by the defense's own witnesses, gentlemen.

The accused has also admitted in this case that he did in fact encounter Paul Meadlo with a group of Vietnamese people as he proceeded through that village. The accused has admitted that he told Meadlo to take care of these people, to waste them. There's no dispute about the fact that Charles Sledge was the accused's RTO [*radio operator*], and that Charles Sledge was with Lieutenant Calley on the day of this operation. There's no dispute about that fact, and that he was in the vicinity of this group of people. That's also established by the accused. There's also no dispute between the prosecution and the defense that the accused in fact came to the irrigation ditch where we have alleged that he killed the people in My Lai. Nor does the defense contest the fact that at least a group of Vietnamese people were placed in that irrigation ditch, and were shot by members of the accused's platoon and the accused himself. The accused also admitted that while he was at the irrigation ditch, he did in fact have a conversation with his men. He did recall that Paul Meadlo was present. He did recall that Jim Dursi was present. The accused and the defense do not contest the fact that the First Platoon had assumed a perimeter position east of the irrigation ditch in the village of My Lai. The accused has also admitted that after he shot into the group of people at the irrigation ditch that he moved north and that he did in fact encounter a man dressed in white, that he did in fact interrogate this individual, that he butt-stroked this man in the face, but he denies that he actually shot this individual.

The accused has denied the fact that he ever picked up a child and threw it in the ditch.

And, gentlemen, we have alleged and have proven in fact that the persons who are shown and depicted in prosecution exhibit 12A [*photograph of bodies*] are in fact the individuals that the accused killed on the north-south trail in the village of My Lai.

We must prove that each of the victims died as a result of the act of the accused on 16 March 1968, and that they died pursuant to his actually having shot and killed them, or someone else at his direction actually having shot and killed these individuals.

We must prove that with respect to each of the specifications that the killings were in fact unlawful and committed without justification or excuse. We must prove that he not only had the specific intent to kill these individuals, but that he had a premeditated design to kill the individuals prior to the time he in fact killed them. This means under the law that he formulated the idea in his mind to take the life before he in fact killed the human being.

First of all, let's take specification one of the charge. Let's look at the specific evidence with respect to that specification.

Judge Kennedy will explain to you that the government has two methods by which it can establish any fact. We can prove a fact beyond a reasonable doubt by presenting to you direct evidence of the fact, or we can prove it by circumstantial evidence. Direct evidence, of course, with respect to a killing would be where an individual actually sees one person shooting another, such as the testimony of Dennis Conti and Paul Meadlo; both testified that they saw the accused shoot the people. We can also prove it by circumstantial evidence, the circumstances involved. For example, in this case, the location of the bodies in relationship to where the accused was seen to those bodies, the fact that they were in his area of operation. We could prove the fact of death of a human being by circumstantial evidence from the nature of the wounds themselves without having a doctor perform an autopsy. So we had available to us both types of evidence, and we have presented both types of evidence to you.

First of all, let's review the direct evidence which we have presented to support specification one of the charge. You will recall the testimony of Dennis Conti—Dennis Conti, truck driver from Rhode Island. He was a PFC [*Private First Class*] at the time of this operation. He was a member of the platoon. Dennis Conti testified that when he got off the helicopter he got separated from the command group, Lieutenant Calley and Charles Sledge, and that he entered the village and ran into Sergeant Bacon who told him that he'd better catch up and get with the command group and get with Lieutenant Calley. That he reached the intersection of the north-south trail and located the command group. He began gathering up people from the hooches in that area at the direction of Lieutenant Calley. They gathered up at least thirty to forty unarmed men, women, and children at the north-south trail intersection. Conti testified that Lieutenant Calley came up and he told Meadlo, "Push the people out in the paddies," and so he and Paul Meadlo pushed the people out in the paddies and put them on the north-south trail and they guarded them like they thought they were supposed to do.

You recall that Dennis Conti said that he assumed a position on the south side of those people, and that Paul Meadlo was on the north side, and he put the people in a squatting position and that while they were waiting, he heard something in the hooches, to the south of where he was, and that he left and went down there and found an old woman and child. He gathered these people up, came back and put them in with the group of people on the trail who w[ere] still waiting there, who weren't resisting, and who weren't armed. He then testified that Calley returned a few minutes later, and said, "Take care of these people," and Calley left. Calley returned shortly and said, "I thought I told you to take care of them." Calley said, "I meant kill them." Then you recall Conti testified that he assumed the position to the rear of Meadlo and Calley, and watched as Calley and Meadlo fired into the group of people as he covered the treeline with his M-79 grenade launcher, not wanting to participate. You recall he testified that Paul Meadlo during the midst of this broke down and started crying, that Meadlo in fact attempted to push his weapon into Conti's hand, but Conti refused to take it, and that Calley and Meadlo shot and killed all of the people on the north-south trail.

Then we have the testimony of Paul Meadlo who also supports the charge, specification one. And what did Paul Meadlo say? He corroborates Dennis Conti, although not identically, sufficiently to show what actually transpired. He also testified that he gathered up thirty to forty people in the same location, at the same spot, and he was told to take these people to a designated area in a clearing. He said substantially the same thing that Dennis Conti said, "Calley came up to me and he said, 'You know what to do with them.' " So the two of them corroborate each other's testimony. Meadlo also assumed, as did Conti, that Calley just meant for him and Conti to guard those people, but then Paul Meadlo says that about ten to fifteen minutes later, Calley returned and said, "How come they're not dead yet?" Meadlo said, "I didn't know we were supposed to kill them." Calley said, "I want them dead." And Calley, according to Meadlo, backed off twenty to thirty feet and fired into this group of people on full automatic, and that he directed Paul Meadlo to join him and Meadlo joined him. You recall that Meadlo said he was very emotionally upset at this time. He became hysterical. He started crying. But Conti didn't fire.

Then we have the testimony of Charles Sledge who was Calley's RTO. He indicated and testified that he joined Lieutenant Calley inside the village as Calley was proceeding south on the north-south trail. He also estimated that the group of people at that intersection was thirty to forty, and he also described them the same way Paul Meadlo and Dennis Conti did—unarmed, unresisting men, women, children, and babies. However, Sledge remembered somewhat differently; that there was an interpreter there, and that Calley in fact asked the interpreter at this location to interpret for him, a fact not recalled by Meadlo and Conti. But he did remember Lieutenant Calley telling Meadlo to waste these people, and that Meadlo in fact fired upon this group of people.

The testimony of Jim Dursi also supports specification one. Jim Dursi found that there was no resistance inside of the village, as had all the other members of the First Platoon. He also recalls that some of these people were still eating breakfast, and he gathered these people up, because he thought that was what he was supposed to do under these circumstances. He described Conti and Meadlo having a group of people, same description of about twenty or thirty in the same general location. He also said that he had his group of people, which he estimated to be about fifteen, in the same general area on a trail on the south side of the village, and that as he was standing there with his group of people on the trail, he saw Lieutenant Calley approach from the right, and that Paul Meadlo had his group of people on the left out in the paddy area. He also heard Lieutenant Calley say the same thing Paul Meadlo and Dennis Conti remembered, asking Meadlo initially if he could take care of that group of people on the trail. Exactly the same thing in substance as Paul Meadlo and Dennis Conti testified to. And then Calley, you recall, returned a few minutes later, and said, "Why haven't you taken care of them?" And then he heard fire from that location.

Now, we have alleged in the specification that the accused killed not less than thirty human beings on the north-south trail. We went to great lengths at the early part of this trial to establish [that] the people shown in prosecution exhibit 12A [*photograph of bodies*] were in fact the people that Calley and Meadlo shot on the north-south trail.

And we presented to you members from all sections of the company, from the mortar platoon and the headquarters element, from the Third

Platoon, who came to this area by various routes, and they all were able to identify that photograph and place it at that location.

The defense raised the question, "Why can't Dennis Conti identify prosecution exhibit 12 as in fact being the group?" Dennis Conti would not say that it was not the group. Why can't Paul Meadlo say that it is in fact the group? What about Paul Meadlo's emotional state at the time he killed those people? Do you think that he was going to look at that photograph and tell you, "That's the people that I killed"? Do you think that he could look at that photograph and admit to himself that that's the people that he killed? How about Dennis Conti? That's not pleasant for those men, gentlemen, and perhaps they have blocked that out of their minds, as you heard one psychiatrist say that an individual could do. And so we wanted to prove it to you by circumstantial evidence, that that is in fact the group of people that were shot there by people who were detached from this event, that Dennis Conti's verification of the location is well substantiated because Dennis Conti, as you will recall, testified that he has since returned to the village of My Lai, went into the village of My Lai on the ground, and in fact located the spot where these people were killed on the north-south trail.

Do you think that Lieutenant Calley would tell you that that was the group of people? Do you think that he would tell you that that was the enemy that he shot? Do you think that he could justify that to you? Do you expect him to admit that that was the enemy he killed?

A lot of people testified concerning their estimates of how many people died and the bodies. Some would say five, some would say ten, some would say fifteen to twenty. But what's the best evidence that you have as to how many people died? The best evidence you have, gentlemen, is prosecution exhibit 12A of the numbers. Look at that photograph when you go back into your deliberation. How many people are shown in that photograph? If you count the number of people in that photograph, you will find not less than twenty-five actually shown in the photograph, nine of which are clearly identified as children, and three of which are clearly identified as infants. Can there be any question about the fact that photograph has been well identified? You've heard twenty people testify before you that they saw that group of bodies on the north-south trail. Twenty out of that company. There can be no doubt about the fact that those people were on the north-south trail and they were in fact dead. Would they be there that long and observed by that many people over that period of time with the wounds that they had and be alive? There is no doubt at all gentlemen, about the fact that Lieutenant Calley shot the people in prosecution exhibit 12A and that they are in fact dead and died as a result of his acts on 16 March 1968.

Let's turn to specification two, the shooting at the ditch. This occurred after the shooting on the north-south trail. Again, we have established this beyond any shadow of a doubt by both the direct and circumstantial evidence. First of all, let's take the testimony of James Dursi, who was also present at the ditch. You recall that Jim Dursi testified that he moved his group east and eventually ended up at the irrigation ditch on the eastern side of the village. He testified that Lieutenant Calley joined him there a few minutes later. He then testified that Paul Meadlo arrived and said Calley told him, "Meadlo, we've got another job to do," which is the same thing that Meadlo said that Calley told him. And here are two men testifying to that fact, both of whom are out of the service, one of whom is from Brooklyn, New York, and the other is from Indiana. Do you think they made something up like that? But they both testified to the same thing. The same statement. And then you recall that Jim Dursi said that Lieutenant Calley ordered them to put the people into the ditch, and that they pushed these people down into that ditch with their weapons at port arms. Jim Dursi said that Paul Meadlo was on his left and that Lieutenant Calley was to the left of Paul Meadlo. He said that the people began to yell and scream as they were put into the ditch, and then Calley gave the order to shoot, "Start firing." And Paul Meadlo and Lieutenant Calley began to fire, and Meadlo, who had been still crying when he came up to the ditch, as described by Dursi, continued to fire at the irrigation ditch. Jim Dursi did not fire. Meadlo turned to Dursi and said, "Shoot." "Shoot." "Why don't you shoot?" Jim Dursi said, "I can't." "I won't." "I will not." Jim Dursi described the people in the ditch vividly for you. Mothers trying to protect their children. People screaming, crying, falling on top of each other as they were shot. And then Dursi said that Calley told him, "Get on the other side of the ditch before you get sick." And so he left the area, they had wounds on all parts of their bodies, and even after he left the ditch, he still heard firing from his rear.

And then we have the testimony of Paul Meadlo, who testified that after he and Lieutenant Calley shot the group at the north-south trail, that he wandered back into the village and gathered up some more people, seven to eight, that he moved out across a ravine, and came back and found Lieutenant Calley there at the ravine with other people. And what did Paul Meadlo say that Lieutenant Calley said to him? "Meadlo, we've got another job to do." The same thing that Jim Dursi said. Then Meadlo described Calley's actions as Calley started shoving the people off into the ditch and he started shooting, and then he said, "He ordered us to shoot them." Meadlo did not know how long he fired.

Meadlo recalled a conversation with Jim Dursi while he was at the ditch, and he also substantiated the fact that he testified that Jim Dursi did not fire into those people. Meadlo estimated that Calley changed magazines ten to fifteen times while he was at that ditch. He remembered that there were about seventy-five to a hundred people there in that ditch. He recalls that these people had blood all over them, and Calley was at the ditch the whole time. Now, Charles Sledge, his account of what transpired was that after the shooting occurred on the north-south trail, he left that area with Lieutenant Calley, and they moved east. And then, as he remembers it, they received a call that Sergeant Mitchell had a group of people at the ditch, and that he and Calley went to this area and found Mitchell, who had twenty to thirty people at the ditch area. He recalled that Calley and Mitchell had a conversation and that after this conversation took place, Calley and Mitchell went over to the ditch, started putting these people into the ditch with their weapons, and then they started firing. He didn't recall that they fired very long, but he did remember that the people were screaming. Sledge also testified that a helicopter landed. He saw the helicopter, saw the accused go over and have a conversation with the helicopter pilot. Calley then returned and said, "He don't like the way I'm running this show here, but I'm the boss." That would be consistent with Lieutenant Calley's testimony, or at least that portion of it.

Then we have the testimony of Dennis Conti relating to specification two. Dennis Conti said that after the shooting on the north-south trail he was stunned by what he had seen, and so he left, because he didn't want to stay with them and wandered back up into the village, that he met two other soldiers up there, and they had a conversation and that he eventually moved to the eastern side of the village where he heard firing. He wanted to find out what the firing was all about, so he moved to the direction from which this firing came, and it led him to the irrigation ditch, and when he got there and he saw what was happening, he didn't stay very long, because he saw Calley and Mitchell, along with other people that he could not specifically identify, firing into the irrigation ditch. He said that he then moved in a northerly direction and set up in the perimeter to the north out in the rice paddies. Dennis Conti did not specifically recall Meadlo being present at the ditch by name. He remembered Calley and Mitchell, but he did not remember the others.

Then you have the testimony of Joseph Boyce who said that after he moved through the village and got to the upper side of the village, somebody brought a group of people up to this general area, and that he was about fifty to a hundred meters away at the time this group was brought up. He remembered that Calley and Meadlo had a conversation there at this irrigation ditch, and that Calley was there, along with other people, and that he saw Meadlo and Calley put the people in, Meadlo firing into the irrigation ditch, and when he saw that, he said he didn't want any part of it and left. We asked him how many people he saw in the ditch. He said he couldn't give an estimate. He said, "You don't look too long at something like that." He said, "I tried to block this out of my memory."

Then we had the testimony of Gregory Olsen, the machine gunner, who was part of their team. He estimated that he saw perhaps two dozen bodies—men, women, and children who had been shot—in the irrigation ditch. He also remembered the helicopter landing and that Lieutenant Calley talked to the pilot, that Lieutenant Calley returned to the ditch area, that he had a conversation with Sergeant Mitchell when he returned to that area, and that then Sergeant Mitchell went to the ditch and he saw Mitchell fire into the ditch—ten to twelve shots semi-automatic.

Then we also presented to you the testimony of Ronald Grzesik, who was the fire team leader. As I indicated to you, he said before he got to the ditch he did encounter Meadlo inside the village, that he was sitting down, and he was crying. He had a conversation with him, and then he moved out. Then he said he exited the village on the south side and proceeded in a northerly direction where he saw the ditch. He said there were several people there at the time, and he estimated that there were perhaps thirty-five to fifty bodies that he saw in the irrigation ditch. He also saw the accused at the ditch. He said that as he walked past, he was then called back, and he remembered being told by the accused, "Finish them off." He remembered being told that twice. He refused, and as he left the ditch he also remembered that a helicopter, a bubble helicopter, was circling low.

Now, as you listened to all of this testimony and you heard varying descriptions, perhaps it appeared to be conflicting. Can you expect anything less than some conflict in the testimony over this period of time?

Isn't it more credible because of the conflicts? What would you have thought if all of these individuals came into this courtroom and told you the same story? If everybody was precise in their detail? Would that be credible to you after this length of time? Think of the number of men who have testified concerning what they saw there at that ditch, who were able to locate it, the fact that the ditch in fact exists, the fact that these men came to you from all parts of the country, the fact that they weren't even questioned about this until after they were out of the service. Did they have an opportunity to fabricate this? There's no way, gentlemen. It has to be the truth, and out of all this testimony, we give you one man whose recollection speaks for itself, whose recall, whose powers of observation tells you and gives you the testimony under which you can resolve all of this. You can resolve all the conflicts and piece together what actually transpired there.

We give you Thomas Turner, student, married in Nebraska. He comes in and testifies before you, he recounts for you vividly what in fact happened. He resolved the conflicts in the testimony. He brings it all together. Why does one man see one number of people in the ditch at one point and another man estimate another number? Why do some people remember seeing some people there at one time and others not? Because, gentlemen, there was more than one group put in that ditch. People were put in over a period of time, and they were seen by different people there at different times, and different people were in fact there at different times. This didn't happen in an instant. What did Thomas Turner tell you, gentlemen? He set up in a position to the north of the paddies after he came out on the southern periphery firing into that ditch, along with other people. You recall that he said there were two groups in the ditch at the time he first got there, there was one group that had already been shot. There was another group just to the north of that that was in fact being shot as he went by, and he recalled that the two individuals were Calley and Meadlo at the time he initially arrived, and he saw those bodies in the ditch, and this other group was kneeling to the north as they were being fired upon. How do you think that they could have put over seventy people or a hundred people into that ditch in one group, but that's what the estimates are? The most reliable estimates are that there were seventy-five to a hundred, perhaps more people who were in that ditch. Thomas Turner testified that groups were brought up at different times.

Twelve members of the platoon placed the accused at that irrigation ditch. Do you think the accused would get on the stand and deny the fact that he was actually there in the face of that testimony? So he said he was there, and he admitted that he fired into that group of people there in the ditch, although he is apparently the only one who can't give you an estimate. He can't even tell you if they were men, women, and children. It wasn't significant. They were just enemy. Out of all those people, he's the only man that can't tell you that. So I ask you to judge the credibility of his story and what happened at the ditch, along with what everybody else says happened at the ditch. The accused's own witnesses don't help when it comes to this area. They can't refute the ditch.

The accused admitted that he was there. We have clearly shown that the people were shot and killed by the accused and the men under his direction in that irrigation ditch. We've satisfied that element of the offense of proving the fact of the death of people in that ditch.

We presented you the testimony of Dr. Lane, the pathologist, who rendered his expert opinion and told you the physiological effects an M-16 rifle fire would have on the human body when fired at close range. This would prove that those people died. We have proved that beyond any reasonable doubt.

But again, with respect to this specification, you have a question to resolve of how many people were killed. The specification alleges that the accused shot and killed there not less than seventy people, but again, the exact number is unknown.

I submit to you that the evidence establishes beyond any shadow of a doubt that there were over seventy people killed in that ditch, by the most reliable evidence, that of Thomas Turner. Paul Meadlo said there were seventy-five to a hundred. People who were detached from this who had an opportunity to observe this, who were not members of the accused's company, verified the number of people who died there.

You heard Jerry Gulverhouse [*helicopter pilot*], who also identified prosecution exhibit 12A and told you that there were at least five times as many people in that irrigation ditch as there are in prosecution exhibit 12A. You heard Hugh Thompson [*helicopter pilot*], whom the accused admits was at the irrigation ditch, who told you fifty to seventy-five.

I submit that the estimates of the helicopter pilots, gentlemen, are the most accurate estimates. Lawrence Colburn who actually went to that ditch and who, along with his crew chief Andriotta, got down in that ditch and rescued that baby—fifty to seventy-five. And perhaps all of these gentlemen would have a natural inclination as human beings to give you a conservative number in this case. Do you think that is something that they want to exaggerate? How many people they saw there? We don't have to prove beyond a reasonable doubt that there were seventy. The evidence is conflicting. We only have to prove that there was just one in that ditch. And we have carried our burden, and you can make an adjustment in the findings and your resolution of this conflicting evidence regarding how many in fact were killed there. Colonel Kennedy [*the trial judge*] will show you how you can do that once you arrive at your own opinion as to how many there were. If you find more than seventy, you have to make no change in the specification. If all of you are able to agree on a specific number, you can reflect that. It's tragic that I would have to stand here and argue before you numbers of people, but we didn't make the facts. So you can resolve that issue, gentlemen, but if you find that there were seventy, that we have proved that, so reflect it.

There are two specifications under the additional charge, and each of these again, the government has the burden of proving beyond a reasonable doubt, specifically in those specifications, that is, that the accused killed them.

Specification one relates to the incident at the northern end of the ditch. You've heard the testimony of Charles Sledge. His presence there in fact was verified by Lieutenant Calley as being his RTO on the day in question. You will recall the testimony of Mr. Sledge that when he moved forward at the end of the ditch, there was a man dressed in white. The accused began to question this man. He refused to answer. The accused butt-stroked this individual and then he blew half his head off. It's a continuous chain of events, gentlemen, a continuous transaction. Lieutenant Calley himself also tells you that he moved to the northern end of the ditch, and there was a man in white, and he was brought to him, and that he did question him. Just as Charles Sledge said he did, and he says in fact that he did butt-stroke the man, but he denies that he shot him. He recognized this man to be a man, gentlemen, as opposed to being something else. He was able to distinguish at least that that individual was a man. He couldn't distinguish between the other people—that they were men, women, and children, but he knew that that one was a man. He said that the man ended up in the ditch, somebody just kicked him. He didn't know whether he lived or died, but that he ended up in the ditch. I submit to you that the testimony of Charles Sledge is more believable, that he in fact blew that man's head off, and from the description that he gave you of the effect that that shot had on that man, there's no question about the fact that that man died at the hands of the accused.

And so who are you going to believe, gentlemen? That's the question that you have to resolve there. Are you going to believe the accused, or are you going to believe Charles Sledge? And why should Charles Sledge lie? What does he have to gain by lying after all this time? But I ask you, what does the accused stand to gain by not admitting it?

Charles Sledge's testimony is also corroborated by Jeffrey LaCross, who said that when he came to the northern edge of that ditch, there was in fact a man dressed in white who he saw lying dead. We submit with respect to that specification and charge we have met our burden that the accused killed the individual by shooting him with a rifle.

What is the evidence relating to specification two of the additional charge? Charles Sledge testified that as they were leaving the ditch area, someone yelled out, "A child is getting away!" Sledge testified the accused went back, picked up the child, threw it in the ditch, and without hesitation, gentlemen, without hesitation, he raised his weapon and he looked down, and he fired. Sledge couldn't see where the baby was, but he threw it out in front of him, out in front of him in the ditch by the arm. Do you think he missed? Do you think he wanted to miss? He didn't hesitate. He just pulled that weapon up and squeezed that trigger, and that baby was at the end of that barrel.

We submit that with respect to all of the specifications, we have clearly established the fact of death of the victims, and that the accused either killed them or he directed that they be killed. We have established those elements beyond any doubt.

Now, we have an additional element that we must satisfy as to all of the specifications: did the accused have the required criminal state of mind at the time he killed these individuals. To be guilty of premeditated murder, gentlemen, you have to intend to kill the victim. You have to intend that he die, and you have to form this intent just prior to the time that you accomplish that act. That's what the law requires. A split second. Just so long as it's before you pull the trigger. If you make up your mind before you fire that the people that you are going to fire into are going to die, that is premeditation. You're going to be given an instruction on what constitutes premeditation, what constitutes premeditated design to kill, and you must find in this case that the accused did in fact premeditate with respect to each of the offenses with which he is charged.

How does the government perceive what a man is thinking? What Lieutenant Calley was thinking on the day in question? How do we show you that? First of all, we rely upon your own common sense and understanding and recognition of the way the human mind functions, recognition of the way people think and act. We rely upon the fact that you can take these facts, you can take his acts, his conduct, the observations of others, and find what he was thinking. We can prove it to you. We have proved it to you, because what is the evidence of a man's intent, what he intends to do? A man's actions [are] the mirror of a man's mind. You can prove intent two ways, just as you can any other element of an offense, or any other fact. You can prove it by direct evidence, and what is that? When a man tells you what he is thinking, that is direct evidence of what he's thinking. You can prove it by circumstantial evidence; even though he doesn't tell you, you know by what he does what he intended.

Now, the defense in this case raised an issue regarding the accused's mental capacity to entertain the required criminal state of mind for these offenses. And you recall how they raised that issue. They raised it with the introduction of psychiatric testimony. They gave you the testimony of Dr. Crane and Dr. Hamman in an attempt to show that the accused's mind, his mental ability, was such that on the date in question and while he was in the village of My Lai he did not have the mental capacity to be able to premeditate, that is, to be able to get an idea in his mind he was going to kill somebody and then kill them after he got the idea. They presented the testimony of these two doctors. The military judge is going to instruct you that under the law, a man can be sane and yet still be suffering from a mental condition which would deprive him of the mental ability to premeditate, and that if you were to find that if there was a mental condition and then if it did in fact deprive the accused totally of his ability to premeditate, then he could not be found guilty of the offense of premeditated murder.

Dr. Crane, as you will recall, testified on the basis of a hypothetical question, which was read to him by Mr. Latimer [*Calley's lawyer*], and at the conclusion of that hypothetical question, he was asked to render an opinion regarding the accused's mental condition on the date of 16 March 1968. Dr. Crane was willing to give you a medical opinion on the basis of a hypothetical question without ever having interviewed the accused, without having the benefit that you've had of observing him, listening to his testimony, without the benefit you've had of listening to what the witnesses who were actually there had to say about what transpired. I point this out to you in this regard as we go through this discussion of the testimony of the experts who testified medical opinions to assist you, gentlemen, in arriving at a medical diagnosis; in effect, a diagnosis of the accused's mental condition on the date in question. The law permits them, because they have expertise, to give you the benefit of their knowledge, but it does not relieve you of the ultimate responsibility of making the ultimate diagnosis, and you're not bound to accept the opinion of any doctor. You must make your diagnosis on the basis of all the facts.

Now, Dr. Crane stated under cross-examination that the accused did in fact have the mental ability to premeditate at the time of the offenses. He said Lieutenant Calley couldn't make a complex decision. We asked him for an example of a complex decision. He said, "Like going to the moon." You don't have to be a genius, gentlemen, to commit the offense of premeditated murder. You don't have to have above-average intelligence to be able to commit the offense of premeditated murder. You don't have to have a college degree. You've just got to have the ability to think and form that intent to kill somebody and form that intent in your mind before you kill them. And Dr. Crane said, "Well, if you're going to give me that literal definition"—and that literal definition, gentlemen, is the legal definition you must make your findings on—Calley had the mental ability to do it on the date in question. Dr. Crane in fact admitted that the accused could form the intent to kill before he pulled the trigger. Then Dr. Crane said that he didn't have the ability to form the specific intent to kill. Does that appear to be inconsistent to you? What is "specific intent to kill"? It's no more than specific intent to kill as opposed to, say, specific intent to wound, as opposed to specific intent to just scaring, as opposed to specific intent just to take away someone's property. That's all it is. It means to take a human being's life. Specific intent to kill as opposed to specific intent to do something else.

They would die, and that he intended their death. He knew when he fired into that ditch that those people were going to die, that he was in fact killing them. Dr. Crane's opinion supports the government's position that he had the mental capacity. He had the mental capacity. He found that the accused was mentally healthy.

Then Dr. Hamman testified. I tell you, gentlemen, that the opinion that is given to you by any man is only as good as the facts upon which it is based, and the facts don't support the opinion of Dr. Hamman. Dr. Hamman, you will also recall, was not a combat psychiatrist. In fact, he said he hadn't read anything about combat psychiatry in two years. He didn't keep up in the field, he hadn't studied in the area. Doesn't Dr. Hamman's testimony indicate that Calley could think? Doesn't it indicate that he was thinking all sorts of things? Just consider all the factors in the accused's own testimony which demonstrate clearly that he not only had the mental ability to think, but that he was thinking on the date in question. He was thinking more complex things than just getting the idea to kill somebody and killing them. Look at the accused's testimony. No evidence that he was in a delusional state at the time. No evidence that he was not aware of what was transpiring around him. He knew where he was that day. He was able to tell you that. He was able to recognize his own men. He was able to give you their names. He was able to recognize what they were doing. He was able to give you an estimate that the helicopter was fifteen feet off the ground, and that he jumped out at five feet. He was able to recognize the subordinate relationships and the relationships of his men to himself, and himself to Captain Medina. He could receive and transmit telephone calls, he could relay information to his men. He was oriented that day as to his direction of travel. He knew where he was going. He was able to communicate, to carry on conversations with others. He positioned his men. You recall him testifying he was positioning the machine guns, directing Sergeant Mitchell to position the machine guns. It was a tactical operation. He recognized there were helicopters in the area. He was able to recognize that there was a man brought to him for interrogation. He was able to rely upon his training in Vietnamese language. He was relying on his training. Anything wrong there with his mental processes?

As the psychiatric testimony of the government's witnesses show[s], in some situations stress can make a man react more efficiently. Did that happen here? Lieutenant Calley testified that while he was there that day, he was thinking about "the logistics of my men, throwing down the volume of fire or picking it up, breaking out into the open, keeping my men down, checking out the bunkers, keeping moving, keeping pre-planned artillery plots at hand. I had two radios that I was working with, the air-to-ground push." He was thinking about all those things, gentlemen. They're complex. Is there any question about the fact that his mind was functioning as a normal human being on the date in question? Do those facts demonstrate someone who was befuddled? They show that he was thinking. If he could think about all those things, he had the mental ability to formulate the attitude that when he pulled the trigger on his weapon, he intended to kill who he shot at, or when he gave the order to Meadlo that he intended for the people to die.

Now, on the issue of mental capacity, you heard from expert witnesses, Dr. Edwards, Dr. Jones, and Dr. Johnson. All of these men were members of the military, all of them were doctors from Walter Reed Army Hospital. You recall what their qualifications were. They were familiar with combat psychiatry. Dr. Johnson had been charged with the responsibility for the mental health program in Vietnam. They were aware of the studies in the area. Dr. Jones had served in Vietnam. He had written in the qualifications of those men with the qualifications of Dr. Hamman and Dr. Crane. I ask you to consider the circumstances under which they were brought here to testify. They didn't volunteer their services, gentlemen; they were directed to conduct an examination, an evaluation of the accused for this court, pursuant to its directive, and operated accordingly. In fact, you recall Dr. Johnson testifying, he wanted to be sure that this was done fairly and impartially, so much so that he disqualified one of his few board-certified psychiatrists from testifying, from sitting on this board, because he in fact had communication with me as trial counsel. You also recall that he testified that I concurred in that man not sitting. They gave you three good medical opinions regarding this man's mental condition, logically and reasonably arrived at. They conducted extensive evaluations of the accused in which the defense participated at Walter Reed. They had available to them the testimony that you heard, and before they rendered their opinions in court, they had available to them the observations of the accused as he testified from the witness stand, which is something which you also saw. And those three doctors' qualifications cannot be contested. They are of the unanimous opinion that the accused did in fact have the mental capacity to premeditate on 16 March 1968, and was not suffering from any mental disease or defects. And you, gentlemen, yourself posed questions to these doctors regarding what factors they had taken into consideration in arriving at their opinion; did they consider the situation in which Lieutenant Calley was in possible stresses of combat upon him. They did. They considered all those facts. They relied upon their experience as soldiers and their knowledge of the military, their knowledge of commanders, their knowledge of the situation, and they gave you three opinions, all of which were the same. But you're not bound by any of that expert testimony, gentlemen. You reject it, as you can the testimony of any witness who has testified in this case. It's offered to help you in making your judgment as to the man's mental ability.

And perhaps the strongest testimony of all is what other people had to say about his actions on 16 March 1968, and what their opinions were of his mental condition at that time in relationship to days that they had observed him before this operation. That perhaps is the strongest evidence, because they were there and they had seen the accused before this operation. The law permits a lay person to give his opinion to you regarding a mental condition. You don't have to be a doctor to know that something is wrong with somebody. You, as a human being, can look around and determine what a man's mental state is, and the law recognizes that a lay witness can make such an observation, permits him to give you his testimony and his opinion regarding the man's mental condition.

It's interesting to note that when Paul Meadlo testified in this case, he was asked by Mr. Latimer, "Lieutenant Calley wasn't raving around that day, was he? . . . He wasn't acting crazy?" Meadlo said, "No."

When we presented to you the testimony of Thomas Turner who said that he had been serving under the accused for three to four months prior to this operation, and he observed him on the date in question, and that the accused's mental condition appeared to him that day as he did every other day.

Jim Dursi, who had also been serving under the accused, said that Calley appeared to be normal to him, that he seemed to be aware of his surroundings.

Dennis Conti also had been serving under the accused, [and] had seen him on a daily basis for four to five months prior to this operation, testified that Calley seemed pretty calm, didn't appear to be upset, just like it was an everyday thing.

In addition to this evidence, the court has also permitted us to present to you evidence which showed that several weeks prior to this operation, a man was captured and interrogated by the accused for over twenty minutes. The accused beat the man during this interrogation, and at the end of the interrogation, shot him. You can also consider that in determining whether or not the accused had the mental ability to form the intent to kill before he killed.

Now, gentlemen, we have proved beyond any shadow of a doubt that the accused had the mental ability to think, to premeditate, and that he did in fact premeditate, and at the time he killed.

With respect to specification one, when you stand up to a group of people with an M-16 and pull that trigger, can you have any other intent? Let's analyze the evidence which demonstrates that the accused not only had the ability but he was in fact premeditating.

First of all, let's take Dennis Conti's version of what transpired. Dennis Conti said that Calley said to Meadlo, "Take care of them," and that when he returned he said that he meant to kill them. This was before any of them were ever killed. He formed the intent to kill them the first time he told Meadlo. He had that same intent fifteen minutes later when he returned. There can't be any clearer case than that. He only had to have the intent a split second. We've got the accused's own statement. We've got direct evidence of what he intended when he made that statement.

Jim Dursi also heard him make the same statement, "Why haven't you wasted them yet?" Paul Meadlo, same statements. Charles Sledge said Calley ordered them to "Waste them." When he gave that order he intended for them to die, and that idea was in his mind before they died, before he pulled the trigger, or before Meadlo pulled the trigger. And that's all the law requires with respect to premeditation.

How about specification two? Don't the facts again clearly show what he intended? He ordered them shot. That means he had to get the idea before the shooting started.

And what about Thomas Turner's testimony that this took place over an hour and a half and they were separate groups?

There's testimony through Paul Meadlo and Jim Dursi, "We've got another job to do." What does that show? And he made that statement before the people were ever placed in the ditch. Fifteen seconds before? One second is enough. How about the fact that he was observed changing magazines?

Gentlemen, the evidence that he in fact premeditated with respect to the people on the north-south trail and at the ditch is just overwhelming. There can be no doubt under those circumstances of what he intended when he started firing, and when he gave those orders. He intended for those people to die, and he formed that intent before he ever killed them, or ordered his men to kill them.

How about specification two of the additional charge? The man in white at the end of the ditch. You don't put that weapon up to somebody's head and pull the trigger. While he was putting it up to that man's head, he had to know that he was going to pull that trigger. He premeditated.

And when he threw that child in the ditch and he raised that rifle, he was premeditating again, and he was premeditating to kill.

And that's what the law requires that we prove. That's what we have proved beyond any doubt.

[Court recessed for the day]

Gentlemen, at the conclusion of the argument yesterday afternoon, I had covered with you, or attempted to do so, a discussion of the evidence as it related to the specifications and the elements of those specifications involving the fact of the deaths of the individuals involved, the numbers of those persons who were killed, and how the evidence showed that the government's theory as to how those facts were proved, the mental capacity of the accused to premeditate, and the evidence which showed that he did in fact premeditate, with respect to each of the specifications with which he is charged.

Now, each of the specifications alleges that Lieutenant Calley killed these individuals with a rifle. The evidence, on the other hand, shows, gentlemen, that Lieutenant Calley was not personally responsible for the death of those victims in the sense that a bullet from his weapon killed every individual that died.

Other members of his platoon were also responsible directly for their deaths, direct in the sense that the bullets from their weapons killed specific people as opposed to the bullets from Lieutenant Calley's weapon. But he is wantonly responsible, for the death of an individual, for the death of a human being, despite the fact that he himself did not actually cause the death by actually having fired the weapon which killed the human being, but was responsible for it in the sense that he directed it.

The military judge will instruct you that an individual who personally perpetrates the act of killing is called a principal, and that likewise, any person who counsels, commands, or procures another to commit an offense that is subsequently perpetrated in consequence of such counseling, command, or procuring is also a principal, and is just as guilty of the offense as he would have been had he actually perpetrated the offense himself. He will instruct you that his presence at the scene where the offense is committed is not essential for him to be in fact guilty of the offense. He will instruct you that the term "counsel" means to advise, recommend, or encourage. That the term "command" imports an order given by one person to another, who, because of the relationship of the parties, is under an obligation, or sense of duty, to obey the order, and that the term "procure" means to bring about, cause, effect, contrive, or induce, and that when the act counseled, commanded, or procured under any of those definitions and when that is done by the person so directed that the person commanding, counseling, or procuring that act to be done, despite the fact that he did not pull the trigger on the weapon which resulted in the individual's death, he is chargeable with only the results that he could reasonably be expected to flow as a probable consequence from that act. If you are satisfied Calley either counseled, commanded, or procured the commission of any of the offenses with which he is charged or any of the lesser included offenses upon which you will be instructed, you may find him guilty of that offense, even though he was not the active perpetrator of the offense.

With respect to specifications one and two of the additional charge, the application of this principle of law is not necessary, because the accused actually pulled the trigger on his weapon, killing the man dressed in white at the northern end of the ditch, and the accused actually pulled the trigger on his weapon, resulting in the death of the child in the ditch.

Where this principle of responsibility has application is with respect to specification one of the charge, referring to the killing of the people on the north-south trail, and specification two of the charge, the killing of the people in the ditch.

With respect to specification one, the evidence is in conflict as to whether or not Lieutenant Calley actually participated in killing those people. The evidence is not in conflict, however, as to whether or not he ordered that those people on the north-south trail should be killed.

Under the testimony of Dennis Conti and Paul Meadlo, the accused actively participated and ordered the killing of the people on the north-south trail. It is not clear under the testimony of Jim Dursi whether or not he actively participated in the killing. Jim Dursi only heard him give the order to "waste" the people, and then left. If under the testimony of

Charles Sledge, it would appear that as Charles Sledge remembers the incident, the order to "waste" was given, but the accused did not fire. Under either theory, gentlemen, the accused is guilty. If you all agree that the accused gave the order to kill those people on the north-south trail, he is guilty. If you all agree that he gave the order and he himself fired into those people on the north-south trail, he is guilty. He is responsible for their deaths. Under either theory, you have two witnesses who gave you direct evidence of the fact that Lieutenant Calley stood there on the north-south trail, directed that those people be shot, and himself pulled the trigger on his weapon.

You have the testimony of Paul Meadlo, a man who admitted his own participation and implicated the accused. Why would he admit that?

With respect to specification two of the charge, you again have the same situation. You have evidence that the accused personally shot at the ditch, that he gave orders to Jim Dursi and Paul Meadlo to shoot into the people in the ditch. Charles Sledge testified that the accused had a conversation with Sergeant Mitchell, and then that Sergeant Mitchell went to the ditch with the accused and began firing into the ditch. What do you think that conversation was about? Do you think that he was commanding that those people die? Do you think that he was telling Sergeant Mitchell, "Shoot those people in the ditch"? Do you think he was at a minimum encouraging him? Or did he have a duty to stop him as a platoon leader, to stop him from acting, or encourage him to kill the people in the ditch?

You also heard the testimony that after the helicopter landed, Calley again spoke to Sergeant Mitchell in the area of the ditch, and that Sergeant Mitchell then went to the ditch. You recall the testimony of Greg Olsen, Mitchell fired ten to twelve shots semi-automatic into that ditch. What do you think that conversation was about?

And then you have the accused's own testimony that he came to the ditch, and even under his version, when he got there his men were firing. He did nothing to stop them. He in fact joined them. He encouraged them, even under his own testimony. The application of that principle of law and the definitions of the terms "command," "counsel," or "procuring" when applied to the evidence which we have presented establishes beyond any shadow of a doubt that the accused was responsible.

Now, the military judge is going to instruct you that in addition to the major offenses with which the accused is charged, that is, the offenses of premeditated murder, that if the government had failed in some way to establish one of the elements of those offenses, the accused could be found guilty of some lesser included offenses.

However, we have clearly shown in this case, and all the facts show that with respect to all of the specifications, that the accused acted with premeditation. And so I say to you that, having established this fact of premeditation with respect to all of these offenses, that the lesser included offenses are not in issue.

The judge will instruct you regarding the offense of unpremeditated murder, which contains the same elements as the offense of premeditated murder with the exception that when the act of killing is committed, the intent to kill is simultaneous with the act of killing. There was no premeditation. He didn't think about it before he did it. It was a spontaneous thing on his part. He formulated the idea of killing simultaneously with the act of killing, a sudden act.

I submit to you that the facts in this case, which establish clearly that the accused premeditated, would show that he in fact intended for these people to die before they were killed, negate any finding on your part of unpremeditated murder. We have established beyond a reasonable doubt that there was premeditation. How can a man give an order to someone to kill someone and not premeditate? The mere fact that he makes the statement before the deaths result show the premeditation. He had to think about it. He had to come up with the idea of killing when he made the statement, which is the direct evidence of the intent, and we don't have to rely upon circumstantial evidence, even though that is abundant.

The judge will also instruct you that another possible, lesser included offense is the offense of voluntary manslaughter. The government submits again that we've shown premeditation. There is no need for you to consider the offense of voluntary manslaughter. If a person acts in a heat of sudden passion, caused by adequate provocation, the law recognizes that a man can be provoked to such an extent by the circumstances that he may kill before he has time to gain control of himself. Again, a spontaneous reaction on his part. The facts negate spontaneous action, the descriptions of those people who were with the accused that he was calm, that he acted like he did on every other day, the time period over which these killings took place. The provocation is not there. His own testimony does not reflect that he was in a rage, that his mind was befuddled by rage, that he acted spontaneously. It shows that he was thinking. It shows that he was premeditating. And where we have shown premeditation beyond any reasonable doubt, there can be no justification for rendering a finding showing any other state of mind than what the facts show.

We also have to establish with respect to each of these offenses that they were committed unlawfully without justification or excuse. In this regard, the accused while denying that he in fact committed the acts which we have alleged in specification one at the trail, he in fact has attempted to justify all of his acts that day under the theory that he was doing his duty, that he was following orders, orders that he had received from his company commander, Captain Medina. This was a combat operation, gentlemen, and the military judge will instruct you that the conduct of warfare is not wholly unregulated by law, and that nations, including this nation, have agreed to treaties which attempt to maintain certain basic fundamental humanitarian principles applicable in the conduct of warfare. And over a period of time these practices have dealt with the circumstances and the law concerning when human life may be justifiably taken as an act of war. The killing of [an] armed enemy in combat is certainly a justifiable act of war. It's the mission of the soldier to meet and close with and destroy the enemy. However, the law attempts to protect those persons who are noncombatants. Even those individuals who may have actually engaged in warfare, once they have surrendered. They are entitled to be treated humanely. They are entitled not to be summarily executed.

The military judge will instruct you that as a matter of law regardless of the loyalties, political views, or prior acts, people had the right to be treated as prisoners once captured until they are released, confined, or executed, but executed only in accordance with the law and the established procedures by competent authority sitting in judgment of the detained or captured individual. A trial, gentlemen, a trial, like the accused has had in this case, a trial at which the guilt or innocence of these individuals can be determined.

He will instruct you that as a matter of law, summary execution is forbidden. He will also tell you that as a matter of law that under the evidence which we have presented in this case, that any hostile acts, or any support which the inhabitants of the village of My Lai may have given to the Vietcong or to the NVA [*North Vietnamese Army*] at some time prior to 16 March, would not justify their summary execution. Nor would hostile acts even that day committed by an armed enemy unit have justified their summary execution, as a matter of law, if those individuals laid down their weapons, held up their arms, and surrendered themselves to the American forces.

He will tell you that as a matter of law, that if unresisting human beings were killed at My Lai while within the effective custody and control of our military forces, their deaths cannot be considered justified, and that any order to kill such people would be, as a matter of law, an illegal order.

We presented in our case in chief no evidence regarding what the orders were for this operation. We wanted to present to you the facts surrounding these deaths. We wanted to present to you, and show to you, show you clearly that the people that were killed in My Lai were unarmed, were unresisting, and offered no resistance to the accused on the date in question, and that they were summarily executed by him. There can be no justification for that. There is none under the law, the law which you have sworn to apply in this case, even despite what your own personal feelings may be regarding this law.

You will be told as a matter of law that the obedience of a soldier is not the obedience of an automaton. When he puts on the American uniform, he still is under an obligation to think, to reason, and he is obliged to respond not as a machine but as a person and as a reasonable human being with a proper regard for human life, with the obligation to make moral decisions, with the obligation to know what is right and what is wrong under the circumstances with which he is faced and to act accordingly.

We submit to you in this case that the accused received in fact no order to have done what he did in My Lai on 16 March 1968. He cannot rely upon an order in the first instance, because there was no order to round up all those men, women, and children and summarily execute them. There was an order, yes, to meet and engage the Forty-eighth VC Battalion in My Lai. We submitted to you all the evidence regarding the preoperational planning for this operation. You heard what the mission of this operation was—to meet and engage the armed enemy unit that they expected to be there. Is there anything unlawful about that order? On the night of 15 March, do you think that they anticipated or intended when they got to the village the next day there would be no one there with weapons, and all they would find would be old men, women, children, and babies, and that the mission was to go in and gather those people up and take them out on that trail and that ditch and shoot them? Do you think that those were the orders on the night of 15 March? Do you think that that was the order that emanated in those task force briefings? There is no evidence to show that any order was given to summarily execute. There is no evidence to show that there was an order given not to take prisoners. There was an order given to meet and engage an armed enemy unit, and this is the order that Captain Medina relayed to his men, to meet and engage the Forty-eighth VC Battalion, and the defense's own witnesses testified to this, as have the government's.

The accused testified that he thought they would come in on a high-speed combat assault, clear My Lai, and make a primary assault on Pinkville and go in there and neutralize Pinkville once and for all. Does that indicate summary execution of men, women, and children? Do you think that was the order issued on the fifteenth of March? Calley said after he received the platoon leaders' briefing that "We were going to go in there and do sustained battle with the enemy and that we would stay with the enemy as long as we could maintain contact with him, and we would try to roll him up." That's what he thought on the night of 15 March.

Was Captain Medina justified in trying to arouse his men to engage the enemy the next day? Shouldn't he have told them, shouldn't he have made them aware of what they could expect? And they expected to meet an armed enemy unit.

And so I say to you that the evidence clearly shows that the accused cannot rely upon any order emanating out of any briefing on the fifteenth of March, 1968, to justify his acts, because no such order was given. Nor can the accused rely upon an order having been given to him the day of the operation. He has testified that he received an order from Captain Medina to "waste" the group of Vietnamese that was detained, and he, gentlemen, alone has testified to that fact.

We have produced both RTOs who were members of that command group; neither one of them heard such an order given. You had the RTO from the Third Platoon, Steven Glimpse, who was on his radio that day. He heard no such order given. You had Jeffrey LaCross, who was the Third Platoon leader, who had no knowledge of such an order being given. You had Charles Sledge who was Lieutenant Calley's RTO; he had no such knowledge of an order being given. The accused and the accused alone said he received that order. You had Captain Medina testify before you under oath that he did not give that order. Do you think that the accused would have called Captain Medina and told him that "I have fifty, a hundred Vietnamese—men, women, and children—none of whom have any weapons." And then would have received an order from his company commander to waste that many. Do you think that he called Captain Medina and told him what he had found in the village and how many people he had under his control, or what type of people they were, or what the circumstances were. He doesn't tell you that. He doesn't tell you, because he didn't do it. He didn't check, and perhaps his conduct is typified by his own statements to Charles Sledge after he talked to Lieutenant Thompson: "He don't like the way I'm running the show here, but I'm the boss." He was running that show, gentlemen, on his own initiative, why did the members of the First Platoon begin to round those people up? Even defense's own witness, Elmer Hanwood, testified that he started gathering them up, because he wasn't receiving any resistance from these people. "I wasn't going to shoot them," Hanwood said. "They weren't doing anything to me."

Sergeant Bacon, another defense witness. He had the same orders for that operation. He sent those people he had rounded up to Lieutenant Calley. Why were they not killed until Calley gave the order? Why did Paul Meadlo not fire until Calley gave the order? And even after Bacon left the first group, gentlemen, he went in and gathered up some more people, seven to eight; he didn't go in and shoot them. He took them to the ditch, and why did he shoot those people? I submit to you that those facts show that Bacon shot those people at the direction of Lieutenant Calley.

And so, gentlemen, the acts are unjustifiable as a matter of law, the accused did not receive any order of any kind which directed him to summarily execute the people on the north-south trail, the over seventy people in that irrigation ditch, the man in white out there at that irrigation ditch, or that child. Let's assume for the sake of argument that he had.

Let's assume that he got an order to waste unarmed, unresisting people in the village of My Lai on the sixteenth of March. The military judge will instruct you that even that is not a justification for his acts, if the accused knew that that order was unlawful. For one to follow such an order, [one] has adopted the same criminal intent of the man who issued it. You're not absolved of your responsibility by the order. There are just two men guilty as opposed to one. The responsibility is joint. He joins in the same criminal purpose when he accepts and follows an illegal order. He has the same criminal intent of the man who gave the order.

The accused testified that this was the second largest military operation he was ever on, that he did his duty that day, that he met and closed with the enemy. His testimony regarding the body count, the great emphasis that was placed on body count within the command, within his company. I ask you, gentlemen, if this was the great battle for the accused, if this was his great day in which he had an opportunity to meet and close with the enemy, wouldn't he have wanted to give a big body count, actual body count of the armed enemy soldiers that he had killed? But he doesn't. He can't even give you an estimate. If they were the enemy, he engaged in honorable combat that day. Do you believe that? And even if you were to find subjectively that the accused believed the order to be lawful, it is still not a defense, if a reasonable man under the same or similar circumstances would have known and should have known that any such order would have been unlawful—a reasonable man, gentlemen, not Lieutenant Calley. A reasonable man is the average man, the average lieutenant, the average platoon leader, with average training knowledge. Would he know that that order was illegal?

The reasonable man, gentlemen, is an objective standard. You represent the reasonable men under the law. The reasonable man charged with knowledge of the law to apply in a given situation. The reasonable man would know and should know, without any doubt, that under the circumstances in which he found himself on the sixteenth of March, 1968, that any order to gather up over thirty people on that north-south trail, and to summarily execute those people is unlawful. It can't be justified. A reasonable man would know that to put over seventy people in that irrigation ditch, like a bunch of cattle—men, women, children, and babies—that to do that is unlawful. A reasonable man not only would know it, he should know it, and he could not rely upon any order to commit that, to absolve himself of criminal responsibility for that conduct.

There can be no justification, gentlemen, and there is none under the law, or under the facts of this case. We have established beyond reasonable doubt every element of every offense that we have charged, and the facts clearly demonstrate that those acts were unjustifiable and without excuse. We have carried our burden, and it now becomes your duty to render the only appropriate sentence, punishments, and adjudications you can make in this case, and that is to return findings of guilty of all of the charges and specifications. Thank you.

Defense counsel, Mr. Latimer, offered the closing argument on behalf of Lieutenant Calley. The following are excerpts from Latimer's closing argument.

The Impropriety of the Prosecution

If the prosecution in this case was necessary to prevent the image of the army from being tarnished, then in my humble judgment, conviction of one lieutenant for the ills and vices occurring in My Lai will sear the image beyond recognition. In excess of one hundred soldiers participated in this assault, and the pages of this record bear testimony of the fact that this was not a one-man carnage. Present indications are that eventually this tragedy, as such, will narrow to be a death race between Captain Medina and Lieutenant Calley, and I am here trying to stop that from happening to my client. . . . I am proud of the United States Army, and it grieves me to see it being pulled apart from within. Whether you consider it as such or not, I do not know, but this case is a vehicle which is hurrying along its destruction. . . . Someone called the wrong signals and something went wrong. Then, the second tragedy occurred. The incident was hushed up by the company commander who ordered it, and those superior to him, and the real truth was forever buried. It cannot be resurrected for memories have dulled. Self-interest has multiplied manyfold and the truth is too easy to avoid. Approximately one year later, the third tragedy occurred, and that involved this prosecution. By this time, many of the members of the company were discharged and insulated from prosecution. They, with the help of army investigators who led the way, pointed the finger of blame toward other members who remained loyal to the service, and were trying to make the army a career, some including the accused, who sought to extend his tour of duty in Vietnam.

The Criminal Liability of Others

All of these people, or most of them, seek to avoid the charge of accomplices, that they were murderers at My Lai; because, let me suggest this to you, good gentlemen, that if Captain Medina shot any of these people or ordered them shot, he is a murderer. If Lieutenant Calley follows in his footsteps, then what about Meadlo? Where is he? He admits having murdered a number of people, and use the word "murder" advisedly, because he was ordered to do it. Does the buck passing stop at Lieutenant Calley or does it go down? In my judgment, every one man who participated if there was an offense committed here, as the government alleges and seeks to prove, there are many that should suffer the same as should those who were convicted.

The Infantryman's Perspective of War

I believe most of the men have a feeling, that are in the infantry, that there is a certain refined distinction which should not be made, but somehow is made, and that distinction is that it's all right for the air force to bomb cities. It's all right for artillery to tear down buildings and wreck the lives of every inhabitant; but somehow or other it's wrong for an infantryman, when he is told to destroy and level a village, to use his mechanical weapons and, after all, you are mechanized, to use his weapons for the same purposes. Oh, surely it can be contended that some of the people like to contend, with their refinements, that the infantryman has a better opportunity to see what he is doing. Well, again, here comes the mental processes to work. Here comes your artillery, your mortars coming in on the village, and you go in with your guns a blazing, M-16s or automatic. You don't shoot them by looking through a peep sight, or you didn't. They are used for mass killing and the philosophy of our war and the philosophy that is taught everybody is fire support and mow them down.

The Inexperience of Calley's Platoon

It's a homebook principle that fear and stark horror is present in a unit on its first assault, combat assault; and when raw troops are used, disaster is courted. That's one of the lessons coming out of My Lai, and I am not surprised about the civilian casualties but I marvel at the unit, that the unit did not kill off most of its own personnel. I'm amazed, gentlemen, because if you take and scale that My Lai, I believe you will find its total length is five hundred yards and its total width, about three hundred yards. I believe you can hear an M-16 anywhere in that village from any other place. I believe you can hear fighting from every nook and corner and when you put a hundred men, less the people who would be in the mortar platoon and attachments, such as that, in that area with guns blazing, I just go back and I wonder why there wasn't a worse disaster.

The Horror and Chaos of Combat

Let's look at the experiences of C Company. These are the experiences just before they go in: a number of reconnaissance and sweep and destroy missions, without ever seeing an enemy; losses of buddies by mines and snipers; never any security from death for it always came from unseen and unknown sources. Darkness, an inability to see, breathes fear. Now, in addition to that, the deaths that were being occasioned to the members of the platoon added to the fear because you never knew when your number was up, and you never knew when the next step might cost you a leg or your life. Always destroyed by a visionary fold, no one you could really see and take a bead on and end his chance to save your life and the life of your buddies. Women and children operating with your enemy, being used to help destroy your unit. That enemy was lethal, but it could not be seen. This is the type of warfare that fends hatred against any enemy and anyone who can aid the enemy, and when the fight starts, it is too late to reason why. It just seems to do or die and everything must go.

Now, let us point out what I have said and superimpose on that the feelings, emotions, and desires of the members of C Company on top of the exhortations given by the commander, and we may reach part of the underlying behavior of good American boys who were trained to kill, sent overseas to kill, ordered to kill, and they were exhorted to go in and level or destroy and they thought their mission must be that. They hadn't been in trouble before. The history of it doesn't show a group of associated murders. This was a one-time incident, and now are they to be tarred and labeled as murderers of My Lai or are they entitled to consideration from the fact that they were doing their job as they saw it? Perhaps too aggressively, perhaps trying too hard, undoubtedly not using good judgment, but do the facts entitle the young American officer to hang by his neck until dead because he was trying to do something there which he thought was required by his mission and by the orders given to him?

The Unreliability of the Participants' Testimony

Now, let's see just for a moment or two what we have in some of these instances. Witnesses like Sledge, Conti, Meadlo, Dursi, Turner, and others. Each one of them recounts substantially different details for the sixteenth of March. Now, who was telling the truth in that connection? Are the memories all dulled, or do any of them actually have a real impression as to what occurred? I would think it's fair to say that as they tried to reconstruct those things and the events of that day and, mind you, this incident was buried for quite a long while, and so, if it is mulled over in the minds of the persons—Captain Daniel said individuals have a tendency to, shall I say, oh, cut down on their estimates.

That's not my experience in human nature. When I start telling my war stories, they start going up and up and up until I start telling them—I embellish them a little bit more, and when a CI [*combat infantryman*] is telling his war experiences, I think the measuring rod for truth would be a little bit short, because I think they have a tendency to move up.

Let's take Mr. Conti, just by way of illustration. Mr. Conti testified he got off and got lost. He got lost. It was some time before he could find out where he was going. He seemed to be doing something besides fighting wars. If you believe the testimony in the record, his accounts of what happened are entirely different from others.

Mr. Meadlo, I think, sits in a category where trial counsel would like to take him as reliable at one time and shed his reliability at another. He's good for certain things, and he's bad for certain things. For my money, Mr. Meadlo would probably have the poorest impressions of anybody, if he was as emotionally upset as they claim he was. In addition to that, Mr. Meadlo found himself in a very peculiar situation. He found himself insulated by having been discharged, but worried about whether he could be prosecuted otherwise by some other forum than a court-martial. Now, his emotional state, as far as I am concerned, makes him one of the most unreliable witnesses.

Now, let's go to another character in this, and I will show you the principal characters upon which the government relies. Mr. Turner is seen as being the epitome of everything in this case. Unfortunately, I can't have that feeling for Mr. Turner. As you recall, Mr. Turner is a witness who said first that he and his counsel had tried to get immunity. I wonder why. I wonder why he would seek immunity if his story is true. I wonder why Mr. Turner would refuse to talk to counsel. He wouldn't talk to either military defense counsel or civilian defense counsel. I wonder why. I think he may be the witness that said he didn't want to become confused. I don't know if his story is true. I don't find witnesses becoming confused when they tell the truth. I think they have trouble when they concoct stories and they are telling impressions that did not, in fact, exist because the next time they try to tell the impressions, they are wrong. Mr. Turner is one of the characters that said Lieutenant Calley stood at the ditch for an hour or an hour and a half, marching people up and mowing them down. Nobody else verified that information or that testimony and everybody contradicts it because they find Lieutenant Calley at other places.

The Chaos and Confusion of Combat

Now, war is confusion, battle is confusion. We only need to read *War and Peace* to go up as high as general and such as that to fight a war. Orders are confusing—radio goes out. Nothing seems to work and in a village—it's been my impression that village fighting is one of the hardest in the world to control your troops.

You have them running into hooches, searching. You have them burning. You have them running here, there, and everywhere, and control of that sort of an operation is most difficult, and then the only way that I know that that can be done is to have training, training, training, so each man can keep track of the other. Each man works as a team. One isn't getting lost out in the tulees. One isn't upon himself, two or three of them running around possibl[y] hurting civilians, others going around looking for women. That's hardly an army or unit that should be sent on a mission such as this.

The Prebattle Intelligence Information

Everybody concurs on the fact that the intelligence information was fantastically wrong. Everybody had a major force in there, and from whence that information came I cannot imagine because they were making some aerial reconnaissance near that area and surely they expected to meet the enemy, to take extra ammunition. They were told to go in aggressively and so I bring myself down to the events with Captain Medina standing in the pit with his shovel, when he starts telling his men what to do tomorrow. "The briefing that I conducted for my company was that C Company had been selected to conduct a combat assault operation into the village of My Lai beginning with LZ time 0730 hours on the morning of 16 March 1968. I told them the VC Battalion was approximately numbered, approximately 250 to 280 men, and that we would be outnumbered approximately two to one and that we could expect a helluva good fight, and we would probably be heavily engaged."

The intelligence reports also indicated that innocent civilians or noncombatants would be gone to the market at 0700 hours in the morning, that this was one of the reasons why the artillery preparation was being placed on the village at 0720. What are innocent civilians? I wonder what Captain Medina had in mind that he repeatedly talks about innocent civilians. I just have never been able to figure out how I, as a CI, or any other CI, would know whether a civilian was innocent or not, and you couldn't tell that merely because they weren't carrying a rifle, because the evidence showed that they have other means of aiding the enemy; but more importantly, he led them to believe that everyone that might be in the village—every civilian that might be in this village, was not innocent.

The Prebattle Orders From Captain Medina

A young man, Sergeant Schiel, testified as follows: "Medina stressed we were to kill everything. Did he mean everything to be— *Question:* Did he mean everything to be killed, men, women and children? *Answer:* Captain Medina answered the question. Captain Medina said, 'Everything was to be killed, men, women, and children, cats, dogs, everything that breathed.' "

Lamartina stated, "Medina said, 'Go into the village and kill everything that breathed.' On March 11, I obeyed that order as I killed everything that moved. I observed others obeying the order. We sprayed the village."

Kinch—this is his impression of what Medina, said: "Everything in that village is considered VC or VCS [*Vietcong sympathizers*]. When he came through the village the next day, he did not want to see anything living." These statements are by CIs.

Flynn: "We were to kill everything that moves, and this was a chance to take revenge. Someone asked Medina if they were supposed to kill women and children and everything, and he answered, 'Kill everything that moves.' "

Fagan: "We were going into Pinkville. We were going on a search and destroy mission. All inhabitants of the village would be killed, livestock slaughtered, all houses burned down. My impression, after the briefing, was that anyone remaining in the village, regardless of whether they were men, women, and children, would be killed."

Alaux: "Anyone remaining in the village on that day would be VC or VCS and that village was supposed to be destroyed and everything in it destroyed. This includes inhabitants."

Meadlo: "We are going to have contact with a heavily armed regiment. He said, 'Everything there is considered VC or VCS and that everybody should be destroyed.' "

Now, when you put those items all in their proper perspective, it just seems to me that despite Captain Medina's denial that he used that language, that certainly it is fair to say that every member of his group that testified, that came here to testify, either said that he said "men, women, or children"; that he was asked whether his phrase included men, women, and children, that he used words from which they inferred that that was what they were supposed to do; and lastly, those that did not testify, testified in the negative that they did not remember whether Captain Medina made the comment about that or not. Now, so you have the positive evidence on one side, the negative evidence on the other, but most of all you have the activity in connection with this extemporaneous construction by the people who heard it. They went in. They went in firing. Insofar as the evidence shows, in every sector of that village civilians were killed.

Captain Medina's Orders to Calley While in the Village

Now, that brings me then to the other question of orders, and that's the two orders Lieutenant Calley said he received from Captain Medina while he was in the center of the village, as to what to do with these civilians. Now, significantly, there are facts which I think tend to show and add considerable light to this question. Number one, my recollection is that Captain Medina said he did call Lieutenant Calley and tell him to hurry up which, in part, verifies what Lieutenant Calley said.

I think Captain Medina said he sat there for two and a half hours with his command post there. He didn't know where his platoons were. He didn't know how far they had gone. He didn't know whether they had reached the east side of the section. Gentlemen, I will tell you, if you look at that map, you will find that Captain Medina could never have been further than about five or six hundred yards away from his lead troops. Now, he sat there and did do nothing about what was going on except the possibility of sending one message down, and I believe that message was something about [how] he had been called by the major about what was happening in the village, and he sent a message down, something to the effect either, "Quit shooting innocent civilians, Eleven" or "Quit shooting innocent civilians," and with that, he let it go.

Captain Medina's Culpability and Cover-up

Captain Medina wasn't interested in going back because he found a lot of reasons for not doing so, but in my opinion those reasons were founded because he didn't want to go back. He'd seen what happened. He thought probably if he didn't go back that night, that somebody might come in and remove the evidence that might be available so that this tragedy could be looked at and investigated and determined right at that time. Now, mind you, had that been done, every living witness to that would have been available to interview. The whole story could have been unfolded long before anybody had any interest in anything but telling the truth and finding out what happened. You know there was a guilty conscience on the part of Captain Medina. He told somebody he was going to go to prison for twenty years. I wonder why. I wonder why if he didn't feel that he had done something wrong, that he had any culpability in the matter. I wonder why he didn't go back and want to clear it up there and then. Well, it's apparent now why he didn't. I think he said four reasons that he gave as to why he didn't want to go back and I'm sorry to have to say, gentlemen, that they ring very hollow to me. Number one, was because of his country. Number two, because he didn't want to degrade the army. Number three, because of his family, and lastly, because of himself. Now, mind you, he knew and if you will read his testimony, you will find out that he stated at that time that he was alarmed at the number of casualties that might have occurred. Yet, he didn't want to go back and in my judgment, if you reconstruct that whole thing, Captain Medina knew how his orders had been interpreted. He sat there for two and a half hours. And he must have been there about the time that the First Platoon hit the south side of the landing zone and watched it go through, and I do not believe there is an area in that village that he could not hear every round that was fired out of an M-16 or out of a machine gun because I do believe that you can hear them fired that far away.

Now, everybody that went through that village said there was shooting. A man could not sit back there with the command post in a place that is not over five hundred to three hundred yards away in area and not know what is going on. The evidence shows that Captain Medina had been a good company commander, but somehow or other self-preservation got into Captain Medina's life at that time and it was necessary for him to take some defensive efforts to protect that. So, when you start to measure the interest, and I will be frank to say that on behalf of both of them, it's terrific; but between he and Lieutenant Calley, because they are both running the last yards, probably to a life or death sentence, and when the stakes are that high, somebody has got to try to escape responsibility.

Medina used a phrase that he was guilty of misprision of a felony by not reporting. Of course, Captain Medina can afford to make that sort of an admission now because he cannot be prosecuted on that charge, the statute of limitations having barred it. Now, gentlemen, for the life of me, I cannot understand why we could take a group of twenty or thirty men out of the United States Army, all good men, all good citizens, at the time they were picked up, put them over there, and have an incident like this happen unless it had been suggested, ordered, or commanded by somebody upstairs. I will leave that up to you good gentlemen to figure out. Why a lieutenant, the lowest man on the totem pole, would be issuing orders like that without having some directive or orders from on high.

Psychiatric Testimony, Captain Medina, and a Soldier's Commitment to Follow Orders

I wanted to get a couple of psychiatrists who had some combat experience to come in and, in their judgment, determine whether or not the influences in effect had been working on Lieutenant Calley during his life and when he got there may somehow or other dull[ed] his mind a little bit so he didn't think as fast, he didn't appreciate as fast because when you get these instructions, you will find out that one of the tests is, in connection with orders, did he understand or fail to understand that it was a legal order. Now, it's easy to stand in a courtroom and point out that there is no impairment there at all, but out in a guerilla warfare, in the type of warfare these people are in, you somehow or other don't have the same freedom of thought. Call it what you want. I don't care about a psychiatric label on it. I don't want to run the gamut from psychoses down to behavioral patterns. All I want you good gentlemen to do and all I brought the psychiatrists here for is, I think they raised the issue, did these things have some impact on Lieutenant Calley, and did they affect his mental processes to a point where he probably did not appreciate that he should tell Captain Medina to go to hell when he got these orders and ignore them.

Captain Medina was a man, a disciplinarian. He wanted orders obeyed. He said that and he didn't brook any denial or disobedience of orders. It may well be that the niceties of the military require that if I have a question about an order, I go to my company commander and say, "Captain, I think this is an illegal order, and I don't think I should obey it," but the other philosophy is that they were saying here, "Obey it first and then go back and find out what about the legality of it," because if you take the former in this situation, your troops might be dead; and if you don't follow out a combat order, then you sacrifice your troops. What a horrid choice to place upon anybody.

The court is also going to instruct on the legality and illegality of orders. You will have it in written form so there is no point in my doing anything more or less than this; that he will define an illegal order and what is an illegal order and he may tell you, in this case, that the killing of civilians—in certain situations, a given order to kill those might be an illegal order, but he also will tell you that that does not end the subject.

That is just a commencement. For, on top of it a man that is involved, whether he uses the subjective or objective test, it must be known to the individual involved that the order and the circumstances—when, where, and why it was given and the facts that control that decision as to whether a person should know whether it's legal or illegal—flow out of his environment, flow out of many things that you have heard in this case, including these things that were bothering this unit on 16 March 1968; and he will tell you that if an ordinary, reasonable person would have done what Lieutenant Calley did, in this case, and obeyed the order; if it was given to him, then, of course, you cannot find Lieutenant Calley guilty because the test that you apply and the measuring rod you use is colored by the facts and circumstances surrounding the giving of the order and if you adopt the philosophy, you obeyed first and asked after in this situation, no one would take that kind of an order and do that, because if they didn't and there was some kind of counterattack here, something happened, then it would be too late.

It may be the difference between winning and losing and so, as you look back on the situation—I could hardly stand here and tell you in good conscience that people, like at Nuremberg, could be excused or justified—but I think when you put untrained troops out in areas and they are told to do certain things, they have a right to rely on the judgment and the expertise, then you are bound to give credence in effect to orders from their company commander; and so when you take that background, the laws of war were tailored in certain respects to meet this very situation, then you will understand that the Congress of the United States and other bodies feel that leeway and latitude should be given to people who were far from home and trying to save the United States of America.

I do not believe that history records another incident when the United States of America ever had a similar situation, nor do I believe that we have taken collectively a group of people who were engaged in a combat mission and what they believed to be a combat mission and put them up before a court for trial. So, you gentlemen are in a situation where you must chart a course for what should be done. You are in a situation where I believe that if ever a presumption of innocence, the personal rights and obligations that are available to protect the men of the armed services ought to be extended in favor of this accused.

They cannot be prosecuted. Sure, they can then come forward with witnesses. They can disclose anything that happened. It's too late to help them, but the man that is in the service, the man that stays in the service and tries to build the morale and efficiency of the United States Army, does not have that protection. To me, I think if I were—if it were possible for me to do it, somehow or other I would give weight to the fact that a man who wanted to make the army a career, who was not told—never a word said to Lieutenant Calley that I can recall, about any of his problems in this case until he had extended in Vietnam and was ordered back to the United States believing he was coming back to a new assignment. There was nothing said to him. All the time, apparently, the finger pointing to Captain Medina, who himself stated that he would probably get twenty years and all of a sudden, times change. Who becomes the pigeon—Lieutenant Calley, the lowest offices. Now, I ask you good gentlemen to give, as I know you will, honest consideration [of] this kid that sits behind me and know there is a difference. There ought to be a difference, and you ought to make the difference between errors in judgment and criminality and so I ask your serious consideration and ask that you let this boy go free. Thank you very much.

Prosecutor Daniel's Rebuttal Closing Argument

If it please the court, counsel for the accused, Mr. President, gentlemen of the court:

It's been a long day, gentlemen. It's been a long trial and my job, truly, is just about over. Again, I thank you for the attention which you have given me throughout this trial. I trust that I will receive your continued attention for the several moments that remain at the end of this case. I am not going to take the time now to reply to every one of Mr. Latimer's arguments. I won't do that. I think the purpose of some was apparent. I am going to take the time to discuss with you again those factual matters which he raised, and those legal matters which he raised, which I feel do need to be responded to.

A point brought out by Mr. Latimer in his argument regarded the offense of voluntary manslaughter and that heat of passion could have dissipated the element of premeditation, citing the classic example of a husband finding his wife with another man and killing under those circumstances, a sudden burst, a sudden reaction to a situation. Whereas, the evidence in this case, as I clearly demonstrated and as the evidence clearly shows, there was no heat of passion. The accused's own testimony shows that he was not acting in a state of heat of passion. Not even he tells you he acted in a heat of passion. Everyone that observed him that day described him to be the same as any other day.

Let's discuss the psychiatric testimony which Judge Kennedy will instruct you is admissible for only one issue and that is the issue of the accused's mental capacity to premeditate, his mental ability to premeditate. In resolving that issue you have had the benefit of live witnesses from this stand. You have had the benefit of observing the accused and you have had the benefit of observing him while he testified, and you have had the benefit of observing him throughout these proceedings. I submit to you that even Dr. Crane [*the defense psychiatric expert*] testified that the accused did in fact premeditate and had the mental ability to do so. Dr. Crane said that Lieutenant Calley intended for the people to die when he pulled the trigger on his weapon. He knew they would die. He had the mental ability.

Mr. Latimer also attacked the credibility of all of the main government witnesses, Charles Sledge, Jim Dursi, Paul Meadlo, and Thomas Turner. He tried to show a reason for bias, prejudice, and why they would lie. He said it was covered up at the time and now the truth will never be known. We will never know what happened. He said that I acknowledged the fact that there were inconsistencies in the testimony and that this showed weakness. Gentlemen, it does not show weakness. It's the strength of this case when almost three years after an event, these men can come into this court from every section of the country and tell you a story and all the pieces fit. They might not fit identically but they fit. They reveal truth, gentlemen; truth which you can't hide, because it's been revealed here in this courtroom over the last three months and it's going to stand forever.

He pointed out that the government witnesses had been caught in numerous inconsistent statements, but he didn't take the time to go to any of those. If they had been important, don't you think he would have done so? And I ask you to verify the record for yourself if you have any questions, because that's what you must do; not rely upon our argument but rely upon the record and the facts as you recall them. And how many government witnesses were confronted with the previous statement about a material matter in their testimony while on the other hand, how many defense witnesses were confronted by the government with inconsistent statements in their testimony? Does he tell you that? How about Sergeant Cowan? I will point that one out to you again. When you talk about inconsistencies in his testimony, here is a man who tells you that he saw nothing, saw no one shoot anybody in My Lai that day, and we present you with the fact that on a previous occasion he told somebody that he did. Sergeant Bacon also was confronted with inconsistencies in his testimony by the government, and Mr. Lloyd was also confronted with a previous statement that he made. All of those were defense witnesses, and if you have any question about it, gentlemen, you can call for the evidence, you can have the testimony reread to check those inconsistencies out against any government witness. The accused has never made any allegation about Thomas Turner or Paul Meadlo as to why these men should testify or why any of these men should want to falsify these stories.

The thrust of their argument, gentlemen, is that what the accused did that day, he did because he was ordered to do it and that he was an American soldier who was doing his duty in a combat situation, and that now he is pitted against Captain Medina, that other men will not be prosecuted for what they may have done, and that you must make a choice between Captain Medina's responsibility and the accused's responsibility in this case. You have only one question to decide and that is the responsibility of the accused. The responsibility of other persons who may have been involved at the time of this incident are not questions to be resolved by you, only the guilt or innocence of this accused for what he did.

The defense attacked everyone. They attacked the CID [*Criminal Investigation Division*]. They attacked the IG [*Inspector General*]. They completely attacked Captain Medina. They attacked the training of the company in one instance and say it was inadequate and rely upon the same training to show that the accused should have followed his orders. They have sought to put the blame everywhere except where it belongs. They have sought to compare the accused with other enlisted men. He was not an enlisted man. He was an officer. He had command. He had responsibility. He had an obligation to think. He had an obligation to his fellowmen and that obligation was not to disregard basic humanitarian principles. He had a duty to do only one thing. He had a duty to obey lawful orders. He had a duty to act as a reasonable man would have acted under the circumstances. He owed that duty to his country. There has been a lot of talk about Captain Medina, about the accused—he's just a poor kid in a tough situation, that he got sent to Vietnam. But there hasn't been anything said in this case about the victims. Who will speak for them, gentlemen?

Mr. Latimer said, "Well, the boys were a little bit aggressive that day. They used bad judgment a couple of times. They used bad judgment." Can you visualize in your mind—we have not been able to create what the people who were on the other end of those weapons felt at the time when they were being shot and placed in that ditch like so many cattle. They tell you that the accused was not the only man responsible. Well, I ask you, did anyone else do any more that day than he did? I submit, gentlemen, that the evidence shows that he did not receive an order in this case. They tell you to disregard the briefings of Task Force Barker, that those have no weight. Do you believe that that task force would have given an order to go in and round up all of those people and shoot them summarily, infants who couldn't even walk? Do you believe that Captain Medina would have given that order and that the accused had received the order, did he show any remorse? Did he mention it to any-one; no he didn't. He said, "I'm the boss and I'm running the show."

If the order was given, gentlemen, he joined in and he is as much to blame as anyone else who would have given that order. And under the law, a reasonable man would not have obeyed that order and could not have obeyed that order without assuming full legal responsibility for his action. What can justify, gentlemen, the shooting in cold blood of an infant or child or any human being who's unresisting and is offering you no resistance? I say to you that your choice is not Captain Medina, or anyone else, and the accused. Your choice is the facts in this case and the law. And the facts in this case prove beyond any shadow of a doubt that the accused is to blame, that he should be held criminally respon-sible. There can be no doubt about that. What happened in My Lai is the truth. You can't hide it. You can't cover it up. It exists. You have taken a solemn oath that you will, with complete impartiality, apply the evi-dence that has been presented to you in this case to the law which Judge Kennedy will give you.

You have sworn, each of you, that you will apply this law regardless of what your personal feelings might be about it. The government has carried its burden and we have established all of the elements of every offense beyond any reasonable doubt. We have proven that the accused gathered up and summarily executed those unarmed, unresisting men, women, and children, and babies in the village of My Lai on 16 March 1968. We knew we had that burden to carry when we came to this court, and we have carried it. There is no question about the fact that he killed them with premeditation. Under the law of this country and the Uniform Code of Military Justice and the laws regulating warfare, all human beings are entitled to be treated humanely. The defense argument would ask you to throw away all of those rules. They would ask you to make us no better than our enemy. They would ask you to legalize murder. How could we as a nation call for humane treatment of our own while condoning inhumane treatment to them? These individuals, these human beings, they are entitled to this under our law, regardless of their race or nationality or their political affiliation. The fact that the accused was an American and these were Vietnamese is irrelevant. They were human beings. It's not just unlawful under our law to take the life of another American. We cannot justify the summary execution of any human being under the law of this country. These people may have been VC. They may have been supporters or sympathizers of the VC. They may have been Vietnamese people who just happened to have been in the wrong place at the wrong time. They may have been people who were under the control of the Vietcong, because they themselves were captives of this country's own enemy. But I ask you, gentlemen, who stopped to ask them? Were they ever asked? Did the accused make any attempt to make that determination? And I ask you, what choice did the children have about the fact that they were in the village that day? Or what about the infants whose only possible crime was the fact that they were born to parents of a village of My Lai?

The accused has been given a fair trial before his guilt could be determined. The people of My Lai were entitled to the same trial to determine if they had committed an offense against this nation, a trial which they never received. Would the evidence presented against those people reveal that they had been guilty of any offense? Would any tribunal in this world have found one of those children guilty of an offense and sentenced him to die? Would the evidence have proven any infant guilty of any offense which could justify his execution? The children, the infants, and the people of My Lai—the children and the infants would never be tried and nothing under the law could justify their execution.

The accused on 16 March 1968 appointed himself judge, jury, and executioner, and he convicted his prisoners without a trial. He assumed the responsibility for determining their guilt and he assumed responsibility for their deaths. The law of this nation and this country did not assume that responsibility. The United States Army did not assume that responsibility. He, and he, alone, made that determination and now he must assume the full responsibility for his unlawful acts.

The laws of this country are only as effective as they are enforced. Without enforcement, they have no meaning, for justice, like discipline, requires that the innocent be recognized and the guilty condemned. Discipline is the backbone of the military. The government and the law also recognize that when the law is disobeyed, it must be exposed and it must be condemned without remorse, without hesitation. It must be quick and it must be sure. The accussed was a commissioned officer of the armed forces of this United States when he slaughtered his innocent victims in My Lai. He has attempted to absolve himself of responsibility by saying that he had his duty there, that he acted in the name of this country and the law of this nation, and I submit to you and the government submits to you that he did not and upon that question there can be no doubt. To make that assertion is to prostitute all of the humanitarian principles for which this nation stands. It is to prostitute the true mission of the United States soldier. It has been said the soldier, be he friendly or foe, is charged with the protection of the weak and unarmed. It is the very essence and reason for his being. When he violates this sacred trust, he not only profanes his entire cult but threatens the very fabric of international society. The traditions of fighting men are long and honorable. They are based upon the noblest of human faith, sacrifice.

You are members of a profession. You have rules governing your profession. Without rules to govern your profession, it's not a profession. Every profession is bound by ethics and the laws of warfare and the principles of humane treatment are the guidelines of the professional soldier. The United States government says to you that the accused failed in his duty, that he did not act in the name of and in accordance with the law of this nation. Within our society and under the law, the value placed on human life is sacred. When the accused put on the uniform of an American soldier and took the oath of allegiance to this country, he was not relieved of his conscience. He was not relieved of his responsibility to know the difference between right and wrong, to know that he should not shoot an unarmed and innocent child or a baby. The accused, when he took the oath of an American officer, was not given a license to slaughter unarmed men, women, and children on his own personal supposition that they were the enemy. Such acts are not now nor have they ever been justified under the law of this country. This accused has failed in his duty as an officer.

Your duty is clear. On the evidence that we have presented to you and under the law, you can arrive at only one decision and still fulfill your duties as a member of this court. You gentlemen, as members of this court, are the conscience of the United States Army. You are the conscience of this country in this case, and you are asked only to fix the responsibility where it belongs. We have carried our burden and the duty is yours to find the accused guilty as charged. Thank you.